JOE BROWN'S PETS

JOE BROWN'S PETS

The Georgia Militia, 1861-1865

∞

WILLIAM R. SCAIFE
and
WILLIAM HARRIS BRAGG

Mercer University Press | Macon, Georgia | ©2004

ISBN 0-86554-883-8
MUP/H655

© 2004 Mercer University Press
1400 Coleman Avenue
Macon, Georgia 31207

Book design by Burt & Burt Studio

Scaife, William R.

Joe Brown's pets : the Georgia Militia, 1861-1865 / William R. Scaife And
William Harris Bragg.— 1st ed.

p. cm.

Includes bibliographical references and index.

1. Georgia. Militia—History—Civil War, 1861-1865.
2. Georgia—History—Civil War, 1861-1865—Regimental histories.
3. United States—History—Civil War, 1861-1865—Manpower.
4. United States—History—Civil War, 1861-1865—Regimental histories.
5. Georgia—History—Civil War, 1861-1865—Campaigns.
6. United States—History—Civil War, 1861-1865—Campaigns.
7. Brown, Joseph E. (Joseph Emerson), 1821-1894.
8. Governors—Georgia—Biography.
9. Georgia—Politics and government—1861-1865.
10. Confederate States of America—Politics and government.
I. Bragg, William Harris.
II. Title.

E559.4.S28 2004

973.7'458—dc22

2004003661

*The engraving opposite the title page, also used as a head-piece throughout the book,
originally appeared on an 1863 State of Georgia $100 bill.*

[The Georgia Militia were] those unique Confederate soldiers who, by the dictum of Governor Joe Brown, were permitted to fight only when an enemy had actually crossed the state line to invade the sovereign soil of Georgia.... They were mostly young boys under seventeen, or elderly men, outside the age limits of the Confederate conscription. As soldiers, they were better than nothing—but not much better.

Stanley Horn, *The Army of Tennessee*

To the

MUCH-MALIGNED MEMORY

of

THE "PETS"

∽∾

No troops in the service
discharged their duty
more nobly and faithfully.

JOSEPH E. BROWN

CONTENTS

Publication of this book

was made possible

by a generous grant

from the

Watson-Brown Foundation, Inc.

PREFACE

At the beginning of the Civil War, Georgia ranked third among the Confederate states in manpower resources, behind only Virginia and Tennessee. Georgia's potential arms-bearing population—some 120,000 to 130,000 white males between the ages of sixteen and sixty—soon became the object of a great struggle between Georgia's war governor, Joseph E. Brown, and the Confederate central government in Richmond. Brown advocated a strong state defense force to serve at the pleasure of the governor, while President Jefferson Davis and the other Confederate authorities looked upon Georgia as a rich source of troops for the Confederate States Army. As the war went on, Richmond imposed ever-increasing quotas on Brown to fill this critical need.

When the war began, most Georgia males of arms-bearing age were members of the Georgia Militia, a statewide organization whose smallest components were company units drawn from militia districts within Georgia's 132 counties. The state's organized militia, however, was immediately disrupted by war volunteering and later drained by conscription; it played a negligible part in the war's first two years. Nonetheless, Governor Brown throughout the war organized whatever men he could assemble into a succession of small state armies for local defense, bearing such designations as the Georgia Army, the Georgia Volunteers, the Georgia State Troops, and the Georgia State Line. During the same period, the Confederacy raised two local defense organizations: the Georgia State Guard and the Georgia Reserve Force.

Many of these state and Confederate organizations were further subdivided into a complicated system of regiments, battalions, brigades, and divisions. For a variety of reasons—including the frequency with which these components were reorganized or disbanded, the similarity of many units'

names, the numerous resignations or deaths of officers whose names had
become part of the units' designations, and the prevalence of indifferent
record-keeping—the precise identity of these units is often difficult to deter-
mine with any degree of certainty. Fortunately from a standpoint of history,
the state forces during this time seem to have been engaged primarily in various garrison duties and thus had little significant impact on the course of
the war.

It was not until 14 December 1863 that the General Assembly approved
a reorganization of the Georgia Militia that would somewhat restore its
strength and take it to the end of the war. The legislation called for an enrollment of available manpower (known as "The Joe Brown Census"),
suspended all contradictory provisions of the Georgia Code of 1861, and
further suspended all militia organizations "theretofore existing."

This new force, designated the First Division, Georgia Militia (but
widely known as "Joe Brown's Pets"), was organized into four brigades of
three regiments each and would be commanded after 1 June 1864 by Major
General Gustavus W. Smith. Under Smith the militia would have its most
significant impact on history, experiencing combat for the first time and providing valuable service during the final phases of the Atlanta Campaign. It
would constitute the major Confederate force at the battles of Griswoldville
and Honey Hill during the March to the Sea and would play a prominent
role in the siege and evacuation of Savannah. When Sherman left Georgia
and embarked on his March through the Carolinas, the militia was primarily
assigned to garrison duty but retained its commander and organizational
structure until the closing days of the war. This work concentrates on the
militia's activities from its final reorganization into the 1st Division, Georgia
Militia, until the end of the war. For a brief account of the earlier incarna-
tions of the militia, as well as of the other state troops mentioned above, refer
to Appendix 3, "Troops of War." Also appended is a series of historical, literary, and satirical descriptions of the Georgia Militia assembled under the
title "The Melish."

We would like to express our appreciation to the many descendants of
Georgia Militiamen who provided diaries, letters, images, and relevant
family history and information for our research on this publication. The list
of such contributors would unfortunately be far too lengthy to include in
this acknowledgment.

Many thanks for vital assistance are also due to Mary Ellen Brooks, director, and the staff of the Hargrett Rare Book and Manuscript Library, University of Georgia Libraries, and to the staff of the Genealogy Room of Macon's Washington Memorial Library, principally the redoubtable Willard Rocker. In locating and securing illustrations, our friends Anne J. Bailey and David Wynn Vaughan provided generous and crucial aid. Andrew M. Thomason and Crystal Hurt did yeoman service assisting with the rosters and the indexes.

In researching the Georgia Militia, the most voluminous single source is a collection from the adjutant general's office of the original rosters of the militia taken at its reorganization as the 1st Division, Georgia Militia. These are found at the Georgia Department of Archives and History in Atlanta, where access to them is limited because of their delicate state of preservation. The condition of these documents and the difficulty in reading, deciphering, and transcribing them made this a lengthy and painstaking task. We are grateful to the staff of the Georgia Archives—most particularly Andy Phrydas, military records archivist—for their exemplary patience and cheerful assistance during this time-consuming process.

Finally, we owe a tremendous debt of gratitude to our wives—Ollie Scaife and Wanda Bragg. They have gone many an extra mile toward making this study possible, and they've been amazingly tolerant, understanding, and good-humored all along the way.

1.
THE WAR GOVERNOR AND HIS MILITIA

Georgia's Civil War governor, Joseph Emerson Brown, was born in the same northwestern corner of South Carolina that had produced John C. Calhoun—fitting for one who would become the most clamorous of the Confederacy's state rights governors. He began his career in 1847 as a lawyer at Canton in Georgia's Cherokee County. But Brown soon discovered that politics, not the law, was his passion, and in 1849 he ran successfully for the Georgia Senate to represent Cherokee and Cobb counties. His presence was almost immediately felt in the state capitol at Milledgeville, and in 1857— due to one of those complicated maneuvers so typical in Georgia politics—the relative newcomer from "Cherokee Georgia" was nominated for governor as a compromise candidate by the state's Democrats. Describing Brown as the "Mountain Boy," the *Augusta Evening Dispatch* wrote that though "not a brilliant speaker or writer," Brown had a "logical, well-balanced mind, and in his moral character exhibits adherence to elevated principles of temperance and morality quite refreshing to find among our professional politicians ...." Nonetheless, the *Dispatch* thought him "a 'lucky dog' to get the nomination," and, while decrying Brown's "political bitterness" and "intense" partisanship, thought him a "good man" who would no doubt make "a competent Governor."[1]

Although Brown's opponent in the 1857 gubernatorial election, Benjamin H. Hill, was praised as "an orator," while Brown was described merely as "a talker," Brown was nonetheless elected (principally by the yeomanry) to his adopted state's highest office. The vote was 57,568 to 46,826, representing an impressive majority for a politician only thirty-six years old. Most of the state's patrician politicians were appalled at Brown's victory and derided his Baptist abstemiousness and uncouth pronunciation. But they saw that he wielded power as if to the manner born, and the people loved him. Moreover, his efficient administration and his popular (and rather Jacksonian) bank war assured reelection in 1859—and he would prevail against his opponents overwhelmingly in 1861 and 1863 as well.[2]

Even before Georgia seceded from the Union, Brown saw the threat of impending war. Consequently, he sought and obtained an appropriation from the legislature of $1,000,000 to recruit and arm 10,000 troops and expand the Georgia Militia—a move that would make Georgia militarily the best-prepared state in the Confederacy when fighting actually broke out.[3]

In order to prevent Federal troops from garrisoning Fort Pulaski at the entrance to Savannah Harbor, Brown on 2 January 1861 sent Colonel Alexander Robert Lawton and the 1st Regiment of Georgia Volunteers to occupy the strategically important fort in the name of the State of Georgia. This prevented Georgia from playing a role similar to that of South Carolina in relation to Fort Sumter, but it was a dangerous act. Brown had seized a Federal installation while Georgia was still within the Union.[4]

Georgia's link to the United States was soon broken, however. On 16 January, two weeks after Pulaski was taken, the Georgia Secession Convention assembled in Milledgeville, and on 19 January 1861, Georgia voted herself out of the Union by a vote of 208 to 89. Brown left no question that Georgia's wartime affairs would be in firm hands as he moved swiftly against the important Federal arsenal at Augusta, garrisoned by troops under Captain Arnold Elzey. Soon Elzey surrendered, and Georgia troops of the Oglethorpe Light Infantry raised the new flag of the Republic of Georgia—a lone red star on a white field—as the Washington Artillery fired a twenty-one-gun salute. Brown then completed the rapid takeover of all-important Federal installations in the state by occupying the United States Mint at Dahlonega. Though long known by his admirers as "Young Hickory," Brown obviously resembled "Old Hickory"—President Andrew Jackson—more as a common's man champion and bank battler than as a defender of the Federal Union. He had taken possession of these Federal facilities with elite state militia units, soon to transfer *en bloc* into Confederate service.[5]

By the time Georgia seceded, Brown had made another important move toward placing his state on a high level of military preparedness. He appointed West Pointer and native Georgian Henry C. Wayne as the state's adjutant and inspector general. Wayne, a Savannah grandee whose revered father remained on the US Supreme Court for the remainder of the war, filled an office unoccupied since 1840. He was principally tasked with overseeing the organization and administration of the state's military strength, divided as it was into the common militia (accessible through the county militia district system) and the elite volunteer militia units.[6]

During the war's first year, Wayne—at Brown's direction—created several small state armies. They were designated the Georgia Army; the 4th Brigade, Georgia Volunteers; and the Georgia State Troops. Most of their men would ultimately enter Confederate service through volunteering or requisition.[7]

During the same period, Brown and Wayne used the machinery of the militia system to fill Georgia's quota of troops sent to the Confederacy, some 60,000 men by April 1862 according to Brown's calculation. Brown enjoyed these recruiting duties. They gave meaning to his constitutional title of commander-in-chief and provided him with an array of appointments that expanded his patronage powers. Moreover, the process of tapping a sovereign state's manpower through the agency of the state's highest elected official fit well with Brown's conception of state rights. Consequently, the Richmond government's understandable move in April 1862 to use the first of the conscription acts to hold the Confederate armies in place—and to recruit their numbers more efficiently through Confederate enrollment officers—seemed to Governor Brown nothing less than an unconstitutional usurpation of state power.[8]

The Conscription Act forever changed Georgia's relations with the Confederate administration. Brown and Wayne obstructed conscription in every way they could. When the governor shielded the militia officers from conscription, Brown's political enemies and the anti-Brown press dubbed them "Joe Brown's Pets," an epithet later to embrace the Georgia Militia in general. But, though Brown did protect the militia officers and expand their numbers, he also reduced them to ranks in early 1863 and sent them to defend Savannah from a Federal attack that never came. The governor also created the Georgia State Line, two regiments of conscription-age men. Though originally mustered as bridge guards on the state's Western & Atlantic Railroad, the men of the State Line were eventually "loaned" to the Army of Tennessee.[9]

Still, neither the "skeleton" remnant of the militia nor the Georgia State Line could be considered a credible defense of the Empire State of the South. Governor Brown determined to reorganize the Georgia Militia into a powerful force that could defend the state when and if the Confederate authorities would not. The spur to his acting on his intent came in mid-1863 during a period of uncharacteristically close cooperation between Milledgeville and Richmond. Since the Confederacy wished to create a temporary Confederate organization to help protect the state, to be called the Georgia State Guard Brown helped the Confederate raise it, even encouraging his militia officers to join. Emboldened by his success in raising thousands of men for the Guard, Brown persuaded the General Assembly to reorganize the militia through an act of 14 December 1863.[10]

Under the terms of the legislation, the militia enrollment would include all white Georgia males from sixteen through sixty, including exempts and conscription-age men not actually enrolled. The reorganized militia would be divided into two parts: the "Militia Proper," composed of those seventeen through fifty years of age—the more active portion of the troops—and the "Militia Reserve," sixteen-year-old boys and men between fifty and sixty who would not even have to drill until the Militia Proper was put into the field. Men from neither class would be legally subject to any requisitions from Richmond.[11]

The information gathered for the militia enrollment was so extensive that the voluminous document created would later become known as the "Joe Brown Census." Enrollees' age and birthplace, as well as any arms, accouterments, horses, or tack they owned, were all recorded.[12]

As in the earlier militia organization, the militia districts within the counties provided the basis of the new system. However, these county militia districts were no longer organized into thirteen two-brigade divisions with corresponding military hierarchies. Instead, the state's forty-four three-county senatorial districts became military districts. In each district, one of the governor's aides-de-camp (with a state colonel's commission and a district surgeon to pass on medical exemptions) and an enrolling officer would enroll the available arms-bearing population. The building blocks of the new regiments, brigades, and, hopefully, divisions, would be produced from the separate three-county districts, with elections of officers held as units organized. Once the enrollment and organization were completed in each district, the "militia organization theretofore existing" was to be declared suspended.[13]

The militia enrolling officers, who carried out their task in early 1864, were allowed three or more assistants to help them enroll their districts, with fifty cents paid for each man enrolled. Because of the war's inroads into the state's arms-bearing population, many districts within various counties could no longer yield a company of men. Consequently, the enrolling officers were empowered to consolidate districts when necessary or to divide districts in the cases of towns whose populations had been swelled by refugees. The state officers found it "impracticable" to conduct enrollments in some of the state's northernmost counties (particularly those near Union-held Chattanooga). They were empowered, however, to enroll men from units of the Georgia State Guard, whose expiration of service was drawing near.[14]

By 7 May 1864, the arms-bearing population with the state of Georgia had been "enrolled, classified, and organized completely." The results were impressive:

MILITIA PROPER—
      3303 (between 17 & 18);
      13,219 (between 18 & 45);
      8301 (between 45 & 50)
      TOTAL: 24,823

MILITIA RESERVE—
      4474 (16 & 17);
      12,101 (between 50 & 60)
      TOTAL: 16,575

GRAND TOTAL: 41,398[15]

These numbers, according to Adjutant General Wayne, yielded eighteen regiments, twenty-one first-class battalions, forty-seven second-class battalions, and eight independent companies, all "ready for service." But, as had been the case with the original Georgia Militia, Confederate legislation wrecked the new organization. The Third Conscription Act had been passed in February 1864, creating new age limits of seventeen to fifty. Furthermore,

Wayne noted that the new act—with its provision of constructive enroll-ment—"absorbing…as it does the Militia Proper" (into either the Confederate army or Howell Cobb's Georgia Reserve Force), left the state "only the Militia Reserve."[16]

"Without expressing any opinion upon the wisdom of the extension of the Conscript Law," Wayne continued, "a political question with which, officially, I have nothing to do, I am at liberty, nevertheless, to say, that it is to be regretted, under the circumstances of invasion pressing upon Georgia, that with a military organization complete in all its parts, the enforcement of the extension had not been suspended, and the unity of force preserved in the State, instead of distracting and dividing it at a critical period."[17]

For his part, Governor Brown argued that "without the interruption growing out the Conscript Acts," Georgia could have fielded, "for her own defence,…a force of some 30,000 men, after making all reasonable allowance for disability, etc." As it was, on 18 May 1864, he was reduced to calling out his militia officers again and sending them to the defense of another threatened Georgia city, in this case Atlanta rather than Savannah.[18]

Joseph E. Brown "Young Hickory," c. 1850, when a rising young lawyer and state senator. (I. W. Avery, *The History of the State of Georgia* [1881])

Henry Constantine Wayne As Georgia's Adjutant & Inspector General, West Pointer and Mexican War veteran Wayne was tasked with administering and occasionally leading Georgia's state troops. A postwar portrait.

(U. S. Military Academy, West Point)

Militia Map One The Military Divisions of Georgia, 1861-1863 [after "Map of
Georgia in 1860" in U. B. Phillips, *Georgia and State Rights* (1902; reprint, Yellow
Springs, Ohio, 1968).]

Until reorganized in 1863-1864 Georgia's militia establishment operated under
the antebellum organization illustrated by the table opposite and the map above.
There were thirteen divisions of two brigades each, commanded by thirteen major
generals and twenty-six brigadier generals respectively. On the map, the brigades
are represented by Roman numerals.

The map's larger divisions represent those areas whose white population was
scattered; smaller divisions represent areas where white population was concentrated. Four counties (Murray, Taylor, Quitman, and Wilcox) were not within the
areas assigned to their brigades.

FIRST DIVISION

First Brigade	Second Brigade
Chatham	Screven
Bryan	Bulloch
McIntosh	Montgomery
Camden	Tattnall
Wayne	Burke
Liberty	Jefferson
Effingham	Emanuel
Glynn	Johnson
Charlton	

SECOND DIVISION

First Brigade	Second Brigade
Richmond	Washington
Columbia	Hancock
Warren	Taliaferro
Glascock	

THIRD DIVISION

First Brigade	Second Brigade
Morgan	Greene
Putnam	Oglethorpe
Baldwin	Clarke

FOURTH DIVISION

First Brigade	Second Brigade
Wilkes	Jackson
Lincoln	Franklin
Elbert	Madison
Hart	Banks

FIFTH DIVISION

First Brigade	Second Brigade	
Jones	Henry	Butts
Jasper	Fayette	Clayton

SIXTH DIVISION

First Brigade	Second Brigade	
Wilkinson	Telfair	Brooks
Pulaski	Irwin	Coffee
Twiggs	Appling	Colquitt
Laurens	Ware	Echols
	Lowndes	Berrien
	Clinch	Pierce

SEVENTH DIVISION

First Brigade	Second Brigade
Habersham	Forsyth
Hall	Lumpkin
Rabun	Union
White	Towns
	Dawson

EIGHTH DIVISION

First Brigade	Second Brigade
Bibb	Monroe
Crawford	Upson
Houston	Pike
Dooly	Spalding
Worth	

NINTH DIVISION

First Brigade	Second Brigade
Meriwether	Coweta
Troup	Campbell
Heard	Carroll

TENTH DIVISION

First Brigade	Second Brigade
Harris	Talbot
Muscogee	Sumter
Chattahoochee	Macon
Stewart	Marion
Taylor	Schley
Webster	

ELEVENTH DIVISION

First Brigade	Second Brigade
DeKalb	Newton
Cobb	Walton
Paulding	Gwinnett
Polk	
Fulton	
Haralson	

TWELFTH DIVISION

First Brigade	Second Brigade
Cass (Bartow from 1861)	Floyd
Cherokee	Murray
Gilmer	Walker
Gordon	Chattooga
Fannin	Dade
Whitfield	
Catoosa	
Pickens	
Milton	

THIRTEENTH DIVISION

First Brigade	Second Brigade	
Decatur	Baker	Dougherty
Early	Thomas	Quitman
Randolph	Lee	Miller
Clay	Mitchell	Wilcox
Terrell	Calhoun	

[Allen D. Candler, ed., *The Confederate Records of the State of Georgia*, 5 vols. (Atlanta, 1909), 2:208-211.]

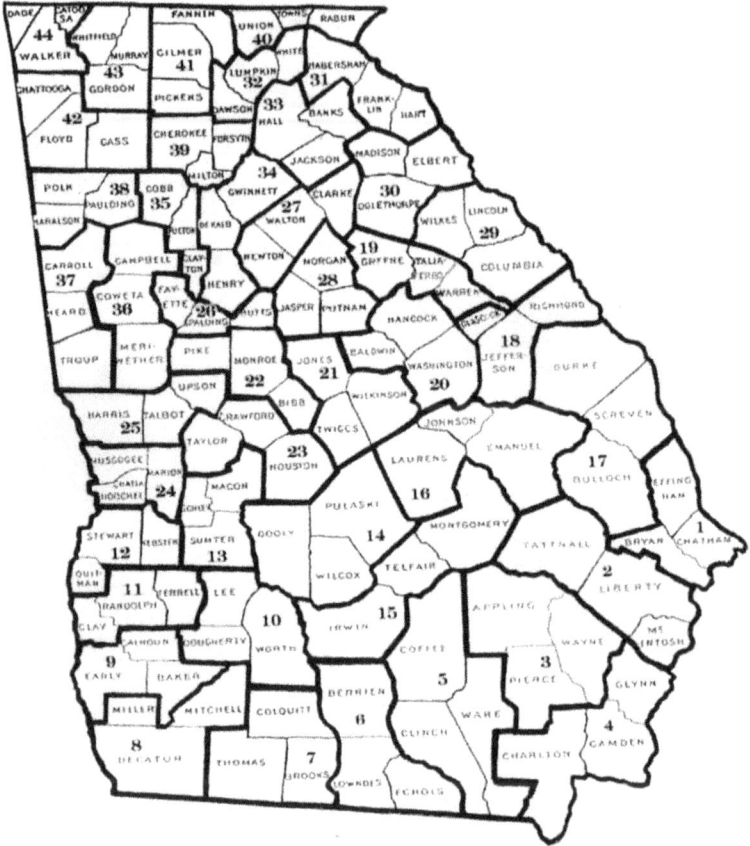

Militia Map   The Military Divisions of Georgia, 1864-1865, under the
Reorganization of 1863 [After "Map of Georgia in 1860" in U. B. Phillips, *Georgia
and State Rights* (1902; reprint, Yellow Springs, Ohio, 1968).]

In mid-December 1863 the Georgia General Assembly passed "An Act to Reorganize the Militia of the State of Georgia." Under this legislation "each Senatorial
District" would "constitute a separate Military District." Once the men in any of
these districts were enrolled and organized, the governor issued an order declaring
"the Militia organizations theretofore existing . . . suspended" and "relieved the
Militia Officers under said previous organizations from their commands."

By June 1864 six regiments and two battalions had been formed from those districts that organized earliest, with efforts obviously made to create regiments from
men drawn from adjacent districts. The original regiments and battalions were as
follows, with districts represented by Arabic numerals: First Regiment (19, 20, 29,
30), Second Regiment (14, 18, 21, 22, 23), Third Regiment (24, 25, 12, 36), Fourth
Regiment (31, 33, 29, 40, 32, 41), Fifth Regiment (6, 7, 8, 9, 10, 11), Sixth
Regiment (26, 27, 28, 34, 35), First Battalion (13, 16, 17, 18), and Second Battalion
(1, 2, 3, 4, 5).

The three-county military districts are shown in the table opposite and on the map above.

1st District	12th District	23rd District	34th District
Effingham	Stewart	Taylor	Gwinnett
Bryan	Webster	Crawford	DeKalb
Chatham	Quitman	Houston	Henry
2nd District	13th District	24th District	35th District
Tattnall	Macon	Muscogee	Cobb
Liberty	Scley	Chattahoochee	Fulton
McIntosh	Sumter	Marion	Clayton
3rd District	14th District	25th District	36th District
Appling	Dooly	Harris	Campbell
Pierce	Pulaski	Talbot	Coweta
Wayne	Wilcox	Upson	Meriwether
4th District	15th District	26th District	37th District
Glynn	Irwin	Fayette	Carroll
Camden	Telfair	Spalding	Heard
Charlton	Montgomery	Butts	Troup
5th District	16th District	27th District	38th District
Coffee	Laurens	Newton	Polk
Clinch	Johnson	Walton	Haralson
Ware	Emanuel	Clarke	Paulding
6th District	17th District	28th District	39th District
Berrine	Burke	Morgan	Cherokee
Lowndes	Screven	Jasper	Forsyth
Echols	Bulloch	Putnam	Milton
7th District	18th District	29th District	40th District
Colquitt	Glascock	Wilkes	Union
Thomas	Jefferson	Lincoln	Towns
Brooks	Richmond	Columbia	Rabun
8th District	19th District	30th District	41st District
Miller	Greene	Madison	Fannin
Decatur	Taliaferro	Elbert	Gilmer
Mitchell	Warren	Oglethorpe	Pickens
9th District	20th District	31st District	42nd District
Early	Baldwin	Habersham	Chattooga
Calhoun	Hancock	Franklin	Floyd
Baker	Washington	Hart	Cass [Bartow]
10th District	21st District	32nd District	43rd District
Lee	Jones	Dawson	Whitfield
Dougherty	Twiggs	Lumpkin	Murray
Worth	Wilkinson	White	Gordon
11th District	22nd District	33rd District	44th District
Clay	Pike	Hall	Dade
Randolph	Monroe	Banks	Walker
Terrell	Bibb	Jackson	Catoosa

[*Acts of the General Assembly of the State of Georgia in 1864* (Milledgeville GA, 1864) 51; "A List of Regiments and the Districts which Compose Them," Executive Secretary Letter Books, 1862-1865, 23; General Orders, Number 12, 7 April 1864, Adjutant General's General Orders.]

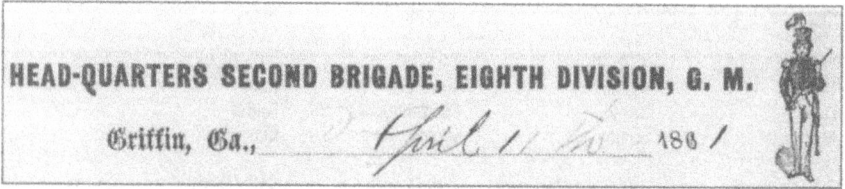

HEAD-QUARTERS SECOND BRIGADE, EIGHTH DIVISION, G. M.

Griffin, Ga.,   186

Militia Stationery Letterhead This letterhead illustrates the Georgia Militia's organization in 1861, as well as the elaborate uniforms favored by some of the units. (Hargrett Rare Book and Manuscript Library, University of Georgia Libraries)

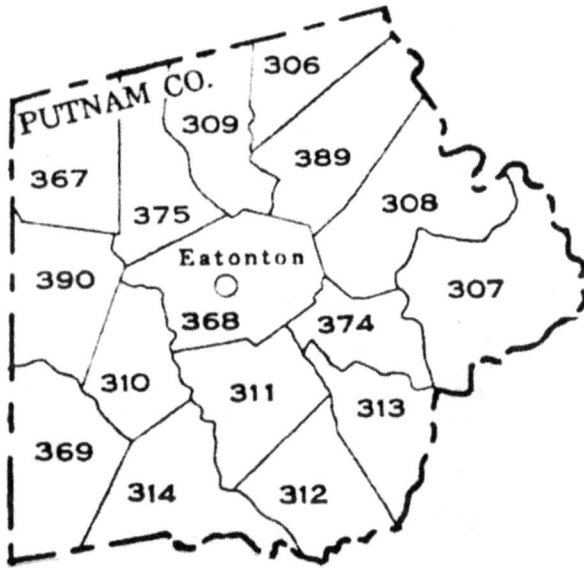

Putnam County Militia Districts This twentieth-century map shows the typical district subdivisions, with these changed only slightly from the Civil War period, as the next illustration shows.

(Hargrett Rare Book and Manuscript Library, University of Georgia Libraries)

Militia Census Record—Putnam County A "census" of Georgia manpower made for the militia reorganization was ordered by the General Assembly in late 1863. As shown by the document reproduced here, a great deal of information valuable to the state was gathered. (Georgia Archives)

Beverly D. Evans Representative of many of Georgia's soldiers, Evans was a member during the war first of a Confederate unit and later served with Georgia's state troops, both the militia and the Georgia State Line. An antebellum portrait.
(Courtesy of the Evans Family)

Howell Cobb As a Confederate counterweight to Governor Brown's state rights
government, General Cobb spent the last two years in constant conflict with the
Milledgeville administration.

(Hargrett Rare Book and Manuscript Library, University of Georgia Libraries)

Jefferson Davis The President of the Confederacy (and his conscription policy in particular) served as a rallying point for the disaffected in Georgia, who created an anti-Davis cabal in the upper reaches of the state government.

(National Archives)

Gustavus Woodson Smith One of several Confederate generals who felt slighted by Davis and his administration, Smith resigned from the army and soon joined Georgia's anti-administration forces. He became the first and only commander of the First Division, Georgia Militia.

(Manuscripts Department, Tulane University Libraries)

The Chatham Artillery at Jackson's Tomb Shown here in June 1859, resplendent in their ornate uniforms, the officers and men of Savannah's Chatham Artillery —"bucks of the blood"—typified Georgia's elite volunteer militia units of the antebellum period. (Georgia Historical Society)

The Common Militia This illustration from *Georgia Scenes* depicts the common militia as they came to be seen by critics and satirists. Characteristic features include the hapless officer, his unsoldierly men, and—a staple of the genre—a militiaman "armed" with an umbrella.

(Hargrett Rare Book and Manuscript Library, University of Georgia Libraries)

Private Ashford M. James, Co. C, Whitehead's Battalion, Georgia Militia. Private James was listed as sixteen in the Habersham County records of the militia reorganization. Shown here armed with a shotgun, he survived the war and lived on until 1934.

(Courtesy of David Wynn Vaughan.)

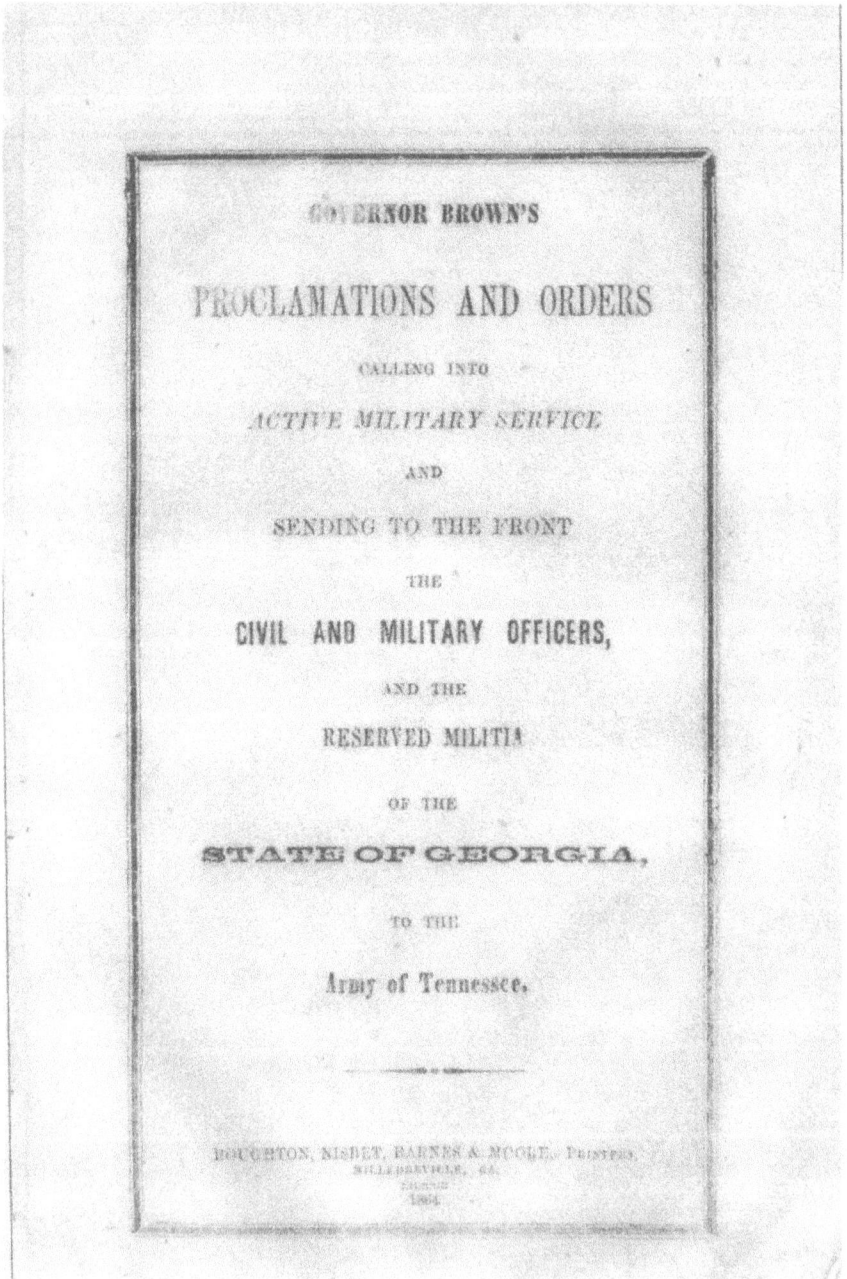

Governor Brown's Proclamations and Orders, 1864 Having been frequently criticized for withholding much of Georgia's manpower from the Confederacy, Governor Brown made a public display of his military assistance to the Confederate army during the Atlanta Campaign.

(Special Collections Department, Robert W. Woodruff Library, Emory University)

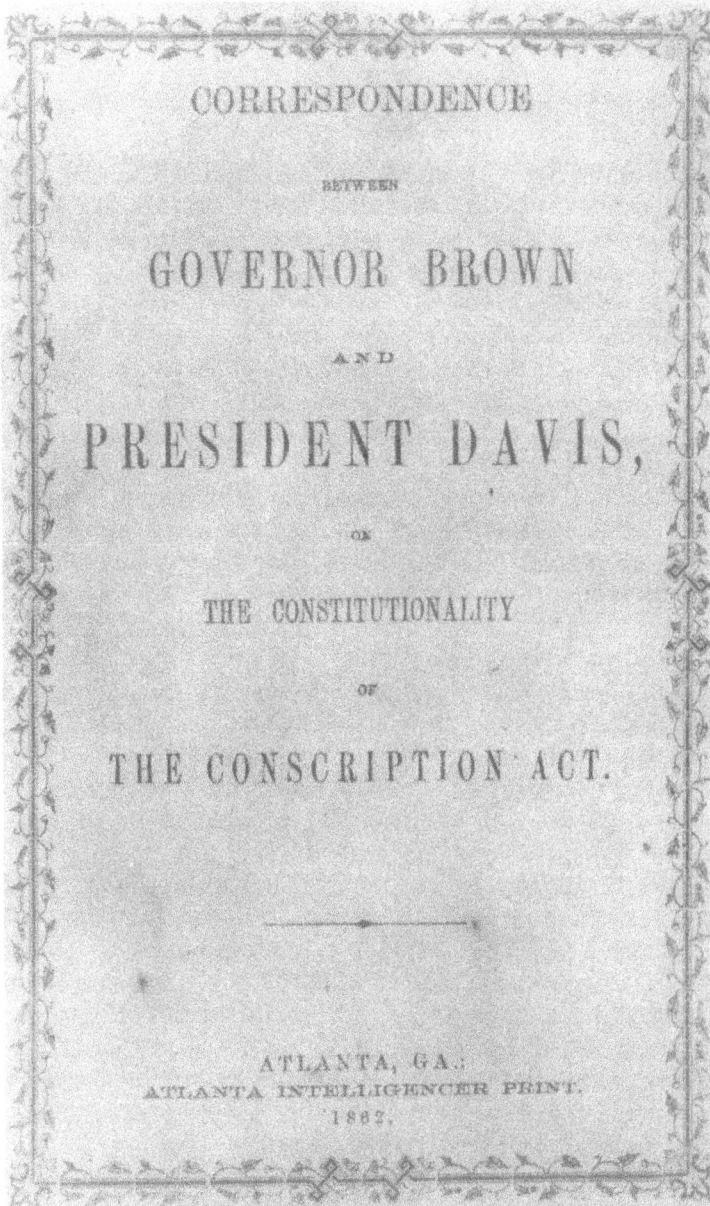

CORRESPONDENCE

BETWEEN

GOVERNOR BROWN

AND

PRESIDENT DAVIS,

ON

THE CONSTITUTIONALITY

OF

THE CONSCRIPTION ACT.

ATLANTA, GA.:
ATLANTA INTELLIGENCER PRINT.
1862.

Conscription Correspondence A controversy that ended only with the war, the conscription conflict generated a huge amount of correspondence between Milledgeville and Richmond. Much of it eventually found its way into pamphlets such as this one.

(Hargrett Rare Book and Manuscript Library, University of Georgia Libraries)

[Ordered 50 copies for the Senate.

AN ACT

To reorganize the militia of the State of Georgia, and for other purposes.

Section 1. Be it enacted by the Senate and House of Representatives of the State of Georgia in General Assembly convened, That each Senatorial District in the State shall constitute a separate Military District, and it shall be the duty of the Governor, as soon as practicable after the passage af this act, to appoint an Aid de Camp, with the rank of Colonel, in each district, who shall be charged with the duties hereinafter set forth.

Sec. 2. Be it further enacted, That within four days after being notified of his appointment, it shall be the duty of each Aid de Camp to commence the enrollment of all free white males resident in his District who are or shall be of the age of sixteen years and not over sixty years, and also those who shall from time to time arrive at the age of sixteen years, or who may come to reside within the District, except those who shall actually be in the army or navy of the Confederate States, or in the State service. The enrollment shall be by Company Districts, and shall show the age, occupation and nativity of each person enrolled, the number of the Company District in which he may reside, and, if any exemption is claimed, the ground of it. For the purpose of facilitating the enrollment, the Aids de Camp shall be authorized to employ, with the approval of the Governor, three or more assistants for each county, who shall receive for their services compensation at the rate of fifty cents for each person enrolled by them. For a failure faithfully to discharge their duties, the assistant enrolling officer shall be liable to removal by the Governor, and if without sufficient excuse, to be judged of by the Governor, shall be liable further to forfeiture of all compensation.

Sec. 3. Be it further enacted That it shall be the duty of the Aid de Camp, within ten days after the enrollment has been completed in his District, to forward complete lists,

---

Draft of the Act to Reorganize the Militia As the militia reorganization legislation made its way through the Senate, this draft was printed to facilitate discussion.
(Hargrett Rare Book and Manuscript Library, University of Georgia Libraries)

HEADQUARTERS, ATLANTA, GA.
July 14, 1864.

J. C. C. Blackburn, Col. and Aid de Camp.

I regret to learn from your letter that men of wealth and influence in your county, who have more property than their neighbors to be defended, and who have Confederate details to remain at home in the pursuit of their ordinary avocations, and performing no military service, express a determination not to obey my late order and report at Atlanta to aid the gallant army under Gen. Johnston in driving back the army of invasion which now threatens to overrun our beloved State, which is the key to the Confederate arch, and to devastate all our homes.

The crops are now generally laid by in the lower half of the State and can be by the 20th of this month in the upper part. The provision supply of next year will not therefore be seriously endangered by the absence of each of those who control plantations, for a short period during the part of the season that is usually one of comparative leisure, after the work in the crop is done. We are now in the midst of the crisis. Our self sacrificing armies have long stood a living breastwork between the enemy and the property of those who you say now refuse to obey my call for the reserve militia. The State officers have nobly responded, and they and the two regiments of the State line have rendered important service on the battle field, and I think the time has come when those who have so long occupied the more comfortable, secure and profitable position in the rear under Confederate details, should step forward meet the enemy and take their share of the danger.

You will, therefore, on and after the 20th day of this month (the day set apart in my proclamation for the militia of your county to leave home) proceed to arrest all such persons as are embraced in my proclamation who may refuse to accompany the balance of the reserve militia of the county, and will send them under arrest to Atlanta to Major Gen. G. W. Smith, where they will be dealt with according to law. To accomplish this object, you are authorized to use all the force necessary. You will not take life unless it is absolutely necessary to overcome resistance. You will temporarily brevet or lance such persons as are necessary to aid in carrying out this order, and will use all non-commissioned officers and all the militia of the county, including all between fifty-five and sixty years of age, with all the guns in the county, if you cannot otherwise enforce obedience to the order contained in my proclamation. All able to bear arms must come to the front and aid in the defence of all that is dear to a people. Those who attempt to skulk from the discharge of this duty, and to hide under exemptions, or details not known to the laws of Georgia, must be compelled to come and do their duty.

The rule laid down for the government of your conduct will apply to all the aids-de-camp of the State, who will be expected to act cautiously and prudently but firmly and decidedly.

Maj. Gen. Smith will send a detail of one or more officers back to each county to aid in enforcing obedience to my orders, who will also act upon the rules above laid down. If armed resistance is made in any county, which is too powerful to be overcome by the militia force at the command of the officer, he will report the facts and sufficient armed force will be sent to overcome force with force and to compel delinquents to do their duty.

The militia who report from each county should see that they bring with them those who refused to come, by sending out details at the time of starting, when necessary to gather them up.

Yours respectfully,
JOSEPH E. BROWN.

☞ Each paper in the State will insert once and send bill.

Militia Broadside Governor Brown himself couldn't always count on obedience to his calls for militia service, as this broadside demonstrates. It also reveals one of his major concerns in withholding militiamen: the agricultural necessity of leaving some of the yeomanry on their farms.

(Hargrett Rare Book and Manuscript Library, University of Georgia Libraries)

Militia Camp This tintype is usually identified showing a militia cavalry camp. If correct, it shows an earlier version of the Georgia Militia, raised before the reorganization that created the First Division, Georgia Militia, in 1864.
(Missouri Historical Society, St. Louis)

STATE OF GEORGIA.

Adjutant and Inspector General's Office.

MILLEDGEVILLE,   1864.

Your application for the exemption of..............:

.....................from the operations of the "Act to
re-organize the Militia of the State of Georgia, and for
other purposes," assented to Dec. 14, 1863, has been received and filed.

As the enrollment prescribed by the Act, will not, of
itself, in any manner interfere with the ordinary avocations
of Citizens; and as they cannot be disturbed, except in
cases of extreme necessity, the Governor declines to grant
any exemptions or details until such contingency may
arise, as shall force him to call the militia into active service. Then he will be better able to judge, whether or
not the public interests, at that time, will warrant special
exemptions or details from service in the field.

Independent or Volunteer Companies are not permitted
by the Law re-organizing the Militia—one uniform military system throughout the State having been prescribed by
that Law.

Very respectfully,

HENRY C. WAYNE,
Adjutant & Inspector General.

Exemption Form The Civil War was certainly a modern war in relation to the
amount of bureaucratic paperwork it involved. This form suggests a fair number of
men attempted to secure exemptions. It also provides the governor's interpretation
of what service under the militia reorganization entailed.

(Hargrett Rare Book and Manuscript Library, University of Georgia Libraries)

TO ARMS!

State of Georgia---
COLONEL'S OFFICE, *Warrenton, Feb. 21, 1862.*

GENERAL ORDER No. 1.

The Captains of the Militia in each District in the counties of WARREN and GLASSCOCK are hereby required to prepare two lists of the men liable to do military duty in their respective districts, and to deposit the same at this office, on or before the 4th day of March next. One list to be composed of the unmarried men, and the other of the married men and widowers.

They are further directed to fill all vacancies of noncommissioned officers immediately, and to direct them to notify every man to be in Warrenton, by 9 1-2 o'clock on the 4th of March next, for a Regimental Parade.

Isaac B. Huff,

February 21.   Colonel Commanding.

Militia Broadside A dramatic example of the workings of the militia organization before passage of the conscription act, this broadside suggests the method by which Governor Brown fulfilled Richmond's manpower requisitions.

2.
THE GEORGIA MILITIA DURING
THE ATLANTA CAMPAIGN

With Atlanta so seriously threatened, Governor Brown's proclamation of 18 May 1864 cast a wide net. It directed "all Commissioned Officers of the Militia of this State, including district Aides-de-Camp," to report to Adjutant General Wayne in Atlanta, along with all civil officers (whom the governor also shielded from conscription), "except those of the State House, the Penitentiary, the State Road, the Judges of the Superior and Inferior Courts, Ordinaries and Solicitors General, and Clerks and Sheriffs of Courts actually in session."[19]

This call, Adjutant General Wayne later noted, "was promptly responded to"; indeed, within a week of the governor's proclamation, the *Atlanta Intelligencer* reported that the militia officers were reporting "in large numbers" and that "a number of the civil officers" had reported as well, with two brigades to act as an "auxiliary force to Gen. Johnston, under the command of that skillful and gallant officer, Gen. Wayne." With General William T. Sherman's massive Federal armies advancing toward Marietta and the Chattahoochee River, General Johnston assigned the militiamen to guard a 100-mile line that stretched along the Chattahoochee River from Roswell, almost due north of Atlanta, to West Point, at the Alabama line. The militia brigades were instructed to hold the line as long as possible and to burn the bridge at Roswell Factory when they could no longer successfully defend it.[20] Patrick McGriff of Company K, 5th Regiment, wrote his wife in Wilkes County from a militia camp near Bolton, close by the Chattahoochee, on 6 June: "We have 55 men in the company. I am 1st Lieutenant. If I had gotten the Adjutant's place I could have a horse to ride…. I am not ambitious, but I would like very much to ride."[21]

By this time, McGriff and his fellow militiamen had reluctantly bidden farewell to General Wayne and received a new commander, Gustavus Woodson Smith. A former Confederate general, Smith had by this time in his wartime career been involved in more controversy than combat. General Smith—a tall, rather massive Kentuckian—had graduated from the United States Military Academy in 1842, taught engineering there for a time, and served in the Mexican War. Later he went into the construction business and eventually became street commissioner for the city of New York. Appointed Major General, C. S. A., on 1 September 1861, Smith had held the highest field command in the Confederate army for a brief time. During the Battle of Fair Oaks (or Seven Pines), he had taken over from the time Joseph E. Johnston was wounded until Robert E. Lee assumed command. His conduct of the battle—"fumbling and overcautious"—was followed by a mysterious bout of paralysis. He had later served as Confederate secretary of war for just four November days in 1862; he was appointed only to bridge the gap between George W. Randolph and James A. Seddon. A friend of Joseph E. Johnston (with "little respect" for Robert E. Lee), Smith feuded with President Jefferson Davis and ultimately resigned from the army on 17 February 1863 after being "overslaughed": six general officers had been promoted to lieutenant general over his head.[22]

One of Smith's primary qualifications for heading the Georgia Militia seemed to be the contempt for President Davis that he shared with Governor Brown. At the time of his appointment to command of the militia, Smith was serving as superintendent of the Etowah Manufacturing and Mining Company, recently destroyed by Sherman's troops; he was in Macon preparing alternate facilities for the manufacture of iron.[23]

Governor Brown fully intended for Smith to become major general, 1st Division, Georgia Militia, so his appointment came on 1 June 1864, with his pro forma election to the position scheduled for shortly thereafter at Camp Georgia, the militia encampment at the fairgrounds near the heart of Atlanta. The governor himself visited the camp at about the time of the election, and, as a correspondent of the *Intelligencer* wrote, Brown began a speech to the militia by exclaiming, "I am exceedingly proud of my Pets. (Immense shouts)." Before he was done, he had also announced himself "ready to march with his Pets, and if need be to die with them."[24] Nonetheless, the *Atlanta Register* of 3 June 1864 reported that the

Militia called out by Gov. Brown exhibited a rather singular freak of fickleness of purpose yesterday, in their election for General. The vote being taken in the morning, Gustavus W. Smith…was elected without any opposition. Later in the day, a letter, it was said, was received in camp, that Adjt. Gen. Wayne would have accepted the position, if he had been elected. The Militia boys, upon hearing this, exclaimed that they had been sold by somebody, and at once, and in a very unparliamentary manner, threw Gen. Smith overboard, and elected Adjt. Gen. Wayne.

If this actually happened, Governor Brown quickly had Smith dragged back aboard, for he was to command the 1st Division for its entire existence.[25]

On 11 June 1864, General Orders, No. 1, issued from the militia's headquarters, announcing Smith's assumption of command and naming his staff officers, among them General Robert Toombs, Inspector General, and Colonel Joseph S. Claghorn (formerly commander of Savannah's Chatham Artillery), chief of artillery and ordnance. Additionally, Linton Stephens, beloved half-brother of Confederate Vice President Alexander H. Stephens, was appointed one of General Smith's aides-de-camp.[26]

Most prominent among these men was Robert Toombs—wealthy planter, brilliant attorney, and one of the greatest of Georgia's public men in the late antebellum years. Since the war he had also been a member of President Davis's cabinet and a general in the Confederate army. He had a lively contempt for West Pointers, however, prominent among them the president himself, and he was an enthusiastic member of the anti-Davis cabal that coalesced in Georgia with Governor Brown as its nucleus. Happily for all concerned, G. W. Smith was almost alone among Southern generals enjoying Toombs's respect.[27] Ever quotable, Toombs had his own unvarnished opinion of the Georgia Militia:

We have a mixed crowd, a large number of earnest, brave, true men; then all the shirks and skulks in Georgia trying to get from under bullets.[28]

In early June the officers and organization of the militia division was announced, the elections for the two militia brigadiers having been held on 3 June. The table of organization showed that the units—at this time composed entirely of the state's civil and military officers—were filling erratically.

The division was composed of Brigadier General R. W. Carswell's 1st Brigade, comprising the 1st Regiment under Colonel E. H. Pottle, the 2d under Colonel C. D. Anderson (later to be a militia brigadier), and the 5th under Colonel S. S. Stafford, with the 1st Battalion, Lieutenant Colonel Henry Kent McCay (another future brigadier), commanding; and Brigadier General P. J. Philips's 2d Brigade, comprising the 3rd, 4th, and 6th Regiments, under Lieutenant Colonel John W. Hill, Colonel Robert McMillan, and Colonel T. J. Burney, respectively. Also organized was an Independent Artillery Battalion under Colonel Carey W. Styles.[29]

This division-in-the-making was soon sent into action. On 27 June, the same day Sherman assaulted Johnston's position on Kennesaw Mountain, Smith was ordered to lead his militia troops in support of Brigadier General William H. "Red" Jackson's cavalry division, posted on the extreme left of the army:

> General Johnston wishes that you would concentrate at some convenient point (say Turner's Ferry) as large an infantry force as can be gathered in your command, with a battery, at short notice (leaving some force at the railroad bridge), and cross the river, moving up so as to place yourself in communication with Brigadier General Jackson. The object is to show an infantry force in connection with Jackson's cavalry as a demonstration calculated to deter the enemy from any further attempt to extend his right flank toward the river. It is not intended nor desired that your troops should become engaged, but simply threaten the right and rear of the enemy without losing your direct communication with the river between Turner's Ferry and Sandtown.
> M. Lovell,
> Major-General[30]

The Smyrna Line was not a particularly strong defensive position. Johnston only occupied it for a few hours in order to move his supply wagons safely across the Chattahoochee River and to deploy his troops in the previously prepared—and much more formidable—Chattahoochee River Line. Smith and his militiamen were only to threaten the right and rear of the enemy without becoming heavily engaged, a rather common assignment in military operations. Consequently, it is difficult to understand how a man of Smith's experience could have failed to comprehend such instructions, but—either through misunderstanding or simple contentiousness—he later wrote:

> *I told General Lovell that I did not believe the small available force of raw militia, acting as a support to the cavalry, could stop Sherman's advance if he choose to move in force around Johnston's left flank; but if I received a positive order from General Johnston to move across the Chattahoochee for the purpose indicated, the order would be obeyed to the best of my ability, without regard to my opinion of the matter.* [31]

In Atlanta, a veteran regular army battery of four twelve-pounder Napoleons under Captain Ruel W. Anderson of Hawkinsville had been refitted for the field. While in the city awaiting orders, Anderson and his artillerists were apparently spotted by Smith. As he moved the militia toward the river, Smith appropriated Anderson's battery for his own command, without, in his words, "other authority than my own, but with the full consent of the officers and men." Crossing the Chattahoochee at James' Ferry, they took a position in open territory, supporting Jackson's cavalry as directed. On 4 and 5 July, the militia (though some were "powerful bad Scared" [*sic*]) conducted an orderly delaying action against Francis P. Blair's Federal XVII Army Corps along Turner's Ferry Road (today's Bankhead Highway) and held a position along the crest of Nickajack Ridge, about 3 miles north of Turner's Ferry on the night of 4 July. At 1:00 A.M. on 5 July, Smith was ordered to withdraw his command at dawn and, first, to fall back into the Chattahoochee River Line, then form in reserve south of the river in the Mason & Turner's Ferry area (near where Charley Brown Airport is located today).[32]

General Smith asserted that the militiamen had executed the delaying assignment thoroughly in their first major combat role, and the militia's commendable performance prompted General Joseph E. Johnston to write Governor Brown on 7 July:

> *To His Excellency J. E. Brown, Governor:*
> *I have the pleasure to inform you that the State troops promise well, and have already done good service. While the army was near Marietta they were employed to support the cavalry on the extreme left and occupied a position quite distinct from any other infantry of ours. According to all accounts their*

conduct in the presence of the enemy was firm and creditable. Such Federal
parties as approached the crossing-places of the Chattahoochee guarded by them
have been driven back. These proofs of their valor make me anxious that their
number be increased. Is it possible? You know that the distinguished officer at
their head [G. W. Smith] is competent to high command.
Most respectfully, your obedient servant,
J. E. Johnston [33]

Two days after Johnston wrote him, Governor Brown called out much
of the Militia Reserve, along with any of the Militia Proper exempted from
conscription and able to serve. He did this, he stated, because his recent correspondence with President Davis had convinced him that Georgia was "to
be left to her own resources to supply the reinforcements" to General
Johnston's Army of the Tennessee. Additionally—beginning another notable
controversy with the Confederate authorities—the governor also decided to
call up those Confederate soldiers in Georgia "not in actual *military service*,"
specifically, "the large number of able-bodied young men who have
Confederate details to attend to various industrial avocations and pursuits."
Many of the young men, however, were not details but boys below conscription age, one of whom was described toward the end of the campaign by an
older militiaman:

[W]e have a little boy 15 years old that has marched the whole distance with us
and toted his gun, cartridges 40 rounds, his blanket and haversack, and has
never fallen out to rest yet. He is in all the cane patches nearly that we pass and
apple orchards. We have a great deal of fun out of him. In passing men that
have fallen out to rest, they say to him: "My little fellow you are too small to be
here." He always says to them: "Yes, and you are too large to be staggering and
straggling out as you do; get up and march. I am one of Joe Brown's colts...." [34]

On the night of Brown's proclamation calling out the Militia Reserve,
General Johnston withdrew the Army of Tennessee from the Chattahoochee
River Line and ordered General Smith to march his militia to Poplar Springs,
two miles southeast of Atlanta, near the Atlanta & West Point Railroad. In
the meantime, the members of the reserve militia that had been called up by
Governor Brown began to join Smith's force. These fresh troops were supposed to be armed and drilled, with a reorganization of the division to follow

soon thereafter. But three days later they were ordered, along with the rest of the militia, to the right of John Bell Hood's corps, where they manned some 2 miles of trenches on the eastern edge of Atlanta.[35]

General Toombs welcomed the arrival in Atlanta of the men of the Militia Reserve and viewed them quite sympathetically:

> *The militia are coming up finely. Twelve hundred of them arrived here this evening, armed and tolerably well equipped. Poor fellows! They are green and raw, undisciplined and badly officered. It keeps us at work day and night to bring order out of this confused mass, and we have but a poor chance. They march right into the trenches, and are immediately under the enemy's fire all day. We shall trust to a kind Providence alone to preserve them from a great disaster, and make them useful to the army and the country. The pressure is so great that we are compelled to put them to the work of veterans without an hour's preparation. I am doing my best to get them in the best possible position.[36]*

On 12 July, one footsore militiaman, Private A. T. Holliday of Company K, 5th Regiment, Georgia Militia, wrote to his wife Elizabeth from "Camp Grease Gut," just north of Atlanta: "I shall try to get into the cavalry as I am worn out walking."[37]

Then, on 16 and 17 July, he wrote her a rather insightful letter, as he found himself bound away from Atlanta and toward West Point on the Alabama line:

> *...You stated in your letter of the 12th instant that you had heard I had been under arrest. It is not so!...I am at this moment at LaGrange. We are on our way to West Point. We left our camp at 8 last night. We had a tolerable comfortable ride considering we had to ride in box cars. We have 13 cars filled inside and out...We only had 5 box cars for our brigade which would make an average of 75 men to the box had all have gone on the inside. Two men fell off the top of the cars in our trip here. I have not learned whether they were hurt much or not.... Some of the brigade have nothing to eat at all. We are seeing hard times sure. The first and fifth regiments do all the work and all the fighting also. We have a shoddy set of officers and our Col. is a perfect fool. I believe if he was ordered to cross the Atlantic Ocean to-night he is just simpleton enough to try it. I will here finish out about the arrest. Gus told me that the Yanks were in a half mile of our Regt. and begged me to turn and go back.*

I was in a two horse wagon. He was nearly broke down and wanted to ride. I
told him I would wait awhile until some more of the boys came up which I did.
They told me also that I had best cross over the river. I did so. Before night an
officer crossed over the river to get up all the stragglers. He came to me and
wanted me to go with him. I would not do it as I had a certificate from the
surgeon exempting me from service. I was sick with bowel affection. The next
day Pottle sent after me. I would not go; he sent again. The next day I felt
better and went to the command and reported to him. There was not a word
said to me. The certificate I had was sufficient and I knew it all the time. So
ended the arrest. You can now make yourself easy. The fool that wrote the lie
was hard pressed for news.[38]

Back at Atlanta on 17 July, at the direction of President Davis, Joseph E. Johnston was replaced as commander of the Army of Tennessee by General John Bell Hood. The Army of Tennessee's new leader lost heavily in his first battle, a badly mismanaged attack at Peachtree Creek on 20 July in which the militia did not participate. Hood then sent Lieutenant General William J. Hardee's corps on a forced night march through the city and eastward. Hardee was ordered to attack Major General James B. McPherson's Federal Army of the Tennessee at daylight on 22 July as it advanced from Decatur along the Georgia Railroad. But Hood miscalculated the time required to make the night march, and the attack, which began the Battle of Atlanta, was not delivered until about noon instead of at daylight as Hood had planned. Despite the delay, Hardee's attack met with initial success. However, the assault eventually stalled, and at 4:00 P.M. Hood belatedly ordered his old corps, then commanded by Benjamin F. Cheatham, to attack from the trenches to the left of the Georgia Militia.[39]

Without waiting for orders, General Smith ordered the militia to join Cheatham's attack, and Smith's men advanced for about a mile to the vicinity of Leggett's Hill (now the intersection of Moreland Avenue and Interstate Highway 20). Smith's report on the Battle of Atlanta was directed to General Hood:

On the 22d of July, while Hardee was attacking the enemy on our extreme
right in the direction of Decatur, you ordered the troops on my left to advance.
Without waiting for orders I closed the intervals in my line, formed line of
battle in the trenches, and moved the militia forward over the parapet more

than a mile against the enemy's strong works in our front. They were directed upon a battery which had annoyed us very much [probably DeGolyer's Black Horse 1st Michigan Battery H]. Captain [Ruel W.] Anderson, who had served with my command beyond the Chattahoochee, volunteered to move his battery with us. He took position in clear, open ground within about 400 yards of the embrasure battery of the enemy, supported by the militia upon his right and left. Within ten minutes the effective fire of the enemy was silenced in our front, and after this they only occasionally ventured to show themselves at the embrasures or put their heads above the parapet. My troops were eager to be allowed to charge the battery, but the brigade upon my left [that of Alexander W. Reynolds of Carter L. Stevenson's division] had given way, and though falling back, was extending still farther to the left. Hardee's fire, on my right, had ceased just after we moved out of the trenches. I considered it useless to make an isolated attack, and therefore held the position, awaiting further developments. In about two hours I received orders from you directing me to withdraw to the trenches. We lost only about 50 men killed and wounded.

The officers and men behaved admirably. Every movement was promptly and accurately made....40

Also impressed was General Robert Toombs: "The militia have behaved with great gallantry. This is sincerely true. They have far exceeded my expectations, and in the fight...equaled any troops in the line of battle. If they stand and fight like men, our homes will be saved. God give them the spirit of men, and all will be well!"41 General Hood added similar plaudits in a brief letter to the governor on 23 July: "The State troops under Major-General Smith fought with great gallantry in the action of yesterday."42 Some of the press also became more appreciative of the state's citizen-soldiers, as indicated by a typical editorial in the *Augusta Chronicle & Sentinel* of 13 July:

Our gallant militia officers have fairly won their spurs.... They have been styled "Gov. Brown's pets," but are now, also, the pets of the army and the people. They have done infinite credit to their patron; and neither he nor they will ever be ashamed of the sobriquet. He has given them a rough handling, for pets, but it has been all the more glorious and advantageous for them. He has been unusually careful of their military education, and they have not failed to profit by their training in the school to which he sent them.43

As July ended, other militiamen "fairly won their spurs," not at Atlanta, but on their way to that city. To facilitate his militia call-up of early July, Governor Brown had split the state of Georgia into southern and northern sections, separated by an east-west line drawn through Macon. Those south of the line were to report to General Smith "with the least delay possible"; those to the north were to leave 20 July, "repairing to Atlanta by the nearest and speediest route."[44]

The response from the southern portion of the state had been over-whelming. One citizen of Macon wrote, "[T]he malitia [sic] are pouring through here by the thousand rushing up without guns & without organization." Consequently, the governor amended his order in a proclamation issued on 21 July 1864 from the 1st Division's Atlanta headquarters: "In accordance with the request of General Hood for the purpose of arming militia in Macon and sending them forward ready for service, thereby avoiding the confusion of having large bodies of unarmed men sent into Atlanta while it is besieged, these headquarters will be moved to Macon." The troops were to "be thrown into camp till they are armed before they are sent to Gen'l Smith."[45]

Ironically, this temporary militia concentration spelled utter ruin for a Yankee raid. Union general George Stoneman planned to take Macon's Camp Oglethorpe prison, free the Federal officers held there, and soon thereafter ride south and break open the teeming Union enlisted men's prison at Andersonville. Delayed by straggling and plundering among his men, Stoneman lost the element of surprise. When he appeared with the bulk of his force—almost 2,000 men—east of Macon on 30 July, the Confederate authorities had been warned by telegraph to expect him.[46]

Governor Brown himself was visiting Macon. Its Confederate commandant, Major General Howell Cobb of the Confederate Reserve Force, found the governor uncharacteristically deferential and eager to assist with the city's defense (despite a longstanding feud between the two). After sending General Wayne with more than 1,000 militiamen east by train to protect the state capital at Milledgeville, Brown immediately turned over command of all militia present to Cobb, and the citizen-soldiers—along with all other disposable troops—were hurried across the river to meet the enemy. Commanding the green militiamen were Confederate officers, many of them convalescents (though some of the militia units had already chosen their officers). All told, the force facing Stoneman roughly equaled his in numbers, though not in training, experience, and weaponry.[47]

Stoneman's axis of approach lay along a road that led west toward Walnut Creek from the tiny village of Cross Keys. Beyond the creek the ground rose to an eminence—crowned by the crude blockhouses of Fort Hawkins, a relic of the Creek Indian Wars—before falling away to the Ocmulgee River, beyond which lay Macon proper and Camp Oglethorpe. Though the bridge into the city had fallen into the river after being undermined by a spring freshet, the railroad bridge downstream had survived and been planked for men and horses. This bridge was Stoneman's immediate goal.[48]

The fight against Stoneman was to be called the Battle of East Macon, after the bucolic suburb on the river's east bank where the battle was waged. East Macon, dominated by the old fort, consisted mainly of cultivated fields, scattered houses, Irish laborers' shanties, and, near the river, a few cotton warehouses. Cobb sent the majority of his force to the heights near the fort, with a strong detachment sent to guard his left, where another road led southwest toward the river from the town of Clinton. The men and boys of Colonel W. J. Armstrong's regiment provided the militia presence on the left, but they would be little occupied during the battle. Their opponents, Unionist Kentuckians whose enlistments were about to expire, had sampled too diligently from the wine cellars and applejack barrels on the way from Atlanta. They attacked only feebly.[49]

The field was much less peaceful on the right. There, near the fort, the defending force was largely militia: Colonel T. L. Holt's regiment went into position left of the road to Cross Keys, with Colonel Charles Jenkins Harris's regiment to the right. When the Federal force swept across Walnut Creek, it concentrated on elevated ground on Captain Samuel S. Dunlap's farm, about a half-mile from the fort. There they unlimbered two Rodman guns in the yard of the captain's house and soon began firing. The Federal artillery was answered by the Confederate battery at Fort Hawkins, and many of the blue cavalrymen dismounted and plunged forward toward the waiting line of militia.[50]

One of the boys in Colonel Holt's militia regiment, nineteen-year-old Sam Griswold (grandson of the pistol maker), remembered vividly what happened in his portion of the line:

[We were] on the left of the road to Cross Keys, in a corn field, and was ordered to lie down in the growing corn. While lying down in this line the skirmishing begun, and to encourage the men, the Adjutant, who had been assigned to the regiment, (he was a convalescent officer of the Confederate armies who had volunteered to go from the hospital, where he was suffering from a wound, to the line and help defend the city) walked up and down in front of them, encouraging them in every way. [Fifty-one-year-old] Uncle Mem Williams was in this line and was somewhat excited, and says to this officer: "Captain, what must an old man, who has got rheumatism and can't run, do?" "Why, we want those who can't run," says he; "You are the very fellow." Soon after the firing began [,] Bob Kingman [,sixteen], who was back of Williams, shot over his head, and it like to have frightened Williams to death. "Oh, you have shot me," he says, "you have shot me." About that time firing became general, and the enemy was shooting their artillery, the shells going over our heads, when from some cause unknown to us the right of the regiment, down next to the road, ran, and the balance of it followed. Uncle Mem Williams was one of the leaders—he forgot his rheumatism.

They rallied after going back a short distance and came around by old Fort Hawkins down to the edge of a pine thicket, and here they skirmished for some time with the Yankees. Bill Brooks[, fifty], who was here behind a fence corner, was shooting at and being shot at by a Yankee behind a tree. Finally Brooks stepped out from behind the fence and straightened himself up and called for the Yankee to come out from behind that tree and give him a fair showing, when some of the boys pulled him back, saying, "You are a goose, Brooks, for that fellow will kill you; he's not coming out." "Well, boys," he says, "I run up yonder, and I am ashamed of it, and I want to show that I am not afraid of them." I forgot to mention that the adjutant was wounded by a ball, soon after talking to Williams and just before the firing began regularly; we heard it strike him and saw him throw his hand to his hip where it struck him.[51]

Some eighty of the other defenders were wounded or killed by the time Stoneman withdrew, and the defenders' lines wavered. But Macon had been saved—principally by the militia, as the governor was quick to note. Stoneman's Raiders, after throwing several shells across the river into Macon, beat a rather addled retreat up the road down which they had come, and many (including Stoneman) were bagged handily by the Confederate troopers who had been pursuing them. Stoneman, now a "dejected and haggard" prisoner, was soon back in Macon.[52]

Another somewhat less reluctant visitor to the city, the recently replaced Joseph E. Johnston, had accompanied General Cobb across the river and witnessed the Battle of East Macon. Johnston observed and applauded the raw militia's baptism of fire, and his brief observations form a fitting summary of the Pets' exploits at Macon: "General Cobb met the Federal forces on the high ground east of the Ocmulgee; and repelled them after a contest of several hours, by his own courage and judicious disposition, and the excellent conduct of his troops, who heard hostile shot then for the first time."[53]

A few days after the Battle of Atlanta, the militia was ordered to the trenches in the northwest quadrant of the city. They remained there—their left extending across the Marietta Road and their right across Peachtree Road—until 1 September, when Atlanta was evacuated. The militiamen were then ordered to march to Griffin, 35 miles south of the city, "guarding the reserve artillery," which they brought in safely. During this march, Smith observed that men over fifty were "not as a class fit for military duty and therefore strongly advised the Governor to withdraw them from continuous military service." G. W. Smith further described his militia troops in reporting to General Hood on their part in the Atlanta Campaign:

> *The militia, although but poorly armed—very few having proper equipments, more than two-thirds of them without cartridge-boxes—almost without ambulances or other transportation, most of the reserves never having been drilled at all, and the others but a few days—all performed well every service required during an arduous and dangerous campaign. They have been in service about 100 days, during at least fifty of which they have been under close fire of the enemy mostly night and day. They have always shown a willing spirit, whether in camp, on the march, working at fortifications, guarding trenches, or upon the open battle-field. They have done good and substantial service in the cause of their country, and have established the fact that Georgia is willing and able to do something effective in her own name beyond furnishing more than her quota to the Confederate armies proper....[54]*

But C. M. Hardy, a veteran of Joseph E. Johnston's Army of Tennessee, wrote his sister on 18 September 1864, referring to the return of the militia from furlough: "They had just as well stay home. They ain't worth a low country cow tick."[55]

A more widely-known and humorous (though no doubt exaggerated) account was written by Sam Watkins of the 1st Tennessee Regiment:

> *By way of grim jest, and a fitting burlesque to tragic scenes, or, rather, to the thing called "glorious war," old Joe Brown, then Governor of Georgia, sent in his militia. It was the richest picture of an army I ever saw. It beat Forepaugh's double-ringed circus. Every one was dressed in citizen's clothes, and the very best they had at that time. A few had double-barreled shot-guns, but the majority had umbrellas and walking-sticks, and nearly every one had on a duster, a flat-bosomed "biled" shirt, and a plug hat; and, to make the thing more ridiculous, the dwarf and the giant were marching side by side; the knock-kneed by the side of bow-legged, the driven-in by the side of the drawn-out; the pale and sallow dyspeptic, who looked like Alex. Stephens, and who seemed to have just been taken out of a chimney that smoked very badly, and whose diet was goobers and sweet potatoes, was placed beside the three hundred-pounder, who was dressed up to kill, and whose looks seemed to say, "I've got a substitute in the army, and twenty negroes at home besides—h-a-a-m, h-a-a-m".[56]*

Though Watkins's famous lampoon makes the militiamen seem a bad bargain, there was someone who wanted them, as Governor Brown found in a letter written in Richmond on 30 August by Secretary of War James Seddon.

> *Sir: The condition of your State, subjected to formidable invasion and menaced with destructive raids in different directions by the enemy, requires the command of all the forces that can be summoned for defense. From recent official correspondence submitted to the Department, it appears on your statement, that you have organized 10,000 or more of the militia of your State, and I am instructed by the President to make requisition on you for that number, and such further force of militia to repel invasion as you may be able to organize for Confederate service. Those within the limits of General Hood's department will report to him; those outside to the commandant of the Department of South Carolina and Georgia [General Samuel Jones].[57]*

This communication, of course, precipitated another battle royal between Milledgeville and Richmond, but before Brown refused Seddon on 12 September (at punishing length), he advised General Hood on 10 September that the Georgia Militia was no longer part of the Army of Tennessee:

> General: As the militia of the State were called out for the defense of Atlanta during the campaign against it, which has terminated by the fall of the city into the hands of the enemy, and as many of these left their homes without preparation (expecting to be gone but a few weeks), who have remained in service over three months(most of the time in the trenches), justice requires that they [the Georgia Militia] be permitted, while the enemy are preparing for the winter campaign, to return to their homes and look for a time after important interests and prepare themselves for such service as may be required when another campaign commences against other important points in the State. I, therefore, hereby withdraw said organization from your command."[58]

Though this news disappointed Hood, it had the opposite effect on William T. Sherman, who wired General Henry Halleck on 15 September, rejoicing that "Governor Brown has disbanded his militia, to gather the corn and sorghum of the State. I have reason to believe that he and [Confederate Vice President Alexander H.] Stephens want to visit me, and have sent them a hearty invitation."[59]

Though there were those in Richmond who considered Joseph E. Brown a traitor and more, a parley with Sherman was not something the governor of Georgia could countenance (nor could Stephens). Consequently, Sherman's planned offer to spare Georgia the March to the Sea in return for withdrawal of Georgia's troops from the Confederacy was never entertained.[60]

Throughout 1864, the fortunes of war had grown progressively worse for the Confederacy. Early in the year, on 12 March, President Abraham Lincoln had made what may well have been his most enlightened decision of the war, naming Ulysses S. Grant to the position of general-in-chief of all the Federal armies in the field. Thus, for the first time during the war on either side, a unified command structure was created. Confederate President Jefferson Davis had in General Robert E. Lee the perfect candidate for a similar post on the Southern side, but failing to show the wisdom of Lincoln,

Davis continued to attempt to control all military operations from
Richmond—in spite of constant criticism from both the army and the
Confederate Congress. His military advisor, General Braxton Bragg, had
resigned in disgrace as commander of the Army of Tennessee following the
debacle at Missionary Ridge in 1863, and Davis himself, although a graduate
of West Point, had never commanded more than a regiment in the field. But
Davis and Bragg would continue management of the Confederate war effort
until near the end of the war. Then, explicitly directed by the Confederate
Congress, Davis would name Robert E. Lee commander-in-chief, though by
that time the outcome of the conflict would no longer be in doubt.[61]

By replacing his archenemy Joseph E. Johnston with John Bell Hood as
commander of the Army of Tennessee in July, Davis had played directly into
Sherman's hands by bringing to an end a Fabian policy that had frustrated
Sherman and probably represented the Confederates' best chance of surviving the Atlanta Campaign. Then following the fall of Atlanta, when
veteran commander William J. Hardee refused to continue to serve under
John Bell Hood, Davis named General P. G. T. Beauregard titular commander of a vague new organization known as the Division of the West,
with three departmental commanders theoretically reporting to him. John
Bell Hood commanded the Department of Tennessee; William J. Hardee
commanded the Department of Georgia, South Carolina, and Florida; and
Richard Taylor commanded the Department of East Louisiana, Mississippi,
and Alabama. But—through this politically-inspired, bureaucratic creation—Davis all but paralyzed the entire western theater of operations, since
Beauregard actually had little authority. Furthermore, the great distances
involved made effective communications so difficult that operations of subordinate department commanders became all but autonomous.[62]

Under this unwieldy command structure, Hood embarked early in
October on a campaign into Tennessee, which he would later claim had the
approval of both Davis and Beauregard. This ill-fated expedition not only
resulted in the destruction of Hood's army at the battles of Franklin and
Nashville, but from its outset left Georgia virtually unprotected and at the
mercy of General William T. Sherman's vast armies.[63]

Hood's preparations for the Tennessee campaign began in September
1864, a month notable for Georgia-Confederate conflict. The fall of Atlanta
had been followed by Richmond's attempt to take over the Georgia Militia,

and later in the month, President Jefferson Davis himself had appeared in Macon, where he denounced Governor Brown in a speech. Hood and Governor Brown had gotten along fairly well during the Atlanta Campaign. However, the governor was more than displeased when, in late September and early October, Hood created a controversy by directing Lieutenant Colonel Richard M. Cuyler of Macon's Confederate States Arsenal to requisition 1,000 Austrian rifles in the town that belonged to the Georgia Militia, then on "agricultural leave." When Governor Brown refused to accede, Cuyler was ordered to take the guns by force if necessary.[64] When militia colonel Lewis N. Whittle informed Brown of this, the governor responded unambiguously: "I shall order Col. Cuyler or any other Confederate officer shot immediately, if he attempts to take the arms of the militia out of the custody of the State by force, and will send force if necessary to execute my Orders. If attempted, inform me at once."[65]

Brown's main military force was, of course, no closer than Milledgeville, so when the rifles were indeed in the process of being taken, Colonel Whittle—also a prominent Macon attorney—took out a possessory warrant, thus buying time by throwing the case into court.[66] Brown meanwhile telegraphed Colonel Cuyler: "If you remove the arms out of the custody of the State, you will do it at your peril and will be held to account in a summary manner."[67]

By 3 October, cooler heads had prevailed. Oddly enough, the coolest head belonged to General Cobb, normally made livid by the very thought of Governor Brown. Before the court could rule on the case, Cobb worked out a compromise through which Brown was promised that a like number of rifles would be sent by the Confederacy to the militia when they reassembled. Gunfire between the Georgia state troops and Confederate forces had been avoided at least, and there was no permanent rupture. Within nine days, General Hood was once again allowed to give orders to the state troops: General G. W. Smith was ordered to reassemble the furloughed Georgia Militia in the vicinity of Macon and—as soon as transportation could be arranged—to make a demonstration against Sherman's forces in Atlanta.[68]

The militia was by then organized as follows:

FIRST DIVISION GEORGIA MILITIA
Major General Gustavus W. Smith

FIRST BRIGADE
Brigadier General Reuben W. Carswell
1st Regiment—Colonel Edward H. Pottle
2nd Regiment—Colonel James Stapleton
3rd Regiment—Colonel Quinton M. Hill

SECOND BRIGADE
Colonel James N. Mann
4th Regiment—Colonel Pleasant J. Philips
5th Regiment—Colonel Henry H. Floyd
6th Regiment—Colonel Frank George

THIRD BRIGADE
Brigadier General Charles D. Anderson
7th Regiment—Colonel Abner F. Redding
8th Regiment—Colonel William B. Scott
9th Regiment—Colonel John M. Hill

FOURTH BRIGADE
Brigadier General Henry K. McCay
10th Regiment—Colonel Charles M. Davis
11th Regiment—Colonel William T. Toole
12th Regiment—Colonel Richard Sims[69]

The numerical strength of the Georgia Militia during summer and fall 1864 has been the subject of considerable conjecture—with revisionist historians in particular greatly exaggerating their numbers. But a copy of the original roster taken in the field near Lovejoy's Station on 31 October 1864 indicates the actual numerical strength of the 1st Division Georgia Militia as follows:

Field and Staff	15
1st Brigade	873
2nd Brigade	572
3rd Brigade	771
4th Brigade	673
Pioneer Corps	79
Aggregate Total	*2,983*
Effective Total	*2,034*[70]

The *Aggregate Total* included those sick, absent on extra duty, or under arrest, while the *Effective Total*, sometimes referred to as so many rifles, consisted only of those armed, equipped, and ready for combat. Within two weeks, the aggregate and effective had declined to 2,882 and 1,949, respectively, but other "available forces" in the vicinity, Confederate and otherwise, would give Smith some 2,800 effectives with which he would begin his foredoomed resistance to Sherman's march.[71]

Still, the larger numbers, evanescent though they proved, had been closer to the mark during the previous summer. Adjutant General Wayne, in reviewing the militia's service during the Atlanta Campaign, noted that the state had armed and sent to the field between 10,000 and 11,000 men (though General Smith asserted that at Atlanta his "greatest number of effective muskets in the trenches at any one time was about 5,000").[72]

Regarding the Georgia Militia, Wayne wrote Brown that they "have done their duty."[73] As Wayne noted, the militiamen had distinguished themseles during the evacuation of Atlanta that and the retreat to Jonesboro and had "received publicly the acknowledgment of their devotion from their eminent chiefs, Generals Johnston and Hood, and merit, deservedly, the thanks of their country." [74]

By this time, of course, their country—in the form of the Confederate States of America rather than the state of Georgia—had tried to gather up the militiamen. Wayne mentioned this in his annual report on the militia, dated 26 October 1864, and noted that, though "[f]urloughed for 30 days by your Excellency's order, from September 10th to October 10th, they are again in the field battling for the independence of their State, for their homes and for their families."[75] In an unusually candid conclusion to his report, Wayne suggested that it was not only Richmond that had trouble tapping Georgia's manpower pool: "While the large body of the militia reported promptly at the Front, a few individuals, I am sorry to say, have failed in their duty, and it is with difficulty that the military machinery of the State can reach them."[76]

More than "a few" obviously were not reached. Though General Smith had advised that the men over age fifty be withdrawn from "continuous active service" since they were "not as a class fitted for military duty," many other men simply seem to have stayed home.[77]

By this time, Hood had already moved with his main army across the Coosa River near Rome, beginning the ill-fated march that would eventually take him all the way to Nashville, Tennessee. Behind him he left Smith's meager militia force of fewer than 3,000 men to demonstrate against Atlanta, garrisoned by at least ten times that number of Sherman's finest veteran troops. Despite the odds, Smith assembled his small force at Lovejoy's Station in preparation for the ordered demonstration against Atlanta. But Hood then proposed that instead of demonstrating against Atlanta, Smith should cross the Chattahoochee River and march northward, destroying the Western & Atlantic Railroad from that river to the Etowah River. Ironically, President Davis's unwieldy command structure may actually have worked to advantage in this case. After Smith had consulted with both Hood and his superior, General P. G. T. Beauregard, reason finally prevailed, and he was ordered merely to remain near Atlanta, observing the Federals' movements and preventing them from foraging beyond the city's fortifications.[78]

When Beauregard had conditionally approved Hood's excursion into Tennessee, he directed that the bulk of Joseph Wheeler's cavalry remain south of the Tennessee River, with Nathan Bedford Forrest ordered to join Hood and replace Wheeler once he had crossed the river on his northward march. Accordingly, Wheeler and his cavalry began arriving at Lovejoy's Station in early November to join G. W. Smith's small militia force.[79]

Atlanta An evening view of the skyline of the city the militia went to help save.(Hargrett Rare Book and Manuscript Library, University of Georgia Libraries)

James Seddon As Confederate Secretary of War, 1862-1865, Seddon was a frequent sparring partner (by telegraph and mail) of Governor Brown.

(Hargrett Rare Book and Manuscript Library, University of Georgia Libraries)

Governor Joseph E. Brown as he appeared engraved on an 1863 Georgia $100 Bill

(Hargrett Rare Book and Manuscript Library, University of Georgia Libraries)

Linton Stephens The half-brother of the Confederate vice president, Stephens was a lawyer-politician who served for a time as an officer in the Georgia Militia.
(Hargrett Rare Book and Manuscript Library, University of Georgia Libraries)

John Bell Hood Commander of the Confederate forces during the siege of
Atlanta, Hood was complimentary of the service of the Georgia Militia.
(Hargrett Rare Book and Manuscript Library, University of Georgia Libraries)

BATTLE OF ATLANTA
July 22, 1864

Battle of Atlanta

(William R. Scaife)

Confederate Macon

(National Archives)

George Stoneman Leader of a Federal raid against Macon, General Stoneman was turned back by a force made up largely of untested militiamen.

(U. S. Army Military History Institute)

Militia Headquarters, Macon The building that housed the Macon headquarters of the Georgia Militia appears in the center of this image, to the right of the tallest structure.

(Middle Georgia Archives, Washington Memorial Library)

Howell Cobb Though Governor Brown was in Macon during Stoneman's Raid, he deferred to General Cobb, who led the defense of the city. At Cobb's side was General Joseph E. Johnston, recently relived of command of the Army of Tennessee.

(Hargrett Rare Book and Manuscript Library, University of Georgia Libraries)

Private James D. Means, 5th Georgia Reserves A youthful member of General Cobb's Macon garrison, Means (born 8 December 1845) served with his unit during the summer of 1864. He died in November 1864 of typhoid fever.

(David Wynn Vaughan Collection)

The Dunlap House In the yard of this structure, Stoneman's battery was emplaced. (Authors' Photograph)

Macon Fortifications These earthworks are the major survival of the defenses on the Dunlap farm. (Authors' Photograph)

Private Moses Speer, Georgia Militia.
(Courtesy of Athens Public Library)

Thomas Hardeman A prominent Georgia politician from Macon, Colonel Hardeman served on the staff of General G. W. Smith. A postbellum engraving.

(Hargrett Rare Book and Manuscript Library, University of Georgia Libraries)

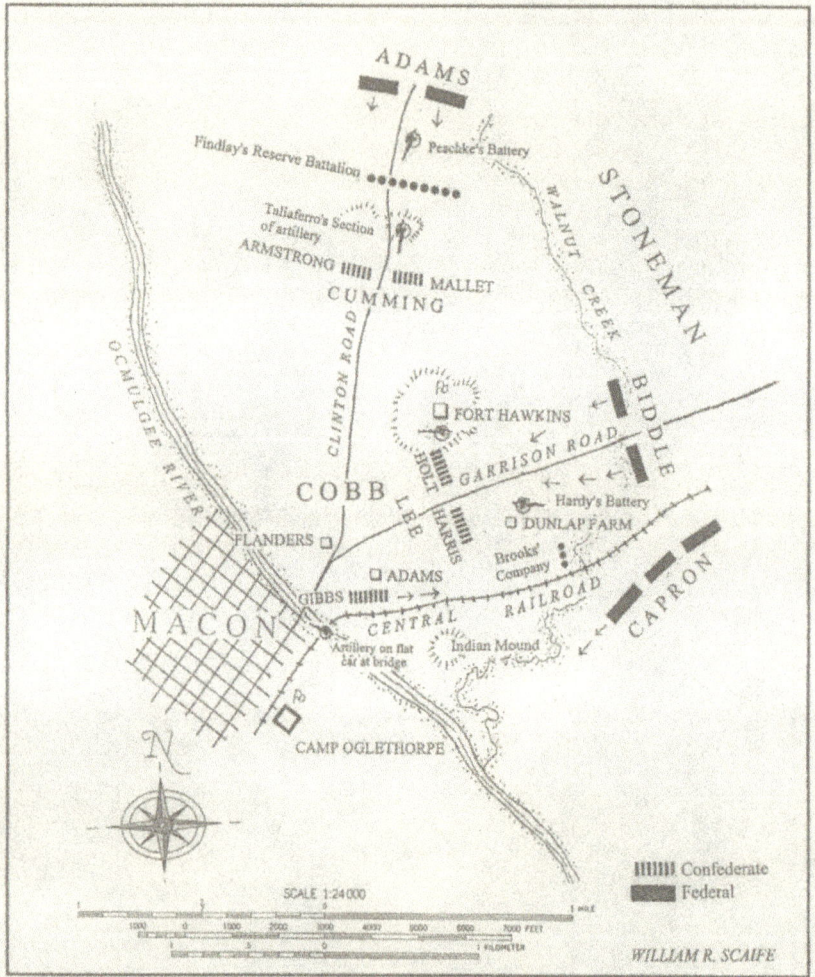

ADAMS

Findlay's Reserve Battalion

Peschke's Battery

STONEMAN

WALNUT CREEK

BIDDLE

Taliaferro's Section
of artillery

ARMSTRONG ||||| ||||| MALLET

CUMMING

CLINTON ROAD

FORT HAWKINS

GARRISON ROAD

OCMULGEE RIVER

COBB

LEE

HOLT

HARRIS

Hardy's Battery

DUNLAP FARM

FLANDERS

Brooks'
Company

CAPRON

GIBBS ||||| →

ADAMS

CENTRAL   RAILROAD

MACON

Artillery on flat
car at bridge

Indian Mound

N

CAMP OGLETHORPE

SCALE 1:24 000

|||||| Confederate
        Federal

WILLIAM R. SCAIFE

BATTLE OF EAST MACON
July 30, 1864

Battle of East Macon

(William R. Scaife)

Alfred Iverson Stoneman and many of his raiders were captured retreating from Macon by the cavalry force of General Iverson, shown here in old age.

(Library of Congress)

READ AND HAND TO YOUR NEIGHBOR.

CORRESPONDENCE

BETWEEN THE

SECRETARY OF WAR

AND

GOVERNOR BROWN,

GROWING OUT OF A REQUISITION MADE
UPON THE GOVERNOR FOR THE

RESERVE MILITIA OF GEORGIA

TO BE TURNED OVER TO CONFEDERATE CONTROL.

BOUGHTON, NISBET, BARNES & MOORE, STATE PRINTERS,
MILLEDGEVILLE, GA.

1865.

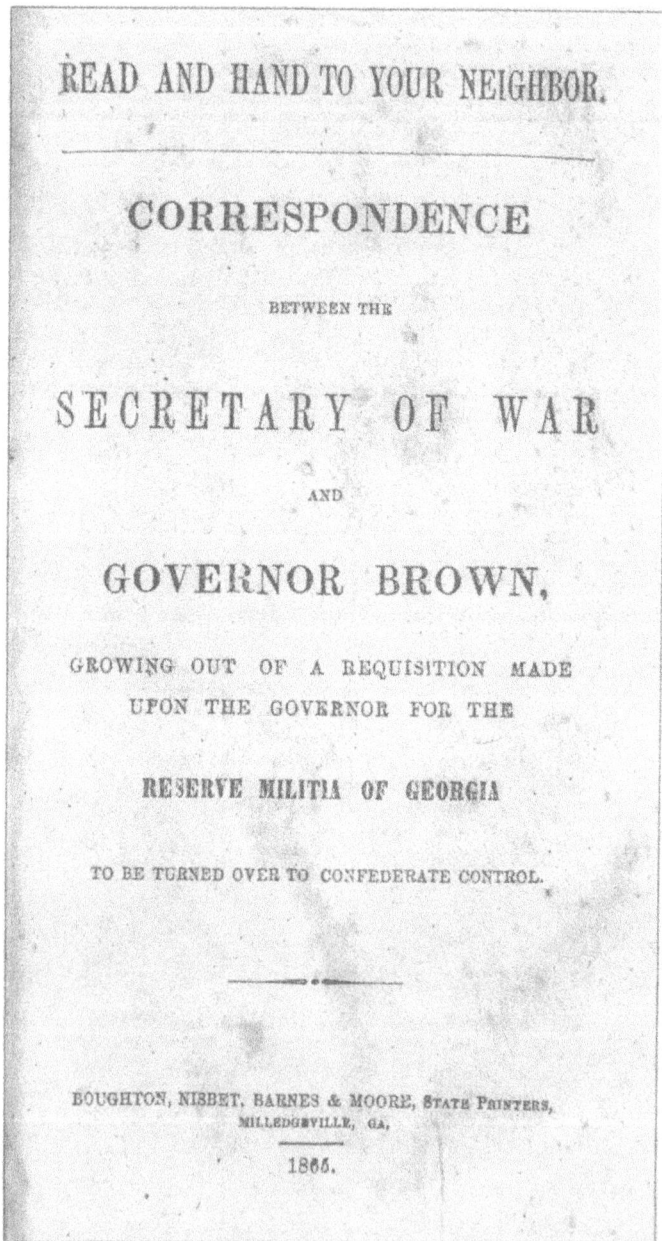

Correspondence between the Secretary and the Governor Richmond's attempt to
requisition the Georgia Militia at the conclusion of the Atlanta Campaign led to
another acrimonious controversy, printed to be distributed as widely as possible.
(Hargrett Rare Book and Manuscript Library, University of Georgia Libraries)

Colonel Richard M. Cuyler Attempting to secure state rifles for Hood's army, Macon Arsenal chief Cuyler begin a controversy with Governor Brown that escalated to threats of force.

(U.S. Army Military History Institute)

L. N. Whittle Governor Brown's representative in the dispute with Cuyler, Whittle
was a prominent Macon attorney, as well as an officer in Brown's militia.
(Middle Georgia Archives, Washington Memorial Library)

3.
CONTESTING SHERMAN'S MARCH:
THE MILITIA AT GRISWOLDVILLE

More than a month before Wheeler's cavalry arrived at Lovejoy's Station, Sherman had crossed the Chattahoochee River with a force of some 40,000 and pursued Hood northward. But his dispatch to General Grant on 9 October indicated that his heart was not really in the chase and that, by that time, he had already formulated his plan for the March to the Sea:

> *It will be a physical impossibility to protect the railroads, now that Hood, Forrest, Wheeler, and the whole batch of devils, are turned loose without home or habitation.... I propose that we break up the railroad from Chattanooga forward, and that we strike out with our wagons for Milledgeville, Millen, and Savannah.... By attempting to hold the [rail]roads, we will lose a thousand men each month, and will gain no result. I can make the march, and make Georgia howl!*[80]

Grant was still anxious that the primary objective of the campaign—the destruction of the Confederate army—be accomplished first. But he finally gave his none-too-enthusiastic approval: "If there is any way of getting at Hood's army, I should prefer it; but I trust your judgement. If you are satisfied the trip to the sea coast can be made, holding the line at the Tennessee [River] firmly, you may make it, destroying all the railroads south of Dalton or Chattanooga as you think best."[81]

Still, Sherman tenaciously continued to push his plan for a March to the Sea and wrote back to Grant on 2 November: "No single force can catch [Hood], and I am convinced the best results will follow from our defeating Jeff. Davis' cherished plan of making me leave Georgia by maneuvering.... If I turn back the whole effect of my campaign will be lost.... I am clearly of

the opinion that the best results will follow me in my contemplated movement through Georgia."[82]

Sherman's persistence prevailed, and General Grant finally overcame his
reservations about this bold and unconventional march through the enemy's
heartland. On 2 November Grant appeared to acquiesce fully:

> *I do not see that you can withdraw from where you are to follow Hood,*
> *without giving up all we have gained in territory. I say, then, go on as you pro-*
> *pose.*[83]

Before beginning the march, Sherman ordered his chief of engineers,
Captain Orlando M. Poe, to destroy all railroads and support buildings,
storehouses, machine shops, mills, and factories within the fortifications of
Atlanta so that—for military purposes—the city would cease to exist. When
Sherman arrived in Atlanta from Kingston on the afternoon of 14
November, he found Poe, with his 1st Michigan and 1st Missouri Engineers,
busy at their task of destruction. Using cleverly improvised battering rams
and powder charges, the engineers leveled the massive masonry walls of the
railroad depot, machine shops, roundhouse, foundry, oil refinery, and freight
warehouse. The unsupported wood framing fell in masses onto the rubble,
and all manner of debris and trash were piled on the wreckage and set on
fire. The flames soon spread to the block of stores near the depot, and the
heart of the city burned into the night. Captain Poe explained that the fire
simply got out of control, but others contended that the conflagration was
deliberately allowed to spread—perhaps even assisted. Whatever the case,
little serious effort seems to have been made to contain the spreading flames.
Ultimately destroyed were the jail, the rolling mill, theaters, fire stations, and
slave markets, along with 4,000 to 5,000 houses and two-thirds of the trees
in the city. The only structures to escape the flames were the city hall,
Masonic Hall, the Atlanta Medical College on Butler Street, five churches
(the Immaculate Conception, Central Presbyterian, Second Baptist, Trinity
Methodist, and St. Philip's Episcopal), one hotel (the Gate City at Alabama
and Pryor Street), and some 400 houses.[84]

With Atlanta's smoldering ruins as a backdrop, the Great March began
on the morning of 15 November. Brigadier General Alpheus Williams's XX
Corps led off to the east by way of Decatur and Stone Mountain, toward

Madison and Augusta. Peter Osterhaus's XV Corps and Francis Blair's XVII Corps formed the right wing under the command of Major General Oliver O. Howard and moved southeastward toward Jonesboro and Macon, with Kilpatrick's cavalry screening their right flank. The next day, the XIV Corps, under Major General Jefferson C. Davis, moved out along the Decatur Road following the same route Williams's XX Corps had taken earlier. These movements were designed to threaten both Augusta and Macon—and thus divide the thinly spread Confederate defenders—then to converge quickly on the state capital at Milledgeville, the real objective of the first leg of the march. Each army corps was expected to cover about 15 miles a day, so that the entire army would be concentrated by 22 November in the vicinity of Milledgeville.[85]

A decade after the war, Lieutenant Colonel Charles Colcock Jones, Jr.— General Hardee's chief of artillery during the December 1864 siege of Savannah—wrote a superb account of the March to the Sea from the Confederate perspective. Therein he described the setting of Sherman's great adventure.

> At this season of the year plantation barns were filled with the newly gathered harvest. Corn, peas, fodder, sweet-potatoes, syrup, hogs, cattle, mules and horses were to be expected without stint. The recent movement of General Hood [into Tennessee], ill-advised and pregnant with naught but disaster, left the state of Georgia fairly open to a Federal advance.... As a military movement this expedition can be justified only upon the hypothesis that it was planned with full knowledge of the weakness of the Confederates. It reached its objective...because General Beauregard was unable to concentrate even a tolerable army of opposition.... That it was not interrupted and totally defeated in its execution, must be attributed to accident—the inability of the Confederates to concentrate an army sufficiently strong to deliver battle along the line of march.[86]

From a somewhat different perspective, Sherman himself described the beginning of the March to the Sea.

> About 7 A.M. of November 16th we rode out of Atlanta by the Decatur Road, filled by the marching troops and wagons of the Fourteenth Corps; and reaching the hill, just outside of the old rebel works, we naturally paused to look back upon the scenes of our past battles.... Behind us lay Atlanta, smouldering

*and in ruins, the black smoke rising high in the air, and hanging like a pall
over the ruined city. Away off in the distance, on the McDonough road, was the
rear of [General Oliver O.] Howard's column, the gun-barrels glistening in the
sun, the white- topped wagons stretching away to the south; and right behind
us the Fourteenth Corps, marching steadily and rapidly, with a cheery look and
swinging pace, that made light of the thousand miles that lay between us and
Richmond....*

*Indeed, the general sentiment was that we were marching for Richmond,
and that there we should end the war, but how and when they seemed to care
not; nor did they measure the distance, or count the loss of life, or bother their
brains about the great rivers to be crossed, and the food required for man and
beast, that had to be gathered on the way. There was a "devil-may-care" feeling
pervading officers and men, that made me feel the full load of responsibility, for
success would be expected as a matter of course, whereas, should we fail, this
"march" would be adjudged the wild adventure of a crazy fool.[87]*

With Sherman's powerful army marching rapidly into the interior of the
state and Hood's Confederate army marching just as rapidly in the opposite
direction, there is little wonder the government and citizens of Georgia felt
utterly abandoned by the Confederate government in Richmond. The situation was so grave that the state legislature abandoned the capital at
Milledgeville on 19 November, only hours after they had passed an act soon
issued to the public in a proclamation by Governor Brown:

*Executive Department,
Milledgeville, Georgia,
November 19th, 1864.
PROCLAMATION.
The whole people understand how imminent is the danger that threatens the
State. Our cities are being burned, our fields laid waste, and our wives and
children mercilessly driven from their homes by a powerful enemy. We must
strike like men for freedom, or we must submit to subjugation.
Death is to be preferred to loss of liberty. All must rally to the field for the
present emergency, or the State is overrun.*

*I, therefore, by virtue of the authority vested in me by the statute of the
State, hereby order a levy en masse of the whole free white male population
residing or domiciled in this State between sixteen (16) and fifty-five (55) years
of age, except such as are physically unable to bear arms, which physical defect*

must be plain and indisputable, or they must be sent to camp for examination, and except those engaged in the Legislature or Judicial Departments of the government, which are by the recent Act of the Legislature, declared exempt from compulsory service.

All others are absolutely required, and members of the Legislature, and Judges are invited, to report immediately to Major-General G. W. Smith, at Macon, or wherever else in Georgia his camp may be, for forty (40) days' service, under arms, unless the emergency is sooner passed.

The statute declares that all persons hereby called out shall be subject, after this call, to all the rules and articles of war of the Confederate States, and on failure to report shall be subject to the pains and penalties of the crime of desertion.

JOSEPH E. BROWN[88]

Once the militia returned from furlough, General Smith entrenched them near Lovejoy's Station and prepared to support Alfred Iverson's division of Wheeler's cavalry, which was opposing a larger force of Federal cavalry under Judson Kilpatrick. But by late afternoon on 15 November, Kilpatrick had driven Iverson southward from Jonesboro to Lovejoy's Station, and General G. W. Smith, fearing his position would be turned, withdrew the Georgia Militia to previously prepared fortifications at Griffin—and there awaited the onslaught. However, by the afternoon of 16 November, it became apparent that Oliver O. Howard's entire Federal Right Wing had veered off to the east through Stockbridge and McDonough, with Kilpatrick's cavalry covering his right flank. Both were heading directly toward Macon.[89]

Since Macon was at that time garrisoned only by a small number of Georgia Reserves under Major General Howell Cobb, Lieutenant General William J. Hardee was ordered to take personal command. He arrived in Macon from Charleston, South Carolina, on the morning of 19 November 19. Meanwhile G. W. Smith marched his militia some 35 miles to Forsyth, where a waiting train took them to Macon. There the Georgia Militia and the two Georgia State Line regiments (which had been assigned to Smith at Lovejoy's Station) were placed first in Macon's defenses on the west bank of the Ocmulgee River, then ordered across the river where they spent the night of 20 November fortifying a new position covering East Macon.[90]

Upon his arrival at Macon, Hardee found the city spiraling into panic. Most businesses were either shut up tight or in the process of closing, and refugees were boarding trains to flee to the south and the west. Though General Howell Cobb had prepared an extensive system of earthworks around the city on both banks of the river, he had no troops to man them. Moreover, Jefferson Davis's complicated new command system had created considerable confusion in the high command of Beauregard's Division of the West. Although Hardee had arrived to take command in Macon on 19 November, General Richard Taylor had been ordered by Beauregard on 16 November to proceed to Macon from Selma, Alabama, to assume command of all the troops in Georgia, in the event Sherman moved toward Macon or Augusta.[91] On 17 November, Beauregard sent a dispatch to Richard Taylor in Selma and to Howell Cobb and G. W. Smith in Macon:

> *Adopt Fabian system. Don't run risk of losing your active forces and guns, available for the field, to hold any one place or position, but harass at all points. Hannibal held the heart of Italy for sixteen years, and then was defeated. Be cool and confident, and all will yet be right. I will join you as soon as possible. G. T. Beauregard.* [92]

But when Taylor was delayed by a railroad accident, Beauregard on 20 November sent the following circular message to Richard Taylor, Joseph Wheeler, and Howell Cobb, adding, no doubt, to the mounting confusion as to exactly who was in charge and for how long:

> *Genl. Hardee will, for the present, give orders for the defense of Georgia, East (South) of Chattanooga. My views are that positions should be defended only so long as not to risk safety of troops and material required for active operations in the field. Meanwhile, remove to safe locality all government property on line of enemy's march, and consume or destroy all supplies within his reach. G. T. Beauregard.* [93]

As Sherman's columns approached, the biggest problem facing Hardee was obtaining reliable intelligence of enemy movements. There were no reports of Federal troops near Forsyth, Griffin, or Barnesville to the north-west, but Kilpatrick's Federal cavalry had cut the telegraph to the east of Macon, breaking all communications with Gordon, Charleston, and

Savannah. On 20 November, Wheeler's cavalry attacked Kilpatrick's Federal cavalry at Clinton, 10 miles to the northeast, and Colonel Charles Crews's 2d Georgia Cavalry attacked Federal troopers at Griswoldville, 10 miles east of Macon, but was driven back. The next day, Wheeler drove Kilpatrick's cavalry from Griswoldville toward Milledgeville to the northeast, but was unable to obtain any definite information on overall enemy movements.[94]

By the afternoon of 21 November, Hardee had concluded that Sherman's true objective was not Macon, but Augusta, with its arsenal and powder mill. There was a choice between two routes for Hardee's troops to follow. The safer (but much longer) route involved a trip of 100 miles southward by rail to Albany in south Georgia, and a 50-mile cross-country march to Thomasville near the Florida line, where the troops would again board trains for Savannah and Augusta. But this route was almost 500 miles long, and there was no assurance the troops could even reach Augusta ahead of Sherman's rapidly moving columns. Hardee therefore elected to take the more hazardous but much shorter route along the Central of Georgia Railroad. Hardee reasoned that the troops could march past the point where Federal cavalry had destroyed the railroad near Griswoldville. After they passed the broken track, they would be met by a train (summoned by Hardee from Savannah) to carry them the fewer than 150 remaining miles to their destination. All communications had been cut east of the Ocmulgee River, and Wheeler's cavalry had been unable to penetrate Kilpatrick's cavalry screening the movements of the Federal Right Wing. Consequently, Hardee had no idea how rapidly Sherman's columns were moving into the interior of the state. Even as Hardee made his plans, the Right Wing was already at Gordon, 12 miles east of Griswoldville, systematically destroying the railroad on which Hardee planned to transport his troops to Augusta.[95]

Griswoldville, the first place of consequence on the route Hardee's troops would follow, was the creation of Samuel Griswold, who had moved from Burlington, Connecticut, to Clinton, Georgia, in 1815. Working first as a tin-ware dealer, he later moved into the manufacture of cotton gins. Around 1850, after the new railroad between Macon and the coast was completed, Griswold had moved his cotton gin factory south from Clinton to the railroad and established the industrial village bearing his name. As Station Number 18 on the Central road, Griswoldville had a depot and a water tank, as well as a long siding north of the main line. Griswold later expanded his operations to include candle, soap, and furniture factories, a grist and saw mill, a brick plant, a general, a church, and more than 100 houses for his workers and slaves.[96]

In 1862, the cotton gin factory was converted to a Confederate pistol works for military production by Griswold and his partner, Arvin Nye Gunnison. The pistol factory produced brass-framed Confederate Colts known as Griswold & Gunnison revolvers. By 1864, Griswold & Gunnison had turned out some 3,500 of these weapons.[97]

Stoneman's Raiders had tried and failed to destroy Griswoldville. But on 20 November 1864, "100 picked men" of the 9th Michigan Cavalry Regiment of Colonel Smith D. Atkins's 2d Brigade, under Captain Frederick S. Ladd, struck the village, destroying the railroad station, factories, the church, and a locomotive with thirteen cars. Every structure in the village was in fact destroyed, except for Sam Griswold's house and one other residence. That night, Colonel Eli H. Murray's 1st Brigade of Kilpatrick's cavalry camped on the east fork of Little Sandy Creek, 2 miles east of Griswoldville, and Brigadier General Charles R. Woods's infantry division, which formed the extreme right of the XV Corps, camped at Mountain Springs Crossing, 2 1/2 miles to the northeast.[98]

At dawn on 22 November, Wheeler's cavalry attacked Murray from the direction of Macon, but Charles C. Walcutt's 2d Brigade of Woods's 1st Division was quickly dispatched to Murray's support. Together the troopers and infantrymen drove Wheeler back through Griswoldville, then Walcutt withdrew to a point a mile and a half east of the village. There his brigade entrenched and erected barricades of fence rails along a ridge overlooking a tributary of Big Sandy Creek (now known as Battle Line Branch), in order to guard the ammunition and supply wagons along Federal right flank.[99]

Back in Macon on the morning of 21 November, General Hardee had put his troops in motion, ordering the 1st Brigade of Georgia Militia (Carswell's), under Colonel James Willis, to proceed as rapidly as possible along the Central Railroad in the direction of Augusta. Major Ferdinand W. C. Cook was ordered to follow with the Athens and Augusta Battalions of General Cobb's Confederate Reserves. The next morning, G. W. Smith was to lead Captain Ruel W. Anderson's battery of light artillery (assigned again to him on 21 November), along with the remainder of his force (the 2d, 3rd and 4th Brigades of Georgia Militia), and the two State Line regiments, commanded by Lieutenant Colonel Beverly D. Evans, toward Augusta. Having issued the orders for these movements, Hardee then left by way of Albany and Thomasville for Savannah. There he would begin preparations for his defense of the coastal city, which he correctly assumed to be Sherman's ultimate objective.[100]

As his troops began their march east on the morning of 22 November, General Smith elected to remain for a few hours in Macon. He occupied himself with completing arrangements for the transportation of ammunition and supplies. In Smith's place, the senior brigadier in the Georgia Militia— Brigadier General Pleasant J. Philips—led the main body of state troops toward Augusta.[101]

In the meantime, Sherman's Right Wing was marching rapidly in a southeasterly direction, only a few miles northeast of Macon. Its line of march put it on a collision course with the Georgia state troops moving toward Augusta. Only Walcutt's barricaded brigade, acting as a flank guard just east of Griswoldville, stood between the Confederates and the entire right wing of Sherman's army.[102]

Since the men of the 1st Brigade of Georgia Militia, Colonel James Willis commanding, had moved out on 21 November—a day ahead of the main militia force—they somehow avoided the main body of Union troops. There is some evidence that they may have returned in a roundabout way to Macon after Wheeler's cavalry was pushed west of Griswoldville on the morning of 22 November.[103]

That same morning at 8:00, Brigadier General Pleasant J. Philips struck out from Macon with the three militia brigades and assorted other troops. Shortly after noon, Philips and his men arrived within a mile of Griswoldville, from which a large column of smoke billowed. There they found the Athens and Augusta Battalions of Cobb's Reserves, commanded by Major Ferdinand W. C. Cook, drawn up in line of battle. Philips quickly deployed his force, with men of the Georgia State Line under Lieutenant Colonel Beverly D. Evans in front as skirmishers. As this formation advanced into Griswoldville, they found the village all but destroyed, with fires being put out at Samuel Griswold's barn, the source of the smoke seen earlier. Philips was told that the Federal cavalry had been fighting Wheeler's men in the vicinity of the village and had set the fire before retiring down the rail line toward Gordon. At that point, Major Cook withdrew his Athens and Augusta local defense battalions from Philips's line and proceeded in the same direction, after informing General Philips that he had previously been ordered by General Hardee to move on Augusta.

Major Cook had only moved down the railroad a little more than a mile when he was confronted by Walcutt's pickets in advance of the fortified Federal line on the ridge east of Griswoldville. Cook formed his battalions in line of battle and, shortly thereafter, was overtaken by General Philips's main column, which had soon followed behind him. Philips again assumed command of all the state troops and for some reason, never adequately explained, prepared for an immediate assault. He deployed his troops with Brigadier General Charles D. Anderson's 3rd Brigade of Georgia Militia on the left, north of the railroad; Brigadier General Henry K. McCay's 4th Brigade of Georgia Militia south of the railroad; and Philips's own 2d Brigade in reserve under Colonel James N. Mann. The 1st and 2d State Line regiments under Lieutenant Colonel Beverly D. Evans formed the center, and Major Ferdinand W. C. Cook's Athens and Augusta battalions formed the extreme right, at an obtuse angle with the Georgia State Line troops on their left. Captain Ruel W. Anderson's battery of four Napoleon twelve-pounders was placed just north of the railroad, less than half a mile from Walcutt's line on the ridge.[104]

Federal Brigadier General Charles C. Walcutt had formed his line along a ridge overlooking the branch of Big Sandy Creek and a large fallow field that stretched toward the railroad (and the gathering troops under Philips). The line extended from the railroad on the right to Big Sandy Swamp on the left, a distance of about a mile through the Duncan farm, whose split rail fences and log farm structures had been dismantled to form barricades. The Duncan farmhouse was located near the center of the line and would become a landmark in the impending battle. About 200 yards west of the ridge, and roughly parallel with it, ran the small, lazy stream that would later become known as Battle Line Branch. A thick fringe of scrubby trees and swamp growth extended a few yards on either side of the stream, but the 200-yard approach from the stream to the Federal position at the crest of the ridge was up a slope and across the open field, some 600 yards wide and easily commanded by Walcutt's riflemen. General Walcutt deployed his forces with the 46th Ohio, 100th Indiana, 40th Illinois, 6th Iowa, 103rd Illinois, and 97th Indiana infantry regiments in line from left to right.

Captain Albert Arndt's Battery B, 1st Michigan Artillery was posted with its
two 3-inch ordnance rifles near the center of the line. Eventually, two regiments of Kilpatrick's cavalry would be sent in to protect Walcutt's flanks: the
5th Kentucky on the right and the 9th Pennsylvania on the left. Colonel
Milo L. Smith's 1st Brigade of Woods's division was entrenched in reserve
about a mile in the rear of Walcutt's brigade at the Mountain Springs
Church, and later in the day the 12th Indiana Regiment would be dispatched to support the right of Walcutt's line.[104]

On the morning of 22 November, Lieutenant General Richard Taylor
finally arrived to take command in Macon. He stepped from his train into a
rare and unseasonable snowstorm, shortly after the last of the militia troops
had started toward Griswoldville.[105] After having the situation explained to
him by Cobb, he immediately instructed G. W. Smith to withdraw his men
to Macon, but Smith's orders to Philips were hardly models of clarity:

> Brig. Gen. Philips:
> General:—Wheeler having retired to the right, keep a close lookout with your
> skirmishers, and avoid a fight with a superior force. You can best judge the
> direction. The wagon train will not leave this evening.
> By command, Gen'l Smith:
> R. TOOMBS, Ch'f of Staff
> P.S. If it be dangerous to get back, take down the Marion Road.[106]

Then, twenty-five minutes later, Smith sent Philips another none-too-
lucid dispatch, conditioned upon the necessity of avoiding a *superior force*:

> General:—Since this note was written a courier has come in from Maj. Cook,
> stating that the enemy were advancing upon him at Griswoldville. The wagon
> train is still here, and it had already been determined not to send it by the route
> you are on before this information came in. If pressed by a superior force, fall
> back upon this place [Macon] without bringing on a serious engagement if you
> can do so. If not, fall back upon the road indicated in General Toombs' note
> [the Marion road]. Anderson's Battery started out this morning—has probably
> joined you. Let me know as soon as possible exactly what is going on in your
> front.
> G. W. SMITH, Maj. Gen'l[107]

But Philips had apparently made his decision to attack by that time. He ordered Ruel Anderson's battery into position on the extreme left, north of the railroad, where he unlimbered his four Napoleons and began firing through an opening in the pines at Walcutt's position on the ridge. Just after Anderson's Battery began firing, G. W. Smith's aide-de-camp, Captain Elijah Hawkins, rode up to General Philips in the field and delivered Smith's second dispatch.[108] Captain Hawkins then reported back to Smith from Griswoldville at 3:20 P.M.:

> *General:—The whole division, including Cook's Battalion, is one mile in advance of this place on the Central R. R. in line of battle, with the State Line Troops thrown out in front skirmishing with the enemy. Anderson's Battery opened upon them just as I rode up to the line, the enemy's battery replying. Gen. Philips does not know what their force is, and on receiving your instructions, concluded not to advance farther. On the movements of the enemy depends whether or not he will fall back to this place, or remain where he now is.*
>
> *Very Resp'tfully, your ob't serv't*
> *E. HAWKINS. A.D.C.*
> *P.S.—I will remain to see any developments which may be made before I report in person.*[109]

But sometime between 2:30 and 3:00 P.M, soon after Captain Hawkins had left the field, Philips gave the order to charge the enemy in his works. Philips's plan called for Ruel Anderson's artillery to rake Walcutt's position at short range, while Charles D. Anderson's 3rd Militia Brigade attacked the Federal right flank, Cook's Athens and Augusta battalions attacked their left flank, and Henry K. McCay's 4th Militia Brigade and Evans's State Line troops attacked them in front. Philips's own 2d Militia Brigade under Colonel James N. Mann would remain in reserve in the rear, there to await further orders.[110]

Captain Ruel W. Anderson's battery was the only regular army unit attached to G. W. Smith's command and would demonstrate its proficiency at the outset of the battle. Many of Walcutt's Federal infantry were armed with Spencer repeating rifles, which he felt confident would give them superior firepower. He therefore instructed them to hold their fire until the advancing Confederate line was in close range, relying on Captain Albert Arndt's section of 3-inch Ordnance Rifles to slow the attackers at long range. As the first Confederate skirmishers began crossing the field toward Walcutt's position, Captain Arndt decided to move one of his artillery pieces to the right, in order to set up an effective crossfire.[111]

While directing this movement, Arndt was struck by one of the first shots fired by the advancing militiamen. Thinking their commander mortally wounded (as did Arndt), the Federal artillerymen became disorganized and almost totally ineffective. The first Confederate shell damaged a caisson, and the ensuing barrage from Anderson's Battery took out of action six artillery horses and half of Arndt's cannoneers. When Arndt belatedly realized he only been struck by a spent ball, his battery section's pat in the battle was already concluded and, to prevent its total destruction, he ordered both guns pulled from the field by their prolonges.[112]

Anderson's veteran Confederate artillerymen thus won the opening artillery duel rather handily. But the less experienced militia infantry would enjoy no such success. Neither of Philips's flanking movements succeeded in their execution, and in essence the poorly coordinated Confederate attack became a direct frontal assault against the Federal right only, rather than along the entire line.[113]

On the extreme left, Brigadier General Charles D. Anderson's 3rd Militia Brigade moved out on an axis north of and almost parallel to the railroad tracks. However—instead of advancing on that line for about a mile before taking a right turn against the Federal flank—they turned almost immediately to the right at the outset, crossing the railroad and advancing against the right center of Walcutt's line. A detachment on Anderson's extreme left was unable to cross a deep railroad cut and became separated from the main force. After the battle had raged for some time (and General Anderson had been wounded in the hand and had two horses shot from under him), he finally led the separated detachment around the Federal flank as originally planned, and made a determined attack, though not in sufficient strength to dislodge the Federals from their strong position.[114]

On the right of Anderson, Brigadier General Henry K. McCay's 4th Militia Brigade moved out south of the tracks on a course that would overlap that of Anderson and bring them both against Walcutt's right center. Lieutenant Colonel Beverly D. Evans's two regiments of State Line troops moved forward against the Federal center as ordered, advancing across the stream and up the slope to within 50 yards of Walcutt's barricaded line. But, to Evans's consternation, he soon discovered that he was receiving fire from the rear as well as the front. Colonel James N. Mann's 2d Militia Brigade had moved out from its position in reserve and advanced behind Evans's State Line troops, then, mistaking them for the enemy, had fired into their rear. Evans in frustration withdrew the State Line back to the cover along the branch, where they were forced to commingle with Mann's militia and attempt to reform their lines.[115]

The Confederate position in the streambed created an angle of fire that sent most bullets over the heads of the Federals on the ridge. On the other hand, Federal fire down the slope from the Spencer rifles was taking a heavy toll. Realizing their best chance lay in attempting to overrun the Federal position, the Confederates, with great courage, repeatedly charged up the slope. But the assaulting troops were mostly old men and young boys, poorly trained and equipped, most under inexperienced officers. In contrast, Walcutt's Federals were the pick of Sherman's Atlanta Campaign veterans, and their Spencers gave them murderously superior firepower. Moreover, unlike the assaulting Confederates, Walcutt's men could be readily resupplied with ammunition as the need arose.[116]

Although Lieutenant Colonel Evans led his partially reformed State Line and Mann's militia troops against the Federal center, they were repulsed by the heavy fire from the repeating rifles of the Federals on the ridge, and Evans himself was wounded. Due to some delay or miscommunication of orders, Ferdinand Cook's Augusta and Athens battalions not only failed to attack the Federal left as planned, but they were also late in advancing on Evans's right, so that the full weight of a simultaneous assault was never brought to bear along the entire Federal line. Consequently, the Federals were able to shift the 46th Ohio Regiment from the extreme left to their extreme right as the battle progressed.[117]

Most of the Federal casualties were inflicted by Ruel Anderson's artillerists, who continued to deliver a "terrific" enfilading fire at relatively short range, for as long as their ammunition lasted. Among the victims of the Confederates' "many telling shots" was the Federal commander himself, Brigadier General Charles C. Walcutt, who was seriously wounded in the leg by shrapnel. An Indiana officer reported, among his casualties, one "struck with a piece of shell" and another's "chin shot off." Additionally, one projectile hit the 6th Iowa Regiment near the center of the line. The explosion killed the color bearer, blowing off the top of his head and saturating the colors with his blood, while also severely wounding eight more men of the regiment.[118]

After Walcutt was wounded and removed from the field, Colonel Robert F. Catterson of the 97th Indiana Regiment took command. Late in the afternoon, Brigadier General Charles Anderson attempted to turn Catterson's right flank with the detachment that had been left at the railroad cut. The militiamen pressed so hard upon the Federals on the right that, as their regimental commander noted, they "fixed bayonets and expressed their desire to hold their line as long as there was a man of them left." Prudently, Catterson called for reinforcements. The 12th Indiana Regiment from Milo Smith's brigade was sent to the extreme right flank under Major Elbert Baldwin, while squadrons of cavalry from Kilpatrick's command were added on each flank. Anderson's threat was thus checked.[119]

When the Confederate artillery finally fell silent, some of the Federal soldiers on the ridge began taunting the Confederates remaining in their front, confidently daring them to make another charge. At twilight, one more charge was made, its primary purpose apparently to provide cover for the removal of some of the wounded from the field. The fight was over; the remaining disheartened Southern troops fell slowly back toward Griswoldville.[120]

When the Federal skirmishers advanced onto the abandoned field before their works, they found a sickening and pathetic scene. On the slopes, in the thickets surrounding the stream, and in the fields beyond, they clearly saw their recent antagonists for the first time. At close range they finally realized that they had been fighting, for the most part, only old men and young boys.[121] Lieutenant Charles W. Wills of the 103rd Illinois Regiment, who thought it "awful the way we slaughtered those men," described what he saw on the killing ground: "Old grey-haired and weakly-looking men and little boys, not over 15 years old, lay dead or writhing in pain.... I hope we will never have to shoot at such men again. They knew nothing at all about fighting, and I think their officers knew as little, or else, certainly knew nothing about our being there."[122]

One of the old men who survived the battle was Alladin T. Newsom of Lumpkin, Georgia. When Sherman's March began, he had been serving as Stewart County's purchasing agent for the Confederate States Army. Responding to the emergency, he had joined Company E of the 11th Regiment as a private, taking with him his Negro servant, John Davis—better known as "Shamrock." While cooking behind the lines at Griswoldville, Shamrock learned that Newsom had been wounded, and he rushed onto the battlefield. There he met Captain Charles C. Humber, commander of Company E and close personal friend of Alladin Newsom. They soon found Newsom, wounded in both arms and legs, and together carried him back to the Confederate lines. However, while helping to carry Newsom to safety, Captain Humber was wounded in the shoulder for the second time during the war, and Shamrock had to return Newsom to safety by himself. Following the war, Shamrock became a well digger, but he was charged in a Stewart County court with cowardice as well as bootlegging. At his trial, Lumpkin attorney Frank Watts declared, "A man brave enough to do what he did at Griswoldville and to earn a living by going down in wells is not a coward." Shamrock was acquitted. One way or another, other slaves also apparently made their way onto the battlefield: one Union officer reported that among the prisoners his skirmishers brought back from the creek bed were "a number of Africans."[123]

The actual fighting at Griswoldville was perhaps best described by the Federal officers participating in the battle. Major Asias Willison, commanding the 103rd Illinois Infantry Regiment, reported: "As soon as they [the Georgia troops] came within range of our muskets, a most terrific fire was poured into their ranks, doing fearful execution Still they moved forward...within 45 yards of [our] works. Here they attempted to reform their line again, but so destructive was our fire that they were compelled to retire."[124]

The wounded General Walcutt's replacement, Colonel Robert F. Catterson, reported his impressions, starting with the opening of the battle:

> He [the enemy] was soon discovered emerging from the woods about 800 yards from our position, and rapidly running across an open field toward us in three lines of battle.... On came the enemy, endeavoring to gain possession of a ravine [the creek bed] running parallel to and about 100 yards [from] our

front, but the fire was so terrible that ere he reached it many of his number were stretched upon the plain. It was at this moment that General Walcutt received a severe wound and was compelled to leave the field. I immediately assumed command, and discovered the enemy moving to the right. I supposed he contemplated turning my right flank. As I had already disposed of every available man in the brigade, and my left being so strongly pressed that not a man could be spared from it, I sent to the general commanding the division [Brigadier General Charles R. Woods] for two regiments. The Twelfth Indiana Infantry [from Milo Smith's 1st Brigade] was sent, and immediately placed in position on the extreme right; also a squadron of cavalry to watch the right and left flanks, but the day was already ours, as the enemy had been repulsed and driven from the field. I immediately sent forward a line of skirmishers, who succeeded in capturing about 42 prisoners and 150 small-arms. The battle commenced at 2:30 p.m. and lasted until sunset. During the engagement the enemy made three separate charges, and were as often repulsed with terrible slaughter.

I would gladly notice the many deeds of daring during the action, but to do so of every man who distinguished himself would be to mention each man by name in the brigade; but suffice it to say, the conduct of both officers and men was most superb.[125]

After dark, General Philips withdrew his battered forces from the field and fell back to a point west of Griswoldville, where trains carried his men to the fortifications surrounding Macon by about 2:00 in the morning. The Confederates reported casualties of 51 killed and 472 wounded, out of approximately 2,300 participating, or 22 percent. Such casualties were heavy, to be sure, but were made worse by a fact reported by General Smith: "Several of the best field officers of the command were killed or wounded." The Federals reported relatively trifling casualties of 13 killed, 79 wounded and 2 missing out of approximately 3,000 present, or 3.1 percent.[126]

Two weeks after the battle, the Confederate field commander, Brigadier General Pleasant J. Philips, described the battle from his perspective.

[After entering Griswoldville,] I soon ordered the command to move down the [railroad] until it should clear the village and halt, to await further orders from Maj. Gen. Smith. The rear of the column had not cleared the village, when firing of small arms was heard.... I ordered an advance of the command, and on arriving, I met Maj. Cook who pointed out to me the enemy, posted on

the opposite eminence in line of battle….I disposed of the forces [thus]: The
Athens and Augusta battalions on our right (owing to the position they then
held), making rather an obtuse angle, with the State Line on their left, and
General McCay's brigade on the left of the State Line, General McCay's left
resting near and south of the railroad. General Anderson's brigade was formed
on the north side of the railroad, his left resting parallel with the railroad, and
posted Captain Anderson's battery of four guns at an eligible site on the rail-
road on the north side. The Second Brigade, under Colonel Mann, was drawn
up in rear of the State Line, and General McCay's brigade in a secure place to
act as reserves.

In this position an advance was ordered. From some misconception of
orders[,] when the general advance was being made, Gen. Anderson's brigade
faced to the right and swept across the Railroad ([save] a small detachment on
his extreme left that was cut off by a deep cut in the Railroad) and participated
with the State Line and General McCay's brigade in the direct attack, where
they, both officers and men, sustained themselves with decision and gal-
lantry….

The order to Major Cook (from some cause of which I am not aware) to
turn the enemy's left, was never carried out, yet his command participated fully
in the action, deported themselves gallantly, and I regret to say, suffered much
from wounds and deaths.[127]

On 6 December, Major General Gustavus W. Smith directed his own
report to General William J. Hardee.

Arrangements for transportation of ammunition and supplies detained me a
few hours in Macon [on the morning of 22 November]…. Information having
been received showing very clearly that a much larger force of the enemy was
near the city than was supposed when you gave the orders for my troops to
move, he [General Richard Taylor] authorized me to direct them to return. My
order reached them on the eve of an engagement with what was supposed to be
a small force of the enemy.

Notwithstanding my order to avoid an engagement at that place and time,
a collision occurred, we being the attacking party; and though the officers and
men behaved with great gallantry, they failed to carry the works of the enemy,
but held a position within 150 yards of their line until after dark, when they
were withdrawn to Macon by my order.[128]

Neither General Philips nor anyone else ever adequately explained why he launched and continued to direct such an all-out assault, despite orders that seemed to instruct him to avoid a major engagement with the enemy. Nonetheless, his instructions from General G. W. Smith on 22 November could hardly be described as clear and timely. Dispatches from Smith at 12:20 and 12:45 only cautioned Philips to avoid a fight with a "superior" force, although General Richard Taylor had by that time ordered the entire movement aborted and Philips's force returned to Macon.[129] It was 4:30 in the afternoon, when the battle was for all practical purposes over, before a clear, unequivocal order "to withdraw...troops immediately to some convenient camp this side of the Cross Keys" was finally issued to Philips by G. W. Smith's assistant adjutant general, Thomas Hardeman in Macon. Hardeman also told Philips to return to Macon and "send a courier" to show when he began his march back.[130]

> *I am directed by the Major General to instruct you to withdraw your troops immediately to some convenient camp this side of the Cross Keys and take a suitable position for the night, unless you receive further orders. You will leave your camp this side of the Cross Keys at daylight to-morrow morning and come back to the fortifications [of Macon]. . . . When you leave to-morrow morning send a courier, stating the time you begin your march . . . .[131]*

An analysis of the strange sequence of events surrounding the tragedy at Griswoldville could hardly overlook the question of why G. W. Smith himself did not command such an important and hazardous expedition as the movement of the militia to Augusta. His delegation of responsibility was particularly inappropriate since Philips's seniority was based entirely on term of service in the militia (he had risen to major before the war), rather than on practical combat experience. Philips's service in the Confederate army had been in large part limited to November 1861-May 1862, spent peacefully at Savannah as colonel of the 31st Georgia Volunteer Infantry Regiment. When on 13 May 1862 the 31st Georgia was reorganized—and Virginia-bound, with Clement A. Evans elected colonel—Philips resigned from the regular army (and Evans, while noting the popularity Philips had enjoyed, also commented that discipline improved after his departure). Philips later commented to General Wayne, "I have served long enough in this war as a

Colonel to satisfy whatever of curiosity and ambition I may have entertained."[132]

Through banking and other interests, Philips had become quite prosperous before the war and, while wishing "to serve his country," also preferred to stay as close to home as possible for the remainder of the conflict. Consequently, in July 1862 he campaigned for and won election to the brigadier generalship of the 1st Brigade, 10th Division, Georgia Militia (embracing his own Muscogee County and three adjacent counties). He served in early 1864 as one of the governor's aides-de-camp and militia-enrolling officers and, after the reorganization, was elected brigadier general of the 2d Brigade. Consequently, his first (and limited) experience of combat had not come until summer 1864.[133]

In contrast, each of the other three militia brigadiers had fought during several campaigns in the Virginia Theater and had returned to Georgia with proven records, honorable wounds, and considerable combat experience. Pennsylvania-born Henry Kent McCay, elected 2d Lieutenant of the 12th Georgia Volunteer Infantry Regiment, eventually rose to captain and assistant quartermaster. Wounded at the Battle of Camp Alleghany, West Virginia, in December 1861 (and there cited for good conduct), he had gone on to fight under Jackson in the Valley, among other campaigns, before resigning in March 1863. Charles D. Anderson of Houston County had served in Alfred Holt Colquitt's brigade in the 6th Georgia Regiment, while Reuben W. Carswell of Jefferson County had been in the 48th Georgia, Ambrose R. Wright's brigade. Both had fought at 2d Manassas, Sharpsburg, and Fredericksburg, as well as later engagements of the Army of Northern Virginia. Anderson, captured at Sharpsburg but soon exchanged, was at Chancellorsville, where he was "frightfully wounded, one shot entering his shoulder, another shattering his left hand, and a third lacerating his bowels." Having reached the rank of lieutenant colonel, he resigned disabled in January 1864. Furloughed briefly to serve in the Georgia legislature during the war (as was Anderson), Carswell received a disabling wound to his right arm at Gettysburg and resigned his commission in November 1863. By all military criteria imaginable (except date of rank), the three were their fellow brigadier Philips's superiors.[134]

Over the years, the little battle at Griswoldville has been the subject of much speculation, and opinions have ranged from those who naively rationalized that the Confederate attack saved Macon from Sherman's forces (and therefore hailed it as a success), to those who contended that Philips was simply drunk and botched the attack. But the Battle of Griswoldville was much more realistically summarized by Colonel Charles Colcock Jones in his classic *The Siege of Savannah in 1864*: "This engagement, while it reflects great credit upon the gallantry of the Confederate and State forces engaged, was unnecessary, unexpected and utterly unproductive of any good. The Battle of Griswoldville will be remembered as an unfortunate accident whose occurrence might well have been avoided by the exercise of proper caution and circumspection."[135]

Blaming Pleasant J. Philips alone for the fiasco at Griswoldville seems a far too simplistic explanation of a less than simple set of circumstances. The delegation of field command of such an important expedition to his least experienced brigadier, and his subsequently issuing ambiguous orders to that subordinate commander, place much of the responsibility squarely upon G. W. Smith. Furthermore, the complex and unwieldy command structure established by President Jefferson Davis in the Division of the West increased the possibility—if not, indeed, the probability—of just such poor field coordination as that which occurred at Griswoldville.[136]

The inexperience and mind-set of the militiamen were certainly factors. Whether known as the "Melish" or "Joe Brown's Pets," these citizen-soldiers had long been ridiculed by the regular army troops and the press alike. While the rank and file were farmers from the yeomanry, or "Yokelry," as they were sometimes called, Governor Brown had "packed" the militia with both military and civil officers of the state, rewarding them for their political support and protecting them from conscription into the regular army. Such a policy understandably generated great resentment among regular army troops who were daily called upon to risk their lives in the front lines.[137]

Also, such an intense, opinionated, and controversial governor as Joe Brown could hardly hope to escape the inevitable ridicule of his "Pets" in the press. Recently furloughed home to harvest the crops, the predominantly agrarian militiamen had been mocked in the newspapers over their "agricultural leave" and lampooned as well in a ditty that has remained popular to this day: "Just before the battle the Gen'ral hears a row / He says, 'The Yanks are coming, I hear their rifles now.' / He turns around in wonder, and what do you think he sees? / The Georgia Militia—eating goober peas!"[138]

General Howell Cobb had perhaps made a subconscious prophecy of an incident such as the Battle of Griswoldville when he wrote that non-regular troops such as the militia dreaded the jeers and sneers of fellow Southerners more than the bullets of the Yankees. The sight of their homeland being pillaged and burned with apparent impunity no doubt increased their sense of outrage, and their "spoiling for a fight" may well have influenced Philips's decision to order such an all-out assault. Whatever the reason, the militiamen appear to have had no shame regarding their loss, since their bravery could no longer be questioned. As one of them put the matter in a letter to one of the newspapers, it was the militia that claimed "the honor of the fight."[139]

ORDER OF BATTLE
FEDERAL FORCES ENGAGED AT GRISWOLDVILLE:
SECOND BRIGADE, FIRST DIVISION
XV ARMY CORPS
    Brigadier General Charles C. Walcutt
    Colonel Robert F. Catterson
    97th Indiana Infantry Regiment
        Colonel Robert F. Catterson
        Captain George Elliott
    103rd Illinois Infantry Regiment
        Major Asias Willison
    6th Iowa Infantry Regiment
        Major William H. Clune
    40th Illinois Infantry Regiment
        Lieutenant Colonel Hiram W. Hall
    100th Indiana Infantry Regiment
        Major Ruel M. Johnson
    46th Ohio Infantry Regiment
        Lieutenant Colonel Isaac N. Alexander
    5th Kentucky Cavalry Regiment (Kilpatrick)
        Colonel Oliver L. Baldwin
    9th Pennsylvania Cavalry Regiment (Kilpatrick)
        Colonel Thomas J. Jordan
    12th Indiana Infantry Regiment (Milo Smith's brigade)

Major Elbert D. Baldwin
1st Michigan Artillery, Battery B
Captain Albert Arndt
(Two 3-inch Ordnance Rifles)

CONFEDERATE FORCES ENGAGED AT GRISWOLDVILLE:
FIRST DIVISION, GEORGIA MILITIA
Brigadier General Pleasant J. Philips

SECOND BRIGADE, GEORGIA MILIITA
Colonel James N. Mann
    4th Regiment—Colonel James N. Mann
    5th Regiment—Colonel S. S. Stafford
    6th Regiment—Colonel J. W. Burney

THIRD BRIGADE, GEORGIA MILITIA
Brigadier General Charles D. Anderson
    7th Regiment—Colonel Abner Redding
    8th Regiment—Colonel William B. Scott
    9th Regiment—Colonel John M. Hill

FOURTH BRIGADE, GEORGIA MILITIA
Brigadier General Henry Kent McCay
    10th Regiment—Colonel Charles M. Davies
    11th Regiment—Colonel William T. Toole
    12th Regiment—Colonel Richard Sims

GEORGIA STATE LINE
Lieutenant Colonel Beverly D. Evans
Lieutenant Colonel James Wilson

ATHENS AND AUGUSTA BATTALIONS, CONFDERATE
RESERVES
Major Ferdinand W. C. Cook

ANDERSON'S BATTERY, PALMER'S LIGHT ARTILLERY
Captain Ruel W. Anderson
(Four 12-pounder Napoleons)

Militia reports seldom include accurate information on troop strength, and few original roasters have survived. Consequently, the number of troops present on the Confederate side at Griswoldville can only be estimated as follows:

2d Militia Brigade	427
3rd Militia Brigade	496
4th Militia Brigade	446
Georgia State Line	469
Anderson's Battery	128
Athens Battalion	180
Augusta Battalion	175

TOTAL EFFECTIVE STRENGTH PRESENT   2,321[140]

Federal forces present at Griswoldville may be determined much more accurately. Division commander Charles R. Woods reported Walcutt's total present for duty as 1,513 men. When the 5th Kentucky and 9th Pennsylvania cavalry regiments of Kilpatrick's division, the 12th Indiana Regiment of Milo Smith's brigade, and the artillerymen in Arndt's battery are added, the total Federal force engaged probably numbered about 3,000 men.[141]

The effective force of the Georgia Militia remained in Macon for two days, recuperating and reorganizing, while their many wounded were distributed to hospitals as far away as Columbus on the Alabama border. On 25 November they boarded trains headed for Sherman's now-apparent objective, Savannah, by way of Albany and Thomasville. Ironically, a more satisfying adventure awaited them beyond Georgia's borders.[142]

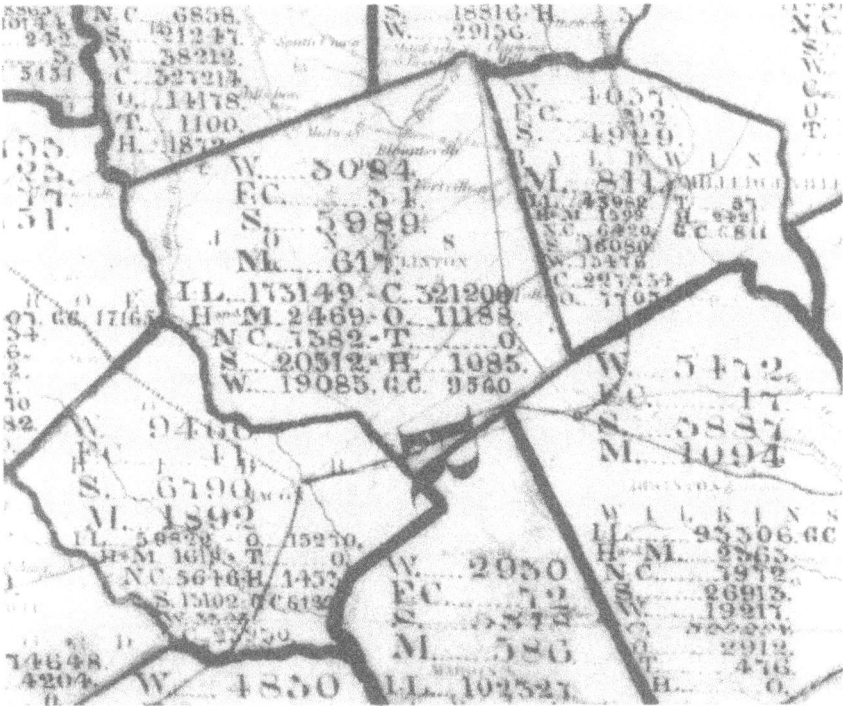

Campaign Map General William T. Sherman had the census bureau prepare a map of Georgia and Alabama for his March to the Sea. As this detail shows, it indicated what Sherman's forces could expect in terms of population , provisions, and provender. (National Archives)

Oliver O. Howard The commander of Sherman's Right Wing during the Savannah Campaign, Howard helped precipitate the battle of Griswoldville. His concern over delays to his wagons led to his sending General Walcutt's force to its meeting with the Georgia Militia.

(Hargrett Rare Book and Manuscript Library, University of Georgia Libraries)

Joseph Wheeler A major fear of the Federal forces was that General Wheeler and his cavalry would destroy vital supply trains.

(Hargrett Rare Book and Manuscript Library, University of Georgia Libraries)

Judson Kilpatrick Wheeler's cavalry's opponent, Kilpatrick's horsemen attacked Macon ineffectually but succeeded in burning Griswoldville.

(Hargrett Rare Book and Manuscript Library, University of Georgia Libraries)

The Bear's Den—Exterior General Cobb's home and unofficial headquarters were located in this residence near the Ocmulgee River, named by its previous owner, Cobb's brother-in-law.

(Library of Congress)

The Bear's Den—Interior The central hallway in the Bear's Den, shown here in the 1930s—much the worse for wear—in better days welcomed such Confederate luminaries as Jefferson Davis, Joseph E. Johnston, Richard Taylor, and P. G. T. Beauregard. (Library of Congress)

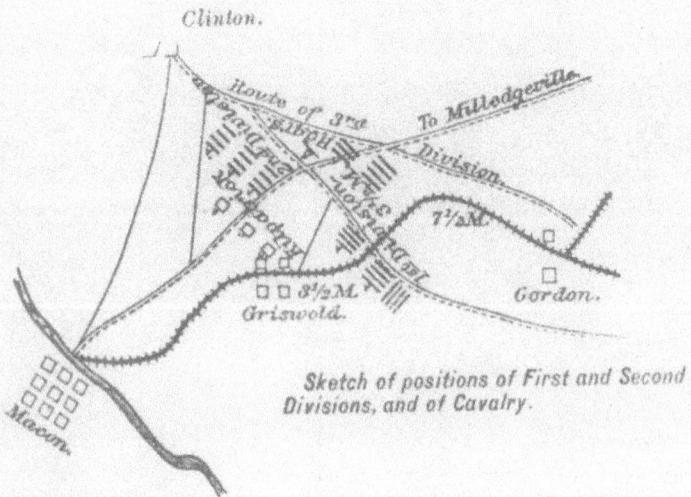

Central Georgia during Sherman's Map This map shows the activities of Kilpatrick's cavalry during an episode of the March to the Sea.

(War of the Rebellion, Series 4, Volume 1)

Samuel Griswold A Connecticut-born industrialist, Griswold founded around 1850 the village that would give its name to the militia's most well-known battle.
(Courtesy of Laura Nelle O'Callaghan)

Griswoldville Pike and Pistol A pike and pistol produced at Griswoldville
([Pike] Virginia Historical Society)
([Pistol] The Museum of the Confederacy, Richmond, Virginia. Photograph by Katherine Weitzel)

Captain Ruel D. Anderson This Confederate artillerist handily won the artillery exchange that began the Battle of Griswoldville.

(Courtesy of the Anderson family)

Philips's Scabbard No image has surfaced of General P. J. Philips, but his sword survives, with the engraving at the top of the scabbard demonstrating (as does his gravestone) that his name was spelled with a single "I."

(Courtesy of Z. Frank Hanner, Director, National Infantry Museum, Fort Benning, Georgia)

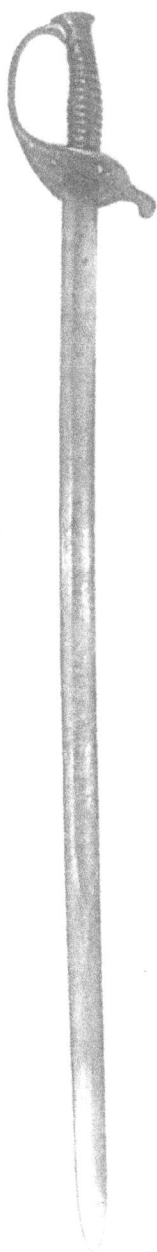

Philips's Sword The blade that Philips came close to having to surrender, it was manufactured by L. Haiman and Brother of Columbus, where Philips is buried.

(Courtesy of Z. Frank Hanner, Director, National Infantry Museum, Fort Benning, Georgia)

Charles D. Anderson One of the militia brigadiers, Anderson was in thick of the fighting at Griswoldville, having horses shot from beneath him and suffering a painful wound himself.

(Georgia Archives)

Griswoldville The field above the tracks at Griswoldville from which Anderson's men were ordered forward.

(Tamara Thompson)

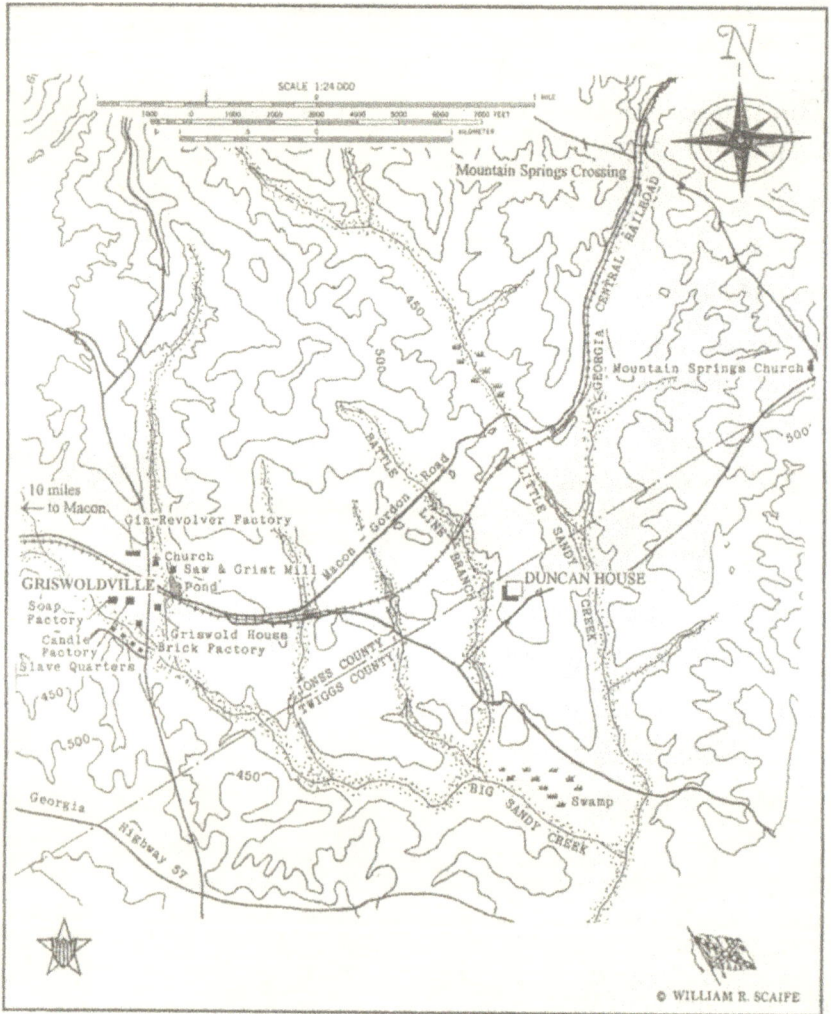

GRISWOLDVILLE BATTLEFIELD

Griswoldville Battlefield

(William R. Scaife)

Beverly D. Evans Commanding the Georgia State Line, Evans participated fully in the action at Duncan's Farm and wrote a detailed account of the battle. From a post-war photograph, presumably taken in Evans's law office in Sandersville.
(Courtesy of the Evans family)

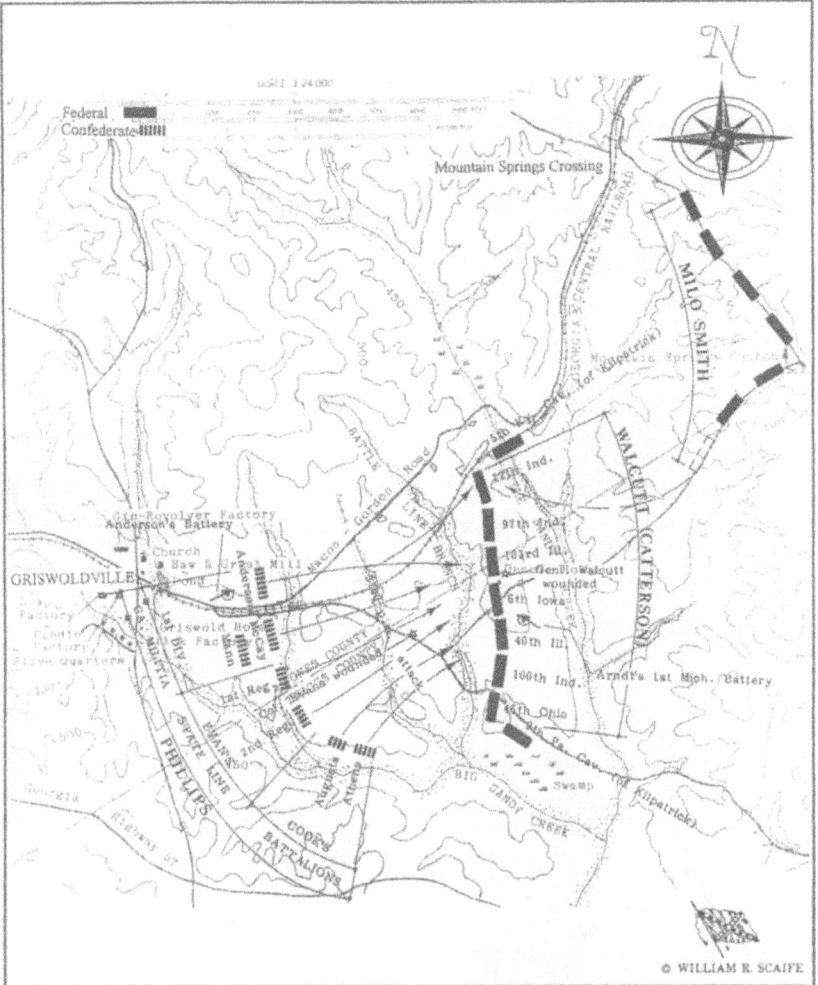

BATTLE OF GRISWOLDVILLE
November 22, 1864

Battle of Griswoldville

(William R. Scaife)

Henry Kent McCay More famed as a Reconstruction judge, McCay, like Samuel Griswold, was an ardent Confederate who had been born in the North.
(Georgia Archives)

A militiaman of McCay's brigade Julius Jefferson Worsham of Macon County was shot in the left side at Griswoldville.
(Athens Public Library)

Charles C. Walcutt Shown in this image seated in the center among members of his staff, Walcutt was one of General Sherman's most trusted subordinates.
(U. S. Army Military History Institute)

Colonel Robert F. Catterson Son of an Irish immigrant, Catterson had a conspicuously martial appearance. He took command of Walcutt's troops when the general
was taken wounded from the field.

(U. S. Army Military History Institute)

William Clayton Hood, G.M. A veteran of the Battle of Fredericksburg, Hood joined the Georgia Militia late in the war and would surrender at Columbus in April 1865.

(Crawford W. Long Museum)

Charles W. Wills Captain of an Illinois regiment, Wills wrote one of the most
affecting accounts of the carnage among the militiamen at Griswoldville.
(U. S. Army Military History Institute)

Eli J. Sherlock Among the Federals wounded by Ruel Anderson's Confederate artillery at Griswoldville was Eli J. Sherlock of the 100th Indiana, whose right foot was ripped open by a shell fragment. As some consolation, a friend presented him with a saber from the battlefield, a trophy of the Union victory.

(U.S. Army Military History Institute)

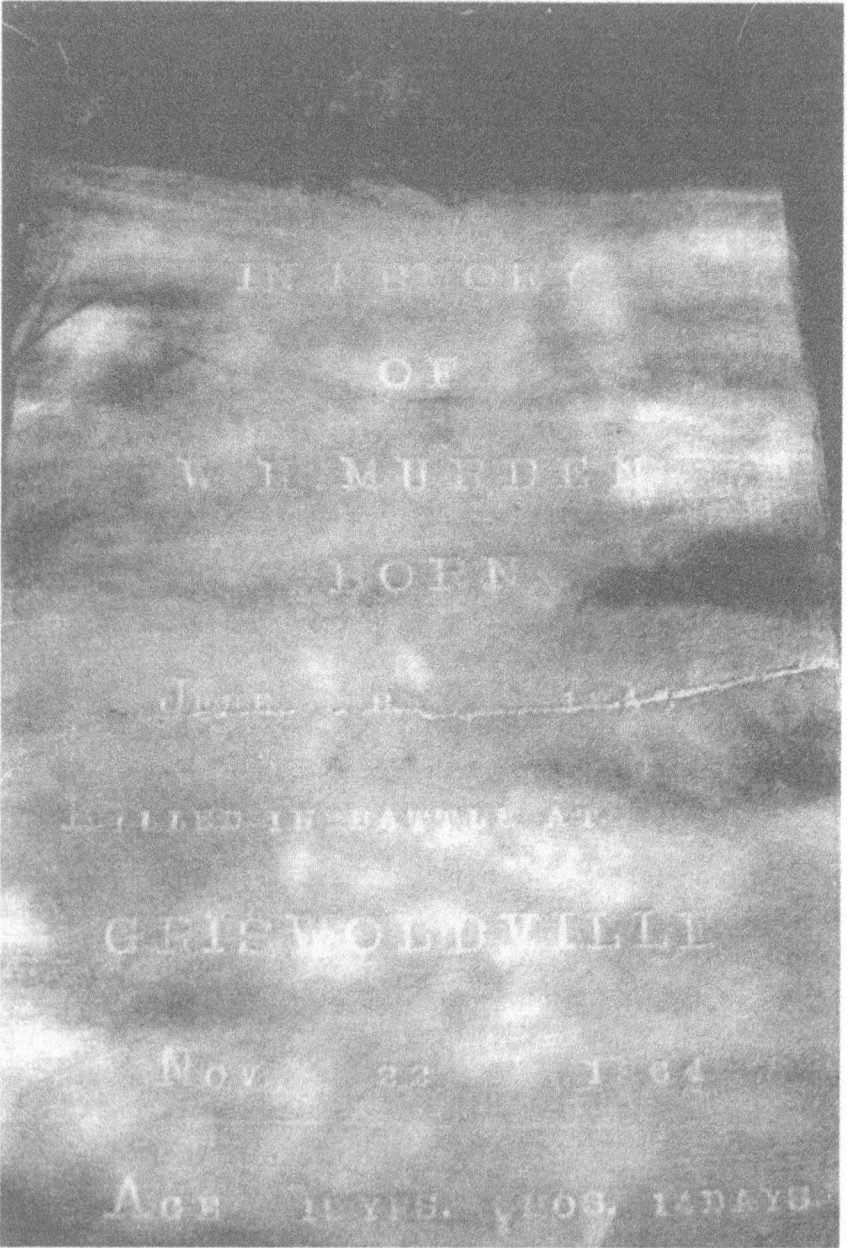

Griswoldville Memorial A memorial to the tragic fate of one of the boys at Griswoldville.

(Courtesy of Bill Moffat)

Joseph E. Brown An engraving of Georgia's war governor at the height of his power. His Macon-bound train steamed through Griswoldville just before it was captured by Federal forces on 20 November 1864.

Sherman's Wagons Escaping the dangerous situation in central Georgia,
Sherman's supply wagons ultimately reached Savannah, where this rather blurry
photograph was taken.

(U. S. Army Military History Institute)

4.
DEFENDING THE CHARLESTON
& SAVANNAH RAILROAD:
THE MILITIA AT HONEY HILL

The Federal Department of the South consisted of a series of outposts stretching along the south Atlantic coast from South Carolina to Florida. Union forces had captured most of the installations during the first two years of the war, and their major function since that time had been to support the Federal naval blockade of the Confederate coast. The department was commanded by Major General John G. Foster and was headquartered at Hilton Head Island, South Carolina.[143]

Prior to the beginning of the March to the Sea, Sherman had written General Henry W. Halleck in Washington requesting that an expedition be sent to cut the Charleston & Savannah Railroad near Pocotaligo, north of Savannah, on or about the first of December. Thus, if Sherman moved on Augusta, reinforcements and supplies could not be sent northward from Savannah through South Carolina—and, if Sherman moved instead on Savannah, supplies and reinforcements from Charleston would be cut off. On 13 November, Halleck therefore directed General Foster to send a force against the Charleston & Savannah Railroad, and the expedition was assigned to Brigadier General John P. Hatch and his 5,000-man Coast Division.[144]

The Federal plan called for Hatch's forces to board transports at Hilton Head and, screened by six gunboats, proceed some 20 miles up the Broad River to an old wharf at Boyd's Neck on the west bank of the river. There they were to disembark and march quickly and quietly some 10 miles westward, cutting the Charleston & Savannah Railroad at a point near a planters' resort called Grahamville. They were to destroy several bridges above and below the lodgment at Grahamville, thus cutting off Confederate supplies and reinforcements to Savannah from Charleston as well as the northward escape route of Hardee's Confederate army—in the event Savannah should fall to Sherman's advancing army.[145]

Hatch's Federal force consisted of two brigades of infantry under Brigadier General Edward E. Potter and Colonel Alfred S. Hartwell, three batteries of artillery under Colonel William Ames, and a battalion of cavalry under Captain George R. Hurlbut—numbering collectively about 5,000 men. A naval brigade of some 500 men under Commander George H. Preble was temporarily attached to Hatch's force and consisted of one battalion each of sailor infantry, marines, and artillery.[146]

Hatch's command embarked from Hilton Head on the evening of 28 November and began arriving by water at Boyd's Neck on the morning of 29 November; however, a dense fog caused many ships to go astray or run aground. The vessels were also spotted early by Confederate pickets, so any hope for a surprise attack was lost. Yet, even with such early intelligence, the Confederates were hard pressed to find a force adequate to resist the Federal movement.[147]

The area was defended by only a few squadrons of the 3rd South Carolina Cavalry Regiment under Colonel Charles J. Colcock, and no men could be spared from already overtaxed garrisons at Charleston and Savannah. The only significant force available was G. W. Smith's 1st Division, Georgia Militia, then on its way to Savannah after the debacle at Griswoldville. Leaving Macon by rail on 25 November, the militia had taken a circuitous route to avoid Sherman's rapidly moving columns. They traveled by rail some 100 miles to Albany, and then they marched to Thomasville, deep in South Georgia near the Florida line—"a distance between fifty-five and sixty miles, in fifty-four hours"—arriving there on 29 November. Five trains were expected to transport them the final 200 miles to Savannah, but only two trains actually arrived to transport them from Thomasville. Consequently, there was only room for the State Line, the Athens and Augusta Battalions, and the 1st Brigade of Georgia Militia. The other three brigades of the Georgia Militia—the 2d, 3rd and 4th, which had been engaged so heavily and suffered such grievous losses at Griswoldville—were temporarily left behind for lack of transport.[148]

It is doubtful that even two trains would have arrived without the intervention of General Robert Toombs, who hurried to Thomasville on horseback in advance of the marching militiamen.[149] General Richard Taylor, who was also waiting for train transport to Savannah, witnessed Toombs ("a man of extraordinary energy") in action:

> [Toombs] took possession of the telegraph and threatened dire vengeance on superintendents and road masters if they failed to have the necessary engines and carriages in time. He damned the dawdling creatures who had delayed me to such an extent as to make them energetic, and my engine appeared, puffing with anxiety to move. He assured me that he would not be many hours after me at Savannah, for Smith did not intend to halt on the road, as his men could rest in the carriages.[150]

General Smith and his Georgia troops arrived in Savannah late on the evening of 29 November, exhausted from their several days of almost constant travel and hoping to finally get much-needed rest.[151] But before General Smith could leave the train, it was boarded by General Hardee's assistant adjutant general, Lieutenant Colonel Thomas B. Roy, who handed him the following peremptory order:

> GENERAL: Lieutenant-General Hardee directs that you proceed at once with the first two trains of your troops which may arrive at Savannah to-night, and in the same cars to Grahamville and Coosawhatchie [in South Carolina], on the Charleston & Savannah Railroad, which places are being threatened by raiding parties of the enemy; and, if you find yourself the ranking officer present, that you command and drive the enemy back to their gun-boats.[152]

According to Smith, he proceeded instead to Hardee's headquarters where he found the commanding general had already retired for the night, and strongly protested his orders. Smith described his men as "almost broken down with fatigue" and pointed out that "a peremptory order from yourself [Hardee] requiring me to take the militia beyond the limits of the State, was in direct violation of the statute organizing and calling them into service." According to Smith, he further informed Hardee that unless he could satisfy him of the necessity of such an out-of-state movement, he would be "under the disagreeable necessity of withdrawing the State forces."[153] Hardee was apparently able to convince Smith of the necessity of the movement, however, and Smith later wrote in his official report to General Hardee, "After a full conference with yourself I was perfectly satisfied that for the purposes intended it was right and proper the movement should be made, and I gave orders accordingly. Notwithstanding some objections made by a portion of officers and men, the order was willingly obeyed."[154]

Consequently, Smith and weary troops spent the rest of the night completing the last leg of their long rail journey and arrived at Grahamville Station, South Carolina, at 8:00 on the morning of 30 November. At Grahamville, General Smith found Colonel Charles J. Colcock, who was in charge of both the 3rd South Carolina Cavalry Regiment and the military district surrounding Grahamville. Both a planter and a railroad man, Colonel Colcock had founded the Charleston & Savannah Railroad before the war and was thoroughly familiar with the area. He was therefore put in charge of selecting and preparing the most suitable defensive position.[155]

Colonel Colcock chose a place called Honey Hill, a slight elevation about 4 miles east of Grahamville. Passing over Honey Hill, the Grahamville road continued east less than 3 miles to a rural chapel called Bolen (or Boleyn) Church, where the road made a right angle with the River Road, which itself made junction with the road to Boyd's Landing. In 1862 General Robert E. Lee had ordered Honey Hill fortified to protect the railroad. The fortification there consisted of twin redoubts on each side of the Grahamville Road, both pierced for cannon; to the redoubts' front was a thick swamp, through which meandered a shallow, sluggish branch. With repairs to the eroded earthworks and the addition of shallow rifle pits, the position could be converted in short order into a suitable defensive line about a mile long. There was precious little time left to prepare such a position, however, since the Federals had landed the day before at Boyd's Neck, only 10 miles away.[156]

Fortunately for the Confederates, the Federals had wasted most of their daylight on 29 November marching and countermarching, trying to find the railroad. Although Federal transports had begun landing Boyd's Neck during the morning of 29 November, it had became obvious by mid-afternoon that the entire Federal force, together with supplies and equipment, would not be ashore until the next day. The Federal commander, Brigadier General John P. Hatch, determined therefore to take part of his force and attempt to cut the railroad at Grahamville before dark.[157]

The Naval Brigade, under Commander George H. Preble, led the advance with the artillery (eight light guns drawn by sailors) under command of Lieutenant Commander Edmund O. Mathews. The artillerymen marched toward Grahamville, supported on the right by the Sailor Battalion under Lieutenant James O'Kane, U.S.N., and on the left by the Battalion of Marines under 1st Lieutenant George G. Stoddard, U.S.M.C. After marching westward for some 2 miles, they encountered Confederate cavalry and pickets near the intersection of Salvesbarg Road and the River Road. When the Confederates withdrew northward along the River Road (today's South Carolina Highway 462), Commander Preble thought they were retreating toward the railroad and followed for some 2 miles before encamping for the night.[158]

The 1st Brigade, under Brigadier General Edward E. Potter, followed the Naval Brigade, and it was not until the 1st Brigade overtook the sailors that the error in direction was discovered. They then countermarched back to the Salvesbarg Road, leaving the Naval Brigade behind, since the sailors— who had been pulling the artillery pieces with drag ropes—were completely exhausted. Potter's 1st Brigade and the 4th Massachusetts Cavalry Battalion, under Captain George R. Hurlbut, continued southward on the River Road for 2 miles to Bolen Church, where the Grahamville Road branched off to the right. Their guide, a frightened slave from a nearby plantation, advised them to follow the left-hand road to reach the railroad. In reality, the left-hand road was a continuation of the River Road and ran almost due south, in the direction of Savannah.[159]

After proceeding some 4 miles, crossing several marshes, and having a number of skirmishes with Confederate pickets, General Potter discovered the second blunder—and countermarched back to Bolen Church. There he and his men encamped on the night of 29 November, having marched more than 15 miles during the day. Their goal, the railroad, remained 7 miles distant. But by the early morning of 30 November, Hatch had most of his forces concentrated at Bolen Church, and at 8:00 he finally began to advance along the Grahamville Road toward Honey Hill and the railroad.[160]

Major General G. W. Smith's Georgia state troops had arrived by rail at Grahamville Station at about the same time Hatch's forces left Bolen Church for the railroad. Consequently, Colonel Colcock had little time to strengthen the Confederate field works at Honey Hill. He therefore sent one

12-pounder Napoleon from Captain Charles E. Kanapaux's Battery, Lafayette South Carolina Light Artillery, under Lieutenant Christopher J. Zealy—along with Company K, 3rd South Carolina Cavalry, under Captain William B. Peeples—to delay the Federal advance while final defensive preparations were completed.[161]

At about 9:30 A.M., the blue column, having traveled only about a mile along the Grahamville Road (now US Highway 278), began crossing the causeway over Euhaw Creek and Swamp. Suddenly, Lieutenant Zealy's field piece opened on them from a small rise, near the entrance to today's Good Hope Plantation. The first shell killed or wounded nine Federal soldiers and threw the advancing column into confusion. Some order was restored as a two-gun section of Mersereau's Battery B, 3rd New York Artillery, was brought up under Lieutenant Edward A. Wildt; an artillery duel commenced at a range of about 600 yards. Zealy's gun was then withdrawn to a second position. When Wildt's Federal section advanced to within 800 yards, the artillery duel resumed, with the Yankees pushing the Rebels steadily back.[162]

The advancing troops had now reached a point where swamps and rice fields gave way to solid ground, allowing skirmishers to fan out and flank the small Confederate advance force. Brigade commander Potter advanced men of the 127th New York on the right and left of the road and sent the 25th Ohio, 157th New York, and 144th New York regiments to their support. Simultaneously, the resourceful Colonel Colcock devised another delaying ploy by having his men set ablaze the fields across which the Federals were advancing. The dry broom grass, fanned by a brisk breeze, flamed up and sped toward the Union troops at head height, temporarily halting their progress. But Wildt's Federal battery made use of the resulting clouds of smoke by running up closer, firing, and killing one of the Confederate cannoneers. Soon after, however, as Wildt once again advanced his guns, "a solid 12-pound shot struck him in the left groin." Inflicting a mortal wound, it bounded on to kill a horse and a foot soldier.[163]

During Colcock's three-hour delaying action, the line at Honey Hill was fully readied, and the Confederates began to occupy the works. To the left were the 1st Brigade, Georgia Militia (commanded by Colonel James Willis in the absence of General Carswell); the Georgia State Line under Lieutenant Colonel James Wilson; and the Augusta Battalion, Major George T. Jackson commanding. These state troops and Confederate reserves had improved the earthworks with headlogs. Beyond them to the left, some dismounted South Carolina cavalry and one gun guarded the flank. In the center of the works and to the right, Major F. W. C. Cook's Athens Battalion was posted, supported by seven artillery pieces. The Confederate line extended thinly beyond the fortifications over a mile to the right, held by a few men and one gun, the ground to their front being practically impassable. To the rear, the 47th Georgia was held in reserve at the direction of General Smith.[164]

Captain Henry M. Stuart, who commanded the Confederate artillery, paced off distances to critical points in the road and swamp in front of the works, calculating how long to cut the fuses on his artillery shells. At about 11:00 A.M., Colonel Colcock reported to General Smith that all was in readiness and tendered his resignation from further management of affairs. But General Smith replied, "No, Colonel, you have prepared so fine an entertainment that you must receive your guests." Having thus deferred command to Colonel Colcock, Smith withdrew to his headquarters in the rear and awaited the outcome of the impending battle. This was the same pattern he had followed at Griswoldville just a week earlier, when he deferred command to Brigadier General Pleasant J. Philips—with disastrous results.[165]

At mid-morning, the Federal column finally marched up the tree-enshrouded swamp road that led to the Confederate defensive line at Honey Hill. In the lead was the 2d Battalion of the 4th Massachusetts Cavalry, followed by the 127th New York Regiment under Colonel William Gurney. Mersereau's Battery B, 3rd New York Artillery, was formed in battery on the road, with Lieutenant George G. Breck's section on the right and Lieutenant George H. Crocker's section on the left.[166] The Confederate field commander, Colonel Charles J. Colcock (who made note of the large number of "old men and boys" who had suddenly come under his command), described the dramatic opening of the battle.

At half past ten o'clock the head of the Federal column appeared around a bend in the road about 120 yards from our breastworks, apparently unconscious of its existence and doubtless anticipating a pleasant morning march to the railroad. They little knew what was in reserve for them. A wild Confederate cheer—a volley from a thousand unerring rifles and six Napoleon guns and the whole of their column went down to their long sleep of death. Not a human

*soul was left, but one mangled mass of dead and dying crimsoned with their
life's blood the little stream of water extending about 20 yards between the bend
of the road and the base of the hill on which our works were located.[167]*

The first salvo exploded two ammunition chests of the right section of
Mersereau's Battery, and one gun recoiled into a ditch. Lieutenant George G.
Breck was so scorched on the hands and face that his section was relieved
and replaced by a section of Lieutenant Edgar H. Titus's Battery F, 3rd New
York Artillery, commanded by 2d Lieutenant Edmond C. Clark. Lieutenant
George H. Crocker, commanding the left section of Mersereau's Battery, was
shot in the right eye and his section lost eight horses and seven cannoneers.
For their part, the Georgia militiamen held firm, as the Union advance
emerged from the cover of the swamp and approached the Confederate
works. Behind "Joe Brown's Pets," one of their officers exhorted them: "Keep
cool, boys, and when they come out of that branch, shoot low."[168]

There is little in any of the official reports to indicate that General
Hatch directed the Federal attack with much skill or forethought. He
appears to have had no overall plan of attack, and the battle consisted primarily of a series of individual assaults or attempted flanking movements in
regimental strength. The Confederate line was never reached or penetrated at
any point. Hatch's rather matter-of-fact report read in part:

> *In front of the enemy's line ran a small creek, bounded by a marsh covered with
> dense undergrowth. This was not impassable, but presented a serious obstacle to
> our advance, being completely covered by the enemy's fire. Potter's brigade was
> quickly formed in line of battle parallel to that of the enemy.... The left of
> Potter's Brigade—re-enforced by the Fifty-fourth and Fifty-fifth Massachusetts
> Volunteers...—made two desperate attacks on the main work of the enemy led
> by Colonel A. S. Hartwell.... They were repulsed with severe loss.[169]*

Brigadier General Edward E. Potter led the first assault with the five regiments of his 1st Brigade, plus the 32d US Colored Regiment of Hartwell's
2d Brigade, supported by the Marine Brigade.[170] The following month
Potter routinely reported the devastating results of the initial attack:

> *I ordered the right of the line [32d US Colored Troops and the Marine
> Battalion] to press forward, swinging round to the left, and if possible to take*

the enemy's works in flank and rear; but after advancing a short distance, the dense undergrowth and deep swamps prevented their further progress. The Thirty-fifth U.S. Colored Troops, which had come up about this time, was pushed out on our right center; but the heavy fire of the enemy and the difficulties of the ground compelled them to withdraw.... On our extreme left, the enemy [the Forty-seventh Georgia Regiment, Confederates just arriving from Charleston] pressed rather heavily, and the left wing Fifty-sixth New York was ordered to take position on the left, and in support of the One hundred and fifty-seventh New York. Here also the deep swamp and abatis in front of the enemy's works prevented the advance of our troops. We maintained the position thus taken until dark....171

For the second assault, Colonel Alfred S. Hartwell, commander of the 54th and 55th Massachusetts Colored Troops, submitted a more candid and detailed report, giving considerably more insight into the confusion on the battlefield:

On arriving near the church orders were received from the commanding general to forward the artillery, which was done; also orders to advance as the troops in front advanced.... About half a mile from the church...[we] went into line in a corn-field on our left as we advanced. Next [we] advanced in the road by the flank, filed into a field on our right as we advanced, and formed column by company, putting out with the pioneers a fire in the grass. Advancing to the brow of the hill, [I] received orders to halt and hold my command compact and ready. Next, by successive orders from the commanding general, [we] advanced over and part way down the hill slowly and keeping the formation in column on right of the road. Received here a verbal order from General Potter to send one regiment in support of the One hundred and twenty-seventh New York, I think, but am not positive, as another order was at the same moment brought from the commanding general [Hatch] for me to advance by the flank down the road in support of the Thirty-fifth U.S. Colored Troops.... The musketry from the enemy was severe at this point; the men whom we had in front of my line along and near the road had come to the rear in confusion.... [T]he strong fire from the enemy's artillery and musketry, aided by the obstructions of the thicket and swamp, forced me back. I was here hit in the hand by a musket-ball.... I advanced [again] until the guns from the enemy's fort threw canister so severely into the head of the column that I was obliged to fall back again....

...On turning the last angle in the road in front of the fort, the grape and canister became insupportable. Captain Crane...was killed, with his horse; Lieutenant Hill...was knocked off his horse by concussion; and my own horse was killed and fell on me. The road seemed to be swept of everything. I was pulled from under my horse and back by an officer and a man of the Fifty-fifth Massachusetts, and during the time was hit in the boot heel by a shot that burned my ankle, and in the side by a spent grape shot that knocked me down and partially stunned me, and lodged in the coat; also, by a spent musket-ball in the back, that lodged in the shirt; in consequence of which, I regret extremely to say, I was unable to give further orders or superintendence, and was taken to the rear.[172]

The last of Colonel Hartwell's forces, the 102d US Colored Regiment, had been landed at Boyd's Neck at 11:00 A.M. and by 1:30 had reached the front at Honey Hill, but was not committed to offensive action. It was instead assigned to remove the guns of the disabled section of Mersereau's Battery from the field. The removal was finally accomplished only after the 102d US Colored Regiment had suffered heavy casualties, among them Captain Arod E. Lindsay killed and Lieutenant Henry H. Alvord wounded. First Lieutenant Orson W. Bennett, with thirty men, finally removed the guns and was subsequently awarded the Medal of Honor for his service.[173]

By mid-afternoon, General Hatch had apparently given up any hope of carrying the Confederate position at Honey Hill and stated in his report, "About 3:00 p.m. 6,000 rounds of musket ammunition was received and issued to those regiments entirely out. It was, however, now certain that the enemy's position could not be carried; and whilst a moderate fire was kept up, arrangements were commenced for retiring as soon as it became dark."[174]

By dusk, Federal ambulance wagons had arrived from Boyd's Neck. As naval howitzers were brought up to lay down a covering fire, the Federal force began falling back to the intersection at Bolen Church. There the pews were removed and the church converted into a hospital to accommodate the large numbers of wounded; in the churchyard "trenches yawned to receive amputated limbs." The Federals reported losses of 89 killed, 629 wounded, and 28 missing (18 captured) for a total of 746 men out of a force of 5,500. The Confederates reported losses of 8 killed and 42 wounded out of a force of 1,400.[175]

The most comprehensive description of the battle from the Confederate perspective was written after the war by Major George T. Jackson, commander of the Augusta Battalion. It was provided at the request of Colonel Charles Colcock Jones for use in the preparation of *The Siege of Savannah in 1864*:

> *My command was an independent Battalion…known as "the Augusta Battalion." It consisted of five (5) companies…A - B -C -D & E commanded respectively in the action by Captain T. H. Holleyman, Lieutenant Miller, Lieutenant Sentell, Lieutenant Ballentine & Captain Adams.*
>
> *I carried into the fight about one hundred and seventy-five (175) men, my force having been reduced by casualties &c. in the engagement at Griswoldville ten miles below Macon, which fight was just one week previous to the one of which I write. My loss [at Honey Hill] was two killed and two wounded—one of the killed was accidentally shot by another of my own men.*
>
> *My position was at right angles with the road—which crossed a small branch about fifty (50) yards in front of our breastworks—a part being on either side of the road. Two pieces of the "Beaufort Artillery" were on either side of the same road.*
>
> *The action took place on Wednesday—30th November 1864. We arrived in Savannah on the morning of that day—having been ordered around by Albany and Thomasville after the fight at Griswoldville…. I learned there was a consultation [in Savannah] between Gen[erals] Hardee and G. W. Smith— (the latter our commanding officer) as to the command of the latter going over into Carolina. This question was raised I suppose from the fact that Gen[eral] Smith's command consisted of the 1st Brigade Ga. Militia, two regiments of the Ga. State Troops [State Line], the Athens and Augusta Battalions—The two battalions being the only Confederate States Troops, the other parts of the command being properly "State Troops," which Joe Brown thought his especial property. However there being no hesitation on the part of either officers or men about going, we were soon again on the cars and crossing the Savannah River. Our men were not in the best fighting condition for besides other reasons they had not had a satisfactory meal since leaving Thomasville, on Monday night. (We were delayed reaching Savannah). After daylight we moved along slowly, fearing we might run into the enemy as they were advancing from their landing place, and we had no definite information as to the precise point of the Charleston & Savannah R.R. they intended to strike.*

At "Grahamville Station" we were ordered to debark from the cars and were furnished with additional ammunition.

My command was tardy in getting off, which called forth a pretty sharp inquiry from General Smith as to the cause. I told him my men were very poorly armed with old muskets, rifles &c. and that I had four different sized calibre of guns which made it necessary to be very particular in distributing the ammunition. We marched about four (4) miles when we arrived at Honey Hill. There I was assigned the position which I have already described. The "Athens Battalion" commanded by Major Cook (who was killed afterwards on the line at Savannah) was on my right, the two regiments of the Ga. State Troops [State Line] on my left, and the 1st Brigade of Ga. Militia on the left of them.

I had my men clear off the weeds from the top of the breastworks in my front, and then ordered them to rest.

We soon knew of the Enemy's advance and one of the "Beaufort Artillery" guns was sent across the creek to give them a shot to entice them on—the artillery had been doing this—firing and falling back all the morning. After a shot or two the piece of artillery returned to its place and we did not have to wait long for a better sight of the Enemy.

They seemed to think now that they had no serious obstacle to their object—the R.R. [railroad]. I had taken a position near the gun that bore directly down the road, and in about twenty (20) minutes and between nine (9) and ten (10) o'clock in the day the head of the column of the Enemy marching "by fours" appeared.

As they neared the branch the order was given to this piece to fire. I watched the sighting of the gun, and the effects of the shot. If the gun had been aimed at a painted target, and the shot had struck the "bull's-eye" it would have not been any better. It was loaded with cannister I think, and certainly did fearful execution. (The artillery was not under my command.) They [the enemy] rallied pretty well, but before they had well formed one of the guns on the left of the road fired and with similar effect. They fell back a little, formed and charged. When they had gotten nearly to the branch, both Artillery and Infantry opened on them and the action soon became general—extending to the right and left, as the Enemy found they had more than the Artillery now to fight. They charged my position repeatedly because I suppose they doubted our strength. Having previously only the Artillery to contend with, and because being the only open part of the line; their Artillery which they had posted opposite ours could support them.

They were not allowed at any time to pass much (if any) beyond the creek.

My position was not changed during the entire day; for while the enemy attempted to flank us repeatedly[,] our men on all portions of the line were equal to the emergency. During the afternoon they attempted a flank movement on our right when parts of the 33rd and 47th Ga. Regiments ("Confederate Troops") came in opportunely and drove them back.

I do not know positively, but it is my impression that a part of the 33rd Ga. came to the scene of action earlier in the day, and that a part of the 47th Ga. came alone in the afternoon.

During the afternoon the Enemy seemed to avoid the road as my men would kill a single man attempting to cross it. I was very much impressed with the singular accuracy of the fire of our men, and have since thought it must have been owing in part to the conformation of the ground, although I could give no reason for it.

The enemy's shells passed over us with few exceptions, and the fire of their small arms as our casualties show was remarkably harmless, while with us every shot seemed to bring down a man. I have been interviewed several times since the war by Yankee Officers who were in the fight; or whose commands were in it[,] as to why their loss was so heavy and ours so light? Evidently they had always doubted the report of our numbers and casualties.

The action continued the entire day, and when it became quite dark their Artillery fired a last Shot and were gone.

The battlefield the next day presented the appearance of a wreck. The Enemy had evidently retreated without any sort of order, and thrown away every thing. I availed myself of the state of affairs to arm my whole Battalion with fine Enfield rifles and turned my old ones over to the ordnance officer.[176]

In his after-action report, General G. W. Smith gave full credit for the victory to Colonel Colcock, to whom it was due (though Colcock would be conspicuously absent from Smith's account of the Honey Hill battle in *Battles and Leaders*). Predictably, Smith recounted the events at Honey Hill with considerably more enthusiasm than he had described the Griswoldville battle the previous week:

…I have never seen or known of a battle-field upon which there was so little confusion, and where every order was so cheerfully and promptly obeyed, and where a small number of men for so long a time successfully resisted the determined and oft-repeated and efforts of largely superior attacking forces…. We had actually engaged five pieces of artillery, and it is due to the South Carolina

*artillerists that I should say I have never seen pieces more skillfully employed
and gallantly served upon a difficult field of battle.*[177]

Having described the arrival of adequate reinforcements in the hours
after the victory—along with Lieutenant-General Hardee himself stepping
from a train at Grahamville Station on the morning of 1 December—Smith
brought his report to a close: "The enemy having been beaten back on the
30th of November, and the Confederate forces having now arrived, there
was, in my judgment, no longer any necessity for retaining the State troops
of Georgia beyond their legal jurisdiction. I therefore asked and obtained
permission to bring these exhausted troops back to their own State."[178]

Brigadier General Lawrence S. Baker arrived with more Confederate
reinforcements later on the morning of 1 December. Almost disbelieving, he
said of the battlefield that he had "never in any previous battle seen such evidence of terrible havoc from Artillery." Another Confederate officer
remarked of the artillerists, with less formality, "It was just wonderful what
the boys did—Why, a rabbit could not have crossed the road."[179]

Luis F. Emilio, in his *A Brave Black Regiment: The History of the Fifty-
Fourth Regiment of Massachusetts Volunteer Infantry, 1863-1865,* quoted a
black veteran of both Honey Hill and the bloody assault on Fort Wagner,
near Charleston as saying, "Wagner always seemed to me the most terrible of
battles, but the musketry at Honey Hill was something fearful. The so-called
'Rebel Yell' was more prominent than I ever heard it."[180]

The Confederate commander in the field, Colonel Charles J. Colcock,
recalled the aftermath of the battle and the carnage and confusion that
marked the field.

> *There were several Reg[imen]ts of negro troops who were terribly cut up.
> Judging from the number of dead found[,] they must have occupied the most
> exposed positions[,] and it is said by persons who examined their bodies[,]
> wounds were found in their backs shewing [sic] that the poor creatures were
> forced into action at the point of the bayonet.*
>
> *The plunder secured on the field [the] next day was a Godsend to our
> half-starved and ill-clad heroes. Thousands of blankets, haversacks, and over-
> coats and any quantity of provisions were strewed over the woods for two miles,
> indicating the thorough defeat and demoralization of the federals.*[181]

G. W. Smith's much-traveled Georgia Militia boarded their trains and were transported back to Savannah, almost as quickly as they had come. They arrived in Savannah by 10:00 P.M. on 1 December. Although nearing total physical exhaustion, they were flushed with enthusiasm over the victory—and filled with satisfaction for having redeemed themselves for the bloody defeat suffered at Griswoldville only eight days earlier.[182]

ORDER OF BATTLE
FEDERAL FORCES ENGAGED AT HONEY HILL
COAST DIVISION
    Brigadier General John P. Hatch
FIRST BRIGADE
    Brigadier General Edward E. Potter
        56th New York Regiment—Lieutenant Colonel Rockwell Tyler
        127th New York Regiment—Colonel William Gurney
        144th New York Regiment—Colonel James Lewis
        157th New York Regiment— Lieutenant Colonel James C. Carmichael
        25th Ohio Regiment—Lieutenant Colonel Nathaniel Haughton

SECOND BRIGADE
    Colonel Alfred S. Hartwell
        32d US Colored Troops—Colonel George W. Baird
        34th US Colored Troops— Lieutenant Colonel William W. Marple
        35th US Colored Troops—Colonel James C. Beecher
        102d US Colored Troops—Colonel Henry Chipman,—Captain Calvin Montague
        54th Massachusetts Colored Troops—Lieutenant Colonel Henry W. Hooper
        55th Massachusetts Colored Troops—Lieutenant Colonel Charles B. Fox

ARTILLERY BRIGADE
    Colonel William Ames
        Battery B, 3rd New York—Captain Thomas J. Mersereau

Battery F, 3rd New York—Lieutenant Edgar H. Titus
Battery A, 3rd Rhode Island—Captain William H. Hanner
2d Battalion, 4th Massachusetts Cavalry
Captain George R. Hurlbut

NAVAL BRIGADE
Commander George H. Preble, U.S.N.
Artillery Battalion
Lieutenant Commander Edmund O. Mathews, U.S.N.
Sailor Battalion of Infantry
Lieutenant James O'Kane, U.S.N.
Battalion of Marines
1st Lieutenant George G. Stoddard, U.S.M.C.

CONFEDERATE FORCES ENGAGED AT HONEY HILL
Major General Gustavus W. Smith
Colonel Charles J. Colcock, commanding in the field
Captain Louis D. DeSaussure, Adjutant General
Lieutenant E. W. Fraser, Assistant Adjutant General
Captain George Elliott
Captain William Elliott
Lieutenant Thomas E. Bessellieu
Lieutenant William N. Heyward

FIRST BRIGADE GEORGIA MILITIA
Colonel James Willis
1st Regiment—Lieutenant Colonel T. A. Walton
2d Regiment—Colonel James Stapleton
3rd Regiment—Colonel L. G. Johnston

GEORGIA STATE LINE
1st and 2d Regiments—Lieutenant Colonel James Wilson

ATHENS BATTALION, CONFEDERATE RESERVES
Major Ferdinand W. C. Cook

AUGUSTA BATTALION, CONFEDERATE RESERVES

Major George T. Jackson
    47th Georgia Confederate Regiment
Lieutenant Colonel Aaron C. Edwards
Major J. S. Cone
Captain Ben S. Williams, Adjutant
    32d Georgia Confederate Regiment
Lieutenant Colonel Edwin H. Bacon
    3rd South Carolina Cavalry Regiment
Major John Jenkins
    Company B—Captain A. L. Campbell
    Company E—Captain H. C. Raysor
    Company I (Detachment)—Captain J. L. Seabrook

ARTILLERY
    Captain Hal M. Stuart
        Section, Beaufort Light Artillery— Lieutenant Barnwell Fuller
        Section, De Pass's Light Battery—Lieutenant John A. Manget
        Section, Earle's Battery—Lieutenant James Furman
        One Section, Kanapaux's Lafayette Light Artillery
    Lieutenant Christopher J. Zealy

On 9 March 1865, during the closing days of the war, the Georgia legislature passed the following resolutions recognizing the Georgia Militia for its gallantry at Griswoldville and Honey Hill:

> *Resolved, by the Senate and House of Representatives in General Assembly met,*
>   *That the thanks of the State are due and are hereby tendered to General G. W. Smith, and to the officers and men composing the first Division of Georgia Militia; and to the officers and men of the Georgia State Line, for their conspicuous gallantry at Griswoldville in this State; and especially, for their unselfish patriotism in leaving their State, and meeting the enemy in the memorable and well-fought battle-field at Honey Hill in South Carolina. The State with pride records this gallant conduct of her Militia, and feels assured that when an emergency again arises, State lines will be forgotten by her Militia, and a patriotism exhibited which knows nothing but our whole country.*
>   *Resolved, That His Excellency the Governor be requested to transmit a copy of these resolutions to General G. W. Smith, with a request that they be*

Robert Toombs This antebellum view of Toombs strongly suggests why he was able to cut through bureaucratic red tape on the militia's journey to Savannah.
(Hargrett Rare Book and Manuscript Library, University of Georgia Libraries)

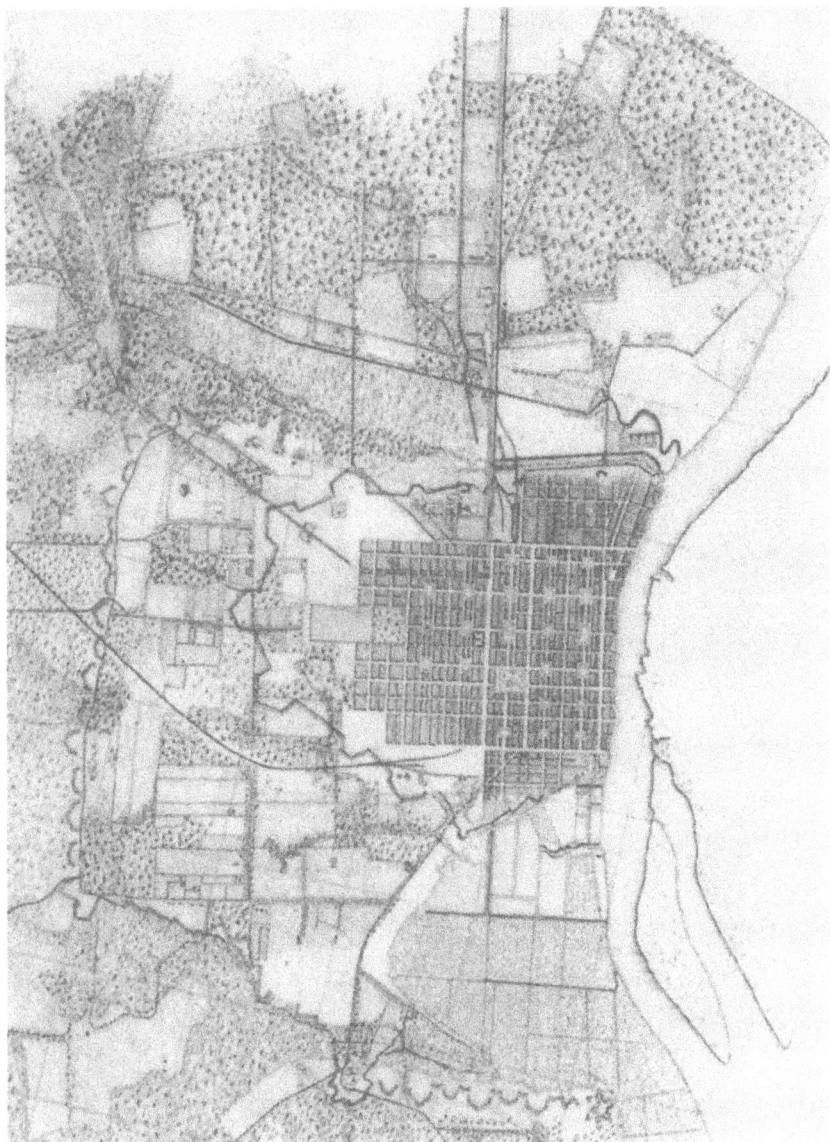

Confederate Savannah and Its Fortifications
(National Archives)

Gustavus Woodson Smith The question of sending Georgia militiamen into South Carolina was predictably debatable to General Smith.

(Library of Congress)

Charleston & Savannah Railroad Georgia troops left their state to protect this vital rail link. (Harper's Weekly)

Honey Hill: Road and Earthworks In this view from the 1980s, the surviving earthworks appear to the right of the old Grahamville Road. (Tamara Thompson)

Charles Jones Colcock The architect of victory at Honey Hill (and, confusingly, a cousin of Charles Colcock Jones), shown in a postwar portrait.

(Courtesy of the Colcock family)

The Swamp at Honey Hill To the front of the earthworks a nameless stream created a broad swamp. (Tamara Thompson)

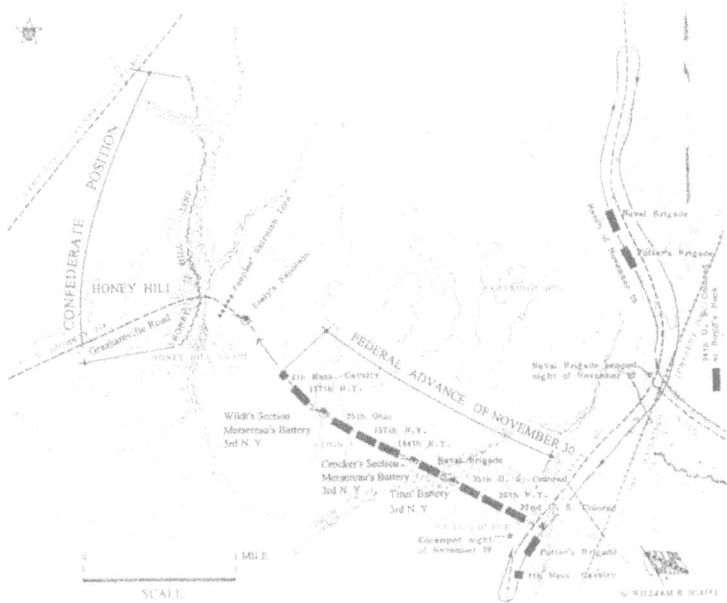

Honey Hill Approach Movements November 29 and 30, 1864.

(William R. Scaife)

Holy Trinity Episcopal Church, Grahamville, S.C. Marching from the Grahamville depot, the militiamen passed this picturesque church, the only surviving structure in the vicinity.

(Tamara Thompson)

General Reuben Carswell Though Carswell's men missed the Griswoldville battle, they were the only militia at Honey Hill.
(From Lawton B. Evans, The Student's History of Georgia [1884])

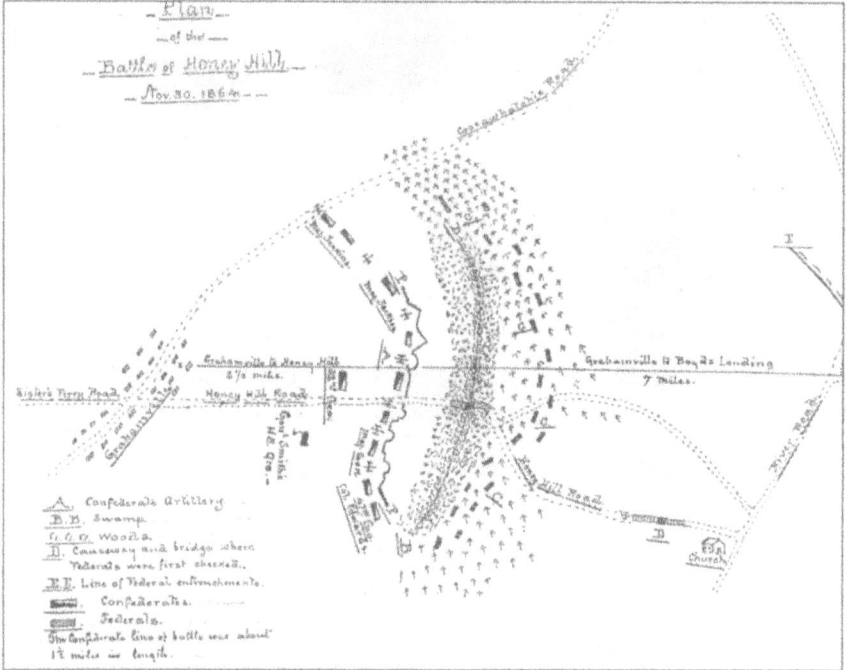

Plan of the Battle of Honey Hill A product of the research and the artistic hand of Charles C. Jones, Jr., this plan illustrated his personal copy of *The Siege of Savannah in 1864.*

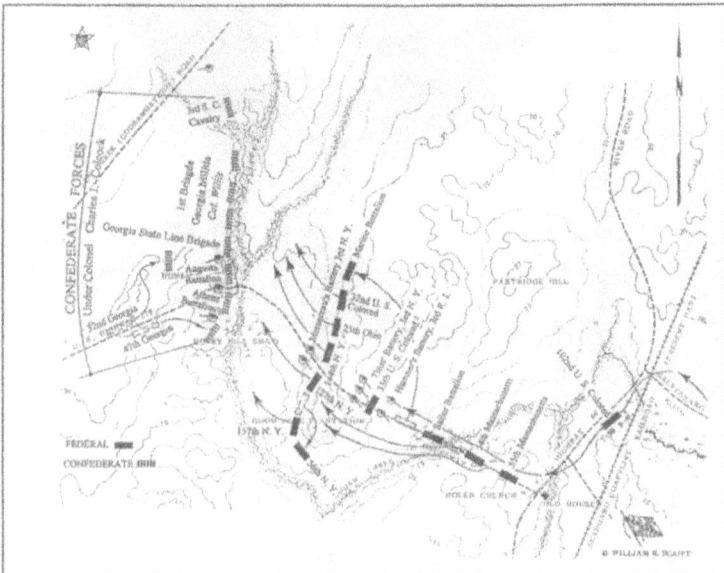

Battle of Honey Hill, November 30, 1864. (William R. Scaife)

Memorial Survivors of Colonel Colcock's command placed this plaque in the
courthouse in Hampton, South Carolina.
(Authors' collection)

Joseph E. Brown Appearing here as if enthroned as sovereign of a sovereign state, Governor Brown felt vindicated by the militia's service at Griswoldville and Honey Hill.

(Georgia Archives)

5.
THE MILITIA AT THE SIEGE OF SAVANNAH AND THE SURRENDER OF MACON

Prior to the Great March, Savannah had been considered reasonably secure from a mainland attack; its defenses had been designed primarily to protect its water approaches against Federal naval forces. Its main defense line consisted of a ring of outposts and fixed water batteries stretching over a distance of more than 20 miles. The line ran from the Red Bluff Battery in South Carolina, 3 1/2 miles above Screven's Ferry on the north, to the Rose Dhu Battery, guarding the Little Ogeechee River on the south. There were fifteen major artillery installations along the line at such places as Fort Jackson, Causton's Bluff, Turner's Rock, Thunderbolt, and Beaulieu.[184]

As soon as it became apparent that the likely objective of Sherman's March was Savannah, a western defense or Siege Line was constructed to protect the city's mainland approaches. This line was laid out by Captain, later Major, John McCrady, chief engineer for the state of Georgia, under the direction of Major General Lafayette McLaws, and by 7 December, Confederate troops began manning the works. Despite the strategic importance of Savannah, Southern manpower and resources were so depleted by late 1864 that the total force available to defend the city was less than 10,000, a substantial number of whom were needed to man the outposts and batteries guarding the water approaches to the city.[185] On 28 November, Savannah's mayor, Dr. Richard D. Arnold, issued the following appeal to the citizens of Savannah:

Fellow Citizens,

The time has come when every male who can shoulder a musket can make himself useful in defending our hearths and homes. Our city is well fortified, and the old can fight in the trenches as well as the young; and a determined and brave force can, behind entrenchments, successfully repel the assaults of treble their number.

The general commanding this division [William J. Hardee] has issued a call for all men of every age, not absolutely incapacitated from disease, to report at once to Captain C. W. Howard, at the Oglethorpe barracks, for the purpose of organizing into companies for home defense.... By manning the fortifications we will leave free the younger men to act in the field....

...The man who will not comprehend and respond to the emergency of the times, is forsworn to his duty to his country.
R. D. Arnold, Mayor [186]

On 1 December, Brigadier General Henry Kent McCay's 4th Brigade was detached from G. W. Smith's militia command and ordered down the coast to guard the Atlantic & Gulf Railroad bridges over the Ogeechee and Altamaha rivers south of Savannah. McCay divided his small brigade, leaving the 12th Regiment of 147 men under Colonel Richard Sims to guard the railroad bridges over the Ogeechee River, as well as the wagon road crossing at King's Bridge. The remaining 220 men of the brigade accompanied McCay to the bridge, where the Atlantic & Gulf Railroad, critical supply route from the south, crossed the Altamaha River near Morgan's Lake and Doctortown. Colonel Leon Von Zinken was ordered to reinforce McCay's 4th Brigade at the Altamaha bridge with 600 local reserve troops from the arsenal and workshops at Columbus, along with Lieutenant Colonel Arthur Hood's 29th Georgia Cavalry, which had been opposing Judson Kilpatrick's Federal cavalry near Midway Church north of the Altamaha River.[187]

On 18 December, Smith D. Atkins's brigade of Kilpatrick's cavalry and Joseph A. Mower's division of infantry—some 2,000 men—attacked General McCay's position, attempting to destroy the critical railroad trestle. McCay, whose force was only half the size of his attackers', had placed two 32-pounder guns on the river bluffs. Another light artillery piece, mounted on a flat car, was pushed out onto the trestle by a locomotive. The part played by McCay's artillerists proved decisive. Unable to take the main bridge after three assaults, the Federals withdrew. Setting fire to the Morgan Lake bridge, they returned to the vicinity of Savannah, having fought "the fiercest and the most intense military skirmish of the war in coastal Georgia."[188]

During the time General McCay and his men were stationed at Doctortown, they had a distinguished visitor: Joseph LeConte, a native of coastal Liberty County, as well as a physician and sometime professor of geology and natural history. Traveling up the railroad in late December 1864, LeConte was attempting to check on his family in Liberty County, where numerous Yankee troopers remained at large, and stopped for the night at Doctortown ("one frame house and two or three log shanties"). LeConte was allowed to sleep in the "only decent house in the place" by its official occupant, Lieutenant Colonel Arthur Hood of the 29th Battalion Georgia Cavalry.[189] Sharing a bed with Colonel Hood and another officer, LeConte fell asleep immediately but was awakened around midnight "by a party of revellers from the Ga. Militia stationed here."

> *They rushed into the room in wild disorder like so many fiends, calling for Col. Hood and demanding something to drink. Col. Hood assured them he had no liquor. After singing "Joe Bowers" and other comic songs with more spirit than melody…they went off as suddenly as they came and we heard them serenading other parties with what success I do not know. I now remembered for the first time this was Christmas Eve.…*
>
> *The troops stationed at this outpost of the Confederate forces are a brigade of militia—"Joe Brown's Pets"—under Gen. McCay, [and several other small commands]—the whole amounting to about one thousand men, nominally under the command of Gen. McCay as the ranking officer. There seems to be, however, but little organization or subordination, for the regulars care little for the militia. There also seems to be much discontent and some desertion among the militia. The regulars have learned to take things as they come—they take no more thought for the morrow than lilies.[190]*

LeConte spent a week in Doctortown before being reunited with his family, and during that period, he recalled, the "dullness of the long evenings was sometimes relieved by long talks around the campfire with Gen. McCay (afterwards Judge McCay), a man of acute and versatile mind, on a great variety of topics—political and social, scientific and philosophic." For his part, McCay and his men remained in the vicinity of Doctortown—guarding that vital spot on the supply route to the south—until May of the following year, and gave themselves up following news that Governor Brown had surrendered the militia to the forces of Major General James H. Wilson.

Doctortown was converted to parole center for Confederate prisoners and occupied by Union troops of Company K, 103rd Colored troops, who issued paroles of honor to McCay and what remained of his force.[191]

During the first week of December 1864, the other three militia brigades, along with the Georgia State Line, were sent to support Adjutant General Wayne at the Central Railroad's Little Ogeechee River Bridge. There Wayne was preparing a delaying action similar to the one he had helped lead from 23 November through 25 November at Ball's Ferry near the Central's crossing of the Oconee River. Among the troops Wayne had brought from the Oconee was the Corps of Cadets from the Georgia Military Institute; for the remainder of the Savannah Campaign the cadets would be posted with the militia. After a brief skirmish on 4 December (during which one of the cadets "brought down the officer...who demanded his surrender"), Wayne and his force, which had grown to 4,000, was withdrawn toward Savannah. Some 4 miles from the city, the militia, State Line, and cadets were joined on 7 December by General Smith, who had just "returned to duty, having been temporarily unwell"—apparently since the Honey Hill fight. Along Savannah's western defenses, or Siege Line, Smith's main force was deployed from the Savannah River at Williams Plantation on the right to within about 100 feet of the Georgia Railroad on the left—a distance of about 2 1/2 miles. Charles D. Anderson's 3rd Brigade of 868 men was on the right, next to the river; then Pleasant J. Philips's 2d Brigade of 492 men, under Lieutenant Colonel Dexter B. Thompson; next was Reuben W. Carswell's 1st Brigade of 906 men; and, finally, on the extreme left, 200 G.M.I. cadets and 469 men of the Georgia State Line under Colonel James D. Wilson.[192]

Lieutenant Colonel B. W. Frobel, a Confederate military engineer, had been ordered to report to Smith for "special engineers service." Frobel found Smith concerned about the water obstruction that fronted his line. It had been created by flooding a rice field and adjacent swamps, so that a vast sheet of water would confront Federal attackers. But Frobel noted:

> It was still possible for the enemy to drain the rice field by cutting the dam near the river. To prevent this a work was necessary in front of the rice field. The position was isolated and exposed and the plan did not meet the approbation of the Com[man]d[in]g Genl nor the Senior Engineer.

It was urged that men could not be spared to garrison the work as they were already full eighteen feet apart in the trenches. Genl G. W. Smith however urged its great importance so warmly that orders were finally given to occupy it, and two hundred militia and fifty negroes were furnished me as a working party. With this force the work was so far advanced in 36 hours as to be tenable. It [Fort Hardeman] consisted of a Lunette (enclosed) with curtains running to the river and rice field, the curtains being so arranged as to be quite as formidable when approached from the rear as from the front. Sand bags were used instead of head logs, and looped so as to allow the men to fire entirely under cover. Before the work was completed the enemy appeared in front driving in the skirmish line and approaching near the main work when a well directed fire from the Militia and Engineer troops drove them back.[193]

By the evening of 9 December, all available Confederate forces were concentrated in the newly constructed Siege Line, which extended from the Savannah River on the right to the Atlantic & Gulf Railroad bridge over the Little Ogeechee River on the left, a distance of more than 13 miles.[194]

The Order of Battle along the Siege Line was as follows:

CONFEDERATE FORCES
MANNING THE SAVANNAH SIEGE LINE
10-21 December 1864
    Lieutenant General William J. Hardee, Commanding
    Lieutenant Colonel Thomas B. Roy, Assistant Adjutant General
    Major John McCrady, Chief of Engineers

FIRST DIVISION, GEORGIA MILITIA (1,899 Men)
    Major General Gustavus W. Smith
        1st Brigade (906 Men)
    Brigadier General Reuben W. Carswell
        2d Brigade (492 Men)
    Lieutenant Colonel Dexter B. Thompson
        3rd Brigade (868 Men)
    Brigadier General Charles D. Anderson
        4th Brigade (367 Men)
    Brigadier General Henry K. McCay

(Detached, guarding Atlantic & Gulf Railroad bridge over the Altamaha River)

GEORGIA STATE LINE (469 Men)
Colonel James D. Wilson

CORPS OF CADETS—GEORGIA MILITARY INSTITUTE (200 Boys)
Major Francis W. Capers

McLAWS'S DIVISION (3,750 men)
Major General Lafayette McLaws
Baker's North Carolina Brigade (2,179 Men)
Brigadier General Lawrence S. Baker
Lewis Kentucky Orphan Brigade (1,571 Men)
Brigadier General Joseph H. Lewis
2d Kentucky Mounted Infantry
4th Kentucky Mounted Infantry
9th Kentucky Mounted Infantry
Worthen's North Carolina Battalion
3rd Battalion Georgia Reserves
5th Battalion Georgia Reserves
1st Regiment Georgia Reserves

WRIGHT'S DIVISION (2,928 Men)
Major General Ambrose R. Wright
Mercer's Brigade (1,200 Men)
Brigadier General Hugh W. Mercer
Athens Battalion, Confederate Reserves
Augusta Battalion, Confederate Reserves
Nisbet's Local Defense Regiment
Brook's Foreign Battalion (Paroled Federal Prisoners)
Jackson's Brigade (1,728 Men)
Brigadier General John K. Jackson
Colonel Leon Von Zinken's Local Reserves
(1,154 Men, From the arsenal and work shops at Columbus)

Ferguson's Dismounted Cavalry Brigade (568 Men)
Brigadier General Samuel W. Ferguson
(From Wheeler's Cavalry)

ARTILLERY
Lieutenant Colonel Charles C. Jones, Jr., Chief of Artillery[195]

Sherman's forces approached the Siege Line on 9 December. Alpheus
Williams's XX Federal Army Corps pressed up close to Smith's position on
the right, but no serious attempt was made to carry it.[196]

As early as 8 December, the Confederate high command had apparently
concluded that the safety of Hardee's small army was of greater importance
than Savannah, as shown by a dispatch on that date from Hardee's commanding officer in Charleston, General Gustave P. T. Beauregard:

> *Lieutenant-General Hardee,*
> *Savannah, Ga.:*
> *Having no army of relief to look to, and your forces being essential to the*
> *defense of Georgia and South Carolina, whenever you shall have to select*
> *between their safety and that of Savannah, sacrifice the latter, and form a*
> *junction with General [Samuel] Jones, holding the left bank of the Savannah*
> *River and the rail road to this place as long as possible.*
> *G. T. Beauregard1*[97]

The earlier decision to sacrifice the garrison at Fort McAllister had been
made on the premise that Savannah would eventually have to be evacuated,
and on 14 December the Confederates began preparations for this difficult
and hazardous withdrawal. Savannah was almost totally enveloped by
Sherman's overwhelming land force on the west and by the Federal fleet on
the south and east. The major lifeline to Charleston and the outside world
was the narrow Union Causeway, which crossed the marshes and rice fields
on the South Carolina side of the river and led to Hardeeville—from which
point the Charleston & Savannah Railroad was still open to Charleston.[198]

The Confederates first planned to evacuate by crossing the Savannah
River at Screven's Ferry and following the Union Causeway to Hardeeville,
but they could not collect sufficient vessels to make the crossing safely and
effectively. Hardee's engineers then selected a line of retreat that entailed (1)

the construction of a pontoon bridge from the foot of Savannah's West Broad Street to Hutchinson Island, (2) a roadway across the island, (3) a second pontoon bridge across the Middle River to Pennyworth Island, (4) another roadway across Pennyworth Island, and (5) a third pontoon bridge across Back River to the South Carolina shore. The escape route then followed Huger's Causeway, little more than a dam running northward through the rice fields and just wide enough to accommodate artillery and wagons. It roughly followed the same course as today's US Highway 17, some distance to the west of the Union Causeway.[199]

One of the most persistent misconceptions of the campaign is that the primary escape route ran along the Union Causeway to Hardeeville, a misconception Sherman unfortunately helped to perpetuate in his 24 December dispatch to Henry W. Halleck. Therein Sherman erroneously assumed the route Hardee had taken. But, to the researcher willing to study contemporary maps of the area—while reading the reports of Federal Colonel Ezra A. Carman and such Confederate officers as General Pierce M. B. Young and Lieutenant Colonel Charles C. Jones—it becomes obvious that the main escape route could only have been along Huger's Causeway.[200]

Since no pontoons were available, rice flats or barges from nearby plantations were collected by Brigadier General Pierce M. B. Young's cavalry brigade and by detailed soldiers sent in steamers by the engineer in charge, Lieutenant Colonel B. W. Frobel. The bridge was constructed under the supervision of Frobel, "whose principal detail for the work consisted of fifty-five Militia under Capt. Gibson and ten Sailors from the Navy under a non-commissioned officer of that service."[201]

The flats were lashed together with ropes and stringers, then anchored in place with railroad car wheels. Wood planking was ripped from nearby wharves and used to floor the makeshift bridges. To deaden the sound of the massive movement, thick layers of rice straw were placed over the planking. By 19 December the last bridge was completed and all was in readiness for the evacuation.[202]

The evacuation began on the night of 20 December 1864. Lieutenant Colonel Frobel, who had gone out "to reconnoitre the enemy's lines," had come back satisfied that Sherman's men, who were fortifying their lines, expected a sortie from the Savannah garrison:

As I returned a long line of wagons and ambulances was crossing the pontoon and stretching away across the flats on the S.C. side. Genl G. W. Smith's division was designated as rear guard and was ordered to move at midnight. As soon as it became dark the troops began to file thro' the town, passing slowly and silently over the pontoon, upon which a quantity of straw had been laid to deaden the sound. At one o'clock the rear guard passed, and no one remained behind except a skirmish line under command of Col. Robert Troup [C.S.A., attached to Smith's Division]. By two o'clock they came up and passed over to Hutchinson's Island, leaving no one in the town but some stragglers and thieves who no doubt fell into the hands of the enemy. We now mounted and took our way toward the bridge. As we reached it, a rocket shot up into the air just behind us—another and another followed. It was a signal…that the city had been evacuated. At the same moment the loud boom of cannon along the lines told that the enemy had discovered the move and were feeling our late position before advancing. Silently we moved along, and as the day broke we reached the high ground on the S.C. shore.203

As a final precaution, holes were punched in the pontoon flats, and they were set adrift in the river to prevent the Federals from pursuing—had they entertained any such intentions. The Georgia Militia, accompanied by the Corps of Cadets and the State Line, marched northward to Bamburg, South Carolina, on the Charleston & Augusta Railroad, where they boarded trains to Augusta. Their supply wagons were left with Hardee's army, which continued northward into the South Carolina interior, accompanied by the militia's former comrades in arms, the Athens and Augusta Battalions (though without the estimable Major F. W. C. Cook, who had been killed during the siege). Nonetheless, the militia's contribution to Savannah's defense and successful evacuation had been considerable. The action at Honey Hill had made it possible for Hardee to resist Sherman's advance until late December. Hardee would recall the daring exit with his troops—an escape that would allow them to fight again—as the most satisfying event of his military life.204

But Hardee realized that the 1st Division, Georgia Militia, had made its last major contribution to the Confederate war effort. On 8 January 1865, he wrote President Jefferson Davis: "I have no reason to expect re-enforcements from Georgia other than Maj. Gen. G. W. Smith's force of militia, now at Augusta, which is rapidly diminishing by desertion, and numbers less than 1,500 muskets."[205]

During this gloomy period of garrison duty in Augusta, with his militiamen steadily filtering away, General Smith reflected on his experiences with Georgia's citizen-soldiers. Looking back over the past eight months, he composed for General Wayne a framework "for the improvement of the state military organization." (As might have been expected, there were no speculations regarding the disastrous problems that could arise from weak leadership at the division level.)[206] Governor Brown had Smith's ruminations published in a pamphlet that collected all the reports relating to his state troops' campaigns in 1864-1865:

> *JANUARY 19TH, 1865.*
> *Memoranda.*
>
> *1st. There is no better established fact in military history than this: "When a Sovereign State determines to keep in service a regular army she must pay the expenses." Money is just as necessary to Militia whilst in service as it is to regulars. The Legislature of this State should make an appropriation at once for the support of the Militia. If this is not promptly done the organization should be given up.*
>
> *2d. All the Militia, or State forces, should be regularly sworn and mustered into the service of the State.*
>
> *3d. At least one permanent Court Martial should be established by law for the trial of Militia who are charged with having committed offences against either the military or civil laws of the State.*
>
> *4th. No officer should be commissioned even after being elected until he had first passed before a Board of competent officers, and received from such Board a certificate stating that he was qualified to perform the duties of the office.*
>
> *All officers now in service should be subject to examination before such Board, on the recommendation of the commander in the field, and when found incompetent should be reduced to the ranks; a good court martial and good examining board[,] both made permanent, their duties defined and habitually holding their meetings in the camp[,] would be of great service.*
> *(Signed) G. W.S.*
> *To Maj. Gen. H. C. WAYNE,*
> *A. & I. Gen'l. Milledgeville, Georgia.[207]*

By 20 January, Smith's dwindling command at Augusta consisted of the 1st Brigade under Reuben W. Carswell; the 2d Brigade, again under Pleasant J. Philips; the 3rd Brigade under Charles D. Anderson; the 12th Regiment of the 4th Brigade (the remainder still at Doctortown), under Colonel Richard Sims; the Georgia State Line under Colonel James Wilson; the Corps of Cadets, Georgia Military Institute under Major Francis W. Capers; a pioneer corps under Captain B. M. Polhill; and Pruden's Battery of artillery under Captain William H. Pruden.[208]

By 4 February, the militiamen still on duty were manning the Briar Creek Line about 25 miles south of Augusta, where they were encamped at Allen's Station on the railroad, as well as at Shell Bluff and Spirit Creek. Four days later they were ordered into Augusta to man the earthworks surrounding the city, and there most would remain until 24 February 1865. On that date, Governor Brown again withdrew the militia from Confederate command and sent them home for the last time—explaining to General Beauregard that the interior of Georgia was in no immediate danger. Nonetheless, from February 1865 the militia took no part in the war as an organized military force, although some units remained on garrison duty in towns such as Macon and Augusta and would participate in the war's final Georgia campaign. As the war wound inexorably toward defeat, "Joe Brown's Pets," once so coveted by the Confederate central government, became inconsequential at Richmond.[209]

There were, of course, a few other half-hearted attempts to requisition the 1st Division, Georgia Militia. In March 1865 General Samuel Jones wrote from the Tallahassee headquarters of his Military District of Florida to request troops to repel Federal raids in West Florida—particularly attempts to ascend the Chattahoochee from the Gulf. During the same month, the governor was informed that "Detailed agriculturists are now ordered into Confederate service in the field," a rather pointed attempt to gather up furloughed militiamen.[210] Brown responded on 13 March, the same day of the request:

> All persons belonging to Major-General Smith's division are in the actual military service of the State. No one of them, whether detailed agriculturists or not, will obey any order from a Confederate officer, unless so directed by General Smith, when he is under orders from me to report to a Confederate general. The

State took the detailed agriculturalists into her military service at a time when,
according to the decision of the [state] supreme court, they were not in the mil-
itary service of the Confederacy, and the Confederate officers can take no
control over them without the consent of the State till they are disbanded by the
State. They are now only on furlough.211

After Sherman had bypassed Macon in November 1864 and moved toward Savannah and the Atlantic coast, Governor Brown set up the executive department in Macon, where it would remain in large part until mid-March 1865—and where other militia-related controversies would arise. General Howell Cobb continued to command a small garrison of Confederate Reserves in Macon, which had become the state's principal town and de facto capital. The city would become the state's political center not only due the governor's presence, but also because the General Assembly would hold its session in the Macon City Hall in the early months of 1865, the Milledgeville facilities having been wrecked by Sherman's troops. On 1 December, Brigadier General William W. Mackall, General Johnston's former chief of staff, was named commander of the post in Macon, and Colonel Isaac W. Avery was put in command of the Macon Home Guard, whom he instructed to round up all Confederate stragglers and return them to duty. The militia having shared headquarters with Cobb's Confederate Reserves on Mulberry Street since mid-1864, General Smith gravitated to Macon after leaving Augusta.212

Governor Brown's tenure in Macon was marked by another attempt at militia organization, parallel to his previous activities, but involving those men not then serving with the 1st Division under General Smith. On 19 November, just prior to escaping Milledgeville for Macon, the governor ordered a levy *en masse* "of the whole free white male population residing or domiciled [in Georgia] between sixteen (16) and fifty-five (55) years of age," exempting only the plainly unfit and state civil officers, along with other classes exempted by the General Assembly. The term of service was to be forty days, "unless the emergency...sooner passed." Confederate detailed men were explicitly stated to be subject to the call, "by the late decision of the Supreme Court of [Georgia]." A subsequent proclamation of 25 November established camps of organization at Macon, Albany, Athens, and Newnan. It also noted that those men who had not rejoined Smith's division at Lovejoy's Station earlier could not go into the new organization but should be rounded up and sent to General Smith. In some cases, small posses of six armed men were sent to "bring up under arrest" those who were subject to the proclamation and had refused to report.[213]

Ironically, the unprecedented circumstance of an armed host marching seaward through the center of the state created a threat to Brown's control of the newly raised militia levies. Returning to Macon on 3 December 1864 from his plantation in southwest Georgia, where his family was taking refuge, the governor found a surprising letter awaiting him. The president of the Georgia Senate, Ambrose R. Wright of Augusta, had written on 24 November to inform Brown that he had created another camp of organization in Augusta and had issued his own proclamation summoning militia levies to that city. Wright's authority for this action was a constitutional provision giving the president of the Senate executive power during the "disability" of the governor, which Wright argued was a consequence of Brown's having been "cut off from communication with the eastern portion of the State."[214]

Brown responded with a somewhat surprising lack of belligerence:

> As the communication between [Macon] and Augusta had not been destroyed, but the line only lengthened by way of Thomasville and Savannah, which was kept open, and in daily use, as shown by your proclamation of the 1st of November, and your order of the 22d, which both referred to my proclamation, dated the 19th [of November], which was published in the Macon paper on the same day, showing that my proclamation and orders published in this city were received in Augusta the second day after they were issued, I cannot admit that the contingency contemplated in the Constitution had happened.... As your orders conflict with both my proclamation and my orders issued..., I cannot approve them.... You may send forward to Major-General Smith all [militia levies] you have organized who are able to do field service, and discontinue the camp at Augusta. I will be much obliged if you will report the muster-rolls of those you have organized to these headquarters.[215]

Wright, also a celebrated Confederate general, did better than that: soon he was commanding troops along Savannah's Siege Line and would be one of the leaders of the troops resisting Sherman's march through the Carolinas. Having instituted the levy *en masse* on 19 November, Brown essentially revoked it on 19 December, sending the Reserve Militia on furlough "until further orders." They were, however, ordered to "perform police and patrol duty" in their respective counties on the "Friday and Saturday in each week," to assist in dealing with the growing "depredations of thieves and marauders." The county reserve militia units were also to arrest and send to the Macon post all absentees from Smith's militia division, so that they could be "forwarded to their command."[216]

On 15 February 1865, Brown addressed the special session of the General Assembly at Macon, with his primary purpose apparently to chastise President Davis for the Richmond government's mishandling of the war. In particular, he wished the General Assembly to approve his actions in not having turned over the Georgia Militia to the Confederate authorities at the conclusion of the Atlanta Campaign, particularly given the fact that Davis had left Georgia "to her fate." Brown once again argued against conscription as unconstitutional, effectively contrasting it with what he identified as the constitutional manner of raising troops, the militia system:

> *This ruinous policy of the administration finds no justification in the Constitution of the country. From the organization of the Government of the United States to the disruption of the Union, the uniform practice was to call upon the States, when more troops than the regular army were needed, to furnish them organized ready for service. This they could readily do, as all the machinery of the State Government could be brought to bear to bring them out. Instead of enrolling officers of the Central Government imported among them, whom they knew not and who were not in sympathy with them, all the militia officers and civil officers of the counties, who are their neighbors and friends, and whom they are accustomed to respect and obey, could be charged with the duty of aiding in the organization. Not only so, but they were permitted to go under officers of their own neighborhoods usually elected by them, to go with their own neighbors and relatives as their associates and companions in arms. This was not only the practical and successful mode, but it was the Constitutional one.*[217]

Since, as Brown contended, Davis had brought the Confederacy to ruin, he also urged that the Confederate Constitution be amended, taking control of the army from the president and placing it under a commander-in-chief, free from the control of the president. Such a change, Brown contended (with a broad hint toward what Davis had done in replacing Johnston with Hood at Atlanta), "would save us in the future from the heavy calamities which have befallen us by the capricious removal of a great commander, at a most critical juncture of an ably conducted defensive campaign."[218]

However well taken the governor's position against Davis might have been, by March 1865 many Georgians had tired of Brown's obsessive and seemingly endless postmortem on the president's conduct of the war and felt the time for effective changes in policy had long since passed. The *Macon Daily Telegraph & Confederate*, for example, published a mid-March editorial that could hardly have been more succinct, nor clearer in its meaning: "If the State must support and take care of him [Governor Brown], be it so: but send him to the Lunatic Asylum, where he will be harmless, if not inoffensive."[219]

Brown, however, was within weeks of being even more effectively removed from the scene. On 22 March 1865, Major General James H. Wilson embarked with three divisions of Federal cavalry (more than 13,000 men) on a raid through the very heart of the crumbling Confederacy. Beginning in the northwest corner of Alabama, he moved in three columns through Selma on 2 April and Montgomery on the 12th.[220] On 15 April, as Wilson neared Columbus, Georgia, on the Alabama line, Governor Brown wrote what was presumably his last letter to his militia commander:

Major-General Smith:
The movements of the enemy in Central Alabama indicate the intention on their part to make an early movement upon Columbus and other points in Georgia. To enable us to meet this successfully, it will require the united efforts of all who are able to bear arms, whether they belong to the State or Confederate service. You are, therefore, hereby directed to order out the militia of the State, subject to your command, to rendezvous at Columbus, as fast as possible. All who are subject to your command under your former orders from the headquarters [Milledgeville] are embraced in this call, and all subject to militia duty under fifty years of age who fail to respond will be turned over to Confederate service. I regret exceedingly to have to require them to leave their crops at this important period, but the movement of the enemy leaves no other alternative.221

From his headquarters in Macon, Smith issued General Orders the same day to attempt to raise and send forward to Columbus (as opposed to lead forward) what militiamen he could. But few had time to respond, since the city fell the next evening between 8:00 and 10:00 P.M. General Howell Cobb had attempted to defend Columbus with a small body of his Reserves and home guards, as well as a few militiamen and the State Line troops (whom Governor Brown had agreed to allow him to take into Alabama if necessary). But Columbus's defenders (calculated by some as between 2,000 and 3,000, but who would translate into only 1,500 prisoners) were easily crushed by some 300 of Wilson's seasoned and daring troopers. Wilson soon turned over the task of destroying much of the city to Colonel Edward F. Winslow, who performed his duty with "detached thoroughness." He obliterated the naval armory and shipyards, two rolling mills, the government arsenal and two powder magazines, the railroad roundhouse, machine shops, 15 locomotives, and 250 freight cars.[222]

Wilson continued through West Point, LaGrange, and Thomaston, approaching Macon from the southwest on 20 April. He planned to concentrate his columns at Macon, destroy the city, and move on to Augusta before joining up with Sherman in North Carolina. But the war would end before he could complete the lengthy circuit.[223]

At dusk on 18 April, Macon was evacuated by much of its population and Eliza Frances Andrews noted in her journal seeing Governor Brown on the eastbound train, his face and manner marked by "preoccupation about his...rather precarious affairs." Two days later, as General Howell Cobb deployed his troops in the trenches west of Macon, he received a telegram from General P. G. T. Beauregard, informing him that in North Carolina Sherman and Joseph E. Johnston had agreed to an armistice that would bring the war to an end. Wilson's cavalry was rapidly approaching Macon, with Colonel Frank White's 17th Indiana Regiment of Robert H. G. Minty's division in the lead. Cobb sent Brigadier General Felix Y. Robertson to intercept Wilson's advancing column some 14 miles southwest of Macon to advise Wilson of the armistice and, it was hoped, bring the fighting and destruction to an end. But Wilson refused to accept the news of the armistice through a Confederate intermediary and continued into the city, demanding its unconditional surrender by Howell Cobb. Since the announcement of the armistice had effectively demobilized Cobb's small garrison, he had no choice but to accept Wilson's demands to surrender, albeit under protest. Captured with the garrison of almost 2,000 men were 350 officers including—in addition to Cobb—Joseph E. Johnston's former chief of staff, William W. Mackall; Brigadier General Hugh W. Mercer; Brigadier General Felix Y. Robertson; and Georgia Militia chief, Gustavus W. Smith, all assembled in Macon to await their fate. Many of the state troops present, including militiamen, were for a time imprisoned in the stockade at Camp Oglethorpe, previously set aside for Federal officers.[224]

Wilson's Selma-Macon Raid had ended the possibility that Jefferson Davis, still at large after the evacuation of Richmond (and not to be captured by Wilson's men until 10 May), could use eastern Alabama and western Georgia as a stronghold for continuing the war. But Augusta, with its massive powder works and other government facilities, had become the most important city in Georgia by late April 1865. At the time of General Johnston's surrender, Governor Brown was in Augusta—and known to be there.[225] Moreover, Mrs. Jefferson Davis, writing to her husband 28 April, assumed that the city was also on the president's itinerary: "Be careful how you go to Augusta. I get rumors that Brown is going to seize all Government property, and the people are averse—and mean to resist with pistols—They are a set of wretches together, and I wish you were safe out of their land."[226]

Though Governor Brown was indeed in Augusta in late April, he seemed in at least one instance far from the self-confident controversialist of old. According to an account by militia brigadier Reuben W. Carswell, "shortly before the surrender of the Confederate armies Brown visited him at his headquarters in Augusta where he expressed the fear that he might be prosecuted for treason, and that he threw himself on a bed and wept."[227]

When Brown ultimately left Augusta on 2 May, he did so because he had been summoned to Macon by General Wilson. Upon Brown's return to Milledgeville, another communication reached him from Wilson. This one, portentously, was addressed to him not as governor of Georgia, but as "Commander-in-Chief of the Georgia Militia," a definition of him as a military, rather than political, personage that no doubt alarmed the captor of Fort Pulaski. As if to underline his political role, Brown called for the legislature to convene, an act that proved to be quite a tactical error.[228]

On the other hand, Adjutant General Henry C. Wayne was getting along famously with General Wilson—a fellow West Pointer, though years the adjutant general's junior. According to Wilson's diary of the period, Wayne admitted to him that he had been a secret Unionist all along and had been manipulating the governor, "using Brown in the Davis quarrel to advance the Union interests." On 5 May, Wayne advised Wilson that Governor Brown would be arriving on the afternoon train from Milledgeville to confer with him in Macon.[229]

After failing to persuade Wilson to visit him in his hotel suite across town, Brown presented himself at General Wilson's headquarters at the Lanier House. According to the general's memoirs, the result was a memorable meeting, though evidence indicates they actually met more than once over several days, since Brown's parole bears a date of 8 May. Wilson—who found Brown "smooth, suave, deferential, and polite, as well as more than usually intelligent"—told the governor at once that he forbade the meeting of the legislature Brown had called for, though he allowed him "an appeal to Washington." At the prospect of surrendering the militia and its officers—along with himself as "commander-in-chief," Brown "at first demurred," fearing that such an act would "rob him of his power and influence."[230]

In Wilson's *Under the Old Flag*, the final exchange between the general and Governor Brown is "as good as a play"—perhaps with good reason. Comparison of Wilson's 1912 memoirs with his diary of the time shows great improvement in both detail and drama in the later account:

> Governor Brown] dwelt complacently on his strenuous opposition to Davis, his devotion to state's rights, and to the organization of the state militia under his chosen commander as an independent force for its defense, and yet he did not seem to appreciate or even to have thought of a parole which would protect him as commander-in-chief from arrest and imprisonment.... I had already directed [preparation] of a drastic document covering Brown's case, and as he was about to take his leave I handed it to him with the remark that perhaps he had better read and sign it.... He then read it carefully with a changing and saddening countenance, and at the end laid it gravely on the table with the remark: "But, General, I can't sign that document."
>
> At this surprising conclusion, I asked why he could not sign the paper....
>
> To this he replied: "Why, General, it requires me to recant and abjure all the political acts and opinions of my life.... If I sign that paper it will destroy my political prospects forever."

That view of the case was novel, and it struck me as indicating the
Governor had not yet fully realized the significance or extent of the Union vic-
tory, and, therefore, rising from my seat and facing him squarely, I said: "My
God! Governor, is it possible that you imagine, in the face of the part you have
taken against the United States for the last four years, you have any prospect in
this country but to be hanged?"
*   ...[He] said, "That view of the matter had not occurred to me."*
Thereupon, sitting again, he deliberately signed the document in duplicate....
*   Taking his leave, with a countenance somewhat "sicklied o'er with a pale* ·
cast of thought," he returned to the hotel, where several leading men were
waiting for him.... They asked at first for the results of his interview, to which
he replied: "Well, gentlemen, General Wilson is a very clever young man, but he
takes the military view of the situation."[231]

The governor's surrender of himself and the state troops was indeed followed by the signing of his parole, though it seems somewhat less "drastic"
than described by Wilson:

Head Quarters Cavalry Corps
M[ilitary] D[epartment of the] M[ississippi]
Macon, Ga., May 8th, 1865.
*   I, Joseph E. Brown, Commander in Chief of the Militia of Georgia and*
State Troops, do solemnly agree and pledge my honor that I will not bear arms
against the United States of America, or give any information, or do any mili-
tary duty whatever against said United States, and further that I will not as
Commander in Chief or otherwise permit so far as it is in my power to prevent
it and will not counsel any other officers or men under my command to do any
act of hostility to the United States or inimical to a permanent peace upon the
basis of the Union under the Constitution and laws of the United States until
regularly relieved by the United States of this obligation by exchange or other-
wise.
Joseph E. Brown
Command in Chief of Militia & State Troops[232]

So, in one of his last acts as Governor (though far from the last of his
political acts, General Wilson to the contrary notwithstanding), Joseph E.
Brown formally surrendered the Georgia Militia, in accordance with the
Sherman-Johnston Convention of 26 April 1865, and accepted his parole.

But, actually, the militia's numerous furloughs, their dwindling ranks, and diminishing importance—together with the surrender of their field commander at Macon on 20 April—had for all practical purposes long since brought an end to the military career of "Joe Brown's Pets."

Artillery Ranges at Savannah from Colonel Jones's personal copy of *The Siege of Savannah in 1864.* (Hargrett Rare Book and Manuscript Library, University of Georgia Libraries)

Major General Smith's Line, Savannah This sketch appears as a large fold-out in Colonel Jones's personal copy of *The Siege of Savannah in 1864.* (Hargrett Rare Book and Manuscript Library, University of Georgia Libraries)

General William T. Sherman Though he moved forward cautiously to take Savannah, Sherman would still be able to present Georgia's largest city to President Lincoln by Christmas.

(Hargrett Rare Book and Manuscript Library, University of Georgia Libraries)

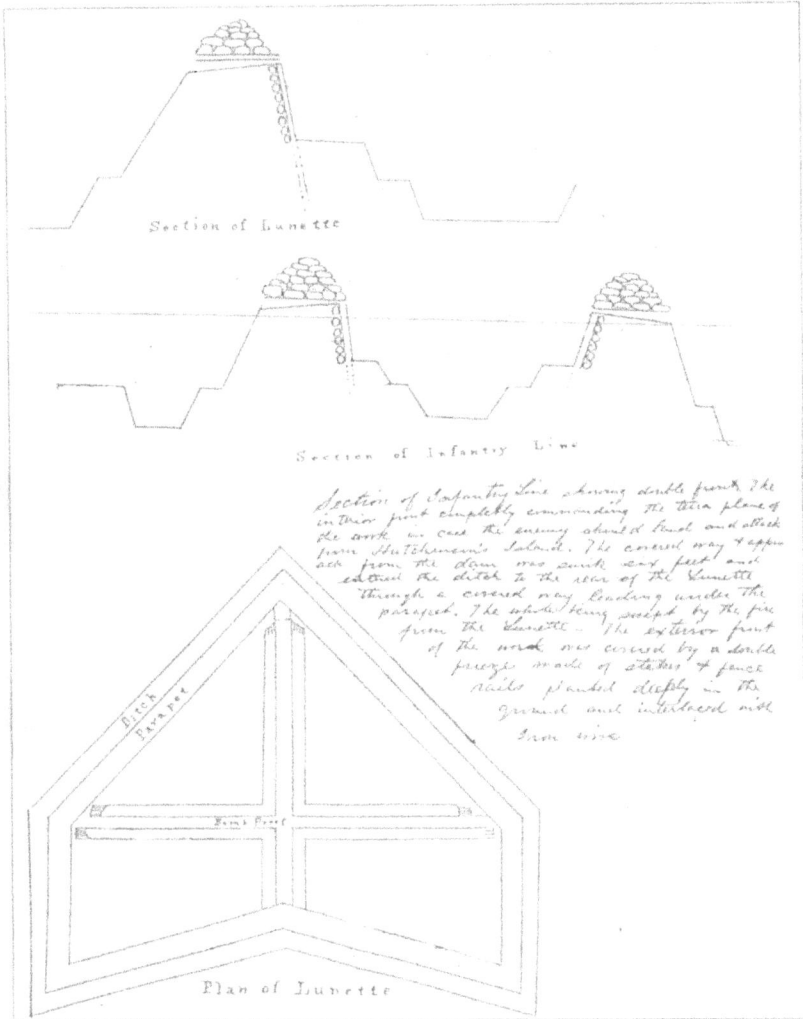

Lunette Plan of Lunette constructed for General Smith's line near Savannah
(Hargrett Rare Book and Manuscript Library, University of Georgia Libraries)

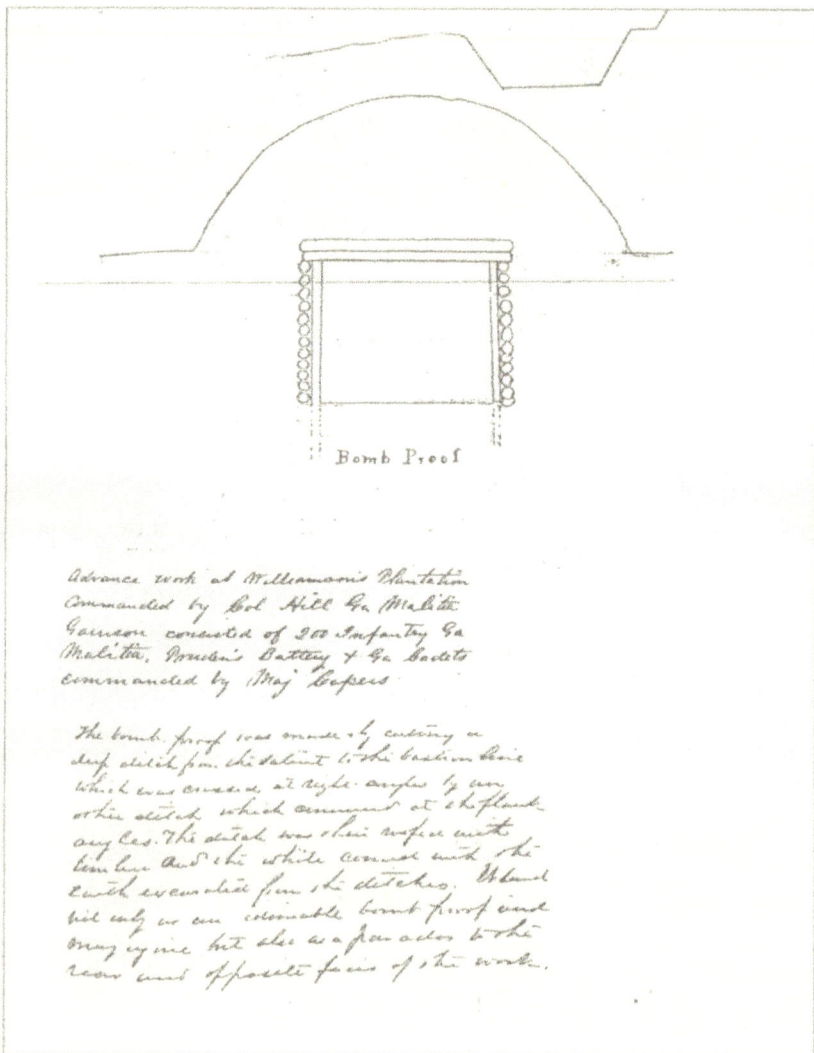

Bomb Proof

*Advance work at Williamson's Plantation
Commanded by Col Hill Ga Malitia
Garrison consisted of 200 Infantry Ga
Malitia, Bowlen's Battery & Ga Cadets
commanded by Maj Capers*

*The bomb proof was made by cutting a
deep ditch from the salient to the bastion line
which was crossed at right angles by an
other ditch which commenced at the flank
angles. The ditch was then roofed with
timber and then while covered with the
earth excavated from the ditches. It stand
... only as an ... bomb proof and
magazine but also as a ... to the
rear and opposite faces of the work.*

Bomb Proof Plan of one of the militia's earthworks near Savannah
(Hargrett Rare Book and Manuscript Library, University of Georgia Libraries)

General William J. Hardee In his later years, Hardee would recall his successful evacuation of Savannah as one of his most satisfying achievements.

General Ambrose R. Wright Though he had been at Gettysburg, General Wright was no doubt unprepared for the racket that ensued when, as President of the Georgia Senate, he suggested that he assume control of eastern Georgia from Governor Brown during Sherman's March.

(I. W. Avery, *History of the State of Georgia* [1881])

Charles C. Jones, Jr. Hardee's Chief of Artillery at Savannah and Georgia's greatest 19th-century historian, Jones in shown here in a postwar likeness to which the uniform has been added.

(Hargrett Rare Book and Manuscript Library, University of Georgia Libraries)

Selected Works of C. C. Jones, Jr. from his Private Library. These sumptuously-bound, lavishly illustrated volumes of Jones's own works numbered among his favorites. (Hargrett Rare Book and Manuscript Library, University of Georgia Libraries)

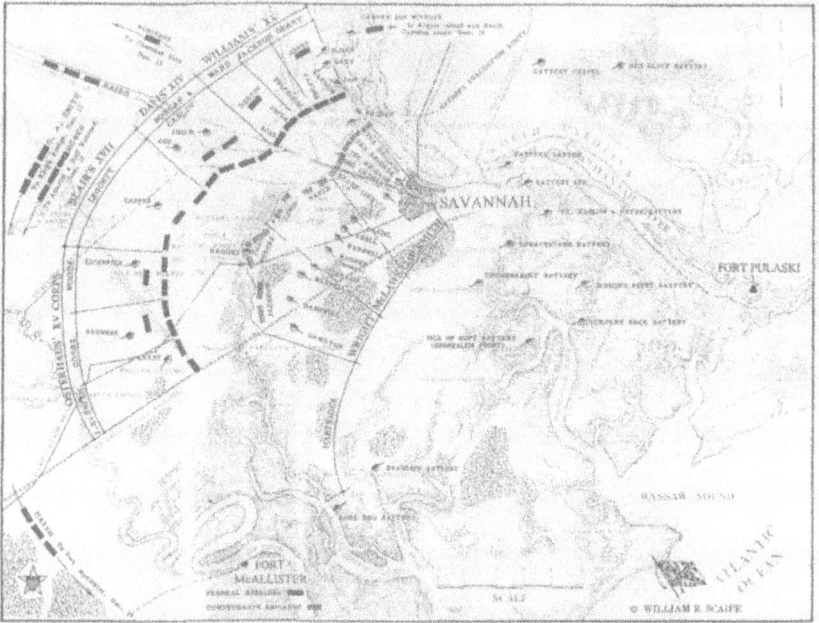

Savannah under Siege (William R. Scaife)

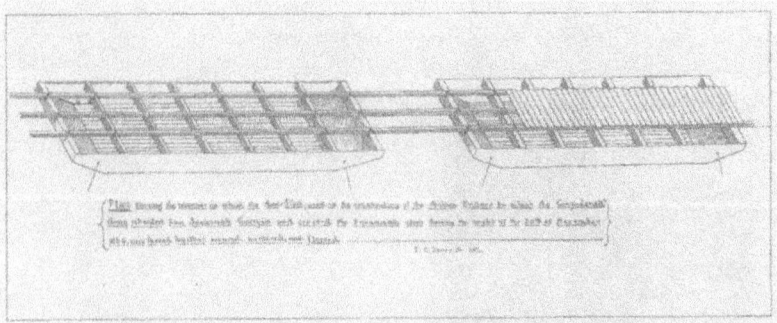

Bridge of Rice-Flats A Section of the Bridge over which Hardee's Army Passed.
From a sketch by Charles C. Jones, Jr.

(Hargrett Rare Book and Manuscript Library, University of Georgia Libraries)

Hardee's Evacuation of Savannah (*Harper's Weekly*)

Augustus B. Longstreet The uncle of James Longstreet, "Lee's War Horse,"
Augustus Baldwin Longstreet served as chaplain of the Georgia Militia. Ironically, his
Georgia Scenes contained one of the most effective lampoons of Georgia's militia.
(Hargrett Rare Book and Manuscript Library, University of Georgia Libraries)

REPORTS

OF THE

OPERATIONS OF THE MILITIA,

FROM OCTOBER 13, 1864, TO FEBRUARY 11, 1865,

BY

MAJ.-GENERALS G. W. SMITH AND WAYNE,

TOGETHER WITH

MEMORANDA BY GEN. SMITH,

FOR THE

IMPROVEMENT OF THE STATE MILITARY ORGANIZATION.

MACON, GA.
BOUGHTON, NESBIT, BARNES & MOORE,
State Printers.

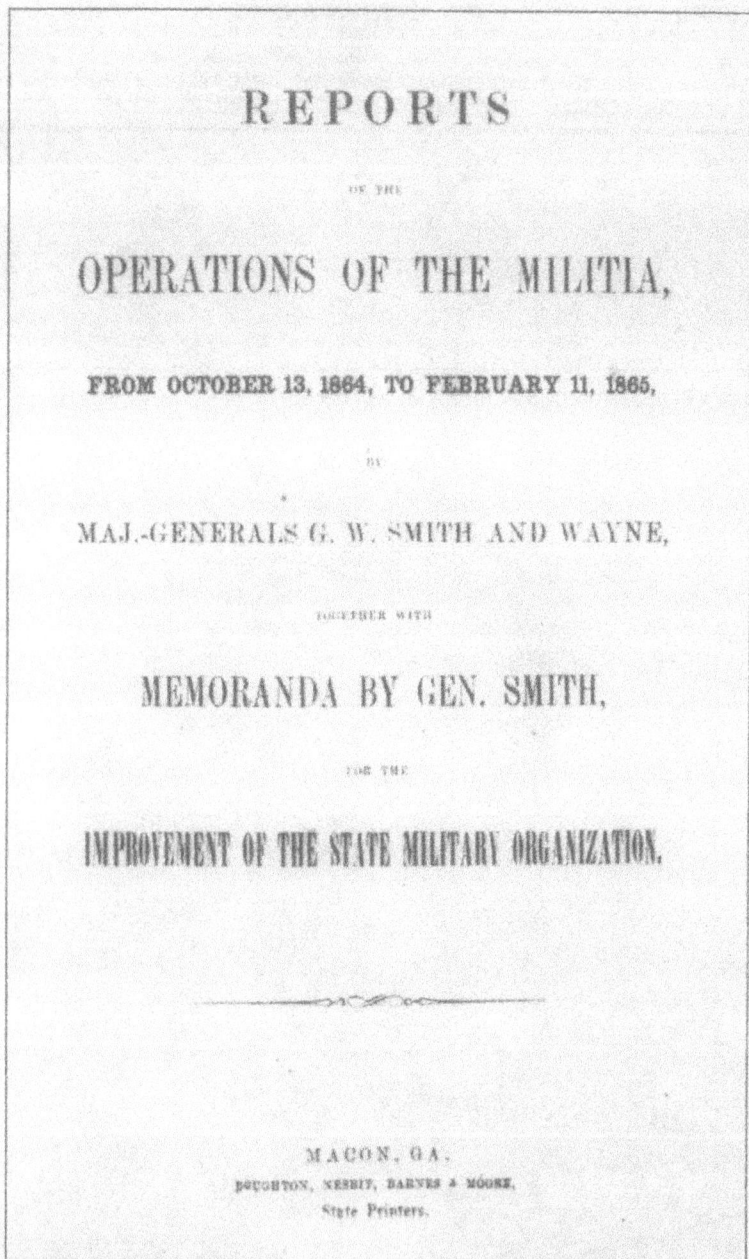

Reports of Operations of the Militia. This pamphlet collects the reports of the actions of the state troops at Griswoldville, the Oconee River, Honey Hill, and Savannah.

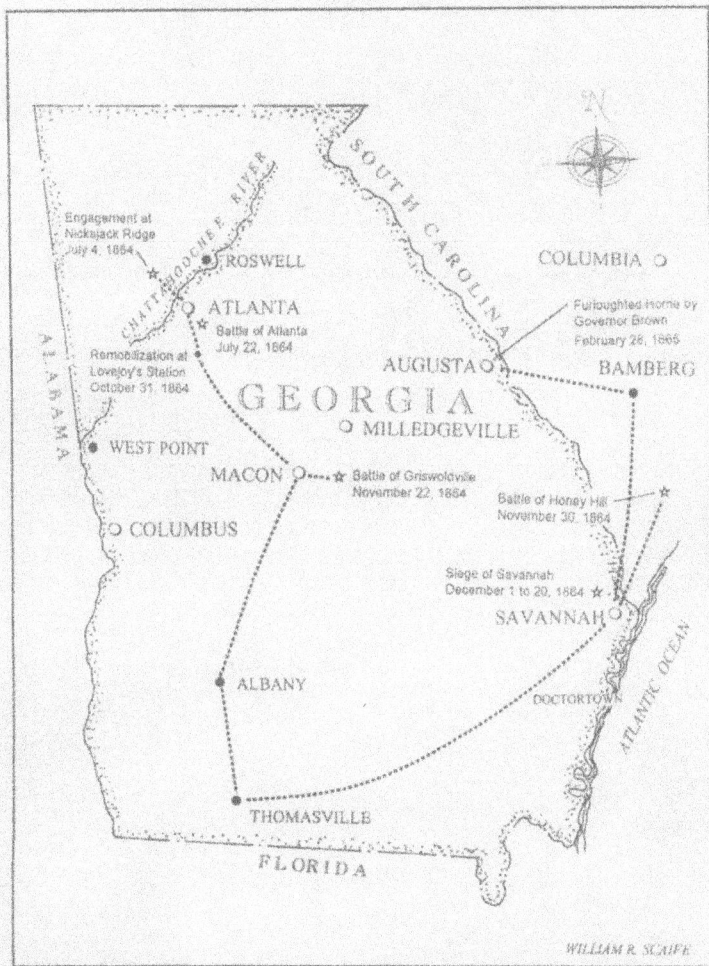

MOVEMENTS OF FIRST DIVISION GEORGIA MILITIA
June 1, 1864 to February 28, 1865

The militia's movements during the war's last year.
(William R. Scaife)

Macon City Hall Shown here on a market day, the Macon City Hall became Georgia's de facto capitol building in the last months of the war. The governor and General Assembly met there after the sack of the State House at Milledgeville by Sherman's troops. (Hargrett Rare Book and Manuscript Library, University of Georgia Libraries)

Macon Terminal Station A familiar sight to the Confederate officers and politicians who frequently visited Macon, the station was also pressed into service as a hospital during the bloodiest months of the war in Georgia.
(Hargrett Rare Book and Manuscript Library, University of Georgia Libraries)

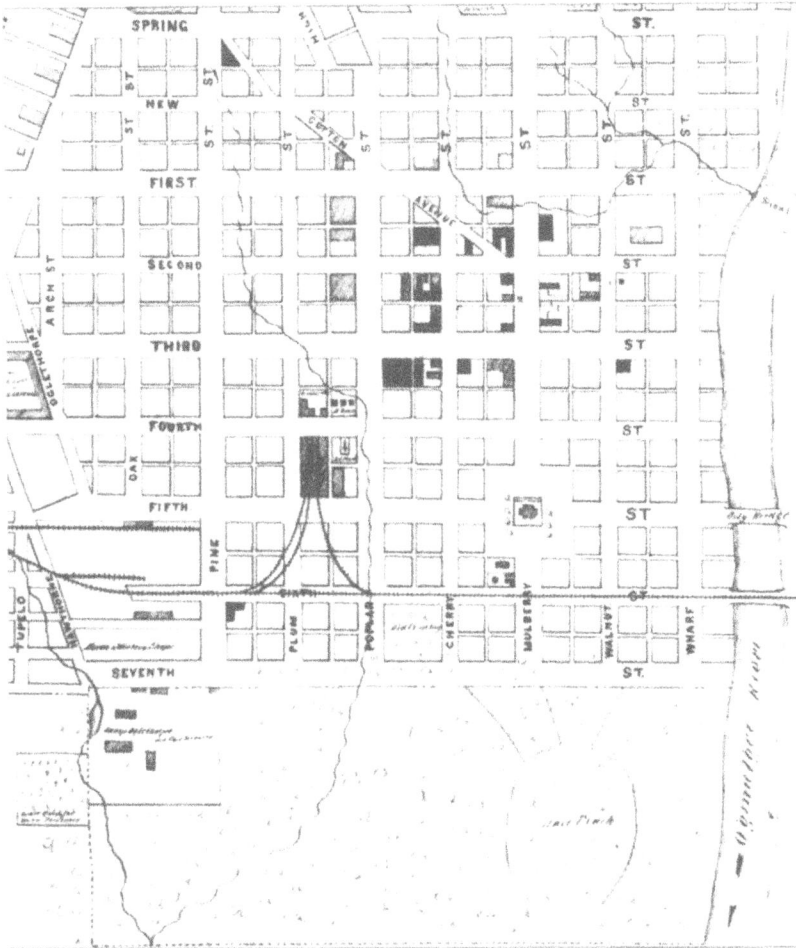

Confederate Macon. In this retouched image, the Bear's Den is marked by the number one on Walnut Street, with the militia headquarters building numbered two on Mulberry.

(National Archives)

Headquarters The Militia Headquarters, a postwar view
(Middle Georgia Archives, Washington Memorial Library)

General James Harrison Wilson This image from late in the war suggests the uncompromising attitude Governor Brown encountered in Macon. When he left Wilson, Brown had surrendered himself and the Georgia Militia.

(U. S. Army Military History Institute)

Joseph E. Brown Here, finally worn down during the war's last days, the governor is graying and almost haggard.

(Courtesy of James W. Enos)

D. H. Hill With G.M.I. dead and the State House empty because of the capital's move to Atlanta, one of Lee's foremost lieutenants, D. H. Hill (shown here to the far left) became president of Middle Georgia Military and Agricultural College (located in the old capitol) in the late 1880s.

(Georgia Archives)

Before and After. A crude but striking image, comparing the Napoleonic finery of the elite militia units of the antebellum period with the reality of four years of service.

(Charles Henry Smith, *Bill Arp's Peace Papers* [1873])

EPILOGUE

Seldom in history have troops in defeat received the accolades bestowed upon the elite Confederate regular army organizations from Georgia. The highly esteemed brigades commanded by George T. Anderson, Alfred Holt Colquitt, Robert Doles, Alexander R. Lawton (later by John B. Gordon and Clement A. Evans), Robert Toombs and William Wofford, along with the Georgia Legions of Augustus R. Wright, Thomas R. R. Cobb, and William Phillips, have become legendary.

But, whether justifiably so or not, the reputation of the Georgia Militia lies at the opposite end of the spectrum. Poorly trained and equipped, often indifferently led, and constantly taunted by members of the regular army and the press alike, the militiamen have over the years been far more frequently ridiculed than praised.

Gustavus Woodson Smith was in one sense a fitting commander for the militia. With impressive credentials and seniority, he was well-connected in high places and might well have been expected to become one of the outstanding Confederate commanders of the war. However, he appears to have suffered from some of the same personality traits that beset Braxton Bragg, from the outset of the war quarreling with his superiors and subordinates alike.

As a field commander, he showed a sometimes alarming tendency to disagree with and complicate even the simplest of instructions from his superiors; he had a corresponding difficulty in issuing explicit and timely instructions to his own subordinates. In both major engagements in which he led the militia, Smith seemed unwilling to assume total responsibility on the field of battle and deferred command to a subordinate officer. At Griswoldville he placed Brigadier General Pleasant J. Philips in charge with tragic consequences, while at Honey Hill he gave way to Colonel Charles J. Colcock, who fortunately led Smith's command to its most decisive and satisfying victory of the war.

The postwar articles written by Smith and published—first in the *Century Magazine* and later in more permanent form in *Battles and Leaders of the Civil War*—were among the few available accounts of the military operations of the militia, and as such might have been expected to provide valuable insight into the militia's history. Unfortunately, those articles, as well as Smith's wartime after-action reports in the *Official Records*, provide far more insight into Smith's own personality than into the role of the militia. The accounts divulge a woeful lack of understanding of the military situations in which Smith found himself—if not a deliberate distortion of the facts. They also expose Smith's insecurity and tender sensibilities, which at times seem to have approached outright paranoia.

Still, the Georgia Militia's general lack of success could not be attributed entirely to incompetent leadership or even to that great Confederate nemesis—political meddling in military matters. The militia's level of proficiency was uniformly low, from G. W. Smith's less-than-brilliant leadership to the awkward, though at times heroic, performance of the untrained old men and young boys so prevalent in the ranks.

In its first major engagement at the Battle of Griswoldville, the militia made a gallant but ill-conceived and poorly directed attack that resulted in a decisive and embarrassing defeat. In sharp contrast, a brilliant performance a week later at the Battle of Honey Hill, South Carolina, would have been a credit to even the most experienced of veteran troops.

The Georgia Militia would hardly go down in history for its military bearing or proficiency in battle, as it demonstrated little of either, but it should in all fairness be remembered for a level of courage and devotion to duty for which any soldier may be proud.

APPENDIXES

APPENDIX 1
TROOPS OF WAR:
AN OVERVIEW OF GEORGIA'S STATE FORCES,
1860-1865

"No State shall…keep troops or ships-of-war in time of peace…." Constitution
of the Confederate States of America, Article I, Section 10.3

The heart of the story of Georgia's militia in the Civil War derived from
the competition between the state government of Georgia and the
Confederate authorities for use of Georgia's "arms-bearing population." This
rivalry grew from conflicting interests, differing views on the role and power
of the central government, and opposite interpretations of various passages
in the Confederate Constitution, such as the one cited above and another—
regarding the militia—found in Article I, Section 8.16.

The manpower pool that was the object of this struggle was vast, relative
to those of most of the other Confederate states. In 1861, one authority calculated that Georgia's white males, aged sixteen to sixty, numbered between
120,000 and 130,000. As late as February 1864, the Bureau of Conscription
calculated that Georgia could "furnish (irrespective of the draft made upon
her by the war) 139,548 men between the ages of sixteen and sixty years;
but, according to the census taken in November last, there were 31,616,
including the exempts from conscription." These various figures suggest
both the considerable size of manpower resources (calculated as third behind
Virginia and Tennessee) as well as the difficulty in making reliable computa-
tions. In fact, the fluid situation and lack of trustworthy figures (or, in some
cases, of any figures at all) made it impossible throughout the war for the
General Assembly to have accurate rosters prepared listing those who had
served, together with those who had been wounded, killed, or had otherwise
died fighting for the Confederacy.

Technically, the entire arms-bearing population of Georgia was in the
state militia. The organization, in its most primitive form, had roots in colo-
nial times, when Georgia's first settlers were expected both to farm and fight.
An Indian agent of the 1770s described the militia of his time as having the
appearance of banditti, and many future descriptions would be similar, down

to and including the Civil War—that is, that the militiamen were motley in dress, spottily accoutered, and armed with a bizarre array of weaponry. These were the so-called common militia, who would travel from their respective militia districts to their courthouse towns for biennial musters. As early as 1778 the newly independent state of Georgia passed an act governing the militia, which would be the basis for other militia laws to come.

A later, parallel manifestation, the volunteer militia, drew from the gentry—particularly its politically ambitious members—and the volunteers (the officers especially) clothed themselves in elaborate uniforms reminiscent of the days of Napoleon's Grand Army (and thereby drew their own share of ridicule). Though not a part of the common militiamen (and exempt from some of their duties), the volunteer units could apply to be added to the militia rolls of the state, which would supply their arms; the volunteer militiamen, were, of course, equally subject to any call-up. When the Civil War began, many of these elite bodies entered Confederate service as units.

For militia organizational purposes, Georgia's counties were subdivided into districts, each of which contained a captain and a company of militiamen, originally restricted "to a maximum of sixty-three men." The counties themselves were then combined progressively into units representing regiments, battalions, brigades, and divisions, each with their own complement of officers. At the time of the Civil War, the state was divided into thirteen divisions of two brigades each.

The decade before the war, however, saw the common militia all but moribund, despite a paper strength of more than 77,000 men. In his farewell speech to the General Assembly in November 1851, Governor George W. Towns decried the militia's weak and disorganized state, particularly in the context of the national crisis of the previous year. He saw the volunteer companies as the "only reliable force" within Georgia and bitterly regretted that "their ardor [had] been checked by [his] inability to furnish arms and equipments." As Governor Herschel Johnson approached the end of his term in 1857, he also castigated the militia system's "inefficiency" and its need for "a more thorough organization of...discipline." The election of Joseph E. Brown that year brought no noticeable change in militia affairs. Even the John Brown Raid of October 1859 drew mainly "burning resolutions" from the legislature, though a Military Convention of Volunteer Companies assembled the following month in Milledgeville, reported to be almost 5,000 strong.

On Christmas Eve 1859, Governor Brown ordered a census of the state's volunteer companies through Special Order Number 22. The results, published the following February, showed a strength of 3,367, with at least 6 of the companies not reporting. The companies follow, alphabetized by principal towns, with each unit's number in uniform placed in parentheses:

Albany, Dougherty County: Albany Guards (50); *Americus*, Sumter County: Sumter Light Guards (48); *Athens*, Clarke County: National Artillery (40); *Atlanta*, Fulton County: Atlanta Grays (52); City Light Guards (No Report); Fulton Dragoons (46); Gate City Guards (42); *Augusta*, Richmond County: Clinch Rifles (60); Irish Volunteers (53); Montgomery Guards (48); Oglethorpe Infantry (64); Richmond Hussars (33); Washington Artillery (41); *Bainbridge*, Decatur County: Bainbridge Volunteers (40); *Beards Creek*, Liberty County: Altamaha Scouts (41); *Buena Vista*, Marion County: Buena Vista Guards (No Report); *Cartersville*, Cass [presently Bartow] County: Etowah Infantry (47); *Columbus*, Muscogee County: Columbus Guards (60); *Covington*, Newton County: Young Guards (54); *Cuthbert*, Randolph County: Cuthbert Rifles (64); *Dalton*, Whitfield County: Dalton Guards (75); *Darien*, McIntosh County: McIntosh Guards (60); *Dawson*, Terrell County: Dawson Volunteers (No Report); *Delhi*, Wilkes County: Delhi Rangers (26); *Eatonton*, Putnam County: Putnam Rifles (37); *Elberton*, Elbert County: Fireside Guards (45); *Forsyth*, Monroe County: Quitman Guards (48); *Fort Valley*, Houston [presently Peach] County: Governor's Guards (60); *Griffin*, Spalding County: Griffin Light Guards (43); *Hawkinsville*, Pulaski County: Hawkinsville Volunteers (No Report); *Homer*, Banks County: Banks County Guards (NoReport); *Johnson's Station*, Liberty County: Liberty Guards (32); *Jonesboro*, Clayton County: Clayton Volunteers (No Report); *LaGrange*, Troup County: LaGrange Light Guards (45); *Lincolnton*, Lincoln County: Lincoln Volunteers (48); *Macon*, Bibb County: Bibb Cavalry (51), Floyd Rifles (69), Jackson Artillery (65), Macon Guards (61), Macon Volunteers (81); *Madison*, Morgan County: Home Guards (45); *Marietta*, Cobb County: McDonald Guards (43); *Midville*, Burke County: Burke Guards (50); *Milledgeville*, Baldwin County: Baldwin Blues (52), Governor's Horse Guards (40); *Newnan*, Pike County: Newnan Guards (40); *Perry*, Houston County: Southern Rights

Guards (45); *Riceboro*, Liberty County: Liberty Independent Troop (38); *Rome*, Floyd County: Floyd Cavalry (40), Rome Light Guards (43); *Roswell*, Fulton County: Roswell Guards (50); *Sandersville*, Washington County: Washington Rifles (40); *Savannah*, Chatham County: Chatham Artillery (44), DeKalb Riflemen (49), German Volunteers (60), Irish Jasper Greens (65), Oglethorpe Light Infantry (95), Savannah Volunteer Guards (148); *Sparta*, Hancock County: Hancock Troop (37), Hancock Van Guards (50); *Springfield*, Effingham County: Effingham Hussars (27); *Starksville*, Lee County: Lee Mounted Rifles (65); *Thomaston*, Upson County: Upson Guards (38); *Thomasville*, Thomas County: Thomasville Guards (30); *Warrenton*, Warren County: McDuffie Riflemen (40); *West Point*, Troup County: West Point Guards (60).

Whatever the state of the volunteer militia, there was no notable improvement in the common militia, despite a decade of complaints and warnings. Less than a month before the portentous presidential election of 1860, Major General J. W. A. Sanford, one of the militia's division commanders, published a letter to Governor Brown that, at great length, described the militia system as a "farce."

General Sanford noted that his own division was "in a state of complete disorganization" and the problems he saw were of "universal prevalence," affecting all the other divisions as well. "For many years," he wrote, "there has been a constantly increasing spirit of repugnance and opposition on the part of the people to the performance of militia duty, until this feeling has at length become sufficiently strong…to subvert the institution itself." Consequently, he continued, "[the militia] ought not to be relied on in its present inoperative condition,…either in suppressing domestic insurrection or repelling foreign invasion." His solution to the problem echoed that of Governor Towns almost a decade past: the General Assembly should promote the formation of additional volunteer militia companies, appropriately armed and accoutered, even if that brought the necessity of taxation, "an execrable sound to the ears of most men."

During the following month, November 1860, Governor Brown began to gather weapons of war, both through purchase and, eventually, by seizure of Federal installations in Georgia. By mid-December he had also secured the appointment of Henry C. Wayne of Savannah as adjutant and inspector general, a post that would make him chief administrator of Georgia's state forces for the duration of the war.

THE GEORGIA MILITIA, 1860-1863

General Wayne's duties quickly overwhelmed him. In fact, his "organizing and instructing regiments and troops for the war and assisting the Confederate authorities" with coastal defense left him apologizing to the governor for the lateness and brevity of his report of his first year's service, submitted in late October 1861. Actually, there was little he wished to report; instead, he wanted to draw the governor's attention "to one point of importance":

> *The Militia System of the State requires careful revision and reorganization. …Based upon the Act of December 19, 1818, and perplexed by subsequent varied and conflicting enactments, many of a special character, it now does not meet the progress of a military organization, science or art. Indeed the legal provisions of the State are in fact suspended by the System of Volunteering now practiced and which, on account of the general inefficiency of the Militia throughout the United States, was initiated during the War with Mexico in 1846.*
>
> *Every exertion has been made to organize the Militia of the State as required by law, but ineffectually. No sooner would a General Officer or Colonel after great personal effort succeed in accomplishing somewhat of a form of organization than his labors would be neutralized by the enrollment of Volunteer companies out of the very material which his energy had collected together. In several instances Generals themselves seeing no prospect of active service in the Militia abandoned their commands and took service with Volunteers [i.e., war volunteers, not volunteer militia].*
>
> *As evidence of the inefficiency of the present system I will state that during the period of my service as Adjutant General, since the 22d say of December 1860 I have enrolled eight hundred and twenty five volunteer companies and issued six thousand three hundred and ninety one commissions, exclusive of those issued to Regular Regiments, the Navy, General Officers, and the General Staff.*
>
> *Many of these enrollments and issues were so much time, labor, paper and postage thrown away, as in several instances the commissions had scarcely*

reached the officers in the Militia elected before they were returned as useless,
the holders having gone into Volunteer service....

He concluded: "Realizing then our present position and measuring by it
to a great extent our future—Reviewing our past political history, and esti-
mating our new and probable future relations, I think it becomes us to
prepare well for the contest we are now in, and for those that may be before
us, by laying the foundation of sound military organization and institu-
tions."

Nonetheless, it would be some time before the militia system would be
overhauled, and the governor's energies in 1861 would be directed toward
the Georgia Army; the 4th Brigade, Georgia Volunteers; and the Georgia
State Troops (to be described below), all of which were composed of militia
in the broadest sense, though destined for Confederate service. Importantly,
however, the militia organization remained in place, with its officers corps
and, apparently, considerable numbers of men who had not joined
Confederate units or volunteered for active state service. Also, during the
first year of the war, when the Confederacy made requisition on Governor
Brown for Georgia's quota of troops, the administrative machinery of the
militia—which reached downward to the company districts within the state's
counties—was used to gather the troops needed to meet the Confederacy's
requisitions. To improve the efficiency of the system, the governor on 21
August 1861 ordered the militia captains to enroll within their districts all
"able-bodied white male citizens, as well as aliens, between the ages of
eighteen and forty-five years." In February 1862 Brown used this machinery
for raising twelve regiments for the Confederacy (preferably from volunteers,
but from draftees if necessary) and then in early April for creating a small
army of thirty companies of militiamen to serve a three-year enlistment
within the state.

But, almost simultaneously, war exigencies—particularly the imminent
expiration of twelve-month enlistments—forced the Confederate government to resort to conscription. The First Conscription Act (16 April 1862)
struck two powerful blows against Governor Brown: it ended his role in
raising Confederate troops (along with the appointment powers he enjoyed),
and it absorbed the militiamen between the ages of eighteen and thirty-five.
Brown succeeded, however, in forcing the Confederacy to accept his exemp-

tion of the militia's officers, who from this time were called "Joe Brown's Pets," a sobriquet eventually applied to the militiamen in general. Theoretically, there were soldiers for the exempted officer to command, for the militia embraced white males between eighteen and forty-five. However, the Second Conscription Act (27 September 1862) soon extended the draft to the upper age range of the militia. Though the governor refused to allow the second act to be enforced until the legislature met, he found little support for his views in the General Assembly, and the state supreme court found conscription constitutional, despite the governor's arguments to the contrary.

The exempted militia officers, previously pilloried for being the governor's favorites, were now ridiculed in the press for being officers without troops. But the ridicule was tempered in spring 1863, when Federal forces once again threatened Savannah, and the Confederate authorities requested reinforcements from Governor Brown. He astounded everyone—not least his militia officers—by ordering "Joe Brown's Pets" to Savannah on 23 February 1863. The governor's order was "relished and approved" even by his opponents; it "transformed Major Generals into Captains of companies, turned Brigadiers into Lieutenants and Captains and Lieutenants into Privates." Those refusing the call were threatened with loss of their exemptions. The call was answered in great numbers, but the peculiar army saw no action and soon returned home. Its major contribution in the short term was to provide the humorist "Bill Arp" with material for two amusing essays. In the long term, the militia officers would furnish the framework for a rejuvenation of the militia and would be instrumental in the reorganization directed by the General Assembly (at the governor's urging, in an act of 14 December 1863).

THE GEORGIA ARMY (THE "SECESSION REGIMENTS"), 1861

From its secession on 19 January 1861 until its union with the Confederate States of America on 16 March 1861, Georgia was a republic. As such, it was as free and independent as Britain, and France and Belgium, to which countries Governor Brown sent an ambassador, identifying himself as "Governor and Commander-in-Chief of the Army and Navy of [Georgia], and of the Militia thereof."

Near the beginning of this heady period, on 25 January 1861, the Secession Convention authorized the governor "to raise and equip a regular military force" for the public defense. Though the force was not to exceed two regiments (the "Secession Regiments"), it was officially known as the Georgia Army. By 20 February skeleton regiments were organized, with William J. Hardee commanding the 1st Regiment, W. H. T. Walker commanding the 2d, and the intention (not to be realized) of brigading the two under the generalship of David E. Twiggs. General Wayne and the officers devoted considerable attention to determining the army's uniform, which included frock coats: "dark blue cloth" for officers and "Georgia cadet gray" for enlisted men.

The Georgia Army set the pattern for Governor Brown's experiences in organizing state forces throughout the war. Important decisions would be made and elaborate plans laid only to be overturned—sooner rather than later—by acts of the Confederate Congress. In this case, the Congress on 28 February 1861 directed President Jefferson Davis "to assume control of all Military operations in every State" and authorized him to receive into Confederate service "such forces now in the service of said States as may be tendered, or who may volunteer." Consequently, within a week of Georgia's joining the Confederate States of America, the Secession Convention passed an ordinance (20 March 1861) transferring "control of all military operations" in the state to the Confederate government and a resolution (23 March 1861) that instructed the governor to tender Georgia's "regular forces" to the Confederacy, with special mention of the transfer of the two regiments of the Georgia Army.

By this time, of course, the leap to arms by the war volunteers had begun and the flood of commissions from General Wayne's office had reversed into a deluge of resignations. Volunteering was now paired with requisitions to fill the Confederate armies. In a letter of 9 March 1861, Confederate Secretary of War Leroy P. Walker had sent Governor Brown a requisition for 2,000 soldiers—coincidentally, the number of two full-strength regiments. Another long-lived pattern now emerged, with the governor wrangling with the Confederate authorities over how the troops would be tendered and how they were to be officered. In mid-March the original regiments lost their colonels to resignation. Thereafter, the companies that had formed within the two regiments were "merged into one," placed under the command of Colonel Charles J. Williams as the 1st Regiment, Georgia Regulars, and sent to fill half the state's requisition.

William J. Hardee Shown here in an antebellum image, Hardee wears blue, as he would have as commander of the First Regiment of the Georgia Army.
(U.S. Military History Institute)

THE 4TH BRIGADE, GEORGIA VOLUNTEERS
(PHILLIPS'S LEGION, C.S.A.), 1861

Though he had lost his first state army before the war had begun, Governor Brown lost no time in creating a new army and, in fact, had begun planning for it in January 1861. Neither did he spend time worrying that subsequent Confederate laws seemed to prohibit him from raising "troops of war" for state defense. His authority for continuing to raise state forces at this point was based on a dubious interpretation of an act of the General Assembly, approved 18 December 1860, now arguably superseded by other legislation. "It will be borne in mind," Brown told the Secession Convention on 15 March 1861, "that the Legislature at its last session authorized the Governor to accept the services of 10,000 volunteers. The Government of the Confederate States has assumed control of all military operations which are to be conducted against foreign powers within the limits of any of the Confederate States. The State has reserved to itself, however, the right to repel invasion or imminent danger thereof." Consequently, he informed them, he planned to create two divisions of 5,000 men each, and he "divided the State into four sections" to yield the necessary brigades. Though the governor planned to have Henry R. Jackson and W. H. T. Walker as division commanders, it ultimately proved "impracticable" to raise more than one brigade, known as the 4th Brigade, Georgia Volunteers, commanded by Brigadier General William Phillips.

The war came on 12 April 1861, but it would be early June before the 4th Brigade went into training at Camp McDonald on the Western and Atlantic Railroad near Atlanta. Governor Brown had by this time filled several Confederate requisitions with "regiments composed of independent companies...enlisted through private enterprise of various captains." But Phillips's brigade had remained "intact as a state organization." Nonetheless, on 28 June 1861, Brown offered the brigade to the Confederacy, describing it as "two regiments of infantry armed with good 1842 model muskets, one battalion armed with new Harper's Ferry rifles, one artillery battalion armed with 1842 model muskets, and a cavalry battalion well mounted and equipped." Brown aimed to circumvent the Confederate law that prevented states from proffering organizations larger than regiments, thus leaving the appointment of generals to the Confederacy. Essentially, his price for giving up his state army was a Confederate brigadier's star for his friend Philips.

Other Confederate governors, like Tennessee's Isham Harris, had managed to achieve similar feats. But Brown failed, despite counteroffers, arguments, and hectoring that lasted until August. Then the brigade was broken up, and a portion of it joined the Confederate army in Virginia as Phillips's Legion, commanded by Colonel, not Brigadier General, William Phillips.

Colonel William Phillips
(From Lawton B. Evans, *The Student's History of Georgia* [1884])

Private Jesse Pendley, a warlike representative of Phillips's men.
(Courtesy of Robert Wilson Bentley, Sr.)

THE GEORGIA STATE TROOPS, 1861-1862

Having lost Phillips and his men in August, Governor Brown waited no longer than the next month to begin organizing his next state force. On 9 September 1861, the governor issued a call for six-month volunteers to report to Savannah for coastal defense. Using the same questionable authority under which he had raised Phillips's brigade, he recruited a division of three brigades, much as he had originally intended to do earlier in the year and using several of the officers he had then planned to commission. Consequently, Henry R. Jackson took command of the division, having resigned a Confederate brigadier general's commission to accept a state major general's commission from Governor Brown. Leading his three brigades were George P. Harrison, F. W. Capers, and the ubiquitous W. H. T. Walker. As one authority has noted, Jackson's division, known as the Georgia State Troops, "operated nominally with the Confederate forces under the command of Brigadier General A. R. Lawton of the Department of Georgia, and did valiant service in the three months campaign around Savannah in the winter of 1861-1862."

When the General Assembly met in late 1861, the House attempted to transfer the state troops to the Confederacy and created a heated controversy by doing so. Not least was the problem of the Confederacy's not accepting organizations larger than regiments, which would break up the division and "divest Major General Jackson and the three Brigadier Generals of their commissions." Surprisingly, the governor enjoyed support from the public and much of the press in this matter, and the troops were ultimately allowed to vote on whether to be transferred, a vote that was overwhelmingly negative. But in April 1892 the First Conscription Act soon did what the Georgia House had failed to do, and most of the Georgia State Troops, originally some 8,000 strong, became Confederate soldiers.

General Henry R. Jackson Major General, commanding Georgia State Troops.
(Hargrett Rare Book and Manuscript Library, University of Georgia Libraries)

Brigadier General Alexander R. Lawton of the Confederate Department of Georgia.
(Hargrett Rare Book and Manuscript Library, University of Georgia Libraries)

Brigadier General George P. Harrison, Sr., Georgia State Troops.
(From Lawton B. Evans, *The Student's History of Georgia* [1884])

Brigadier General W. H. T. Walker, Georgia State Troops.
(Library of Congress)

Thomas A. Watson A Fannin Countian, Watson served as a corporal in the
Georgia State Troops before deserting and joining the Union army
(Georgia Archives)

Surgeon Joseph Barnett Carlton, 2nd Battalion, Georgia State Troops
(David Wynn Vaughn Collection)

THE GEORGIA STATE LINE, 1862-1865

After conscription took the Georgia State Troops in April 1862, Governor Brown created only one other state military organization that was not a form of militia, in the widely accepted sense of the term. This body of conscription-age men was known as the Georgia State Line (or "Georgia State Line Regiments"), apparently because its original responsibility was guarding the state-owned Western & Atlantic Railroad, often called the State Line. The Georgia State Line was composed of two regiments. They grew from two companies of bridge guards that had served along the W&ARR from May 1862 until the State Line's regimental elections in late February 1863.

Edward M. Galt of Whitfield County was elected colonel of the 1st Regiment, Georgia State Line ("Galt's State Line"), which drew its men mainly from the North Georgia mountains. Wilkinson County's Richard L. Storey became commanding officer of the 2d Regiment, Georgia State Line ("Storey's State Line"); his men came from counties along the Chattahoochee or scattered across the central potion of the state. In March 1864, 100 men were withdrawn from the 1st Regiment to create a cavalry company that would serve until war's end. It was variously known as "Cowen's Cavalry," "State Scouts," and "Talbot's Scouts."

The State Line served at Savannah (and, in the case of some detachments, at Charleston, South Carolina) during the Federal operations in early 1863. By May of the same year, the State Line companies were distributed along the length of the W&ARR from the Chattahoochee to near Chattanooga. Both regiments were attached to the Confederate Army of Tennessee from mid-1864 throughout the Atlanta Campaign, and men of the State Line fought at such battles as Kolb's Farm, Peachtree Creek, and Atlanta (where John M. Brown, the governor's brother and an officer of the Line, was killed). During fall 1864, the regiments resisted Sherman's March and fought at both Griswoldville and Honey Hill, South Carolina. The State Line, much reduced by deaths, wounds, and desertion, spent the balance of the war in garrison duty in Augusta, Milledgeville, and elsewhere, but some of its men fought in the last major battle on Georgia soil in Columbus in mid-April 1865 before being surrendered by Governor Brown to Union General James H. Wilson on 7 May 1865.

Colonel Richard L. Storey, Second
Regiment Georgia State Line
(Hargrett Rare Book and Manuscript Library,
University of Georgia Libraries)

Private John Barnes,
Company D, First State Line
(Lumpkin County Public Library)

Colonel John M. Brown, First Regiment, Georgia State Line One of the governor's younger brothers, Brown was killed at Atlanta. His funeral service was conducted at the Executive Mansion.

(Courtesy of James W. Enos)

Private Elias Bentley, Company K, Second State Line
(Courtesy of Robert Mitchell)

THE GEORGIA STATE GUARD (C.S.A.), 1863-1864

The Georgia State Guard was an unusual organization raised in summer 1863, following a request to Governor Brown from Secretary of War James Seddon of 6 June 1863. The troops raised served from 1 August 1863 to 1 February 1864 and were commanded by Confederate Major General Howell Cobb.

A guard was formed in other states as well, principally among men not of conscription age, for the Richmond authorities wished to take the Confederate governors' penchant for creating state armies and turn it to a more useful purpose. President Davis hoped that the creation of the state guard organizations would become for the Confederate central government "an opportunity to take over local defense, secure control of the various state military organizations, and, through uniformity, proper discipline and training, and the centralization of command, increase the efficiency of all the forces of the Confederacy."

But, through skillful negotiation, Governor Brown created his own version of the state guard, a temporary body of troops that was to be left undisturbed except during military emergencies. Many members of the guard, however, were summoned to the north of the state during the emergency presented by the Chickamauga Campaign of August-September 1863.

Brown claimed to have almost doubled Georgia's quota of 8,000 by providing the Confederacy with 15,000 troops, though the Confederate authorities felt these numbers were inflated. In any case, Brown swelled the numbers by urging the militia and civil officers of the state to join, gave them furloughs to do so, and had them use the draft apparatus of the militia to raise some of the troops.

Unsurprisingly, the Georgia State Guard produced more controversies between Governor Brown and the Confederate authorities, particularly over Brown's again claiming power to appoint officers. The governor also complained that the men called up were kept in the ranks after the emergency of the state's invasion had passed and cited this as one reason for terminating the service of the Georgia State Guard in February 1864.

Major General Howell Cobb, Commander, Georgia State Guard.

Captain Barnard Curley, 5th Regiment, Georgia State Guard
(Athens Public Library)

Waid Hill, Georgia State Guard
(Athens Public Library)

Private James Cowart, 22d Cavalry Battalion, Georgia State Guard
(Courtesy of Frank Jasek)

THE GEORGIA RESERVE FORCE (C.S.A.), 1864-1865

The Georgia Reserve Force, created under the Third Conscription Act, was also commanded by Major General Howell, who began organizing it in April 1864. This force drew its numbers from men seventeen to eighteen and forty-five to fifty. The Reserves were stationed mainly at Macon (Cobb's headquarters) and at other principal towns. At the time Sherman's March began in November 1864, Cobb reported having 900 men near Atlanta and 600 at Macon (including convalescents and conscripts), plus, at Augusta, Columbus, and elsewhere, a "nominal strength" of "about six thousand men," including "men unfit for duty in the field and men engaged in the work shops," and the "four most effective regiments," which "were kept at Andersonville as a guard to that prison—about two thousand strong."

General Cobb faced many challenges in recruiting for the Reserves, not the least of which was Governor Brown. The governor had been energized by his success in fielding the Georgia State Guard, a success that persuaded him that the time was right to create a new militia force. This put Cobb and Brown in competition for some of the same men, and the governor was an extremely cunning opponent. Cobb's presence in Georgia was in part to have a sound pro-administration man in the state as a counterbalance to Brown. But, as one authority has noted, "Cobb was probably an unwise choice" because of "the enmity between him and Governor Brown," based as it was in politics, personality, and class. Cobb, the planter-aristocrat, looked down on the yeoman-class Brown as an opportunistic parvenu.

Though Cobb's men were supposed to go about their jobs except in military emergencies, the Confederacy's manpower needs in Georgia demanded that many of them be on permanent service on guard or garrison duty. When military emergencies did occur during the Savannah Campaign, the Reserves were in the forefront of the action, fighting in several of the battles during the March to the Sea. Some of them eventually left the state with the Confederate army in December 1864 and were surrendered in North Carolina at war's end.

Major General Howell Cobb, Georgia Reserve Force
(Hargrett Rare Book and Manuscipt Library, University of Georgia Libraries)

Colonel Allen D. Candler, 4th Georgia Reserves. Later governor of Georgia from 1898 to 1902, Candler famously spent his last years compiling Georgia's records, in particular those of Georgia in the Confederacy.

Harry Cook, Athens Battalion, Georgia Reserves
(David Wynn Vaughan Collection)

STATE OF GEORGIA,

Adjutant and Inspector General's Office.

MILLEDGEVILLE, OCT. 13, 1864.

GENERAL ORDERS, }
No. 31.. }

Attention is hereby called to the accompanying Orders of Major General Howell Cobb, commanding Georgia Reserves and Military District of Georgia, by which it will be seen that no person belonging to the Georgia Militia under Major General G. W. Smith, will be permitted to join the local Companies invited to organize under a former Order of General Cobb; and that all detailed men in this State, not in service, are required to join the Militia under General Smith, or their details will be revoked, and they be required to unite with the Regiments of Reserves formed for the war under Major General Cobb: The Governor therefore orders,

1st. That all Aids-de-Camp, and all persons belonging to the Militia Reserves over fifty years of age, who are detailed to remain at home on police and patrol duty, and to arrest and send forward deserters, stragglers and skulkers, do also promptly arrest and send to General G. W. Smith all persons belonging to his command, who have attached themselves to local Companies, and shall neglect or refuse to report at Macon.

2d. The Governor also orders, that persons having Confederate details, not in actual service, who fail to report to, and connect themselves with one of the Regiments of Reserves under Major General Cobb, within five days after the publication of these Orders, be arrested by the Aids-de-Camp and Police above mentioned, and sent to Major General Smith at Macon without delay.

3rd. All details and furloughs granted by any Aid-de-Camp or other Officer, not approved at these Head Quarters, are hereby revoked and declared null and void; and all such granted in future will be likewise void, as it is the duty of these Officers to send men to the front, and not to grant furloughs or details.

4th. All persons detailed by General Smith whilst at Atlanta, to send forward parties subject, who remained at home, are likewise ordered to report forthwith at Macon, as the duties heretofore discharged by them are now devolved on the Policemen and men over 50 years of age, of the respective Counties,

By order of the Commander-in-Chief:

HENRY C. WAYNE,
Adj. & Ins. General.

General Orders, No. 31, 12 October 1864. Such messages from General Wayne demonstrated the competition between the Reserves and the Georgia Militia over Georgia's dwindling manpower pool.

THE BATTALION OF CADETS,
GEORGIA MILITARY INSTITUTE, 1864-1865

Founded at Marietta in 1851, near the recently-completed Western & Atlantic Railroad, the Georgia Military Institute boasted an enrollment of 150-plus in early 1861. The cadets' numbers plummeted when the war came, however, as many cadets entered military service. Early in the war, those who remained on campus were pressed into service as drill instructors for the recruits at Georgia camps of instruction, particularly at Camp McDonald, located at nearby Big Shanty. The cadets' numbers appear to have grown after passage of the first conscription act, and G.M.I. came to be criticized—in a fashion similar to that directed at the Georgia Militia—as a haven for conscription dodgers. No doubt this was true in some cases, but many cadets apparently wished for active duty and military action within the state with their corps.

Governor Joseph E. Brown gave notice to the Richmond government that he considered the cadets exempt from conscription, but the pertinent laws provided no such protection for cadets, and the Davis administration offered no exemption. Though Brown was capable of shielding the young men from Confederate enrolling officers with his usual tactics—bombastic arguments and threat of force—he found a novel way to give cover to the young men of G.M.I. Brown named G.M.I.'s superintendent, Francis W. Capers, to be Chief Engineer of the state of Georgia, while at the same time transforming the cadet corps into the state's Engineer Corps. This act placed all involved under the exemption Brown claimed, arguably within the language of the conscription legislation, which exempted officers of the state government.

The presence among the cadets of the martially-named Julius Brown, the young son of the governor, created controversy throughout the subsequent life of the battalion. Some cadets charged that the governor's desire to keep his son out of harm's way explained the delay in allowing them to enter active service, as well as their extended periods of garrison duty at Milledgeville.

The cadets, now styled the Battalion of Cadets, finally realized their ambition of entering active field service during the Atlanta Campaign. Their commander's account of their service in summer and fall 1864 follows.

HEADQUARTERS BATTALION OF CADETS,
AND GEORGIA MILITARY INSTITUTE,
Milledgeville, Oct. 27th, 1864.
MAJ. GEN. H. C. WAYNE,
Adj. and Inspector General of Georgia.
SIR—Your order of the 12th, May 1864, to report myself to General Jos. E. Johnston commanding the Army of Tennessee and "to hold the corps of Cadets in readiness, to obey his orders during the present emergency," was joyfully received and promptly executed. The Cadets of the Georgia Military Institute, have sought active field service from the beginning of the war. This desire has become almost a passion. Under its influence we had lost our higher classes and might have lost the existence of the Institute, but for the hopes inspired by your reply to the petition of last year and their positive realization in your order of May 12th.

The service of the battalion has been as follows. On the 27th of May, under a special field-order from General Johnston we reported to you in Atlanta, where you were organizing the militia. By your order the Battalion was sent to West Point, where we remained until the third (3d) of July, when by order of Maj. Gen. G. W. Smith, we reported for duty at Turner's Ferry on the Chattahoochee. There, for the first time, the Cadets exchanged shots with the enemy. I remember with pride that the style of their march across the river on the afternoon of the 6th, under fire, elicited applause from veterans.

On the 12th July the following special order from General Johnston, detached the Battalion from General Smith's command, viz:

HEADQUARTERS ARMY OF TENNESSEE,
July 12th, 1864, 11 A.M.

GENERAL:
General Johnston directs you to send the Battalion of Georgia State Cadets, Maj. Capers commanding, to West Point Georgia, without delay.
Most respectfully your obedient servant,
(Signed) A. P. MASON
Major & A.A.G.
On the 25th July the Battalion was ordered back to the Division; and marched to position in the trenches of Atlanta in the night of the 27th.

On the 14th August the Battalion was ordered here by his Excellency the Governor.

In no single instance, whatever may have been the duties assigned them or the position occupied by them, have our expectations been disappointed in either the bearing or efficiency of the command. There was fatigue and blood and death in their ranks but no white feather.

Considering the nature of our service in the trenches and on the picket lines of Atlanta, we have reason to be grateful to God that our list of casualties is so small. We report as follows:

Killed or Mortally Wounded.

Cadet A. H. Alexander, Monroe County, Ga., Aug. 6th.

Color Corp'l. J. K. Anderson, Edgefield, S.C., Aug. 12th.

Died of disease contracted in service.

John McLeod, Burke Co., Ga., at res., of Gen. S. P. Myrick.

Ringgold Commander, Marianna, Fla., at res., of R. McCombs.

E. D. Jordan, Hancock, Ga., at home.

W. J. Mabry, Wayne Co., Ga., at home.

W. H. Smith, Knoxville, Ga., at home.

W. Baker, Troup Co Ga., at home.

Wounded.

Cadet Sam'l Goode, Stewart Co. Ga., slightly in shoulder.

Cadet Lt. F. E. Courvoisie, Savannah, Ga., seriously in hip.

Cadet Samuel Griffin, Lowndes Co. Ga., slightly in face.

I have the gratification to report that the number of absentees on the sick list is rapidly diminishing, and the health of those present in ranks is good. The organization of the Battalion is as follows:

Field and Staff.

F. W. Capers Maj. Commanding.

1st Lt. L. J. Hill, Adjutant.

Capt. J. C. Eve, acting Quartermaster.

Dr. W. H. Hardeman, Jr. Surgeon.

Co. A.—Capt. Jas. S. Austin.

Cadet Lieutenants—J. R. McClesky, P. Faver, F. E. Courvoisie, S. M. White.

Co. B.—Capt. V. E. Manget.

Cadet Lieutenants—C. H. Solomon, P. A. Hazlehurst, J. P. Harris.

The Aggregate number present and absent is one hundred and eighty-five.

Very respectfully,

Your obedient servant,

F. W. CAPERS.

Major Commanding.

From the end of the Atlanta Campaign to the beginning of the March to the Sea, the cadets formed part of the Milledgeville garrison. As such, they were occasionally drilled by Adjutant General Wayne himself on the capitol grounds, where they occupied a small tent city. The cadets served at Milledgeville reluctantly, however; their discipline deteriorated, and they agitated once more for active duty in the field. Sherman's advance into central Georgia answered their prayers, and the battalion was sent as part of a ragtag force—including paroled penitentiary convicts—to resist Sherman's right wing at the Oconee River crossings; five were wounded. Attached to the Georgia Militia during the Siege of Savannah, the cadets saw minor action along General Smith's lines before joining the evacuation. Serving with the militia once again as part of the Augusta garrison for a time thereafter, the cadets soon returned to Milledgeville. There they were observed by Fanny Andrews:

> *Late in the afternoon we went out and saw the Georgia cadets on dress parade in front of the capitol.... [W]e had a fine time. Among the cadets we recognized Milton Reese, Tom Hill, and Davy Favor, from Washington, and as soon as the drill was over, we went into the capitol with them and saw the destruction the Yankees had made. The building was shockingly defaced, like everything else in Milledgeville.... The boys told us that the cadets are so hot against the governor for not ordering them into active service that they had hung him in effigy right there in the capitol grounds. His son is among them, and the boys say the governor won't let them fight because he is afraid Julius might get hurt. The truth is, they all ought to be at home in their trundle beds, Julius with the rest, for they are nothing but children.*

Hanging effigies to the contrary notwithstanding, the cadets remained in Milledgeville until the last week of the war. Then they were once again sent to help guard the military-industrial complex at Augusta, and it was there that they were finally disbanded.

Despite several attempts, the institute was never resurrected. Its buildings had been destroyed in November 1864 by Sherman's troops; its moveable property, including books, had been sent to Milledgeville for safekeeping and was there destroyed during Sherman's occupation of the capital. Ironically, cadets of another institution were marching across the old capitol grounds before long. By 1880, with the state's capital having been moved to

Atlanta, the Middle Georgia Military and Agricultural College (predecessor of present-day Georgia Military College) had taken over capitol square, a location G.M.C. still occupies.

Major F. W. Capers, Battalion of Cadets
(From Lawton B. Evans, *The Student's History of Georgia* [1884])

G. M. I. Cadet "There was fatigue and blood and death in their ranks," noted General Capers, "but no white feather." Shown here is James Appleton Blackshear, who was attending G.M.I. "at the outbreak of the war."

(Courtesy of Jim Beacham)

Unidentified Sergeant, G.M.I.
(David Wynn Vaughan Collection)

THE 1ST DIVISION, GEORGIA MILITIA, 1864-1865

At the extra session of the Georgia General Assembly in spring 1863, the legislature directed Adjutant General Henry C. Wayne "to prepare a System of Military Laws, in accordance with the Constitution and Laws of the Confederate States" and Georgia's Constitution. By late October 1863, this had proved impracticable, in large part, Wayne wrote, because "the present condition of the country and its military laws [rendered] impossible...the operation of any military system within the state." And even if a militia system had been practicable, he noted, "it would not be advisable to order elections under it, while the larger portion of our citizens qualified to command, are absent from the State in active service in the field."

Nonetheless, between June and October 1863, the Georgia State Guard had been raised, more than 18,000 strong, and the availability of so many men for service (whether or not considered part of the surviving militia system) apparently encouraged Wayne and Governor Brown to propose a reorganization of the Georgia Militia, which the General Assembly approved on 14 December 1863. To Adjutant General Wayne's great satisfaction, this legislation suspended all contradictory provisions of the Georgia Code of 1861, which had drawn Wayne's "serious objections," and another bill, passed the same day, raised the adjutant general's rank from colonel to major general.

As in the earlier militia organization, the militia districts within the counties would be the basis of the new system. But these county militia districts were no longer organized into thirteen two-brigade divisions with corresponding military hierarchies. Instead, the state's forty-four three-county senatorial districts became military districts, in each of which one of the governor's aides-de-camp (with a state colonel's commission and a district surgeon to pass on medical exemptions) would enroll the available arms-bearing population. The building blocks of the new regiments, brigades, and, hopefully, divisions, would be produced from the separate three-county districts, with elections of officers held as units organized. Once the enrollment and organization were completed in each district, the "militia organization theretofore existing" was to be declared suspended.

The militia enrolling officers, who carried out their task in early 1864, could have three or more assistants to help them enroll their districts, with fifty cents paid for each man enrolled. Because of the war's inroads into the state's arms-bearing population, many districts within various counties could no longer yield a company of men. Consequently, the enrolling officers were empowered to consolidate districts when necessary—or to divide districts in the cases of towns whose populations had been swelled by refugees. No enrollment was conducted in the northwestern counties of Chattooga, Catoosa, and Dade, near Union-held Chattanooga, but units of the Georgia State Guard, whose expiration of service approached, were to be enrolled.

One of the most interesting aspects of the 1864 enrollment was its inclusion of conscription-age men. In fact, the act ordering the reorganization showed little deference to conscription legislation: it called for enrolling "all free white males…who are or shall be of the age of sixteen years, and not over sixty years. and…those who shall from time to time arrive at the age of sixteen years…*except those who shall actually be in the Army or Navy of the Confederate States, or in the State service*" [emphasis supplied].

It also provided that "any person subject to service" under the act could "volunteer in the military or naval service of the Confederate States" or in any of the Confederate local defense companies, though any such would be subject to the act "when his term of service as a volunteer shall have expired." Almost as an afterthought, one of the final sections of the act stated that "no person shall be enrolled…who is subject to conscription…; if the State enrolling officer has doubt whether any person within his limits is subject to enrollment as a conscript, he shall report the fact to the Confederate enrolling officer of the Congressional district, and if said Confederate officer does not cause such person to be enrolled within twenty days after such notice is given, the State enrolling office shall enroll him…." Obviously, there was a class of men within the state who were exempt from Confederate service for various reasons, but it is difficult to believe that exempts accounted for the 13,219 men, aged 18-45, who were enrolled.

These men, according to the act, were to be part of a class designated the Militia Proper, "composed of those between seventeen and fifty years of age"; the Militia Proper would be "first liable and subject to perform all the military duties contemplated" by the legislation. The other class, designated the Militia Reserve, was to include "those between sixteen and seventeen years of age, and between fifty and sixty years of age." Though they were to be organized with the Militia Proper, they would not "be required to drill or perform any of the military duties" of the Militia Proper until that class was "called into active service." Moreover, the Militia Reserve was not to be "subject or liable to any draft or other compulsory process to fill any requisition for troops" that might be made by President Jefferson Davis on Governor Brown.

Since the legislation directed the enrolling officers to gather much more information than age, the 1864 enrollment came to be known as the "Joe Brown Census." Enrollees were not only classified by occupation and nativity, but they were also required to report whether or not they owned a horse, what tack they had available for it, and whether they owned a "rifle, musket, or shot-gun." The enrolling officers recorded more than 5,000 rifles, more than 9,000 shot guns, and more than 12,000 horses, though tack was unavailable for some 500 of them.

By 7 May 1864, the arms-bearing population with the state of Georgia had been "enrolled, classified, and organized completely." The results were impressive:

MILITIA PROPER—
    3,303 (between 17 & 18);
    13,219 (Between 18 & 45);
    8,301 (Between 45 & 50)
TOTAL: *24, 823*
MILITIA RESERVE—
    4,474 (16 & 17);
    12,101 (Between 50 & 60)

TOTAL: *16, 575*

GRAND TOTAL: *41, 398*

These numbers, according to Adjutant General Wayne, yielded, "ready for service," eighteen regiments, twenty-one first-class battalions, forty-seven second-class battalions, and eight independent companies. But, as had been the case with the original Georgia Militia, Confederate legislation wrecked the new organization. The Third Conscription Act, with its provision of con-structive enrollment, Wayne noted, "absorbing…as it does the Militia

Proper" (into either the Confederate army or Howell Cobb's Georgia Reserve Force), left the state "only the Militia Reserve."

"Without expressing any opinion upon the wisdom of the extension of the Conscript Law," Wayne continued, "a political question with which, officially, I have nothing to do, I am at liberty, nevertheless, to say, that it is to be regretted, under the circumstances of invasion pressing upon Georgia, that with a military organization complete in all its parts, the enforcement of the extension had not been suspended, and the *unity* of force preserved in the State, instead of distracting and dividing it at a critical period."

For his part, Governor Brown argued that "without the interruption growing out the Conscript Acts," Georgia could have fielded, "for her own defence,…a force of some 30,000 men, after making all reasonable allowance for disability, etc." As it was, on 18 May 1864, he was reduced to calling out his militia officers again and sending them to the defense of another threatened Georgia city, in this case Atlanta rather than Savannah. His proclamation directed "all Commissioned Officers of the Militia of this State, including district Aids-de-Camp," to report to Adjutant General Wayne in Atlanta, along with all civil officers, "except those of the State House, the Penitentiary, the State Road, the Judges of the Superior and Inferior Courts, Ordinaries and Solicitors General, and Clerks and Sheriffs of Courts actually in session." This call, Adjutant General Wayne later noted, "was promptly responded to"; indeed, within a week of the governor's proclamation, the *Atlanta Intelligencer* stated that the militia officers were reporting "in large numbers" and that "a number of the civil officers" had reported as well, to act as an "auxiliary force to Gen. Johnston, under the command of that skillful and gallant officer, Gen. Wayne." The governor claimed these officers "rendered effective service," observing also that they "constitute[d], in a great degree, the remaining active militia force left to the State by the different acts of conscription." In the view of the Confederate authorities, the force was not negligible; by late 1864 they estimated that Georgia had exempted from conscription more than 5,400 civil officers and more than 2,700 militia officers

More important, Governor Brown on 9 July 1864 decided to call out much of the Militia Reserve, along with any of the Militia Proper exempted from conscription and able to serve. He did this, he stated, because his recent correspondence with President Davis had convinced him that Georgia was "to be left to her own resources to supply the reinforcements" to General Joseph E. Johnston's Army of the Tennessee. Also, beginning another notable controversy with the Confederate authorities, the governor decided to call up those Confederate soldiers in Georgia "not in actual *military service*," specifically, "the large number of able-bodied young men who have Confederate details to attend to various industrial avocations and pursuits."

By this point, Gustavus Woodson Smith had entered the history of the Georgia Militia; he would command the first and only division to be created from the militia reorganization. A Confederate general of checkered past and, not coincidentally, an ardent member of the anti-Davis cabal, Smith had arrived in Georgia in 1863. By late May he had been made one of Governor Brown's aides-de-camp, and soon he was planning fortifications for the railroad bridge over the Etowah River. Near the river on a spur rail line, Smith superintended the Cooper Iron Works until Sherman's forces destroyed them in May 1864.

Governor Brown intended for Smith to be major general, 1st Division, Georgia Militia, so his appointment came on 1 June 1864, with his pro forma election to the position shortly thereafter. On 11 June 1864, General Orders Number 1 issued from the militia's headquarters, announcing Smith's assumption of command and naming his staff officers, among them General Robert Toombs, inspector general, and Col. Joseph S. Claghorn, chief of artillery and ordnance. By this time, the officers and organization of the 1st Division had also been announced: Brigadier General R. W. Carswell's 1st Brigade, comprising the 1st Regiment, Colonel E. H. Pottle, commanding; the 2d Regiment, Colonel C. D. Anderson, commanding (later to be a militia brigadier); the 5th Regiment, Colonel S. S. Stafford, commanding, and the 1st Battalion, Lieutenant Colonel McCoy, commanding; and Brigadier General P. J. Philips's 2d Brigade, comprising the 3rd Regiment, Lieutenant Colonel John W. Hill, commanding; the 4th Regiment, Colonel Robert McMillan, commanding, and the 6th Regiment, Colonel T. J. Burney, commanding. Also organized was an Independent Artillery Battalion, Colonel Carey W. Styles, commanding.

This early incarnation of the 1st Division won the approval of General Joseph E. Johnston, who wrote Brown on 7 July that the militiamen "promise well, and have already done good service." Essentially, however, this was little more a skeleton organization, "a little over 3,000 men," that would need to be fleshed out by militiamen from either class who would obey Governor Brown's order of 11 July1864 to report to Atlanta. The governor split the state into a southern section and a northern section, separated by an east-west line drawn through Macon. Those south of the line were to report to General Smith "with the lest delay possible"; those to the north were to leave 20 July, "repairing to Atlanta by the nearest and speediest route." The response from the southern portion of the state was overwhelming. One citizen of Macon wrote, "[T]he malitia [*sic*] are pouring through here by the thousand rushing up without guns & without organization." Consequently, the governor amended his order in a proclamation issued on 21 July 1864 from the 1st Division's Atlanta headquarters: "In accordance with the request of General [John B.] Hood for the purpose of arming militia in Macon and sending them forward ready for service, thereby avoiding the confusion of having large bodies of unarmed men sent into Atlanta while it is besieged, these headquarters will be moved to Macon." The troops were to "be thrown into camp till they are armed before they are sent to Gen'l Smith." This concentration of troops would await Union general George Stoneman on 30 July and thwart his plan of freeing Union officers imprisoned in Macon. General Joseph E. Johnston, then in Macon after his replacement by Hood, observed and applauded the raw militia's conduct during the battle against the Yankee raiders.

Plaudits came from General Hood as well, who wrote to the governor on 23 July that the militia had fought "with great gallantry" at the Battle of Atlanta. The press also became more appreciative of the militia, as indicated by a typical editorial in the *Augusta Chronicle & Sentinel* of 31 July:

> *Our gallant militia officers have fairly won their spurs. … They have been styled "Gov. Brown's pets," but are now, also, the pets of the army and the people. They have done infinite credit to their patron; and neither he nor they will ever be ashamed of the sobriquet. He has given them a rough handling, for pets, but it has been all the more glorious and advantageous for them. He has been unusually careful of their military education, and they have not failed to profit by their training in the school to which he sent them.*

General Smith forwarded the governor his assessment of his command on 5 September 1864 after the loss at Jonesboro and the evacuation of Atlanta. By this time, the 1st Division totaled four brigades, as shown in the appended roster. During the retreat the militiamen had the responsibility of "guarding the reserve artillery," which they brought safely to the town of Griffin. Of his men, Smith wrote,

Without time for drill and inspection—with very incomplete and imperfect organization—inadequately supplied with transportation, equipment and all that pertains to the "Materiel" of an army, these men were first distributed upon the Chattahoochee to guard the passages of the river from above Roswell to West Point. When Gen. Johnston held Kennesaw Mountain with the right of his army, we by his order, concentrated and crossed the river, taking position on his left, supporting the cavalry upon that wing in the vicinity of Marietta—We fell back with the army to the Chattahoochee and then across that river, from which time until now we have formed a component part of the army, and have borne our full proportionate share of all its dangers, hardships and labors; and I have every reason to believe that, upon the battle field, on the line of march, in laboring upon fortifications and defence of intrenchments, the militia of Georgia, in the past hundred days of active service, (most of the time in the immediate presence of the enemy and under fire,) have won the respect and esteem of the gallant officers and men composing the regular army under General Hood. You are well aware of the embarrassments arising from conflict in legislation upon the part of Congress and the Georgia Legislature, and can appreciate the spirit of concession and forgetfulness of self, by which all seem to have been actuated, and which have resulted in procuring harmony and con-cert of action when there was such opportunity and cause for well founded complaint and real difficulty. The recent march was severe upon the men who had no experience in frill, and were not inured to fatigue. This was particu-larly the case with the old men. The command, however, came into camp in good condition. Some were weary and foot-sore, but all in fine spirits.... The militia in this army have done good service, and are entitled to the thanks of the State of Georgia and of the Confederate States."

Adjutant General Wayne, in reviewing the militia's service during the Atlanta Campaign, noted that the state armed and sent to the field between 10,000 and 11,000 men (though General Smith asserted that at Atlanta his "greatest number of effective muskets in the trenches at any one time was about 5,000"). "Of the services of this body of citizen soldiery," Wayne wrote the governor, "in the trenches around Atlanta, and during the evacua-tion of that city and retreat to Jonesboro..., it is needless for me to speak

here. It is enough to say that the Militia have done their duty nobly and efficiently, and have received publicly the acknowledgment of their devotion
from their eminent chiefs, Generals Johnston and Hood, and merit,
deservedly, the thanks of their country."

By this time their country, in the form of the Confederate States of
America rather than the state of Georgia, had tried to gather the militiamen
up, and Brown had promptly given them "agricultural leave" to prevent it.
But Adjutant General Wayne noted, in his annual report on the militia,
dated 26 October 1864, that, though "[f]urloughed for 30 days by your
Excellency's order, from September 10th to October 10th, they are again in
the field battling for the independence of their State, for their homes and for
their families." In an unusually candid conclusion to his report, Wayne suggested that it was not only Richmond that had trouble tapping Georgia's
manpower pool: "While the large body of the militia reported promptly at
the Front, a few individuals, I am sorry to say, have failed in their duty, and
it is with difficulty that the military machinery of the State can reach them."

More than "a few" obviously were not reached. Though General Smith
had advised that the men over fifty be withdrawn from "continuous active
service" since "not as a class fitted for military duty," many other men simply
seem to have stayed home. In any case, once gathered at Lovejoy's Station at
the beginning of what became the Savannah Campaign, the 1st Division on
31 October 1864 showed only 2,034 effective muskets present out of an
aggregate present of 2,983. Within two weeks, the total had declined to
1,949 and 2,882, respectively, but other "available forces" in the vicinity,
Confederate and otherwise, gave Smith some 2,800 effectives, with which he
began what would be a foredoomed resistance to Sherman's march.

The militiamen fought in two engagements in November 1864, in both
of which they formed the majority of the force deployed. At Griswoldville,
near Macon, they lost the only infantry engagement of the March to the Sea,
while showing foolhardiness and bravery in equal measure. At Honey Hill,
South Carolina, they won a notable victory over Union troops who were
trying to break Savannah's rail link with Charleston. By the end of December
1864, the 1st Division, Georgia Militia, had formed part of Savannah's garrison and had evacuated with the rest of General William J. Hardee's troops.

In early 1865, General Smith and some of his troops were stationed near
Augusta (now arguably Confederate Georgia's most important city, given its

mammoth powder works). Reflecting on his experiences with the Georgia Militia, Smith composed for General Wayne a set of memoranda "for the improvement of the state military organization."

During this period the General Assembly was generous with praise, rather than funds. In early 1865 the legislators passed a joint resolution lauding the men of the Georgia Militia for "conspicuous gallantry at Griswoldville…and especially for their unselfish patriotism, in leaving their State, and meeting the enemy on the memorable and well fought battlefield at Honey Hill in South Carolina."

For the duration of the war, for those militiamen who remained in the ranks, mainly garrison duty awaited, though a few of them fought in the last major battle in Georgia at Columbus. Finally, on 7 May 1865 at Macon, Governor Brown surrendered the Georgia Militia to Union general James Harrison Wilson, along with himself as their commander-in-chief.

NOTES

(Sources are listed in order of citation.)

Introduction: James Horace Bass, "Georgia in the Confederacy, 1861-1865," Ph.D. dissertation, University of Texas, 1932, 106-109; US War Department, comp., *The War of the Rebellion: A Compilation of the Official Records of the Union and Confederate Armies,* 128 vols. (Washington, DC: Government Printing Office, 1880-1901) ser. 4, vol. 3, p. 100 (Hereafter cited as *OR.*); James M. Johnson, *Militiamen, Rangers, and Redcoats: The Military in Georgia, 1754-1776* (Macon GA: Mercer University Press, 1992) 85; Alex M. Hitz, "Georgia Militia Districts," *Georgia Bar Journal* 18 (February 1956): 1-2; George R. Lamplugh, *Politics on the Periphery: Factions and Parties in Georgia, 1783-1806* (Newark: University of Delaware Press, 1986) 22-23, 26; *Acts of the General Assembly of Georgia…1841,* 204-205 (Hereafter cited as *Acts,* with pertinent year); Philip Katcher, *American Civil War Armies (5): Volunteer Militia* [Men-at-Arms ser. 207] (London: Osprey Publishing, 1989) 3; Lyle D. Brundage, "The Organization, Administration, and Training of the United States Ordinary and Volunteer Militia, 1792-1861," Ed.D. dissertation, University of Michigan, 1958, 69-70; Hitz, "Georgia Militia Districts," 2; T. R. R. Cobb, *A Digest of the…Laws…of Georgia* (Athens GA: Christy, Kelsea, & Burke, 1851) 737-39; *Confederate Records of the State of Georgia* (Hereafter cited as *CR.*), 2:208-11; *Southern Recorder* (Milledgeville GA), 6 November 1851 and 7 July 1857; I. W. Avery, *The History of the State of Georgia from 1850 to 1881* (New York: Brown & Derby, Publishers, 1881) 103; "Report of the Number of Members in Uniform in Each Volunteer Corps of Georgia," [1860], Box 21, Governor Brown's Incoming Correspondence, GDAH; *Southern Recorder* (Milledgeville GA), 16 October 1860; *Federal Union* (Milledgeville GA), 16 October 1860; Louise Biles Hill, *Joseph E. Brown and the Confederacy* (Chapel Hill: University of North Carolina Press, 1939) 48-49, 42 n100; Bass, "Georgia in the Confederacy, 1861-1865," 207.

1. The Georgia Militia, 1860-1863: Henry C. Wayne to Joseph E. Brown, 29 October 1861, Adjutant General's Letterbook (Hereafter cited as AGLB) 4, pp. 35-38, Georgia Department of Archives and History (Atlanta GA) (Hereafter cited as GDAH.); Adjutant General's General Orders No. 13 (21 August 1861), GDAH (General Orders hereafter cited as AGGO); AGGO No. 2 (13 February 1862); *CR* 2: 213-16; Hill, *Joseph E. Brown and the Confederacy,* 80-81, 83-84, 86-87; AGGO No. 1 (23 February 1863); Avery, *History of the State of Georgia,* 256-57; [Charles Henry Smith], *Bill Arp, So Called*

(New York: Metropolitan Record Office, 1866) 41-51 [book publication of war-time newspaper columns]; *Annual Report of the Adjutant and Inspector General of the State of Georgia* (Milledgeville GA: Boughton, Nisbet, Barnes, & Moore, 1864) 4 (Hereafter cited as *AGAR*, with pertinent year.). The Adjutant General's General Orders for the period after April 1862 call for numerous elections for militia officers, suggesting that considerable numbers of them did not take advantage of their exemptions and perhaps joined the Confederate service rather than being conscripted.

2. The Georgia Army (The "Secession Regiments"), 1861: *CR* 2:19-20; *CR* 1:710-11; Henry C. Wayne to Francis S. Bartow, 19 February 1861, AGLB B-44, GDAH; AGGO No. 1 (9 February 1861), No. 4 (15 February 1861, giving the "*Uniform, Dress* and *Equipment* of the two Regiments of Infantry in the regular Service of the State"), No. 5 (20 February 1861, listing the officers of the Georgia Army, with David E. Twiggs as brigadier general), and No. 11 (19 July 1862, on the death of Twiggs and his decline of the proffered brigadier generalship), GDAH; *Statutes at Large of the Provisional Government of the Confederate States of America* (Richmond VA: R. M. Smith, Printer to Congress, 1864) 43; *CR*, 1:726-27, 737-38; Joseph H. Parks, *Joseph E. Brown of Georgia* (Baton Rouge: Louisiana State University Press, 1977) 134, 136-37; AGLB B-49, pp. 113-15; *CR* 3:20; Joseph T. Derry, *Georgia*, vol. 6 in Clement A. Evans, ed., *Confederate Military History*, 12 vols. (Atlanta GA: Confederate Publishing Company, 1899), 16; Avery, *History of the State of Georgia*, 661. For the Georgia Navy, see Henry C. Wayne to Commander C. M. Morris, 16 February 1861, AGLB B-44 (I), GDAH, and other February 1861 correspondence; AGLB B-49, passim; and Charles C. Jones, Jr., *The Life and Services of Commodore Josiah Tattnall* (Savannah GA: Morning News Steam Printing House, 1878) 130-32.

3. The 4th Brigade, Georgia Volunteers (Phillips's Legion, C.S.A.): *OR*, ser. 4, vol. 1, p. 168; AGGO No. 2 (10 January 1861); *Acts of the General Assembly of the State of Georgia* (Milledgeville GA: Boughton, Nisbet, Barnes, and Moore, 1860) 49-51 (hereafter cited as *Acts*, with pertinent year); *CR* 2:89-92; Bass, "Georgia in the Confederacy, 1861-1865," 213-14; "Camp McDonald, A School of Instruction for the 4th Brigade Geo. Volunteers" (map), in Bowling C. Yates, *History of the Georgia Military Institute* (Marietta GA: n.p., 1968), between pp. 15 and 16; Bass, "Georgia in the Confederacy, 1861-1865," 215-17; Thomas Lawrence Connelly, *Army of the Heartland: The Army of Tennessee, 1861-1862* (Baton Rouge: Louisiana State University Press, 1967) 32, 37; Parks, *Joseph E. Brown of Georgia*, 152-55.

4. The Georgia State Troops, 1861-1862: *CR* 2:52-55, 69-70, 93-94, 131-32, 138, 146; *CR* 3:146-47, 170-71; Bass, "Georgia in the Confederacy, 1861-1865," 220-27; Avery, *History of the State of Georgia*, 227-31, 236-41. Henry R. Jackson's letter and order books and other materials are in the papers of the adjutant and inspector general's office, location numbers 3340-18 and 3340-06, GDAH. In the same repository, extensive rosters of the Georgia State Troops are found under location numbers 3297-18 (box 90) and 3298-01 (boxes 91 and 92).

5. The Georgia State Line, 1862-1865: William Harris Bragg, *Joe Brown's Army: The Georgia State Line, 1862-1865* (Macon GA: Mercer University Press, 1987), passim. The GDAH holds extensive man-uscript materials on the Georgia State Line, including but not limited to muster rolls and correspondence with the governor and adjutant general.

6. The Georgia State Guard (C.S.A.), 1863-1864: *CR* 2:456-62; *CR* 3:339-46, 374-77, 618-19, 637; Hill, *Joseph E. Brown and the Confederacy*, 166-77; Horace Montgomery, *Howell Cobb's Confederate Career* (Tuscaloosa AL: Confederate Publishing Company, 1959) 99-110. Some material on the Georgia State Guard is found in the records of the Adjutant General's Office, location number 3337-06, Box 1, GDAH, and numerous personnel records from separate commands are found throughout the National Archives Microfilm Publication *Compiled Service Records of Confederate Soldiers Who Served in Organizations From the State of Georgia*.

7. The Georgia Reserve Force (C.S.A.), 1864-1865: *CR* 3:503-507; *OR*, ser. 4, vol. 3, pp. 178-79, 473-75; Montgomery, *Howell Cobb's Confederate Career*, 115-21; Howell Cobb to Charles C. Jones, Jr., 17 September 1867, Charles C. Jones, Jr., Papers, Duke University Library; Parks, *Joseph E. Brown of Georgia*, 285-86; Hill, *Joseph E. Brown and the Confederacy*, 92-93. Personnel records of the Georgia Reserve Force, many recording the surrender in North Carolina, are also found scattered among the *Compiled Service Records.*

8. The Battalion of Cadets, Georgia Military Institute, 1864-1865: Keith Shaw Bohannon, "'Not Alone Trained to Arms But to the Science and Literature of Our Day': The Georgia Military Institute, 1851-1865," master's thesis, University of Georgia, 1993; Keith Bohannon, "Cadets, Drillmasters, Draft Dodgers, and Soldiers: The Georgia Military Institute during the Civil War," *Georgia Historical Quarterly* 79 (spring 1995): 5-29 [essentially an illustrated version of ch. 4 of Bohannon's definitive study of G.M.I., cited above]; Bowling C. Yates, *History of the Georgia Military Institute* (Marietta GA: n.p., 1968); Lynwood M. Holland, "Georgia Military Institute, The West Point of Georgia: 1851-1864," *Georgia Historical Quarterly* 43 (September 1959): 225-47; Francis W. Capers, *Official Report on Services [of the Battalion of Cadets, Gerogia Military Institute]* (Milledgeville GA: n.p., 1864); Eliza Frances Andrews, *The War-Time Journal of a Georgia Girl, 1864-1865* (1908; reprint, Atlanta: Cherokee Publishing Company, 1976) 164; James C. Bonner, *Milledgeville: Georgia's Antebellum Capital* (Athens: University of Georgia Press, 1978) 240-44.

9. The 1st Division, Georgia Militia, 1864-1865 [Please note: for reasons of completeness, this survey of the service of the First Division, Georgia Militia, incorporates some portions of the main text.]: *AGAR* (1863), 10-11; ibid., 7-8; *Acts* (1862-1863), 51-58; Henry C. Wayne to Joseph E. Brown, 18 March 1863, AGLB 14; R. H. Clark, T. R. R. Cobb, and D. Irwin, *Code of the State of Georgia* (Atlanta: John H. Seals, 1861) 199-204; *Acts* (1862-1863), 51-53, 55; *AGAR* (1864), 4; Georgia Adjutant General, Statistical Analysis of Militia Enrollment under 1864 Reorganization, location number 3341-07, GDAH (includes original manuscript listings for all counties except the three in northeast Georgia and Glynn, Glascock, Jefferson, Bibb, Monroe, Pike, Franklin, Habersham, Hart Henry, and Campbell—though the counties named above are represented by statistics in table 1 of the *AGAR* [1864]); *Acts* (1862-1863), 51, 57; *AGAR* (1864), table 1; *Acts* (1862-1863), 54, 56; *AGAR* (1864), 4 and table 1; OR, ser. 4, vol. 3, pp. 178-83; *AGAR* (1864), 5; *CR* 2:774; ibid., 703-704; *AGAR* (1864), 5; *Columbus* (GA) *Times*, 26 May 1864 (quoting the *Atlanta Intelligencer*); *CR* 2:710-12; *OR*, ser. 4, vol. 3, pp. 868-70; Henry C. Wayne to Gustavus W. Smith, 23 May 1863, AGLB B-49, GDAH; *OR*, ser. 1, vol. 38, pt. 3, p. 969; *Atlanta Intelligencer*, 4, 15 June 1864; *The Countryman*, 21 June 1864, 347 (quoting the *Atlanta Register*, 3 June 1864); *Atlanta Intelligencer*, 15 June 1864; *Governor Brown's Proclamations and Orders Calling into Active Military Service and Sending to the Front the Civil and Military Officers, and the Reserved Militia of the State of Georgia, to the Army of Tennessee* (Milledgeville GA: Boughton, Nisbet, Barnes, and Moore, 1864) 8 (Hereafter cited as *Governor Brown's Proclamations*.); *OR*, ser. 1, vol. 38, pt. 3, p. 969; *CR* 2:711-12; J. J. Gresham to "Dear Brother," 21 July 1864, Gresham E. B. & J. J., Folder, Georgia Miscellany 1, Special Collections, Robert W. Woodruff Library, Emory University; *CR* 2:717; Joseph E. Johnston, *Narrative of Military Operations* (New York: The Century Publishing Company, 1874) 370; *Governor Brown's Proclamations*, 15; *Augusta Chronicle & Sentinel*, 31 July 1864; *Milledgeville Confederate Union*, 20 September 1864; *AGAR* (1864), 5-6; *OR*, ser. 1, vol. 38, pt. 3, p. 971; *AGAR* (1864), 6; *OR*, ser. 1, vol. 38, pt. 3, p. 971; Morning Report, 1st Division, Georgia Militia, 31 October 1864, and Tri-Monthly Report, 1st Division, Georgia Militia, 10 November 1864, GDAH; *Reports of the Operations of the Militia from October 13, 1864, to February 11, 1865, by Maj. Generals G. W. Smith and Wayne, together with Memoranda by Gen. Smith, for the Improvement of the State Military Organization* (Macon GA: Boughton, Nisbet, Barnes, and Moore, 1865) 3-8; *OR*, ser. 1, vol. 49, pt. 2, p. 663.

APPENDIX 2
THE "MELISH": A SELECTION OF HISTORICAL AND LITERARY DESCRIPTIONS OF THE GEORGIA MILITIA, 1807-1864, SATIRICAL AND OTHERWISE

Any mention of the Georgia Militia and the Civil War remains likely to provoke a smile. This is not surprising; the rich possibilities for ridicule inherent in almost any militia organization have always produced gibes from commentators, and the militiamen of the Northern states were not exempt from such raillery. The Georgia Militia merely provided one of the later, more well-known targets in this "perennial subject for humor." No doubt the earliest such lampoons are found in hieroglyphics or on baked clay tablets. But, given the British heritage of the United States, British history provides precursors aplenty of the lack of respect and confidence that citizens often displayed in the citizen-soldiers they found themselves depending upon for protection. One of the more poignant, from the English Civil War, describes public unease with a defending force of militia without "soldiers' faces," who "had hardly known how to use the muskets hurriedly put into their unpracticed hands." A famous later example shows the basic similarity of all militiamen, even when an ocean apart. In Thomas Hardy's *The Trumpet-Major* (1880), the author was caught describing an English militia drill of the early 1800s with anecdotes traceable to a satirical attack on the Georgia Militia of the same period.

Another aspect of America's British heritage—fear of standing armies—also contributed to the stereotypical presentation of the militia. Beginning during the Constitutional Convention and lasting for decades thereafter, there was a spirited debate over whether America was to rely on militiamen or professional soldiers for its defense, with proponents of standing armies eager to place the militia in an unfavorable light. This particular anti-militia attitude forms part of the substructure of the most famous of the early lampoons of the Georgia Militia, apparently brought to print for the first time around 1807 by its author, Oliver Hillhouse Prince (1787-1837). Its title gives an excellent idea of its content: *The Ghost of Baron Steuben; or, Fredonia in Arms! Being a Description of that most Bloody Campaign, Styled the*

*Alexandro-Caesaro-Eugenio-Frederico-Bonapartic Campaign out Napoleonised;
or, a Georgia Training, In which the Most Exquisite Discipline, Subordination,
Military Knowledge, Fortitude, Temperance, and Patriotic Preparation, Are
Clearly Exemplified, and Particularly Recommended to Those Who Are Opposed
to the Uselessness and Mischief of a Standing Army.*

By 1835, when A. B. Longstreet included a version of Prince's sketch in
Georgia Scenes, militia satires were, in the words of Edgar Allan Poe, "rife in
the land," both North and South. But a major reason for some of these pro-
ductions—other than those aforementioned—was narrowly political (and
sectional), for some opponents of President Andrew Jackson found the officers of the militia in particular to be irresistible whipping boys. As Kenneth
S. Lynn noted, "it is not surprising that militia officers should have seemed
to the Whig mind the incarnate spirit of Jacksonism, or that the comic possibilities of Southern military life were capitalized upon by conservative
humorists from the early '30's on. In dozens of sketches, back-country officers were depicted as militarily inept braggarts, incapable even of drilling
soldiers, let alone of leading them into battle. One of the best [that of
Prince]...told of a militia company drill that began in soldierly pomp and
ended in a tanglefooted mess."

Obviously, there was also a political thrust to much of the criticism and
ridicule of the Georgia Militia of 1861-1865, for the opponents of "Young
Hickory," Joseph E. Brown, were no less eager to score points than the enemies of Old Hickory had been. This is particularly obvious in any survey of
the newspapers of the period. Predictably, the pro-Brown organs were more
likely to view the militia with some seriousness and appreciation, while the
anti-Brown press seldom failed to draw on what was by then a rich tradition
of poking fun at the militia or (in the abbreviation of the time) the "Melish."

Although the following excerpts show the range of literary and historical
commentary on the Georgia militia from around 1807 through the Civil
War. The effect that the two classes of description had on each other is a
matter for speculation, the influence on public attitudes toward the militia
seems certain.

A GEORGIA MILITIA COMPANY
ON A RURAL DRILLING FIELD, C. 1807

The men had been notified to meet at nine o'clock, "armed and equipped as the law directs;" that is to say, with a gun and cartridge box at least, but, as directed by the law of the United States, "with a good firelock, a sufficient bayonet and belt, and a pouch with a box to contain no less than twenty-four sufficient cartridges of powder and ball.'

At twelve, about one third, perhaps one half, of the men had collected, and an inspector's return of the numbers present, and of their arms, would have stood nearly thus: 1 captain, 1 lieutenant; ensign, none; fifers, none; privates, present, 24; ditto, absent, 40; gunlocks, 12; ramrods, 10; rifle pouches, 3; bayonets, none; belts, none; spare flints, none; cartridges, none; horsewhips, walking canes, and umbrellas, 10. (From A. B. Longstreet, Georgia Scenes (New York, 1957, originally published 1835), 131.)

A. B. Longstreet (1790-1870) served as chaplain of the Georgia Militia during the Civil War. The Oliver Hillhouse Prince sketch that Longstreet used in *Georgia Scenes* was originally printed as early as 1807, both in a Georgia newspaper and in pamphlet form under the title *The Ghost of Baron Steuben*, containing "some curiously graphic drawings," apparently meant to represent a bird's-eye view of the disorganized marching of the militia company. Prince's sketch was also published as *Captain Clodpole, or The Oglethorpe Muster*, and was reprinted (oddly, as an example of a militia muster in Charleston, South Carolina) in John Lambert's *Travels through Lower Canada, and the United States of North America, in the Years 1806, 1807, and 1808*, 3 vols. (London: Richard Phillips, 1810) 2:431-41; and, as an example of militia in discipline in America, in C. H. Gifford's *History of the Wars occasioned by the French Revolution*, 2 vols. (London: W. Lewis, 1817) 2:968-70. It was in the last-mentioned that Hardy found the version he paraphrased for the English muster in *The Trumpet-Major*.

THE GEORGIA MILITIA AGAINST THE CREEK INDIANS,
29 NOVEMBER 1813, THREE VIEWS

[I] Georgia, no less patriotic than Tennessee, soon came to the relief of her brethren of the Mississippi Territory. Brigadier-General John Floyd crossed the Ockmulgee, Flint, and Chattahoochie, and advanced near the Tallapoosa with

an army of nine hundred and fifty militia and four hundred friendly
Indians.... Before sunrise, on a cold and frosty morning, Floyd attacked the
Creeks, who were assembled in great force at the town of Auttose.... The
Indians at first advanced, and fought with great resolution, but the fire from
the artillery, with the charge of the bayonets, drove them into the out-houses
and thickets, in rear of the town.... (From Albert James Pickett, History of
Alabama and Incidentally of Georgia and Mississippi, from the Earliest
Period, 2 vols. [Charleston SC: Walker and James, 1851] 2:557-58)

[II] Some particulars of the battle...fought on the 29th, Nov. under the
command of Gen. Floyd on our part. After three days march, the
army...encamped on the night of the 28th, with 8 miles of the Ottessee town
the place of battle. The next morning it marched so soon as to exhibit itself to
the surprised an astonished Indians, about half way between day break and
sunrise; at this period the contest commenced.... The battle lasted 2 and a half
or 3 hours. Nine of our men were slain on the fields, some say 100, some 200
and some 300 of the enemy.... Two of their kings shared the fatal portion of
many of their subjects.... (From the "Journal of James A. Tait [, Georgia
Militia,] for the Year 1813," Georgia Historical Quarterly 8 [September
1924]: 234, 235)

[III] You were not wrong in your conjecture that the next information you
received would be of a severe battle with the Indians; such a one has never
before been fought with the Creeks.... At day light we were in sight of the
enemy, who it seems, were apprized of our approach, and from the order of our
movements calculated that we would not reach their town before the middle of
the day, not presuming that we would move at night. The sereneness of the
morning, the yells of the savages, the firing of our artillery and the incessant
prattling of the musketry and rifles; the dead laying promiscuously over the
field, and the rolling pillars of smoke issued by the devouring flames preying on
the savages' dwellings, in addition to the columns produced by the repeated discharge of our artillery, and the lighter sheets produced by the discharge of small
arms, were in various figures fantastically floating in the air.... The attack
upon this town was a daring undertaking when it is known to be situated in
the heart of the war party! (Major General John Floyd, Georgia Militia, to
Mary H. Floyd, 5 December 1813, from "Letters of John Floyd, 1813-1838,"
Georgia Historical Quarterly 33 [September 1949]: 235)

MILITIA VOLUNTEERS IN CHEROKEE GEORGIA, 4 AUGUST 1836

This morning, while we were at breakfast, a company of Georgia Mounted Volunteers rode through this place [Spring Place, Murray County, Georgia] on their way to the Cherokee Council. All had their coats off with their muskets and cartouche-boxes strung across their shoulders. Some of the men had straw hats, some of them white felt hats, others had old black hats on with the rim torn off, and all of them were as unshaven and as dirty as they could well be. The officers were only distinguished by having Cherokee fringed hunting shirts on. Many of the men were stout young fellows, and they rode on, talking, and cursing and swearing, without any kind of discipline. Upon the whole it was a picturesque sight, and brought to my recollection the descriptions of the condottieri of ancient times. (From George Featherstonhaugh's A Canoe Voyage Up the Minnay Sotor, *2 vols. [London: R. Bentley, 1847] 2:229)*

A MILITIA MUSTER IN ATHENS, CLARKE COUNTY, GEORGIA, 24 JUNE 1839

On the Monday after our arrival, we witnessed a grotesque exhibition of the militia muster.... By the law of the State, every male citizen between the ages of eighteen and forty-five, not legally exempted, must be enrolled as a militiaman, and attend the stated musters throughout the year, under penalties for noncompliance. As this is felt here, as elsewhere, to be a duty as irksome as it is thought useless, and one from which the great majority of the community would gladly relieve themselves if they could, there seems an universal determination to bring these muster into contempt. Accordingly, while the commanding officer, under whose review they were to pass, was dressed in a field-officer's full uniform of blue and silver, and mounted on a fine charger richly caparisoned; the battalion that marched before him was as grotesque as the most ingenious caricaturist could make it. About a dozen of the whole number had muskets, some with bayonets and some without; and these were carried in as many different ways as there were pieces. The rest of the troop, about one hundred in number, carried sticks, umbrellas, waggoners' whips, and large planks or rails. Their dresses, too, were as varied as their arms; some wore cloth coats, others white cotton jackets, and many were in their shirt sleeves; while hats of all kinds, black, white, and straw, broad-brimmed and narrow, made up the motley dress of this strange company; and in marching, the aim seemed to be to make the line as irregular as possible, and cause every man to step out of time. In short, they seemed to labour under the influence of sym-

metrophobia, and to do everything in the opposite way to that in which it should be done. (From J. S. Buckingham's The Slave States of America, *2 vols. [London: Paris, Fisher, Son, and Company, 1842) 2:69-70)*

WILLIAM TAPPAN THOMPSON'S MAJOR JOSEPH JONES MUSTERS THE MILITIA AT "PINEVILLE," GEORGIA, 1842

You know I said in my last [letter] that we was gwine to have a betallion muster in Pineville. Well, the muster has tuck place, and I reckon sich other doins you never hearn of afore.

I come in town the night before, with my regimentals in a bundle, so they couldn't be siled by ridin, and as soon as I got my breckfast, I begun rigin out for the muster. I had a bran new pair of boots, made jest a purpose, with long legs to 'em, and a cocked hat like a half moon, with one of the tallest kind of red feathers in it, a blue cloth regimental coat, all titivated off with gold and buttons, and a pair of yaller britches of the finest kind. Well, when I went to put 'em on, I couldn't help but cuss all the tailors and shoomakers in Georgia. In the fust place, my britches like to busted and wouldn't reach more'n halfway to my jacket, then it tuck two niggers and a pint of soap to git my boots on; and my coat had tail enough for a bed-quilt, and stood straight out behind like a fan-tail pidgin.—It wouldn't hang right no how you could pull it. I was never so dratted mad, especially when ther was not time to fix things, for the fellers wer comin in town in gangs and beginin to call for me to come out and take the command. Expectation was ris considerable high, cause I was pledged to quip myself in uniformity to the law, if I was 'lected Majer....

[Major Jones approaches the muster where his men, "settled like bees on a bean-pole, pretty considerable straight," have been ordered to salute at his approach. But his horse becomes spooked by his rattling sword, the racket of a fife and drum, and the hurrahs of the crowd out to view the muster.] My hoss [was] wheelin and pitchin worse than ever, right up to the muster—and, before I could draw my breth, bang! bang! bang de bang! bang! bang! went every gun in the crowd, and all I knowed was, I was whirlin, and pitchin, and swingin about in the smoke and fire till I cum full length right smack on the ground, "in all the pride, pomp, and circumstances of glorious war," as Mr. Shakespeare ses.

Lucky enough I didn't git hurt: but my cote was split clean up to the coller, my yaller britches busted all to flinders, and my cocked hat and fether all nocked into a perfect mush. Thunder and lightnin! thinks I, what must be a man's feelins in a rale battle whar they're shootin bullets in good yearnest!

Cum to find out, it was all a mistake; the men didn't know nothing about military ticktacks, and thought I meant a regular fourth of July salute.

I had to lay by my regimentals.—But I know'd my caracter was at stake as a officer, and I termined to go on with the muster. So I told Skinner and Cullers to git the men straight agin, and when they was all in a line I sorted 'em out. The fellers what had guns I put in front, then what had sticks in the rare, and them what had no shoes, down to the bottom by themselves, so nobody couldn't tramp on ther toes. A good many of 'em begun to forgit which was ther right hand and which was ther left; and some of 'em begun to be very diffikilt to manage, so I termined to march 'em out to a old field, whar they couldn't git no more licker.... (From William Tappan Thompson's Major Jones's Courtship, rev. ed. [New York: D. Appleton, 1872] 25-26, 28, 29. The original edition was published in Philadelphia in 1840.)

RICHARD MALCOLM JOHNSTON'S COLONEL MOSES GRICE MUSTERS THE MILITIA AT ANTEBELLUM DUKESBOROUGH [POWELTON, HANCOCK COUNTY, GEORGIA]

Colonel Moses Grice, of the Fourteenth Regiment Georgia Militia,...was a man thirty-five years old, over six feet high, of proportional weight, owned a good plantation with about twenty negroes, and had seen the theater as many as three times in the city of Augusta.... The colonel...had a wife, but no child (a point on which he was, perhaps, a little sore), was not in debt, was hospitable, an encourager (especially in words), of public and private enterprise, and enthusiastically devoted, though without experience in wars, to the military profession, which—If he might use the expression—he would call his second wife. Off the muster-field he habitually practiced that affability which is pleasant because so rare to see in the warrior class. When in full uniform at the head of the regiment, with girt sword and pistol-holster, he did indeed look like a man not to be fooled with; and the sound of his voice in utterance of military orders was such as to show that he intended these orders to be heard and obeyed. When the regiment was disbanded, the sternness would depart from his mien, and, though yet unstripped of weapons and regalia, he would smile blandly, as if to reassure spectators that, for the present, the danger was over, and persons might approach without apprehension....

It was muster day for the battalion. Colonel Grice always felt it his duty to be at these occasions, preparatory to the great regimental parade. The exercises, after many hours, were coming to an end, as the companies marched, with short intervals between, down the one street of the village, preparatory to dis-

bandment. Alternately had the colonel been complimentary and censorious, as he rode, sometimes in a walk, other times at full gallop, up and down the lines.

"Peerter, peerter, major," he remonstrated with Major Pounds, respectfully indeed, but with a warmth that seemed difficult to repress—"peerter; make them captains peerten up them lines. My blood and thunder! my Juberter and Julus Caesar! if the enemy was to come upon us with fixted bannets—Oh, you've done your part admarably, major. It's them captains."

It was just before the final halt that the colonel addressed Captain Collins, whose company was in the center, and then immediately in front of Bland's store. "Ah, Cap'n Collins, look to your rar. It's so fur behind that it looks like two companies 'stid o' one. That sergeant o' yourn you'll have to talk to and drill in private. He's arfter makin' twins out o' your company. Sergeant Williams is a great man for twins, you know, cap'n. But you better tell him to make 'em keep his cubs at home. We want solid columes when we come to the field of battle."

The warrior enjoyed his jest, that had been heard by all in the company, and others besides. But he did not allow himself even to smile when at the head of the military forces of his country, in order to keep himself ever on the alert against sudden attacks of her enemies. His gloomy brow indicated indignation at the thought that a petty subaltern, from some vain notion of making his own domestic status the model of the nation's principal means of defense, sought to demoralize it, and actually invite invasion. (From Richard Malcolm Johnston's Dukesborough Tales *[New York: D. Appleton, 1892], 246, 247-48, 274-75. In 1857 Johnston began publishing his tales of middle Georgia [based on his reminiscences of rural Hancock County in the 1820s, 1830s, and 1840s], and he added to them during and after the Civil War.)*

BILL ARP ON ANTEBELLUM MILITIA COLONELS AND MUSTERS

We used to have general musters all over the State twice a year. The militia were ordered out to be reviewed by the commander-in-chief, which was the governor. The constitution required him to review 'em, and as he couldn't travel all around in person, he had to do it by proxy, and so he had his proxy in every county, and he was called the governor's aid-de-camp with the rank of colonel. This gave the governor over a hundred aid-de-camps, and they all took it as a compliment and wore cockade hats with red plumes, and epaulets, and long brass swords, and big brass spurs, and pistols in their holsters, and rode up and down the lines at a gallop, reviewing the meelish. The meelish were in a double crooked straight line in a great big field, and were armed with shotguns

and rifles, and muskets, and sticks, and cornstalks, and thrash-poles, and
umbrellas, and they were standing up and setting down, or on the squat, or
playing mumble peg, and they hollered for water half their time, and whisky
the other; and when the colonel and his personal staff got thorough reviewing
he halted about the middle of the line and said, "Shoulder arms—right face—
march," and then the kettle drums rattled and the fife squeaked, and some guns
went off half cocked and the meelish shouted awhile and were disbanded by the
captains of their several companies. (Charles H. Smith, Bill Arp's Scrap Book
[Atlanta: James P. Harrison & Co., Publishers, 1884] 226)

MILITIA PARADES IN SAVANNAH, CHATHAM COUNTY, GEORGIA, C. 1840

Just hearing the sound of martial music, I am reminded of the appearance and
manner in which military parades are conducted in the South. In the first
place all their musicians are colored men, for the white gentlemen would con-
sider it quite beneath their dignity to perform such a piece of drudgery as to
play for a company while doing military duty. These colored musicians are
dressed in the full uniform of the company to which they belong, and, on the
morning of the day in which the several companies are to be called out, each
band in uniform, one at a time, marches through all the streets to summon all
the soldiers to the parade ground. This performance also calls out servants that
can obtain permission to attend the training, and it is not a few of them that
not only follow but go before the companies wherever they march. They are
excessively fond of such scenes, and crowds of men, women and children never
fail of being present on all such occasions, some carrying their masters' young
children on their heads and shoulders, while many are seen with large trays on
their heads, loaded with fruit, sweetmeats and various kinds of drinks to sell to
those who always wish to purchase on such days. In Savannah there are five of
that kind of companies that exist in all the states and are called by all names,
composed of all such persons as only perform military duty because they are
obliged. In Savannah they are called ragmuffins [sic], and I never heard a
name more appropriately applied. Scarcely any two men are dressed alike or
took the same step, and, whenever I saw them approaching, some with a shoe
on one foot and a boot on the other, some with their guns wrong end up and
others with them on their shoulders, wearing their knapsacks bottom up and
wrong side out, I could not help thinking one might suppose they were learning
how to catch up their guns and knapsacks and effect the most speedy escape in
time of danger instead of facing an enemy." (From Emily P. Burke's

Reminiscences of Georgia *[Oberlin OH: James M. Fitch, Publisher, 1850]*
92-94.)

THE GEORGIA MILITIA'S OFFICERS REDUCED TO RANKS AND
SENT TO GENERAL P. G. T. BEAUREGARD IN SAVANNAH,
FEBRUARY-MARCH 1863: BILL ARP'S VIEW OF A DEPARTURE
AND RETURN, AS DESCRIBED BY A REDUCED MILITIA OFFICER

(I) The Officer Goes Forth. *"How in the dickens can Joe Brown reduce a*
major to a private when he hasn't done anything? What sort of an army regu-
lation do you call that? Joe Brown's new tactics, I reckon.... I thought from the
way he pitched into Jeff Davis about trying to enroll his militia officers, that we
wouldn't have to fight nothing for the next twenty-five years. Now, you see, he's
conscripted the whole concern himself, all at once in a pile, and reduced 'em all
to ranks. He's a devil of a Governor-Commander-in-Chief. Blame his old hide
of him; I'll bet he don't appear at Savannah, not him. Durned if I don't go
anywhere he'll risk his carcass. Not him.... Bet my ears if old Bory once gets his
French paws on a militia officer, he'll hold him during the war and fight him
some afterwards just for the fun of it. When this fuss is over he will take 'em to
Arkansas to fight the Indians. Better believe he hasn't any love for Joe Brown's
pets."

(II) The Officer Returns. *"Did you suppose it was going to take a year to*
whip a parcel of blue-bellied Yankees? They knew we was coming after their
codfish, and they retired—yes, sir, they evacuated. We have now fallen back to
recruit. You see,...we are the reserve. We occupy the post of honor, which you
know is the post of danger. We are the 'reliable gentlemen,' as the editors say.
The militia of Georgia now stand conspicuous as the Old Guard of Napoleon
Bonaparte, and Joe Brown is old Bony himself come to light—regenerated, res-
urrected, reconstructed—and I am one of the militia myself, I am. I've been to
Savannah and stood on the ramparts....

"Durn that luck, I ain't no fool muself, and I know we aint out of the
woods. Joe Brown just called us to Savannah to how docile we were. Well, we
got to Atlanta, and he said 'halt,' *and we halted. Then he said* 'counter-march,
go home,' *and we got ready for the cars in double-quick. Then he cried out,*
'counter-march to Savannah,' *and to Savannah we went* straight forthwith.
Now here we are again, but where we will be day after to-morrow, no mortal
fool knows except Joe Brown. Blame the militia. Dad burn old Brown. What
security has a man got for his liberty! What satisfaction is there in living
between hawk and buzzard? Who cares about traveling on the railroad when
every impertinent dog on the way can stand off and point and say, 'Thar go the

Melish; yonder come the Melish; do you see that Melish?'" (From Charles H. Smith, *Bill Arp, So Called* [New York: Metropolitan Record Office, 1866] 41, 42, 46–47, 48)

MAJOR GENERAL D. H. HILL, C.S.A., ON EXEMPTS, WITH PARTICULAR REFERENCE TO MILITIA OFFICERS AND MILITIAMEN, 24 APRIL 1863

How much better is it...to deserve the thanks of the country by your courage and patience, than to skulk at home as the cowardly exempts do. Some of these poor dogs have hired substitutes, as though money could pay the service every man owes his country. Others claim to own twenty negroes, and with justice might claim to be masters of an infinite amount of cowardice. Others are stuffy squires—bless their dignified souls. Others are warlike militia officers, and their regiments cannot dispense with such models of military skill and valor. And such noble regiments they have. Three field officers, four staff officers, ten captains, thirty lieutenants, and one private with a misery in his bowels. Some are pill and syringe gentlemen, and have done their share of killing at home. Some are kindly making shoes for the army, and generously giving them to the poor soldiers, only asking two months' pay. Some are too sweet and delicate for anything but fancy duty; the sight of blood is unpleasant and the roar of cannon shocks their sensibilities. When our independence is won, the most trifling soldier in the ranks will be more respected, as he is now more respectable, than an army of these skulking exempts. (From OR, *ser. 1, vol. 51, pt. 2, p. 694)*

THE GEORGIA MILITIA NEAR THE CHATTAHOOCHEE, JULY 1864

On the 3d day of July [1864] we fought General Schofield's Corps nearly all day, fighting and falling back (as they were pushing down a road leading to Sand Town, a crossing on the Chattahoochee River), passing through a line of breastworks on the crest of a ridge crossing the road at right angles, erected and occupied by the Georgia Militia, about the middle of the afternoon. As we passed into the breastworks one of our men was killed by a long-range ball. The militia had never been under fire and had never seen a man killed before. We were instructed to form a line in their rear and rest, and to support them if the enemy should come; but beyond throwing a few shells over the works and skirmishing at long range, we had no farther trouble with the enemy that afternoon. Our men were very much amused at the sayings and doings of the *militia at this time, but subsequently the Georgia militia were commanded by General G. W. Smith, an experienced officer, and after this day they acted very gallantly in battle. (*From S. H. Barron, *The Lone Star Defenders: A Chronicle of the Third Texas Cavalry, Ross' Brigade* [New York: The Neale Publishing Company, 1908] 197)

A GLIMPSE OF GENERAL TOOMBS AND THE GEORGIA MILITIA DURING THE SIEGE OF ATLANTA, 1864

[4 August 1864] Yesterday I saw an aged man of corpulent dimensions riding behind the lines and telling the Georgia troops to "stand by the artillerists and you will whip the Yankees like the devil." His remarks "took" so promptly that an involuntary cheer was raised, and I walked near the individual to get a close view of him. It proved to be Hon. Robert Toombs, of Georgia, who in better times had figured largely on the political stage in the capital at Washington, and who had a wide reputation as a debater and statesman. He is no longer known as a Senator but now goes by the title of General of Militia. It was to the Georgia militia that he was addressing himself....

[6 August 1864] There was a brisk fire on the left of our lines, and Sherman is working as usual to avoid attacking our fortifications. Heavy rain fell this evening while the raw militia were in the street preparing to go into the trenches on picket for the first time. They appear ready to do their duty as well as the best fighting they know how. It is laughable, however, to see their awkward motions and blunders at the simple military evolutions. But in two months they will prove good soldiers. (From the diary of Thomas J. Key, Calvert's Battery, Hotchkiss's Battalion, C.S.A., as printed in Wirt Armistead Cate, ed., *Two Soldiers* [Chapel Hill: University of North Carolina Press, 1938] 108, 110)

SAM WATKINS'S OBSERVATIONS ON THE GEORGIA MILITIA DURING THE ATLANTA CAMPAIGN

"Old Joe Brown's Pets.

By way of grim jest, and a fitting burlesque to tragic scenes, or, rather, to the thing called 'glorious war,' old Joe Brown, then governor of Georgia, sent in his militia. It was the richest picture of an army I ever saw. It beat Forepaugh's double-ringed circus. Every one was dressed in citizen's clothes, and the very best they had at the time. A few had double-barreled shot-guns, but the majority had umbrellas and walking sticks, and nearly every one had on a

APPENDIX 2: THE "MELISH"

duster, a flat-bosomed 'biled' shirt, and a plug hat; and, to make the thing even more ridiculous, the dwarf and the giant were marching side by side; the knock-kneed by the side of the bow-legged; the driven-in by the side of the drawn-out; the pale and sallow dyspeptic, who looked like Alex. Stephens, and who seemed to have just been taken out of a chimney that smoked very badly, and whose diet was goobers and sweet potatoes, was placed beside the three-hundred-pounder, who was dressed up to kill, and whose looks seemed to say, 'I've got a substitute in the army, and twenty negroes at home besides—h-a-a-m, h-a-a-m.' Now, that is the sort of army that old Joe Brown had when he seceded from the Southern Confederacy, declaring that each state was a separate sovereign government of itself; and, as old Joe Brown was an original seces-sionist, he wanted to exemplify the grand principles of secession, that had been advocated by Patrick Henry, John Randolph, of Roanoke, and John C. Calhoun, in all of whom he was a firm believer. I will say, however, in all due deference to the Georgia militia and old Joe Brown's Pets, that there was many a gallant and noble fellow among them. I remember on one occasion that I was detailed to report to a captain of the Fourth Tennessee Regiment.... He was a small-sized man, with a large, long set of black whiskers. He was the captain, and I the corporal of the detail. We were ordered to take a company of the Georgia militia on a scout. We went away around to our extreme right wing, passing through Terry's Millpond, and over the old battlefield of the 22nd, and past the place where General Walker fell.... We passed on, and as soon as we came in sight of the old line of Yankee breastworks, an unexpected volley of minnie balls was fired into our ranks, killing this captain of the Fourth Tennessee Regiment and killing and wounding seven or eight of the Georgia militia. I hallooed to lay down, as soon as possible, and a perfect whizz of minnie balls passed over, when I immediately gave the command of attention, forward, charge and capture that squad. That Georgia militia, every man of them, charged forward, and in a few moments we ran into a small squad of Yankees, and captured the whole 'lay out.' We then carried back to camp the dead captain and the killed and wounded militia. I had seen a great many men killed and wounded, but some how or other these dead and wounded men, of that day, made a more serious impression on my mind than in any pre-vious or subsequent battles. They were buried with all the honors of war, and I never will forget the incidents and scenes of this day as long as I live. (From Sam R. Watkins, *"Co. Aytch," Maury Grays, First Tennessee Regiment; or, A Side Show of the Big Show,* 2d ed. [Chattanooga: Times Printing Company, 1900] 175-76.)

THE MILITIA'S WOUNDED AFTER GRISWOLDVILLE, NOVEMBER 1864

26 NOVEMBER 1864, C.S.A. HOSPITAL, COLUMBUS, GEORGIA]

There has been quite a battle near Macon, and we have had wounded from it; but I have not seen them. They are militia.

I hear the men telling a good many jokes on them. One poor boy, when he came to the hospital, said that the battle was the most terrible *of the war. It was quite a severe fight. The enemy set a trap, and the unsophisticated militia were caught in it. I believe there were at least one hundred killed and many wounded, and I am told they were nearly all old men. The* veterans *whom I have heard speak of the fight say that old soldiers never would have rushed in as the militia did.*

'Joe Brown's Pets' have done much better than any one expected; they have fought well when they have had it to do. (From Kate Cumming, Kate: The Journal of a Confederate Nurse, *ed. Richard Barksdale Harwell [Baton Rouge: Louisiana State University Press, 1959] 241.)*

NOTES TO THE INTRODUCTION AND ANNOTATIONS, IN SEQUENCE

B. R. McElderry, Jr., introduction to A. B. Longstreet's *Georgia Scenes* (New York: Sagamore Press, 1957) viii; John K. Mahon, *History of the Militia and the National Guard* (New York: The Macmillan Company, 1983) 9; C. V. Wedgwood, *The King's War* (New York: The Macmillan Company, 1959) 80; Thomas Hardy, *The Trumpet-Major* (New York: Oxford University Press, 1991) 353-54 n.4; Mahon, *History of the Militia and the National Guard*, 11; Walter Millis, *Arms and Men* (New Brunswick NJ: Rutgers University Press, 1981) 47; Russell F. Weigley, *History of the United States Army* (New York: The Macmillan Company, 1967) 86-88, 93-94, 109; Carlton B. Smith, "The American Search for a 'Harmless Army,'" *Annual Collection of Essays in History* 10 (1964-1965): 29-43; John Donald Wade, *Augustus Baldwin Longstreet* (Athens: University of Georgia Press, 1969) 178-80; Kenneth S. Lynn, *Mark Twain and Southwestern Humor* (Boston: Little, Brown, and Company, 1959) 86; *Augusta Chronicle & Sentinel*, 31 July 1864; *Macon Telegraph* (GA), 5 and 16 August 1864; *Atlanta Daily Intelligencer*, 1 October 1864; Wade, *Augustus Baldwin Longstreet*, 344-45 (Longstreet as Chaplain, Georgia Militia); Hardy, *Trumpet-Major*, 353-54 n.4; Henry Prentice Miller, "The Background and Significance of Major Jones's Courtship," *Georgia Historical Quarterly* 30 (1946): 268 n.7; Bert Hitchcock, *Richard Malcolm Johnston* (Boston: Twayne Publishers, 1978) 13-14, 45; David B. Parker, *Alias Bill Arp* (Athens: University of Georgia Press, 1991) 51; *Milledgeville Southern Recorder*, 10 March 1863 ("An Interesting Dialogue," a newspaper appearance of what was later printed as "The Militia Officers Reduced to Ranks, and Ordered to Savannah" in *Bill Arp, So Called*).

The Attack on Autossee An early heroic image of the Georgia Militia from the Creek War of the early 1800s. (Hargrett Rare Book and Manuscript Library, University of Georgia Libraries)

Muster of the common militia. A more customary caricature of a muster of the common militia (Engraving by "Porte Crayon" for "Old Time Militia Musters," *Harper's New Monthly Magazine*, July 1878)

APPENDIX 3
"GOOBER PEAS"

Although "Goober Peas" was sung during the Civil War, there is no evidence that it was published before 1866, when a version was brought out by A. E. Blackmar of New Orleans. The song apparently derived from a "spontaneous camp melody." As a cheerful lampoon of the Georgia Militia, "Goober Peas" has proved incredibly long-lived.

The sheet music attributes the words and music to humorous pseudonyms: A. Pindar, Esq., and P. Nutt, Esq, repsectively. Colloquially in the South, pindars, peanuts, and goobers all referred to the same popular ground nut, with pindar (or pinda) and goober having been borrowed from the Gullah language of the Georgia and South Carolina coast. (Richard Barksdale Harwell, *Songs of the Confederacy* [New York: Broadcast Music, Inc., 1951] 100-101)

Sheet Music

(Hargrett Rare Book and Manuscript Library, University of Georgia Libraries):

GOOBER PEAS:

WORDS
BY
A. PINDAR, Esq.

MUSIC
BY
P. NUTT, Esq.

NEW ORLEANS:

Published by A. E. BLACKMAR, 167 Canal Street.

Entered according to Act of Congress, A.D. 1866, by A. E. Blackmar, in the Clerk's Office of the District Court of the Eastern District of La.

GOOBER PEAS.

Words by A. PINDAR, Esq.

Music by P. NUTT, Esq.

1. Sit-ting by the road-side on a sum-mer day, Chat-ting with my mess-mates
2. When a horse-man pass-es, the soldiers have a rule, To cry out at their loud-est

pass-ing time a - way, Ly-ing in the shadow un-der-neath the trees.
"Mis-ter here's your mule," But an-oth-er pleasure en-chant-ing-er than these, Is

Good-ness how de - li - cious, eating goober peas!
wear ing out your Grinders. eating goober peas!

Peas! Peas! Peas! Peas!

Chorus.

eat - ing goo - ber peas! Goodness how de - li - cious, eating goober peas!

End with Prelude

3.

Just before the battle the General hears a row,
He says "the Yanks are coming, I hear their rifles now,
He turns around in wonder, and what do you think he sees
The Georgia Militia, eating goober peas!

Chorus.

4.

I think my song has lasted almost long enough,
The subject's interesting, but rhymes are mighty rough,
I wish this war was over when free from rags and fleas,
We'd kiss our wives and sweethearts and gobble goober peas!

Chorus.

APPENDIX 4
ROSTER OF THE GEORGIA MILITIA [233]

The following is a roster of troops serving with the Georgia Militia from the time of the reorganization under Major General Gustavus W. Smith on 1 June 1864 until released from duty and furloughed home by Governor Joseph E. Brown on 24 February 1865.

1ST DIVISION—GEORGIA MILITIA

Major General Gustavus W. Smith
Brigadier General Robert Toombs, Inspector General
Colonel Thomas Hardeman, Adjutant General
Major William Anderson, Aide–de–camp
Captain Elijah Hawkins, Aide–de–camp
Captain L. T. Toby, Assistant Adjutant General
Colonel Joseph Cleghorn, Chief of Artillery
Dr. Thomas Raines, Medical Director
Dr. William Holt, Staff Surgeon
Colonel Bushrod W. Frobel, C.S.A., Chief Engineer

1st Brigade
Brigader General Reuben W. Carswell
Colonel James Willis

1st Regiment
Colonel Edward H. Pottle
Lieutenant Colonel T. A. Walton
R. F. Robinson, A.A.G.

Company A—Catoosa & Wilkes Counties
Captain T. R. Willis
Private A. J. Alexander
Private W. P. Andrews
Private J. H. Arnett
Private W. I. Austin
Private Martin Ball

Private William D. Binns
Private W. F. Blackstock
Private Bailey Bone
Private Benjamin F. Barksdale
Private R. A. Bedingfield
Private Freeman Brewer
Private Benjamin Bryant
Private George C. Cosby
Private David A. Danner
Private David L. Dinesmore
Private John Etris
Private James B. Gerald
Private William Goff
Private L. C. Green
Private John L. Haines
Private Isaac S. Hendrix
Private William R. Hester
Private James A. Hill
Private J. H. Holland
Private John T. Huguley
Private A. T. Holliday [234]
Private Herman B. Ivey
Private James Ivey
Private Ezra Jacobs
Private James Johnson
Private James M. Jolley
Private John B. Jones
Private W. S. Lane
Private William Lansdell
Private Patrick Henry Mansfield
Private Jack Martin
Private Owen Martin
Private Brian McGuire

Private Joel W. Moore
Private William W. Moore
Private R. J. Morrison
Private Thomas O. O'Keefe (Wounded in back at Honey Hill)
Private W. J. Owens
Private John L. Pate
Private Alexander A. Perkins
Private Edward Perkins
Private James A. Perry
Private William Davis Pittard
Private F. H. Powell
Private R. C. Sale
Private Green Franklin Smallwood
Private J. W. Smith (Wounded left shoulder at Honey Hill)
Private Thomas E. Smith
Private W. R. Smith
Private William Smith
Private James N. Spriggs
Private W. P. Thompson
Private Benjamin Thurmond
Private James R. Underwood
Private John H. Walton
Private Simeon A. Ware
Private H. J. Wolfe (Wounded at Honey Hill)

Company B—Columbia, Washington, & Paulding Counties
Captain William L. Benton
2d Lieutenant W. M. Willingham
2d Lieutenant Edward Jones
Sergeant Major H. C. Weaver
Private S. F. Bagwell
Private James H. Bawyer
Private William Butler
Private G. W. Brayer
Private Asa Brown
Private Turner L. Brown
Private Thomas J. Cliatt
Private John P. Fair
Private Simeon Farmer
Private Richard Foster (Wounded in back at Honey Hill)

Private Thomas J. Fulton
Private Charles Gann
Private Thomas M. Garrett
Private Stith E. G. Hardaway
Private Thomas Hardman
Private Jeptha Hatcher
Private William J. Hayes
Private Albert Hewell
Private George B. Hunnicutt
Private Thomas J. Hutchinson
Private J. S. Jacks
Private Edward W. Jones
Private Charles M. King
Private David Land
Private William G. Langston
Private George E. Larkin
Private Y. M. McAdams
Private John McDuffie
Private G. W. McMichen
Private G. W. Martin (Wounded in breast at Honey Hill)
Private Theodosius E. Massengale
Private William D. Mattox
Private A. S. Merritt
Private Allen M. Morgan
Private John C. Mosley
Private Asa Moss
Private William B. Neal
Private John Newton
Private John New
Private Joseph T. Newman
Private Thomas J. Ogle
Private J. F. Osborn
Private William C. Pearson
Private George L. Reville
Private James V. Reese
Private Samuel Wilson Ruddock
Private J. M. Sikes
Private Hugh Smith
Private Jesse Thurmond
Private David Vaughn
Private William B. Washington
Private Richard Ward
Private Peter Wright (Wounded left thigh at Honey Hill)

Company C—Effingham & Wilkes Counties

Captain J. H. Walton
Private Willis Powell Anderson
Private James A. Anderson
Private W. T. Anderson
Private William Andrews
Private Thomas J. Bowers
Private Z. T. Bryant
Private S. P. Callaway
Private J. J. Camp
Private Coleman C. Cochran
Private T. L. Cofer
Private C. P. Dalton
Private Cecil Day
Private James M. Defoor
Private Wiley C. De Nard
Private W. L. Dunaway
Private Z. T. Dunaway
Private W. L. Eckles
Private Bryan Fanning
Private Webster Fanning
Private G. T. Fife
Private Thomas E. Fortson
Private W. R. Gillis
Private John W. Harper
Private William A. Harris
Private William H. Heard
Private William House
Private M. L. House
Private R. W. Hinton
Private James J. Johnson
Private J. T. Jones
Private John T. Lindsey
Private James C. Martin
Private Elijah J. Norman (Wounded right thigh at Honey Hill)
Private William Reynolds
Private George W. Sherrer
Private Terry P. Sherrer
Private John D. Shumate
Private W. M. Sims
Private William L. Standard
Private William M. Talley
Private Gideon A. Turner

Private J. T. Thurmond
Private James B. Thurmond
Private William R. Willis

Company D—Lumpkin & Talliaferro Counties

Captain William Henry Hausman
Private Simeon Abee
Private Franklin Acree (Killed in trenches of east Atlanta, 20 July 1864)
Private Edward Bailey
Private John Barnes
Private Elijah Blackman
Private Isaac Brown
Private William S. Brown
Private John Collins
Private Garland Cosby
Private Jesse Darden
Private David Ennis
Private Hamlin Fogarty
Private George T. Hatfield
Private Singleton Henry
Private William R. Hutchinson
Private Benjamin F. King
Private Robert Lott
Private John W. Newsome
Private Wiley Phillips
Private Ben Pearce
Private William H. Poss
Private Thomas Rhodes
Private W. B. Roebuck
Private William Sansdell
Private John Swan
Private Robert Taylor
Private J. G. Thomas
Private J. W. Wall
Private J. A. Walton
Private James M. Watts
Private J. H. Wilkins

Company E—Greene, Miller, Warren, & Meriwether Counties

Captain Wiley W. Swain
Ensign M. Fitzgerald
Private James Allen

Private John L. Burkhalter
Private E. L. Cawthon
Private John N. Chapman
Private Henry Cook
Private Allen Davis
Private Phillip Gaddy
Private George W. Granada
Private Henry Garner
Private Obediah Godwin
Private Newton Gunn
Private W. R. Haney
Private Mark W. Hardaway
Private S. E. G. Hardaway
Private James Humphries
Private Quintilus Kennedy
Private Walker Knight
Private O. R. Lasetor
Private Robert G. Maddox
Private Andrew M. McDaniel
Private Daniel McKinney
Private William G. McLain
Private James W. Mathews
Private Robert Montgomery
Private Solomon Norris
Private Sterling T. Roberts
Private James Scruggs
Private W. W. Swain
Private Samuel Tovel
Private A. H. Winter
Private Henry Wynn

Company F—Franklin County
Captain J. H. Payne
1st Lieutenant Thomas Skelton
2d Lieutenant Thomas Davis
3rd Lieutenant Thomas Higgins
2d Lieutenant John Coswell (Wounded at
    Honey Hill)
1st Sergeant J. H. Chappslear
2d Sergeant J. W. Williams
3rd Sergeant E. C. Vandiver
4th Sergeant J. W. Crump
Private William Alexander
Private James W. Asbury
Private George Atkinson

Private Jeptha Atkinson
Private E. P. Ayers
Private Buford Bird
Private Weaver Barrett
Private Jack Beadman
Private Newton Bellamy
Private S. Bellamy
Private L. D. Bolding
Private J. W. Bond
Private Jack Burgess
Private George Cartledge
Private T. Cawthorn
Private William Cawthorn
Private William Champion
Private Thomas D. Chapman
Private John Crenshaw
Private David Cromer
Private G. B. Cromer
Private J. P. Cromer
Private J. N. Chapman
Private Stephen Crawford
Private Oliver P. Darby
Private J. E. Darden
Private Allen P. Davis
Private E. S. Davis
Private J. O. Dean
Private Z. T. Dean
Private William M. Denton
Private William Lee Dobson
Private M. H. Duncan
Private Joseph Davidson
Private Allan Davis
Private T. R. Echols
Private Wiley C. Elam
Private A. G. Evans
Private Jack Edwards
Private Jack Elrod
Private H. W. Fulbright
Private Morgan Guess
Private Posey Guess
Private John Harman
Private Roderic Harper
Private Thomas S. Hutchinson
Private John Thomas Henning
Private John Henning

Private Robert Hunnicutt
Private William Kesley
Private _____ Knox
Private Joe Henry Lankford
Private Joseph Lankford
Private S. Ledbetter
Private J. M. Little
Private Thomas Little
Private Bolen F. Lunceford
Private David H. Lunceford
Private B. J. McCain
Private J. B. McMurray
Private William T. Moody
Private F. Nalley
Private William Neese
Private W. D. Ogletree
Private John Osborn
Private W. Owen
Private John Phillips
Private W. W. Prather
Private Jack Prather
Private Morrison Ramsey
Private William C. Rhodes
Private Jack Scott
Private A. J. Scott
Private Chap Sewell
Private David Sewell
Private L. D. Sewell
Private Russ Sewell
Private T. Sewell
Private J. R. Skelton
Private E. P. Smith
Private J. R. Smith
Private T. K. Smith
Private Pinckney Smith
Private William Smith
Private W. Stephens
Private Welcome Stone
Private Henry T. Stovall
Private J. Striblong
Private W. M. Sullins
Private Jesse Taylor
Private Capel Towns
Private B. P. Vandiver
Private David Vaughn

Private T. Vaughn
Private Ed Verner
Private James Whitlow
Private A. J. Witt
Private John Witt
Private Major Witt
Private Thomas Wilkinson
Private J. W. Williams
Private Robert Wright
Private Robert Wyly

**Company G—Greene, White & Pike
Counties**
Captain Littleton Stephens
Lieutenant E. A. Burgess (Wounded right
  leg at Honey Hill)
Lieutenant B. S. Wright
Private George P. Ashmore
Private William E. Bennett
Private James Blackburn
Private James M. Blair
Private Jasper C. Brown
Private J. L. Clarke
Private Ephram Collins
Private Greenberry Dodd
Private J. W. Dodd
Private John Gay
Private James A. Hardy
Private Benjamin Head
Private John H. Holland
Private Wiley T. Jones
Private John P. Kenney
Private James A. King
Private John P. Kinney
Private William W. Kemp
Private Mountain Kendrick
Private E. S. Lynch
Private C. C. Oliver
Private William Mitchell Patton
Private James Phillips
Private Andrew J. Williams
Private Z. S. Willingham

**Company H—Gilmer, Chatham, &
  Lumpkin Counties**
Captain James Bryan
1st Sergeant Lesse Tunnell
Private James Bennett
Private B. F. Ellington
Private F. H. Ellington
Private Perry Grogan
Private William Grogan
Private John Hunter
Private Wesley H. Hutchinson
Private Mike McKinney
Private William G. McWilliams
Private William Moore
Private J. H. Neely
Private Charles C. Norton
Private Nicholas Sorrow
Private John Ward
Private W. G. Williams

**Company I—Fayette, Warren, &
  Whitfield Counties**
Captain Wiley W. Swain
Private W. E. Anderson
Private Jasper J. Bales
Private James W. Bone
Private John A. Bradley
Private James Buchanon (Wounded in
  trenches of Atlanta, 20 August 1864)
Private Thomas Buchanon
Private J. L. Burkhalter
Private J. W. Cash
Private Rufus H. Cleghorn
Private J. S. Cole
Private B. T. Crenshaw
Private John Deaton
Private John E. Dye
Private James S. Elliott
Private James R. English
Private W. E. English
Private G. W. Farr
Private S. H. Fowler
Private George Grande
Private H. L. Hamilton
Private John Hitchcock

Private Russell Johnson
Private James Jones
Private Stephen Kinsey
Private A. A. Langford
Private John W. Lay
Private Silas Mayes
Private James A. McGibony
Private T. J. Murphy
Private Robert A. Offutt
Private John Parrott
Private Thomas F. Persons
Private J. M. Phillips
Private W. B. Pool
Private Benjamin F. Reynolds
Private John P. Sturdivant
Private Lemon Schell
Private J. K. P. Smallwood (Died 10
  September 1864 of unknown cause)
Private N. D. Twilley
Private M. S. Weaver
Private George Wheeler

**Company K—Lincoln & Richmond
  Counties**
Captain Daniel N. Gibson
1st Lieutenant William Landrum
3rd Lieutenant R. S. Wright
Corporal Robert Davy (Wounded right
  shoulder at Honey Hill)
Private A. J. Bentley
Private Joseph D. Byrd (Wounded both feet
  at Honey Hill)
Private E. W. Brown
Private John E. Benton
Private George W. Booker
Private R. A. Blanchard
Private J. M. Cartledge
Private Thomas Cobb
Private W. R. Cunningham
Private Zack B. Dallis
Private Wiley Denard
Private George Dunaway
Private Isaac Dunaway
Private Thomas J. Graves
Private J. W. Greerson

Private William Hagan
Private Anthony Taylor Harmon
Private James W. Hawes
Private William Henderson (Died 16
    September 1864 of unknown cause)
Private William B. Hensley
Private Hilliard G. Helton
Private William Hogan
Private C. F. Holcomb
Private M. Ivey
Private John B. Kemp
Private Marion L. Kinney
Private Carter Langford
Private George V. Lowery
Private A. L. Murry
Private John M. Newton
Private John McCracken
Private J. C. Moncrief
Private Eugene Parks
Private L. G. Parks
Private W. E. Parks
Private Lett Reeves
Private Joseph Roney
Private Sam Smith
Private William Smith
Private F. A. Thompkins
Private Felix Thurmond
Private Augustus Verdery
Private William Henry Warr

2d Regiment
Colonel James Stapleton

Company A—Forsyth County
Captain Randolph Stanley
Captain James Carroll
Private Stephen Barrs
Private W. T. Boggs
Private George W. Boozer
Private John A. Bradwell
Private Isaac M. Brownlow
Private George G. Cartledge
Private William Cooper
Private John S. Drew
Private James A. Eberhart

Private R. J. Ellison
Private Thomas Giles
Private W. Grant
Private George W. Gresham
Private W. R. Hubbard
Private Edward Kuykendall
Private Oliver McGinnis
Private Daniel P. Major
Private H. G. Morris
Private W. T. Nix
Private J. W. Spivey
Private James A. Thomas
Private James B. Thompson
Private Isaac Toole

Company B—Terrell County
Captain B. F.Saunders
Lieutenant James L. Fulcher (Wounded in
    head at Honey Hill)
Private Walter Beeks
Private William Davis
Private Joseph Woodward

**Company C—Johnson & Paulding
    Counties**
Captain James C. Suell
Private J. M. Anderson
Private Dirrell Braswell
Private L. H. Cook
Private David Z. Douglas
Private G. W. Earwood
Private C. N. Gray
Private J. M. Hightower
Private John Jenkins
Private C. B. McClung
Private James Mathews
Private William A. Meeks
Private Reuben Perdue
Private C. J. Roberts
Private J. A. Rowland
Private William C. Smith
Private James C. Snell
Private Alexander Sumner
Private John Toler
Private W. H. Toler

Private Dan Williams
Private David Williams
Private L. C. Woodward

Company D—Bulloch, Talbot, Thomas, Walton, & Upson Counties
Captain R. L. Worrill
Private Dirrell Braswell
Private L. H. Cook
Private David Z. Douglas
Private John Dye
Private G. W. Earwood
Private C. N. Gray
Private J. M. Hightower
Private C. B. McClung
Private James Mathews
Private William A. Meeks
Private Reuben Perdue
Private C. J. Roberts
Private J. R. Rollins
Private W. C. Smith
Private James C. Snell
Private John Toler
Private David Williams

Company E—Burke & Harris Counties
Captain J. C. Snell
Captain William T. Morgan
1st Lieutenant L. W. Cook
2d Lieutenant P. G. Smith (Wounded Battle of Atlanta, 22 July 1864)
3rd Lieutenant D. C. Smith
1st Sergeant L. J. Snell
2d Sergeant Charles Wheeler
3rd Sergeant Shaade Williams
1st Corporal Persy Crofton
2d Corporal P. S. Winton
3rd Corporal S. Meeks
Private J. Anderson
Private John T. Bass
Private A. D. Belcher
Private Wesley J. Brown
Private James Capland
Private P. C. Capland
Private James M. Crews

Private Dan Dailey
Private John Dailey
Private H. Y. Douglas
Private Henry Fountain
Private Dennis T. Glisson
Private James M. Godbee
Private John G. Heath
Private William Hightower (Killed at Battle of Atlanta, 22 July 1864)
Private R. W. Hillis
Private Benjamin Lee
Private Thomas W. Lott
Private Nile Low
Private Jacob D. Moon
Private John Parker
Private Martin Raines
Private George W. Reynolds
Private J. Smith
Private Jacob T. Snell
Private Isom Stevens
Private A. A. Sumner
Private R. C, Sumner
Private Noah Tison, Sr.
Private John Toler
Private Thomas A. Wallace
Private H. Williams

Company F—Burke, Newton, & Wilkinson Counties
Captain Malachi Richardson
Captain A. A. Beall
Private John Thomas Bivins
Private Zachariah W. Collins (Wounded in trenches of Atlanta, 8 August 1864)
Private Seaborn J. Fountain
Private Green H. Hatfield
Private William Hatfield
Private James R. Hicks
Private Charles G. Johnson
Private Brittain B. Jordan
Private Orin D. Lassiter
Private David Lesley
Private James M. McCurdy
Private Henry Mercer
Private John P. Nichols

Private W. P. Wheeler
Private Isaac Withers

Company G—Jefferson & Newton Counties
Captain Notley Maddox
Corporal John Barrow (Wounded in face at Honey Hill)
Private James Adkins
Private Bryant Beasley
Private G. M. Beddingfield
Private Robert Cameron
Private F. L. Covena
Private Isaac Eubanks
Private John M. Goodowns
Private John Hancock
Private Bennett Herrington
Private J. C. Hudson
Private Vince Irby
Private Reuben A. Jones
Private John Lynch
Private James G. Maddox
Private T. H. Marshall
Private Thomas M. Moseley
Private Moses E. Mead (Wounded in face at Honey Hill)
Private J. Vining (Wounded right arm at Honey Hill)
Private William L. Peek
Private R. J. Pope
Private Martin V. Quinie
Private T. F. Ridenhour
Private H. W. Rucker
Private John Russell
Private M. M. Scruggs
Private J. E. Smith
Private John L. Thompkins
Private Joe Tompkins
Private Jasper Vining
Private Thomas J. Watt

Company H—Emanuel & Warren Counties
Captain Alfred Coleman
1st Lieutenant E. J. Coleman
1st Sergeant W. R. King
1st Sergeant John W. McArthur (Wounded in side at Griswoldville)
Private L. M. Adams
Private Matthew B. Adams
Private Thomas B. Adams (Wounded in head at Griswoldville)
Private A. H. S. Anderson
Private W. B. Beacham
Private Math Bell
Private A. H. Birdsong
Private John Bragg
Private Zeb Camp
Private M. E. Chapman
Private E. J. Coleman
Private J. A. Coleman
Private Thornton Coleman
Private Joseph E Davis
Private A. T. Durden
Private Jerry Dixon
Private Zack Douglas
Private Lott Durden
Private Jesse J. Duggan
Private James H. Edwards
Private J. J. Evans
Private John Flynn
Private Benjamin F. Harris
Private Jonathan Hart
Private Robert Hood
Private William D.Hooks
Private W. R. Kemp
Private Thomas Kent
Private Joseph H. Kitchen
Private George Martin
Private Robert F. McWilliams
Private Coleman Mobley
Private John J. Munford
Private B. W. Odom
Private Wilson Pettis
Private Martin Radford

Private Allen Roundtree (Wounded left
shoulder at Honey Hill)
Private J. W. Spinks
Private James Stinson
Private J. G. Thompson
Private William Underwood
Private Thomas M. Waldrop

**Company I—Clayton, Carroll, Glascock,
& Fulton Counties**
Captain John Neal
1st Lieutenant Barthelamew C. Kitchens
2d Lieutenant John Coywell
2d Lieutenant David Aldred
1st Sergeant Gale Harris
Sergeant Charles Kitchens
Corporal James M. Braddy
Corporal William Lockhart
Private O. A. Bannister
Private George Barfield
Private Jacob Beckworth
Private Taylor Beckworth
Private David Blankinship
Private Linton Braddy
Private Thomas J. Braddy
Private Elias Branch
Private Benjamin F. Brown
Private Davis Buchanan
Private Turner Chalker
Private F. A. Chandler
Private Shadrack Cooper
Private Washington Cooper
Private _____ Culpepper (Killed in trenches
of Atlanta, 20 July 1864)
Private A. J. Chambers
Private D. C. Daniel
Private Lee R. Daniel
Private John Davis
Private James Dickens
Private George English
Private Joel English
Private Wilson Glover
Private Noah Grace
Private Benjamin Hadden
Private Elisha S. Hanes

Private Levi Harrell
Private Joda Harris
Private Joe Harris
Private Robert Henderson
Private D. H. Hendley
Private James Hewett
Private Frank Hopkins
Private Joseph E. Hopkins
Private W. R. Hunter
Private Jesse Hutchinson
Private V. A. Irby
Private Allen B. Johnson
Private James Johnson
Private John Kelly
Private B. M. Kitchens
Private William H. Lockhart
Private Henry May
Private Hezikiah C. McElhenney
Private Henderson Morgan
Private Augustus Neal
Private James Neal
Private John C. Nazworth
Private Arch E. Newsome
Private A. T. Newsome
Private Green Shelton
Private A. G. Simpson
Private Columbus Usry
Private James Usry
Private Thomas Wilcher
Private William Wilcher
Private John B. Williams
Private Madison Williams

3rd Regiment
Colonel Q. M. Hill
Colonel L. G. Johnston

Company A—Fulton & Glynn Counties
Captain Charles T. Bayless
Private Tillman L. Babb
Private W. H. H. Barnes
Private Charles Bayne
Private W. D. Berger
Private Thomas Bloodworth
Private Thomas M. Collinsworth

Private Samuel W. Davis
Private A. A. Fambrough
Private Thomas Finch
Private George W. Haines
Private Charles J. Hawkins
Private Elbert C. Joyner
Private C. P. Kitchens
Private W. B. Langford
Private Baldwin Ledlaw
Private J. T. McClendon
Private W. W. McCurry
Private William O'Briant
Private R. E. Odums
Private Allen Porterfield
Private Henry W. Roberson
Private Job Sosebee
Private David B. Thompson

Company B—Madison County
Captain Patton Griffith
Corporal Oliver Griffith (Killed at Honey Hill)
Private M. V. Bagwell
Private G. H. Bird
Private Zechariah Brookins
Private John Burroughs
Private R. B. Bynum
Private John W. Campbell
Private Robert Carithers
Private William D. Carrington
Private Isaac Chandler
Private James Cook
Private W. F. Croombs
Private Thomas W. Dean
Private J. W. Duffell
Private William T. Evans
Private M. D. Ghalston
Private J. C. Hairston
Private O. P. Hopkins
Private William S. Johnson
Private J. B. McDowell
Private Reuben T. McGinnis
Private George H. O'Kelley
Private M. J. Patton
Private John W. Porterfield

Private Joseph Pittman
Private James Porterfield
Private William L. Sharp
Private William W. Shipp
Private Bennett Simmons
Private C. M. Smith
Private G. J. Wynn

Company C—Hancock, Thomas, & Sumter Counties
Captain Benjamin Franklin Floyd
1st Lieutenant A. S. Butts
(Wounded left leg at Honey Hill)
Private Thomas Applewhite
Private Jesse Bosman
Private McDonald Boyer
Private James A. Brantley
Private William H. Brown
Private James Carter
Private Fabian Cone
Private R. Walter Davis (Wounded in groin at Honey Hill)
Private Sterling Evans
Private Abe Forman
Private John Grace
Private John Griffin
Private Major Griffin
Private John Gripher
Private D. A. Hix
Private William R. Humphrey
Private Henry W. Johnson
Private Thomas Mack
Private Joseph Mason
Private William McAuley
Private James McCrary
Private Clarke McCraw
Private Lovett McGuire (Wounded at Honey Hill)
Private Lorick Newton
Private Taylor Owens
Private James Page
Private Horace Parramore (Captured Columbus GA, 16 April 1865)
Private James Porter
Private Samuel Sherrod

Private Luther G. Smith
Private Tharpe Spence
Private Jesse Stone
Private Patrick Thomas (Wounded at Honey
   Hill and captured at Columbus GA, 16
   April 1865)
Private Sherrod Thompson
Private James A. Walker
Private A. M. Warren
Private Gus Young (Captured at Columbus
   GA, 16 April 1865)

Company D—Glynn, Washington,
   & Macon Counties
Captain J. B. Martin
Ordnance Sergeant W. H. Armstrong
(Wounded in left breast at Honey Hill)
Corporal Thomas A. Orr (Wounded at
   Honey Hill)
Private N. L. Bran
Private Henry Brock
Private Felix Augustus Dougherty
Private Thomas Gibbs
Private James Hughes
Private Thomas P. Loyd
Private R. A. McCallum
Private S. H. McCallum
Private. E. F. Orr (Wounded left knee at
   Honey Hill)
Private William D. Pittman
Private A. T. Powell
Private Z. T. Prescott
Private F. C. Rawlings
Private B. P. Sharpe
Private Wyley Stephens
Private W. A. Stone
Private John Taylor
Private Aliphon H. Trawick
Private J. P. Ward
Private J. P. Wood

Company E—Hancock & Upson
   Counties
Captain E. A. Spivey
Private Wesley Bass

Private G. F. Boatwright
Private Addison Brooks
Private J. Brown (Wounded right arm and
   shoulder at Honey Hill)
Private Green B. Burton
Private R. P. Bynum
Private John Culver
Private Seaborn B. Hutchings
Private Columbus A. Johnson
Private Samuel P. Johnson
Private John Knowles
Private John W. Ledbetter
Private Frank L. Little
Private W. E. Martin
Private J. W. Mathews
Private Andrew Jackson Morris
Private John T. Murphy
Private John Noble
Private S. E. Pearson
Private J. P. Reed
Private W. K. Smith
Private J. T. Snell
Private George P. Spears
Private LeRoy Turner
Private William N. Veal

Company F—Elbert & Washington
   Counties
Captain Albert L. Roughton
1st Lieutenant James F. Smith
2d Lieutenant Elijah Peacock
3rd Lieutenant William Fulgham
4th Lieutenant W. P. Smith
1st Sergeant Thomas R. Smith
2d Sergeant Matthew Fulgham
3rd Sergeant J. D. Williams
4th Sergeant C. T. Smith
5th Sergeant Josiah Jones
1st Corporal Zack Peacock
2d Corporal W. G. Bryan
3rd Corporal R. H. Wicks
4th Corporal A. M. Riddle
Private H. Achord
Private L. L. Adams
Private Littleton Adams

Private A. Atkins
Private J. T. Baks
Private C. G. Barnes
Private James Barron
Private A. J. Barwick
Private A. A. Beall
Private S. Blackburn
Private N. H. Bowen
Private J. M. Brantley
Private Jesse M. Brantley
Private E. D, Brown
Private B. F. Brown
Private William Bryant
Private W. L. Canty
Private F. H. Cato
Private J. B. F. Chappelar
Private Burwell Chester
Private W. S. Collins
Private J. Daniel
Private H. H. Davis
Private R. O. Echols
Private J. R. Elton
Private J. Eubanks
Private Ivy Fountain
Private J. M. Fulghum
Private W. W. Gaines
Private Anderson Griffin
Private A. Guin
Private J. C. Harrison
Private K. A. Harrison
Private William Hart
Private Bur Hartley
Private Kaif Hartley
Private A. Jackson
Private M. Johnson
William Johnson
Private John King
Private I. C. Lewis
Private Strozier Linceford
Private T. Lord
Private William Lozier
Private M. M. Mathis
Private W. E. Martin
Private H. M. Martin
Private William N. McPherson

Private N. A. Morgan
Private S. F. New
Private J. W. Newsom
Private N. J. Newsom
Private James Noles
Private W. B. Pool
Private Jesse Pounds
Private G. W. Prince
PrPrivate J. F. Rogers
Private Zachery Roughton
Private Ned Ryan (Wounded, no date indi-
  cated)
Private C. H. Shepperd
Private J. H. Shurling
Private William Sinquefield
Private E. W. Smith
Private Ed Smith
Private H. O. Smith
Private R. D. Smith
Private T. L. Smith
Private William T. Smith
Private W. A. Smith
Private W. R. Smith
Private Isaac Turner
Private Thomas Tanner
Private W. A. Taylor
Private S. S. Thomas
Private C. J. Trussell
Private Joseph Vincent
Private William Warthen
Private Bryant Watkins
Private Elbert West
Private J. R. Wicker
Private T. A. Wood
Private J. C. Yates
Private Robert Young
Private William Young

Company G—Elbert County
Captain Gus Bailey
Private Thomas McClure
Private W. C. Faulkner (Wounded left wrist
  at Honey Hill)
Private William E. Hammock
Private J. M. Harper

Private James Moon
Private William R. Parker
Private Jarriett E. Prather
Private B. S. Stamps
Private T. F. Willis

Company H—Elbert County
Captain Clark Mattox
1st Lieutenant T. J. Fortson (Wounded in head at Honey Hill)
2d Lieutenant R. E. Adams
Private John Adams
Private W. H. H. Adams
Private Thomas R. Alexander
Private Alfred P. Anderson
Private Stephen H. Black
Private Asa Candler Fortson
Private Horatio Goss
Private James C. Harper
Private E. B. Heard
Private James L. Heard
Private J. B. Jones
Private J. M. Jones
Private Miley A. Jones
Private Thomas Jones
Private William T. Kelley
Private Clark Mattox
Private David J. Maxwell
Private A. W. Mayfield
Private John L. Mize
Private J. J. Morrison
Private David M. Sanders
Private James H. Thompson
Private John Warren
Private Lafayette Wheless
Private J. C. Young

Company I—Elbert County
Captain W. H. Johnson
Private J. H. Alveston
Private William Brooks
Private Jesse T. Gainey
Private William A. Hooten
Private John C. Jenks
Private E. W. Johnson

Private H. W. Johnson
Private William G. McNair
Private Joel Thomas Olive
Private James Thomas Petty
Private William Spradley (Died 3 December 1864 of unknown causes)
Private John L. Winfrey

Company K—Oglethorpe & Upson Counties
Captain G. A. Cunningham
Private W. J. Bell (Wounded in back at Honey Hill)
Private William P. Broach
Private Milton Brown
Private Benage Crowley
Private W. J. Draper
Private Jacob Eberhardt
Private Frederick M. Gardner
Private Thomas H. Glenn
Private Thomas Graham
Private W. H. Graham
Private C. R. Hitchcock (Wounded in face and left shoulder at Honey Hill)
Private M. L. Hitchcock
Private Charles M. Huff
Private Mat G. Pass
Private C. H Thornton
Private Jasper M. Tiller
Private John W. Tiller
Private Washington I. Tinsley
Private Robert H. Turner
Private W. A. Turner
Private Charles M. Witcher

2d Brigade
Brigadier General Pleasant J. Philips
Colonel James N. Mann

4th Regiment
Colonel James N. Mann

Company A—Dawson, Lumpkin, Monroe, White, & Meriwether Counties

Captain Samuel Harben
1st Lieutenant W. E. F. Shelton
2d Lieutenant W. H. Findley
3rd Lieutenent W. H. Logan
4th Lieutenant A. M. Jackson
Lieutenant J. J. Findley—Aide–de–camp
1st Sergeant William Crisson
2d Sergeant C. P. Cragg
3rd Sergeant H. J. Hill
4th Sergeant Erby Cannoa
5th Sergeant John Quarles
1st Corporal M. T. Kenimer
2d Corporal Robert M. Barrett
3rd Corporal D. C. Freeman
4th Corporal Phillip Cantrell
Private James Barker
Private J. M. Beavers
Private Isaac Black
Private C. C. Blalock
Private C. G. Burt
Private John Byers
Private James Chambers
Private James Cooper
Private Elijah Cragg
Private William R. Crisson
Private J. M. Dean
Private Jacob Dick
Private Albert Edwards
Private Nathan Elder
Private J. J. Findley
Private Daniel L. Freeman
Private T. S. Gamblin
Private Tirey Harben
Private A. J. Hill
Private Herbert J. Hill
Private A. R. Jackson
Private W. B. Langford
Private Samuel Floyd Littlejohn
Private Richard P. Lumsden
Private J. C. Maxey
Private William A. Miller
Private George G. Morris

Private J. F. W. Osborn
Private John Palmour
Private L. D. Penny
Private George Roper
Private George Smith
Private C. M. Stovall
Private Thomas Stowers
Private M. H. Vandyke
Private E. G. Williams
Private J. F. Wood
Private David Woodall

Company B—Newton & Paulding Counties

Captain Wilson Davis
1st Lieutenant Henry T. Henry
2d Lieutenant A. K. Richardson
3rd Lieutenant George M. Cunningham
4th Lieutenant Lucius Middlebrooks
1st Sergeant Sam Pickens
2d Sergeant J. Robinson
3rd Sergeant McIntosh Bower
4th Sergeant Simeon Stallings
1st Corporal W. F. Gardner
2d Corporal D. A. Thompson
Private Sam Akin
Private S. C. Avery
Private Tom Avery
Private William Avery (Killed in Battle of Atlanta, 22 July 1864)
Private Richard Aycock
Private W. L, Bebee
Private Lewis H. Beck
Private Alexander Bohanan
Private Lemon Brown
Private Jasper Bryan
Private Samuel Chaffin
Private C. G. Chestnut
Private Samuel Chestnut
Private Rufus Christian (Discharged for overage, August 1864)
Private John Comer
Private John Conner
Private James Cook
(Discharged for overage, 1864)

Private William T. Cowan
Private Henry T. Gann
Private John Glass
Private William Glass
Private Avin Hailey (Discharged for overage,
    July 1864)
Private Henderson Harris
Private LeRoy Harris
Private Thomas R. Hawthorne
Private Thomas Hay
Private Thomas Hayden
Private F. M. Hays
Private Eli Franklin Hearn
Private F. M. Hodgens
Private John Horton
Private Jackson Howell
Private Isham Kelly
Private Addison Kennon
Private John C. King
Private J. H. Kinny (Captured 22 July at
    Battle of Atlanta)
Private W. F. Kirkpatrick
Benjamin Kitchens
Private William B. Lee
Private Joseph Lewis
Private W. H. Mabry
Private Enoch McCullough
Private Asa McDonald
Private Thomas Meriwether
Private W. S. Montgomery
Private Josiah C. Morgan
Private Ephriam Moss
Private Francis Moss
Private Frank Moss
Private James Nolen
Private John Norton
Private Anderson Owens
Private Mayfield Owens
Private Hilliard Parker
Private E. J. Piper
Private Smith Piper
Private James Rakestraw
Private John D. Reynolds
Private Henry R. Robinson
Private John Ross

Private James H. Sappington
Private Joseph Stockwell
Private S. N. Stallings
Private Henry Stanton
Private Devency Swann
Private D. A. Thompson
Private John Thompson
Private Rucker Tinsley
Private William Turnbull
Private Samuel Weldon
Private William Weldon
Private Harmon Wheeler
Private William Wright
Private Hamp Wylie
Private W. H. Wylie

**Company C—Fayette, Fulton, &
    Gwinnett Counties**
(Commander not recorded)
Private B. Adams
Private William P. Archer
Private William Brann
Private W. S. Brown
Private W. C. Davis
Private Thomas J. Edmonston
Private F. M. Hodges
Private Ransom Hutchins
Private Francis P. Jones
Private S. G. Jones
Private James W. Lynch
Private Enoch McCullough
Private Thomas C. Malone
Private William Malone
Private J. G. Morris
Private Benjamin F. Paxson
Private John D. Reynolds
Private T. J. Spurlin
Private Richard T. Thomas
Private T. P. Tiller
Private William Whatley (Wounded at
    Griswoldville)

Company D—Hall & Heard County

Captain R. F. Pitman
Private J. J. Batchlor
Private R, G, Baxter
Private Thomas S. Campbell
Private Nathaniel Delk
Private J. H. Edson
Private Jeremiah Hawkins
Private Joshua Jarrell
Private J. F. Long
Private Robert McClure
Private T. B. Montgomery
Private T. C. Moore
Private Hugh Partin
Private Isiah[ISAIAH?] Partin
Private E. D. Pittman
Private Noah Pittman
Private Rasmon Rogers
Private A. H. Talley
Private Thomas L. Watson

Company E—Gwinnett County

(Commander not recorded)
Private S. E. Bailey
Private John W. Bates
Private James M, Brawner
Private J. A. Brock
Private Christopher Coleman
Private William C. Evans
Private John J. Morton
Private Thomas J. Pilgrim
Private William M. Potts
Private G. R. Simmons
Private James Tidwell
Private Hugh C. Ward

Company F—Meriwether County

Captain Willis Goodwin
Captain J. W. Payne
Private Joe N. Ard
Private J. M. Blankinship
Private J. M. Brannan
Private William F. Burroughs (Wounded in head at Griswoldville)

Private James Credille (Wounded at Griswoldville)
Private Porter Fears (Wounded at Griswoldville)
Private Joseph Few (Wounded at Griswoldville)
Private James A. Gaddy
Private Willis Goodwin
Private James Gregory
Private Felix Pryor
Private James Sorrell
Private George Stovall (Wounded in neck at Griswoldville)
Private Seaborn Walker (Wounded in thigh at Griswoldville)
Private James W. Watkins
Private Anguish Weaver
Private W. A. White
Privtae Walter L. Zachry (Wounded in leg at Griswoldville)

Company G—Heard & Talbot Counties

Captain J. M. Lane
Private L. Z. Bradberry
Private Allen Cook
Private Marcus Craine
Private Jonathan Dial
Private James S. Gregory
Private William Hodges
Private Isaac Moore
Private George Reynie
Private James Reynie
Private David Thaxton
Private William White

Company H—Troup & Walton Counties

Captain Dock Owens
Captain Joseph J. Prather (Wounded at Griswoldville)
1st Lieutenant Thomas Gibbs
2d Lieutenant J. B. Abercrombie
3rd Lieutenant Johnson Verner
4th Lieutenant William Mitchell (Mortally wounded at Griswoldville)
1st Sergeant Thomas Colquitt

Private T. A. Abercrombie
Private William Adair
Private Barnett Adcock
Private Joseph Adcock
Private Simon Adcock
Private W. M. Adcock
Private Henry Baccus
Private J. H. Barfield
Private Fred Barrett
Private Albert Burton
Private Eldridge Burton
Private Horace Burton
Private Robert Carter
Private Mitchell Conner
Private W. M. Copeland
Private W. B. Crowell
Private Joshua J. Eckles
Private James Edmonds
Private James Garrett
Private Joseph Gibbs
Private William Greeson
Private Jesse Griffin
Private Jacob Hawk
Private Benjamin Higginbotham
Private Richard Hobbs
Private Willington Hughes
Private William H. Jones
Private Richard King
Private George Knox
Private Peter Knox
Private William A. Langford
Private James Long (Wounded at
    Griswoldville)
Private Joseph Long (Wounded at
    Griswoldville)
Private William Lunsford
Private George Malcom (Captured at
    Griswoldville)
Private James Malcom
Private John Malcom
Private Thomas Malcom
Private William Malcom
Private Alexander McIntosh
Private Elick McIntosh, Sr.
Private Elick McIntosh, Jr.

Private Anderson Michael
Private W. F. Mitchell (Died 11 January
    1865 of unknown causes)
Private Lemuel Mitchum
Private James Mobley
Private Ed Nolan
Private John Nunnally (Wounded at
    Griswoldville)
Private Dock Oats
Private Wright Perkins
Private Henry Peters
Private John M. Peters
Private Monroe Peters
Private W. H. Powell
Private Benjamin Preston
Private Longino Pulley
Private Adolphus Ross
Private Eugene Ross
Private Daniel Ruff
Private Russell Shepard
Private James Simmons
Private Walton D. Sims
Private Coleman Taylor
Private John R. Thompson
Private Jonathan Williams
Private Junius Williams (Wounded at
    Griswoldville)

Company I—Carroll County
(Commander not recorded)
Private William B. Crowell
Private Lewis Green
Private Lucius Harvey
Private James Hendricks
Private R. H. Hightower
Private M. L. Lacky
Private B. O. McDaniel
Private J. H. Mills
Private William Florence Moss
Private Sanders Williams
Private Hamp Young

5th Regiment

Colonel Henry H. Floyd
Lieutenant Colonel John Thomas Bowdoin
(Wounded in foot at Griswoldville)
Surgeon Thomas Gelzer
Lieutenant J. M. Bonner (Killed at
Griswoldville)
Sergeant Major William A. Gatewood
(Wounded in leg at Griswoldville)
Private William Hawkins (Wounded in hip
at Griswoldville)
Private H. Raldin (Wounded in neck at
Griswoldville)

Company A—McIntosh County

Captain J. P. A. DuPont
Sergeant W. C. Caldwell (Mortally wounded
ast Griswoldville)
Private G. G. Carthage
Private R. T. Chandler
Private Jonathan Hollifield
Private William H. Johnson
Private Spencer C. Kicklighter
Private J. P. Looney
Private W. Sawyer (Died 4 December 1864
from unknown causes)
Private W. W. Watson

Company B—Burke & Muscogee
Counties

Captain H. S. Parks
Private W. H. Baker
Private James Blackstock
Private George Brom
Private William Bryant
Private C. T. Burgess
Private T. C. Chandler
Private L. V. Forbes
Private J. M. Hancock
Private M. W. Kennedy
Private William G. Parks
Private William J. Tillman
Private A. A. Turk
Private F. H. Wright

Company C—Clay, Hart, & Muscogee
Counties

Captain D. G. Johnson
1st Lieutenant John Herndon
2d Lieutenant S. V. Brown
3rd Lieutenant J. W. Suit
4th Lieutenant J. B. Stevenson
1st Sergeant J. A. Barron
2d Sergeant John Teasley
3rd Sergeant M. H. Adams
4th Sergeant N. R. Bryant
5th Sergeant A. W. McCurry
Corporal J. W. Brown
2d Corporal J. B. Alford
3rd Corporal B. L. Hilliard
Private M. F. Adams
Private T. B. Adams
Private W. M. Alford
Private J. D. Bailey
Private C. H. Barron
Private A. J. Brown
Private Rucker Brown
Private S. C. Carlton
Private Richard Carnes
Private D. O. Chapman
Private E. Chapman
Private S. H. Cheek
Private W. J. Cole
Private J. M. Crump
Private William Davis
Private B. Dickerson
Private J. F. Duncan
Private M. A. Duncan, Sr.
Private M. A. Duncan, Jr.
Private W. E. Duncan
Private T. I. Durrett
Private E. B. N. Fleming
Private Peter L. Fleming
Private L. F. Frost
Private Jefferson Gaines
Private John Gaines
Private Wesley E. Gaines
Private W. I. Ginn
Private J. P. Gurley
Private J. B. Hall

Private John S. Herndon
Private G. C. Holland
Private P. Human
Private W. B. Jackson
Private I. M. Johnson
Private J. A. Johnson
Private J. F. Johnson
Private M. A. Johnson
Private R. A. Madden
Private S. M. Martin
Private A. J. McCullar
Private Isham Luther McCurry
Private J. A. McGarity
Private William McGarity
Private A. J. McMullan
Private J. P. McMullan
Private W. A. Mewborn
Private J. L. Mize
Private A. B. Moore
Private T. H. Murray
Private W. F. Patterson
Private Yancy Pickens
Private Thomas Prichett
Private J. E. Pruitt
Private Andrew Ray
Private Bynum Reed
Private Aaron Rice
Private Blackstone Richardson
Private S. W. Richardson
Private Martin Roberts
Private James Scott
Private Richard Shirley
Private W. J. Skelton
Private Asa Smith
Private John Snow
Private J. Stidman
Private J. W. Suit
Private R. G. Swearingen
Private J. A. Teasley
Private Benjamin Thornton
Private K. B. Thornton
Private G. P. Tyler
Private J. H. Tyner
Private James A. Vickery
Private T. E. Vickery

Private William Vickery
Private J. Weldon
Private N. G. W. White

Company E—Emanuel, Muscogee, Pulaski, & Jackson Counties
Captain Arch Pittman (Killed at Griswoldville)
Private Benjamin Adair
Private Washington Arnold
Private Hugh Atkins
Private E. P. Ayers
Private Milton Bailey
Private S. E. Bailey
Private M. P. Barnett
Private Hosea Bennett
Private J. F. Bowden
Private H. H. Brock
Private David Burger
Private John Chapman
Private Albert Cook
Private Calvin Cox
Private Frank David
Private Haden David
Private Jones Duke
Private Marshall Duke
Private A. N. Elrod
Private John P. English
Private William F. Frazier
Private Thomas Hardy
Private Perry Harrison
Private T. P. Harrison
Private J. H. Head
Private Cap Highfill
Private J. H. Highland
Private Mans Hinton
Private Carey Johnson
Private James Kea
Private A. Lemons
Private David LeSueur
Private T. A. Little
Private Mation Lott
Private Byrd Lyle
Private David Lyle
Private William Lyle

Private Joseph Marlow
Private John Martin (Killed near Griffin,
   August 1864)
Private John McCune
Private Stewart McElhannon
Private J. G. McLester
Private John J. Mitchell
Private Henry Moody
Private Alsa Moore
Private J. A. Moore
Private Robert Morris
Private William Murray
Private Thomas Nix
Private Sanuel Pressley Orr
Private Pompey Page
Private Sell Parks
Private Cobb Pittman
Private William Potts
Private J. W. Pruitt
Private J. H. C. Randolph
Private James E. Randolph
Private James Reynolds
Private Stephen Roberts
Private Blake Rogers
Private Francis Washington Segars
Private Jack Segars
Private Mark Sell
Private Sam Smith
Private T. J. Stapler
Private Adison Storey (Discharged 17 August
   1864 with malformed left foot)
Private C. T. Storey
Private J. A. Story
Private James Thompson
Private L. Thurmond
Private James Vandiver
Private George Walker
(Wounded at Griswoldville)
Private Press Walker
Private Lute Watkins
Private William White
Private Frank Wilbanks
Private Sanford Williamson
Private L. C. Wilson
Private W. W. Wofford

Private Abraham Yearwood

Company F—Dougherty, Lee, & Worth
   Counties
Captain William A. Harris
1st Lieutenant D. McClelland
2d Lieutenant Addison Harris
3rd Lieutenant Quarles Dickerson
1st Sergeant William Bauldey
1st Sergeant Thomas Phillyaw
Corporal Shade Adkinson
Corporal Frank Harris
Corporal J. H. T. Calhoun
Private William Ammons
Private Barney Bass
Private C. K. Chestnut
Private Robert Ford
Private William Ford
Private George Goulding
Private W. H. Harden
Private James Harris
Private Thomas Harris
Private William Henderson
Private M. C. Horn
Private William Johnson
Private George Lyons
Private William Mitchell
Private W. P. Neese
Private James H. Parrish
Private P. W. C. Spencer
Private John Spring
Private Gordon Sumner
Private William Tillman
Private Richard Townsend
Private Moses Tyson
Private Theophitus W. Tyson
Private Major Whitt
Private Daniel Willis
Private Thomas Young

Company G—Bulloch & Pulaski
   Counties
Captain James DeLoach
Captain C. E. Clark
Private E. L. Anderson

Private Elijah Anderson
Private Zachariah J. Brown
Private J. B. Deffnal
Private Matthew T. DeLoach
Private William E. Fields (Died 4 December 1864 from unknown causes)
Private George W. Weaver

Company H—Putman County
Captain Benjamin F. Adams
1sr Lieutenant H. T. Lawreull
2d Lieutenant Thomas Whitfield
3rd Lieutenant Wiley Simmons
4th Lieutenant James Nelson
1st Sergeant J. A. Davis (Killed at Griswoldville)
2d Sergeant T. J. Howard
Private J. M. Adams (Wounded in arm at Griswoldville)
Private M. T. Ashurst
Private Howell Baldwin (Wounded at Griswoldville)
Private John Baugh
Private Joseph Boswell
Private E. Z. Brown
Private James Bullard
Private Thomas Bynum (Died of unknown causes, Atlanta, July 1864)
Private Carroll Caswell (Killed at Griswoldville)
Private Sidney Causby
Private B. W. Clark
Private James Cochran
Private Joseph Coker (Died of unknown causes, Atlanta, July 1864)
Private Robert Coker
Private D. A. Davis (Killed at Griswoldville)
Private Jeff Davis
Private R. R. De Jarnette
Private John Drew
Private Z. J. Edmondson
Private R. N. Edwards
Private J. W. Farley
Private James Garner
Private N. T. Garrard

Private Richard Griffin
Private John Hancock
Private William Hawkins (Mortally wounded at Griswoldville and died 4 December 1864))
Private W. T. Hearn
Private A. J. Hilburn
Private Henry Howard
Private Wilbur Jenkins
Private R. L. Jones
Private Ralph Jones (Wounded in foot at Griswoldville)
Private N. A. Jordan
Private W. B. Jordan
Private William Jordan
Private Madison Kilpatrick
Private W. G. Kimbrough
Private Jerry Lawrence
Private Charles E. Leonard
Private Reid Leverette
Private Davis Little
Private W. F. Little
Private Asa Martin (Wounded in side at Griswoldville)
Private T. B. Meriwether
Private James Middleton (Wounded in shoulder at Griswoldville)
Private Richard Moore
Private A. O. Mosley
Private A. S. Mosley (Missing at Griswoldville)
Private Augustus Mosley
Private James Mosley
Private Matthew Overstreet
Private Samuel Paschal
Private Clay Pearson
Private Mage Perryman
Private W. C. Phillips
Private David Reddick
Private Amos Register
Private Alexander Reid
Private John A. Reid
Private Mark Rivers
Private Thomas S. Robins

Private William Seals (Killed at
Griswoldville)
Private Irby H. Scott
Private W. H. Sparks
Private Eli Spikes
Private Mitchell Strange
Private C. C. Tucker
Private Zadduck Turner
Private W. M. Vaughn
Private P. P. Vincent
Private Joseph Whaley
Private Elijah Wheeler (Killed at
Griswoldville)
Private Paul Wheeler (Killed at
Griswoldville)
Private John Wilson (Killed at Griswoldville)
Private R. J. Wynn

**Company I—Pulaski and Screven
Counties**
Captain Fleming Jordan
Private Alexander Bohannan
Private Dewitt Blackwell
Private J. L. Burkhalter
Private William Digby
Private Robert F. Edenfield
Private W. E. English
Private J. N. Ezell
Private L. D. Ezell
Private Robert F. Ezell
Private Samuel H. Fowler
Private James T. Goodman
Private Joseph Graham
Private John W. Grubbs (Wounded and dis-
abled at Griswoldville)
Private J. C. Hancock (Died 10 August 1864
of unknown causes)
Private Alfred N. Huff
Private Francis Ivey
Private D. P. Johnson
Private Fleming Jordan
Private E. H. Jordan
Private Seaborn C. Kelly
Private John D. Lovejoy
Private Grief Lynch

Private S. B. Malone
Private James Marks (Died 6 December
1864 of unknown causes)
Private W. J. McClendon
Private Green Lee McMichael
Private John W. Morgan
Private J. H. Morten
Private N. G. Pate
Private R. P. Penn
Private Thomas Piper (Wounded at
Griswoldville)
Private Thomas J. Portwood
Private C. A. Pye
Private J. T. Roland
Private I. T. Wyatt

**Company K—Morgan & Taliaferro
Counties**
Captain James Bostwick
Private H. J. Almond
Private John D. Dickinson
Private Thomas Knight
Private William C. Morris
Private Thad Pennington
Private Thomas Pennington
Private John Sturgis
Private George R. Wilson
Private C. R. Zachry

6th Regiment
Colonel J. W. Burney
Lieutenant Colonel Frank George (Mortally
wounded in shoulder at Griswoldville and
died 4 December 1864)
Sergeant MajorThomas Hay

Company A—Muscogee County
Captain T. C. Reedy
Private William Blanton
Private H. A. Brooks
Private John Connally
Private Ferdinand S.Drewry
Private James M. Edwards
Private T. N. Epps
Private Leonard G. Haines

Private Andrew J. Harris
Private William J. King
Private William T. Pool
Private John C. Reedy
Private Humphrey Reid
Private Thomas J. Ritch
Private R. N. Simpson
Private J. D. Steele
Private M. A. Thomas
Private John White

Company B—Clayton & Chattahoochee Counties
Captain Washington Mann
1st Lieutenant James Allums
2d Lieutenant Andrew Harp
3rd Lieutenant Daniel Codery
1st Sergeant Thomas Howard
Corporal Philip Adams
Private James P. Adams
Private T. M. Adams
Private Benjamin F. Bagley
Private William Bagley
Private Samuel Barron (Mortally wounded at Griswoldville)
Private William Bartlett
Private John Booth
Private Christopher Burke
Private Wiley Burke
Private Duncan Cannon (Killed at Columbus GA, October 1864)
Private John Cates
Private Sanders Cates
Private Abner Christian
Private Jack Clark (Wounded at Griswoldville)
Private Jake Clark
Private Henry Crawford
Private Thomas Creed
Private I. F. Dent
Private R. H. Debt
Private Thomas De Wolf
Private Zach Edwards
Private Tillman A. Farr
Private C. K. Fortson

Private David Fusselle (Wounded at Battle of Atlanta, 22 July 1864)
Private Caleb Gallops
Private Benjamin George
Private Frank George
Private Elijah Glass
Private George Gordy
Private Jack Hale
Private S. D. Harp
Private Thomas Harper
Private Francis B. Hascall
Private Robert Helms
Private Benjamin Hickey
Private J. B. Huff
Private David Huie
Private R. S. Huie
Private Edmond Jenkins
Private James Jones
Private William Lane
Private William Langford
Private Jesse Lauson
Private J. H. Lee
Private Thomas J. Lee
Private James Lilse
Private Si Lunsford
Private Henry J. Marshall
Private B. F. Mathews
Private James Dee McConnell
Private David McGlaun
Private Elijah Morgan
Private Leonard Nelson
Private John Pate
Private M. J. Pate
Private Marion Pate
Private William Phillips
Private Lee Pollard
Private Chappel Roberts
Private William T. Roberts
Private Hardy Royals
Private James M. Sizemore
Private James H. Smith
Private Russell Smith
Private John Stephens
Private John Stewart
Private Horton Turney

Private James Whipple
Private John Wilkinson
Private Burrell Williams
Private B. D. Williams
Private William Willis (Wounded at
   Griswoldville and later elected captain)
Private Wilson Wright

Company C—Jasper County
Captain John Phillips
Private J. F. Adams
Private Norman Bedingfield
Private G. W. Brown
Private George Dillard
Private E. J. Dooling (Wounded and lost leg
   at Griswoldville)
Private J. C. Forehand
Private J. M. Graham
Private John Hamner
Private Benjamin H. Ivey
Private C. G. Lumsford
Private J. T. Rutherford
Private Zachariah Sims
Private Joseph Stringfellow
Private C. W. Varnadoe

Company D—Marion & Upson Counties
Captain James Wiggins
Private J. W. Benson
Private Zachariah W. Hardage
Private Jesse M. Duke
Private J. F. Green
Private W. F. Greenway
Private John Hanner
Private Zachriah Hardage
Private J. R. Minter
Private E. A. Moore
Private J. F. Rushin
Private John T. Rushin
Private J. F. Ruskin
Private Joseph C. Scott
Private J. Smith (Wounded at Griswoldville)
Private E. M. Tharpe

**Company E—Columbia, Pike, &
   Wilkinson Counties**
Captain William H. Byrom
Private J. F. Adams
Private L. D. Agnew
Private C. G. Bellflower
Private J. E. Coleman
Private J. H. Cross
Private Charlie Dillard
Private E. J. Dooling
Private J. L. Duncan
Private William Fudge
Private Jeptha J. Hammock
Private Emanuel James Hicks
Private William Kaigler
Private J. W. Lashley
Private William Lewis
Private John D. Lovejoy
Private Eli McFail
Private O. P. Randall
Private Martin D. Simpson
Private James P. Spradley
Private Stephen Strickland
Private Alonzo Sumerford
Private John J. Taylor
Private J. P. Walters
Private William T. Westbrook

Company F—Gwinnett County
Captain T. M. Peeples
Private John N. Adkins
Private W. I. Butler
Private S. H. Cannon (Wounded at
   Griswoldville)
Private A. B. Davis
Private James M. Dees
Private John T. Dickerson
Private George G. Golden
Private William J. Harvard
Private Cornelius McDaniel
Private J. L. Murray
Private John S. Pate
Private J. H. Smith
Private T. K. Smith
Private J. H. Swearingen

Private W. T. Thomas
Private John D. Williams
Private J. W. Wright

Company G—Washington County
Captain W. H. Byram
Private Edward W. Ammons
Private D. N. Carmichael
Private Thomas Harkness
Private Franklin Malone
Private Benjamin F. Mason
Private L. M. Pettigrew
Private William Short
Private Thomas Spears

Company H—Butts, Jones, & Newton Counties
Captain Fleming Ward
1st Lieutenant Henry Fletcher
2d Lieutenant N. H. Woodward
3rd Lieutenant Samuel McKibben
1st Sergeant William Hodges
1st Sergeant Jelson Barnes
2d Sergeant Thomas Gregory
3rd Sergeant W. A. Elder
Private John Adams
Private Ellington Allmond
Private Gus Bankston
Private Jesse Bankston
Private Jack Bennett
Private John Bledsoe
Private John Brady
Private Richard Byers
Private Fred Cargile
Private John Cargile
Private Carter Carmichael
Private David Carmichael
Private Poney Carson
Private Thomas J. Collins
Private Marcus Craine
Private James Crittenden
Private Lott Durden
Private W. A. Elder, Sr.
Private Riley Fears (Elected Captain 1864)
Private William Fletcher
Private James Fogg

Private Joseph Freeman
Private Josiah Freeman
Private James Gilmore
Private Lucius Goddard
Private John Goodman
Private M. Graham
Private John Gray
Private Monroe Gray
Private James Gregory
Private Thomas Hammond
Private Thomas Harkness
Private Thomas Harris
Private Chester Hay
Private H. Henderson
Private Alexander J. Hewit
Private James W. Jackson
Private Paschal Jackson
Private Samuel Johnson
Private Thomas J. Kent
Private Barney Kinard
Private George W. King
Private Larkin Lee
Private Edward A. Lester
Private Thomas Lewis
Private Fernando Mackey
Private Emory Maddox
Private Arch Mayfield
Private J. W. McCord
Private Hezekiah McElhaney
Private Robert McGough
Private F. McKay
Private James McMichael
Private Jeff McMichael
Private LeRoy McMichael
Private Reese McMichael
Private T. J. McMichael
Private B. McNeer
Private Flem Mobley
Private Isaac Moore
Private Kit Moore
Private Stephen Moore
Private Virgil Moore
Private William Moore
Private Virgil P. Moore
Private Ezekiel P. Newton

Private Isaac Nolan
Private Edward O'Neal
Private Daniel Oxford
Private Robert Oxford
Private Lewis Pettigrew
Private William Redman
Private R. E. Rhyner
Private Jack Rich
Private Norman Shirey
Private John Singley
Private F. V. Smith
Private Sam Smith
Private T. Y. Smith
Private William Sparks
Private Keith Thomas
Private John Thompson
Private Green Turner
Private Alfred Watkins
Private B. Watkins
Private Joel Watkins
Private R. T. Watkins
Private William Watkins
Private Green Westbrooks
Private William White
Private Joseph Woodward
Private Robert Woodward

Company I—Upson County
1st Lieutenant R. B. Johnson
Private J. K. Adkins
Private Harmon P. Exley
Private Aaron G. Frier
Private Lloyd Jolly
Private Fleming Jordan
Private Joseph Martin
Private J. S. Scott
Private William R. Smith
Private Shade Thornton
Private Lewis C. Wilcox
Private John Williams

Company K—Fulton County
(Commander not recorded)
Private Amariah Bowen
Private George P. Brightwell

Private Albert Howell
Private William L. Johns
Private J. J. Pope
Private Lewis Pope
Private Carter Shepherd

**Company L—Laurens, Tattnall, & Wayne
Counties**
Captain M. B. Holland
1st Lieutenant H. B. Gould
2d Lieutenant F. Millikin
2d Lieutenant H. B. Roberson
3rd Lieutenant Richard Carter (Deserted 15
August 1864)
1st Sergeant T. R. Yeomans
1st Sergeant J. Clary
3rd Sergeant D. C. Dowling
4th Sergeant H. Saxon
Corporal R. Pendavis
2d Corporal D. S. Carter
3rd Corporal T. E. Lyon
4th Corporal R. J. Davis
Private William Ballard
Private I. Bennett
Private W. J. Bennett
Private C. Boatwright
Private Elias Branch
Private James Griffin
Private Gideon Hoteton
Private Sebron Hoteton
Private William Hunter
Private James Johnson
Private John Johnson
Private Andrew Knight
Private Abraham Leggett
Private John Lynn
Private John McClellan
Private Alex McSwain
Private Joshua Middleton
Private James Milton
Private Britton Mims
Private Thomas Moodie
Private William Overstreet
Private George Raddish
Private Isham Raddish

Private William Russ
Private Burrell Taylor
Private Henry Taylor
Private Willis Taylor
Private Absalom Thomas
Private Berry Thomas
Private James Willis

3rd Brigade
Brigadier General Charles D. Anderson
(Wounded in hand and had two horses
shot from under him at Griswoldville)

7th Regiment
Colonel Abner F. Redding (Killed at
Griswoldville)
Lieutenant Colonel Zachariah Fryer
Major J. F. M. Hanson
Captain _____ Adams (Wounded at
Griswoldville)
Lieutenant _____ Hamilton (Wounded at
Griswoldville)

Company A—Fulton & Monroe Counties
Captain Charles F. Gibson
Lieutenant Wiley Sikes[235] (Wounded in leg
at Griswoldville)
Lieutenant O. L. Woodward
Lieutenant _____ Hamilton (Wounded at
Griswoldville)
Sergeant Thomas Dumas (Wounded in arm
at Griswoldville)
Private Lee B. Alexander
Private Miles Burnham
Private Elias Cox
Private E. F. Dumas
Private William Evans (Wounded in foot at
Griswoldville)
Private J. M. Harville
Private Lawrence Jones
rivate Marion Kemp
Private Pat McCallum
Private John McClure
Private Leonard C. Martin
Private Arthur Newton

Private Andrew Russ
Private S. H. Singleton
Private Patrick Williams
Private R. H. Williams
Private J. B. Willis
Private Robert T. Wood

Company B—Monroe & Tift Counties
Captain J. B. Collier
Corporal A. C. Colvard (Wounded in foot at
Griswoldville)
Corporal J. A. G. Phinazee (or Phinizy)
(Wounded in breast at Griswoldville)
Private John Chambliss
Private J. T. Childs (Wounded in foot at
Griswoldville)
Private J. J. Conner
Private John Fogg
Private T. A. Gaar
Private Nathan J. Goggans
Private John G. Mays
Private John A. Parker
Private John R. Simons
Private William Walker
Private G. L. Watson
Private John Webb
Private R. Whatley (Wounded in thigh at
Griswoldville)
Private C. M. Williamson
Private John Willis
Private John G. Willis
Private John Winn (Missing at
Griswoldville)

Company C—Montgomery & Randolph Counties
Captain John J. McArthur
1st Lieutenant Lewis "Gipp" Wilcox[236]
2d Lieutenant Walter T. McArthur
(Wounded at Griswoldville)
3rd Lieutenant J. W. Vaughn
4th Lieutenant W. Wilcox (Wounded in
thigh at Griswoldville)
1st Sergeant M. C. Adams

Sergeant John W. McArthur (Wounded in
side at Griswoldville)
Sergeant William R. Ryals (Wounded in
knee at Griswoldville)
Private G. W. Adams
Private John Adams
Private M. B. Adams
Private Thomas B. Adams (Wounded in
head at Griswoldville)
Private R. A. Bedgood
Private Isham Cannifax
Private Martin Cauey
Private Littleton Clark
Private Orien J. Clark
Private Cornelius Clements
Private Groves Connor (Killed at
Griswoldville)
Private James J. Connor
Private J. B. Connor
Private Joseph K. Connor
Private Andrew Coursey
Private Andrew J. Gillis
Private Elkana Haralson (Killed near Griffin)
Private Archibold Martin
Private J. B. Manry
Private Addison C. McArthur (Killed at
Griswoldville)
Private Allen McArthur
Private John J. McArthur (Wounded &
missing at Griswoldville)
Private Daniel Q. Morrison
Private David Morrison
Private Duncan McRae
Private W. D. Penick (Wounded in foot at
Griswoldville)
Private Seaborn Rainey
Private John D. Roberts
Private William Ryals (Killed at
Griswoldville)
Private Uriah Sears
Private C. R. Vaughn
Private M. K. Wilco (Wounded at
Griswoldville)
Private Frank H. Williams

Company D—Cobb, Fayette, Monroe, & Richmond Counties

Captain J. G. Green

Corporal T. G. King (Killed at Griswoldville)

Private Alexander Burnett

Private Obadiah Edge (Wounded in ankle at Griswoldville)

Private Thomas J. Hood

Private Andrew J. Inglett

Private Thomas Knowles

Private James E. McCord

Private James M. Redding

Private William M. Redding

Private Alex Spicer

Private John Taylor

Private William Thompson

Private T. L. Turk (Wounded in arm at Griswoldville)

Private F. L. Watts

Private James White (Wounded in foot at Griswoldville)

Private Lewis Wimberly

Company E—Cobb & Houston Counties

Captain John Power

Private James Bevel

Private John Branch

Private William A. Goodson

Private William Morris Haman

Private William Hayman

Private Peyton F. Horton

Private J. F. Johnson

Private S. C. Nicholson

Private John Roberts

Private John Ross

Company F—Clayton & Lee Counties

Captain R. G. Fulgam (Wounded in leg at Griswoldville)

Lieutenant A. C. McPhail (Wounded and missing at Griswoldville)

Sergeant D. H. Henley (Wounded in thigh at Griswoldville)

Private Jordan Brown

Private David Douglas

Private J. M. Fogg

Private G. W. Giles

Private Irwin B. Hamilton

Private Benjamin Harrell

Private G. F. Hendricks

Private L. L. Hargrove

Private John King (Wounded in thigh at Griswoldville)

Private Moore Lee

Private Les Moore (Died 24 August 1864 of unknown causes)

Private Hilliard L. Morrow

Private S. J. Poole

Private J. T. Rawlins

Private George W. Stapleton

Private James Vaughn

Private D. B. Willis

Company G—Baker & Wilcox Counties

Captain J. B. Ware

Captain S. D. Fuller237

Private Benjamin T. Boman

Private Samuel Brown

Private James Davis

Private J. A. Gibbs (Wounded and missing at Griswoldville)

Private R. A. Gibbs (Wounded in shoulder at Griswoldville)

Private Darling Grain (Wounded and missing at Griswoldville)

Private Lewis Hancock

Private L. A. Houston

Private LeRoy Johnson

Private William L. Lovett

Private Moses Lovette

Private Allen Marshall (Wounded in thigh at Griswoldville)

Private John T. Marshall

Private J. B. Mitchell

Private James M. Mixon

Private Bird Owens (Died 7 September 1864 of unknown causes)

Private A. F. Reid

Private Elisha B. Royal

Private S. D. Smith
Private J. A. Stubbs
Private W. D. Swain (Wounded and captured at Griswoldville)
Private John Swinney
Private George W. Young (Wounded and missing at Griswoldville)
Private Samuel Young

Company H—Spalding County
Captain Charnel C. Hightower (Wounded in foot at Griswoldville)
Lieutenant B. D. Hardaway
Private T. J. Barnett
Private Jack Bussey (Wounded in shoulder at Griswoldville)
Private Thomas J. Bussey
Private Osborn Cannafax
Private James E. Coppedge (Wounded in thigh at Griswoldville)
Private James R. Cotton
Private W. H. Davis
Private George Gardner (Killed at Griswoldville)
Private C. C. Hightower
Private Calvin Lynch
Private Archibold J. Moon
Private H. C. Morris
Private Allen Reid
Private J. N. Sikes
Private W. J. Sikes
Private Andrew J. Tyler
Private William C. Yarbrough

Company I—Telfair & Terrell Counties
Captain Daniel Fraser McRae (Wounded in arm at Griswoldville and later promoted to major)
1st Lieutenant John A. Powell (Mortally wounded at Griswoldville)
2d Lieutenant Stephen Boney (Later promoted to Captain)
2d Lieutenant Thomas McDuffie (Mortally wounded at Griswoldville)

Sergeant William F. Williams (Wounded in breast at Griswoldville)
Corporal Thomas J. McRae (Wounded in hand at Griswoldville)
Private Green Brewer
Private Henry Brewer
Private James Brown
Private Simon Browning
Private Miles A. Burman
Private William W. Clements
Private Wright Colline
Private John Cravey
Private Allen W. Dean
Private Henry P. Dopson
Private Thomas C. Fletcher
Private William M. Fletcher
Private William Harrell
Private Allen Hulett
Private Blount Keel
Private James W. Lancaster
Private T. C. Leslie
Private James H. Lindsey (Wounded in right shoulder at Griswoldville)
Private D. H. Maloy
Private Walter T. McArthur
Private Alexander McEachen
Private Cornelious McKinnon
Pvt. John McKinnon
Private John C. McLean (Killed at Griswoldville)
Private Archibald McMillan
Private G. M. McRae
Private William T. McRae
Private John McRaine
Private Archie Mims
Private John Mims
Private A. B. Mixon
Private James Parker
Private John A. Powell
Private Isaac Rawlins
Private Allen Ray
Private Isaac Rollins
Private Mike Rushing
Private Uriah Sears
Private Freeman Selph

Private John B. Studstill
Private T. S. Swain
Private Thomas Varnedoe
Private J. S. Walker
Private. Jermiah Walker (Wounded near
   Atlanta, July 1864)
Private Gideon L. Watson
Private J. G. Williams
Private W. F. Williams
Private Jordan Wombler
Private John Wooten
Private W. S. Wooten (Furloughed home
   with malaria, 5 February 1865)

Company K—Randolph & Terrell
Counties
Captain W. T. Morgan (Wounded at
   Griswoldville)
Captain S. H. Singleton (Wounded in head
   at Griswoldville)
Sergeant Blanton Nance (Wounded in
   shoulder and neck at Griswoldville)
Private T. M. Chandler
Private J. V. Davis
Private E. Erwin (Missing at Griswoldville)
Private Peyton Horton (Wounded in leg at
   Griswoldville)
Private H. Johnson (Missing at
   Griswoldville)
Private William Kersey
Private Thomas J. Lowe
Private D. P. McArthur
Private Arthur R. Newton (Wounded in
   head at Griswoldville)
Private Samual H. Singletary
Private William Warren (Missing at
   Griswoldville)
Private D. Wartz (Missing at Griswoldville)

8th Regiment
Colonel Willam B. Scott
Captain Mack E. Boatwright, Adjutant

Company A—Crawford & Fannin
Counties
Captain John W. Wellons
1st Lieutenant B. F. White238 (Wounded
   both knees at Griswoldville)
Private Robert M. Bond
Private William Boone
Private W. T. Braswell (Wounded both lungs
   at Griswoldville)
Private James Bryant (Wounded at
   Griswoldville)
Private Andrew J. Burnett
Private E. F. Bryant
Private William Burnett
Private Samuel Causey
Private Benjamin Finney
Private James Fry (Wounded at
   Griswoldville)
Private John L. Goza
Private William Hamlin
Private John Harrison
Private Andrew J. Head
Private Francis M. Head
Private George M. Hedden
Private Steve Willis Johnson
Private Nathan Jones
Private H. D. McCrary
Private J. J. McCrary
Private John McGee
Private Peter Monroe
Private John Moose
Private O. T. Myoch (Wounded in shoulder
   and missing at Griswoldville)
Private Owen Myrick
Private James Parham
Private Robert Parham
Private Stephen Rigdon
Private Mack Robinson
Private Edward Rowell
Private William R. Sandifer
Private Augustus Sealy
Private John Searcy
Private R. S. Smith
Private James Henry Steadman
Private T. M. Tarpley

Private Elbert Vinson
Private Thomas Vinson
Private C. H. Walker
Private C. F. White (Mortally wounded at
  Griswoldville)
Private Samuel Wilson
Private Steve Wilson
Private John Worsham

Company B—Emanuel County
Captain D. A. Green
Private Miles Fitzgerald
Private William Flanagan
Private E. B. Gilbert
Private Obediah Lewis
Private M. J. Nelson

**Company C—Floyd, Taylor, & Lumpkin
· Counties**
Captain Zachariah Beland
1st Lieutenant M. Jones239
Sergeant B. F. Fenney (Wounded in jaw at
  Griswoldville)
Private Pickens Byrd
Private Zack Beeland
Private C. Catton (Wounded through leg at
  Griswoldville)
Private Delmus Cicero
Private William Christopher
Private A. B. Daniel
Private Hagan Dial
Private Osborn L. Downing
Private M. C. Howell
Private G. W. Ingram
Private John F. Jinks
Private Joseph King
Private James T. Lucas
Private George W. McDaniel
Private B. M. C. Taunton
Private Gilbert Simpson
Private Spurgeon Simpson

**Company D—Bibb, Monroe, &
  Wilkinson Counties**
Captain Eli Cummings
1st Lieutenant W. L. Adams
2d Lieutenant Augustus Brown
2d Lieutenant Alex Stuckey (From
  September 1864)
3rd Lieutenant J. B. Hall
Surgeon Alex Cumming
1st Sergeant Mack E. Boatwright
2d Sergeant James Butler
3rd Sergeant J. M. Boone
4th Sergeant E. T. Miller
Sergeant L. M. Peacock (From September
  64[???])
Sergeant William R. Ryals (Wounded in
  knee at Griswoldville)
Private Urias E. Adkins (Mortally wounded
  at Griswoldville)
Private Jack Allen
Private P. A. Ashley
Private James Barlow
Private William Barrett
Private Alex Baum
Private J. R. Bellue
Private John David Boone
Private George F. Brack
Private Joel Harris Branan
Private W. C. Brannan
Private A. M. Brown
Private Anderson R. Brundage
Private Jesse Brundage
Private John Burke
Private Nimrod Burke
Private Frank Burney
Private George Butler
Private J. A. M. Butler
Private Joel Butler
Private George L. Carswell
Private John Carswell
Private Matthew Carswell
Private Rufus H. Carswell
Private Andrew Chambers (Wounded in
  thigh at Griswoldville)
Private Bryant Chambers

Private Amos Cook

Private William Cook

Private Amos Cox

Private Alexander Cummings

Private Greenberry Daniel

Private Calvin Dean

Private Bogus Doke

Private Perry Dominy

Private T. J. Dominy

Private John E. Duncan

Private William Ethridge

Private Ben H. Fordham

Private Wyley Fordham

Private Wilbur Gilder

Private George Green

Private Jesse Green

Private Lyman A. Hall

Private Iverson Harville

Private Samuel W. Hatfield

Private Jesse Holder

Private William Holder

Ptrivate J. M. Holliman

Private W. E. Holliman

Private W. S. Holliman

Private James M. Howard

Private L. L. Jenkins

Private Edwin Johnston

Private Eli B. Johnston

Private Iverson Jones

Private John Jones

Private Kirby Jones

Private Seaborn Jones

Private J. F. Keel

Private John Kemp

Private Walter Lee

Private Zachariah Lee

Private William G. Lewis

Private J. H. Lord

Private James M. Manson (Killed at
    Griswoldville)

Private John Mason

Private Theophitus A. Mason

Private Richard Martin

Private Arch McCallum

Private Silas McIntyre

Private Henry H. Miller

Private Charles Moore

Private Bozeman Morgan

Private James N. Nesmith

Private Wiley Nesmith

Private W. H. Ogburn
    (Wounded at Griswoldville)

Private Meredith Pace

Private J. N. Parker

Private Ben F. Pate

Private George Washington Payne

Private Levi Milton Peacock

Private Lewis M. Peacock

Private John J. Perkins

Private James Pierce

Private Thomas Porter

Private James R. Rawls

Private O. H. P. Rawls (Wounded in thigh at
    Griswoldville)

Private J. L. Renfroe

Private Dexter Rozar

Private Joseph Rozar

Private Franklin C. Rutherford

Private H, H. Rye

Private William Shepherd

Private James Simpson

Private M. D. Simpson

Private C. C. Smith

Private H. H. Smith

Private J. J. L. Smith

Private Jasper Smith

Private Joel A. Smith
    (Wounded left side at Griswoldville)

Private L. W. Smith

Private R. S. Smith

Private W. L. Smith (Wounded in hand at
    Griswoldville)

Private Edward M. Stanley

Private James Stevens

Private Alex Stuckey

Private R. J. Stuckey

Private Grimsley Thompson

Private Robert Trapp

Private Joshua Walker

Private Jasper Wall

Private James Walters
Private James D. Waye
Private W. W. Whitaker
Private John Wiggins
Private David Williams

Company E—Gilmer County
Captain Jacob Pearcy
Sergeant _____ Beckom240
Private John R. Bragg
Private Samuel Bragg
Private A. F. Bryant
Private Elias Champion (Killed at
   Griswoldville)
Private Thomas W. Henderson
Private Jack Martan
Private Addison May
Private John M. Mills
Private J. D. Tharp (Wounded in arm at
   Griswoldville)

**Company F—Chattooga, Jones, & Walker
   Counties**
Captain Robert H. Barron
Captain Robert Cameron
1st Lieutenant G. W. Thames241
2d Lieutenant Henry Edmondson
2d Lieutenant Thomas Cochran
Sergeant Jesse Jones
2d Sergeant James Hendricks
3rd Sergeant Oliver York
Private E. E. Broadwell
Private Richard Brooks
Private E. E. Bryant
Private S. F. Bryant (Wounded at
   Griswoldville)
Private John Childs
Private B. A. Crutchfield
Private James L. Fisher
Private John Humphries
Private James Hutto
Private Jackson Morton
Private James Vaughn
Private Elbert Vinson
Private John R. Pearce

**Company G—Houston, Milton, Newton,
   White, & Lumpkin Counties**
Captain Charles N. Roundtree
1st Lieutenant _____ Hollaman242
1st Lieutenant M. L. Thurmon
2d Lieutenant John Staley
3rd Lieutenant J. H. Pollock
4th Lieutenant James Harrison
1st Sergeant Thomas Killen
Corporal W. R. Gilbert (Wounded both
   thighs at Griswoldville)
Private James Altman
Private William Anderson
Private James Aultman
Private Joe Baskin
Private J. W. Belvin
Private Joseph Carr
Private William Carr
Private Henry Chancey
Private H. D. Conyers
Private John Cook
Private H. D. Cunyus
Private Charles David
Private M. Dominac (Wounded in both
   arms at Griswoldville)
Private William Dupree
Private Joseph Ellis
Private Lem Everette
Private McD. Felder
Private Joseph Floyd
Private S. J. Fordhand
Private D. C. Fountain
Private A. A. Geter
Private Julius Gilbert
Private John Giles
Private William Green
Private Dan Gunn
Private Thomas Gurr
Private Thomas Halliburton
Private John Hancock
Private John Harper
Private Joe Harris
Private Joel Harris (Wounded in leg at
   Griswoldville)
Private Ben Harrison

Private Nathan Head
Private Major Henderson
Private John Howard
Private Elijah Hulsey
Private A. A. Jeter
Private Clay Jones
Private Thomas Judge
Private Kindred Kemp
Private John King
Private James Knight
Private Frank Litty
Private Absalom Marshall
Private Humphrey Marshall
Private William McLemore
Private Tom Murphy
Private Henry Neal
Private John Nepier
Private John Pearce
Private Wiiliam Peavy
Private Burton Pitts
Private J. G. Pollock
Private David Riley
Private William Simmons
Private George Singleton
Private George Smith
Private William Smith
Private Isaac Taylor
Private Benjamin Franklin Vinson
    (Wounded in ear at Griswoldville)243
Private William Wagnon
Private Thomas Warren
Private George White
Private B. B. Yates

Company H—Whitfield County
Captain R. H. Barron
1st Lieutenant Jonathon Baker (Wounded in
    wrist at Griswoldville)
2d Lieutenant Jonathon Humphrie
    (Wounded in left hand at Griswoldville)
Private J. E. Anderson
Private R. S. Bowden
Private William C. Branan
Private Levi Chewning
Private James Cobb

Private William Harris
Private J. S. Humphries
Private F. M. Hunt
Private William H. Jolly (Killed at
    Griswoldville)
Private Roberrt H. Kingman, Sr.
Private Uriah Mitchell
Private N. Morris (Wounded in right arm at
    Griswoldville)
Private William Morris
Private M. E. Souther
Private Wiley Vinson
    (Wounded in side at Griswoldville)

Company I—Newton & Pickens Counties
Captain John T. Lingo
Private A. Chambers
Private John Comas (Died 12 September of
    unknown causes)
Private James Council
Private S. I. Dennard
Private Sam Griswold
Private Alexander D. Hall
Private J. M. B. Hall
Private E. B. Johnston
Private John Martin
Private Elijah Pruett
Private Daniel J. Ryles
Private M. M. Sanders
Private Newton Sanders
Private James Snow
Private James Stevens
Private Henry T. Stinson
Private Henry A. Wood (Captured at
    Griswoldville)

Company K—Fannin & Union Counties
Captain T. M. Hunt
2d Lieutenant John Baker (Wounded left
    arm at Griswoldville and died 2
    December 1864)
Private James Baker
Private W. Cairy (Wounded in hand at
    Griswoldville)

Private W. D. Darm (Wounded in side and
arm at Griswoldville)
Private Thomas J. Fields
Private John W. Harkins
Private J. Hawkins (Wounded in hip at
Griswoldville)
Private James Hunt
Private James H. Hurt
Private Thomas J. Huse
Private John J. Kitchens
Private Nathan Morris
Private William Morris
Private L. S. Morse
Private George W. Souther
Private J. Van Zant (Wounded both knees at
Griswoldville)
Private Wiley Vinson
Private John W. Ward
Private John W. Wood (Discharged for
overage at Griffin GA, September 1864)

9th Regiment
Colonel John M. Hill
Lieutenant Colonel T. S. Sherman
(Wounded in shoulder at Griswoldville)
Major W. A. Turner (Wounded in leg at
Griswoldville)
Dr. J. S. Henry, Surgeon (Wounded at
Griswoldville)
Lieutenant A. B. Howard, Adjutant

**Company A—Putnam & Richmond
Counties**
Captain James L. Turner
1st Lieutenant J. K. Smith
2d Lieutenant S. S. Langston (Promoted to
captain, 1864)
Private A. P. Barfield
Private Z. T. Crawford (Wounded in thigh
at Griswoldville)
Private Robert DeLeon
Private Bennett O. Estes (Captured near
Atlanta, 22 August 1864)
Private J. C. Forbes (Killed at Griswoldville)
Private Tyre Hagwood

Private Edward Hett
Private John Leaker (Missing at
Griswoldville)
Private S. L. Lorger (Wounded left arm at
Griswoldville)
Private Thomas J. Nixon
Private Henry J. Patterson
Private William A. Paul
Private John H. Pennington
Private John Henry Pennington
Private A. W. Phillips (Killed at
Griswoldville)
Private L. Shell (Wounded in thigh at
Griswoldville)
Private Jacob B. Smith
Private James L. Smith
Private John C. Smith
Private Joseph B. Smith
Private R. D. Smith (Wounded in elbow at
Griswoldville)
Private W. H. Speir
Private W. P. Thackston
Private Burton Weaver

**Company B—Marion & Meriwether
Counties**
Captain W. H. Hinton
Corporal W. T. Bussey (Wounded both feet
and arms at Griswoldville)
Private William Barnes
Private M. B. Braswell
Private Z. T. Bonner
Private John G. Brown
Private James Callaway (Killed at
Griswoldville)
Private L. M. Chunn (Wounded in shoulder
at Griswoldville)
Private A. J. Cooksey
Private A. J. Cooper
Private George W. Eubanks
Private T. J. Hardaway (Wounded right knee
at Griswoldville)
Private Thomas Hattaway (Mortally
wounded at Griswoldville)
Private William H. Hinton

Private John Knott
Private D. A. Maqouirk
Private R. M. McCaslan
Private Franklin M. McClung
Private J. B. McDowell
Private John R. O'Cain (Wounded in
shoulder at Griswoldville)
Private John B. Pope (Wounded in shoulder
at Griswoldville)
Private P. Strozier (Wounded in hip and
shoulder at Griswoldville)

Company C—Sumter County
Captain W. H. Chambliss
Lieutenant J. B. Chamblis (Wounded in
both feet at Griswoldville)
Sergeant R. M. Canton (Wounded in arm at
Griswoldville)
Private John T. Gaddy
Private J. W. Hammock (Wounded in head
and hand at Griswoldville)
Private Eli Hubbard
Private T. E. Huff
Private Walton A. Inglett
Private G. M. Kellum
Private Walter Paine
Private James M. Robertson
Private W. Rothermel (Mortally wounded at
Griswoldville)
Private Benjamin F. Smith
Private Benjamin J. Smith
Private H. M. Smith (Mortally wounded at
Griswoldville)
Private H. M. Snead (Missing at
Griswoldville)
Private A. Teal (Missing at Griswoldville)

Company D—Whitfield County
Captain Clark Mattox
Lieutenant L. Farmer (Killed at
Griswoldville)
Lieutenant _____ Semms (Mortally
wounded at Griswoldville)
Lieutenant Thomas Swint (Wounded at
Griswoldville)
1st Sergeant _____ Lee (Wounded in hip at
Griswoldville)
Private R. E. Adams
Private John Anderson (Wounded at
Griswoldville)
Private William Dent
Private _____ Dykes (Wounded at
Griswoldville)
Private J. R. Getton (Wounded in leg at
Griswoldville)
Private Charles G. Moon
Private Henry L. Samples
Private Ira Scoggins (Wounded at
Griswoldville)
Private John I. Scoggins (Wounded right
foot at Griswoldville)
Private A. Simmons
Private B. J. Smith
Private B. F. Tigner

**Company E—Meriwether & Walton
Counties**
Captain E. F. Strozier (Killed at
Griswoldville)
1st Lieutenant John L. Strozier
Lieutenant Robert Parker
Sergeant Thomas Michain (Wounded in arm
at Griswoldville)
Private W. M. Boyd
Private Jefferson Castleberry
Private T. J. Folds
Private G. W. Grant
Private N. S. Hamby
Private W. S. Hamby
Private C. F. Humphries
Private John W. Matthews (Wounded in
thigh at Griswoldville)

Private James Patillo
Private Nat A. Ray
Private C. J. Reeves
Private Wade Stewart (Wounded at
  Griswoldville)
Private E. F. Strozier
Private John L. Strozier
Privaate R. C. Strozier
Private William P. White
Private John Wesley Willingham

Company F—Upson & Walton Counties
Lieutenant William C. Bray
Sergeant R. B. Lyle (Missing at
  Griswoldville)
Sergeant R. F. Patillo (Wounded at
  Griswoldville)
Corporal H. M. Jackson (Missing at gris-
  woldville)
Private H. T. Butts (Killed at Griswoldville)
Private G. W. Childs (Wounded in thigh at
  Griswoldville)
Private W. I. Cole (Mortally wounded at
  Griswoldville)
Private T. A. Dallas (Missing at
  Griswoldville)
Private C. H. Green (Wounded at
  Griswoldville)
Private B. G. McKenney (Wounded at
  Griswoldville)

**Company G—Clarke, Harris, &
Richmond Counties**
Captain John Kennon
1st Lieutenant Hillard W. Pitts
2d Lieutenant Jesse F. Sutton
3rd Lieutenant Brit Johnston
Sergeant Henry Harris
Private Frank M. Bazemore
Private Willis Beall
Private B. F. Benning
Private B. E. Berrong
Private J. D. Binns
Private James Blow (Missing at
  Griswoldville)

Private Benjamin Boddi (Wounded at
  Griswoldville)
Private Bennett Boddie (Mortally wounded
  at Griswoldville)
Private Monroe Bradshaw
Private Cephus Brannan
Private S. M Brannen
Private James Bray
Private Joseph Bray
Private William P. Bridges
Private Allen Brooks
Private J. W. Calvin
Private Abe Coates (Wounded at
  Griswoldville)
Private J. A. Cook
Private William D. Cook
Private George W. Cooke
Private John Copeland (Wounded at
  Griswoldville)
Private Monroe Davidson
Private William Davis
Private John M. Delay
Private Hamp Dewberry
Private George Dozier
Private David Evans (Wounded at
  Griswoldville)
Private Arthur Farley
Private James H. Freeman (Missing at
  Griswoldville)
Private Thomas H. Freeman (Wounded at
  Griswoldville)
Private G. W. Gordon
Private C. M. Grant (Wounded at
  Griswoldville)
Private J. M. Grant
Private Wilkerson Grant (Wounded at
  Griswoldville)
Private W. Griggs
Private Henry Hargett
Private L. C. Hargett
Private Robert Y. Harris
Private Thomas Harris
Private William A. Harris (Killed at
  Griswoldville)
Private Noah Harvey

Private Dennis Henderson

Private W. Hightower

Private L. J. Horn

Private L. H. Horne

Private James Hubbard (Wounded hip and arm at Griswoldville)

Private Jonathon H. Hubbard (Wounded at Griswoldville)

Private W. J. Hudson

Private Hugh Ingram

Private Bishop Jennings

Private W. C. Johnston

Private Mason Jones

Private Willis Jones

Private A. C. Jordan

Private George Madison Kilpatrick

Private _____ Kinsey

Private John Lawson

Private James W. Layton

Private Henry Livingston

Private Kirk McDaniel

Private _____ McFarland

Private Seaborn Meadows

Private R. C. Milner

Private A. L. Moore

Private Elijah C. Moultrie

Private J. W. Murphy

Private James P. Murrah

Private Pickens Murrah

Private Andrew J. Nunnery

Private Reuben W. Page

Private Hartwell Passmore (Wounded in knee at Griswoldville)

Private Hudson Pitts

Private Isaac H. Pitts

Private Joe Pollard (Missing at Griswoldville)

Private Milton Roberts

Private W. S. Saxon (Wounded in leg at Griswoldville)

Private Charles Smith

Private William Snell, Sr.

Private William Snell, Jr.

Private T. N. Sparks

Private Henry Spear

Private Albert O. Trammell

Private John Turner

Private Mathew Walker

Private Augustus Whitehead

Private W. Whitehead

Private B. C. Williams

Private Bedford Williams

Private Benjamin H. Williams

Private C. Williams (Missing at Griswoldville)

Private Robert Wimpy

Company H—Clarke County

Captain B. Gray (Wounded at Griswoldville)

Lieutenant J. D. Thurman (Wounded at Griswoldville)

Sergeant J. B. L. Watson (Wounded at Griswoldville)

Sergeant A. N. Camp (Wounded at Griswoldville)

Corporal G. Hall (Wounded at Griswoldville)

Private W. J. Boles (Died 14 December 1864 of unknown causes)

Private J. R. Cotton (Wounded at Griswoldville)

Private J. W. Moore (Wounded at Griswoldville)

Private J. W. Odom (Wounded at Griswoldville)

Company I—Harris County

Captain H. E. Moss (Wounded at Griswoldville)

1st Lieutenant L. C. Hargett, Jr.

2d Lieutenant E. G. Tucker (Wounded at Griswoldville)

3rd Lieutenant James Swint

1st Sergeant J. E. Hogan

2d Sergeant H. A. Goodman

3rd Sergeant James Patillo

1st Corporal A. F. Truett (Wounded at Griswoldville)

2d Corporal Wilson Hargett

3rd Corporal Joel A. Huling

Private E. A. Adams
Private James Allen
Private Willis Beall
Private David Blackman
Private W. P. Bridges
Private J. M. Calhoun
Private H. C. Cameron
Private Andrew Clines (Killed at Griswoldville)
Private R. A. Cotton, Sr.
Private R. A. Cotton, Jr.
PrivateDuncan Cox (Deserted 1 September 1864)
Private John T. Cox (Deserted 1 September 1864)
Private John Daniel
Private C. F. Davidson
Private J. W. Davidson (Killed at Griswoldville)
Private Major Davidson
Private J. L. Davis
Private J. L. T. Davis
Private Thomas DeLoach (Killed at Griswoldville)
Private Thomas Dillamer (Killed at Griswoldville)
Private Henry C. Emory
Private Jackson Evans
Private Benjamin Gamble
Private Robert C. Gaylor
Private T. V. Gibson
Private John S. Goodman (Wounded at Griswoldville)
Private Samuel C. Goodman
Private William T. Goodwin
Private John B. Griffin
Private H. C. Hargett
Private Laney C. Hargett
Private Wilson Hargett (Mortally wounded at Griswoldville)
Private _____ Hogg
Private Jeff Horn
Private James Huey
Private Joel A. Hulling (Wounded in leg at Griswoldville)

Private Seaborn Jones
Private Jonathan McClung
Private Sam M. Mills
Private H. T. Murphy
Private W. L. Owen
Private Ezekiel King
Private John T. King
Private John Laney
Private Abner Ledbetter
Private J. A. McCurry
Private J. R. McDaniel (Wounded in hand at Griswoldville)
Private Edward Middlebrooks
Private John A. Middlebrooks
Private Bennett H. Moore
Private Jasper Mullins
Private J. M. Nelson
Private W. T. Nelson
Private James M. Oliver
Private J. M. Pratt
Private Anderson Reeves
Private George M. Riser
Private Francis Marion Talley
Private Andrew Jackson Teel
Private A. F. Truett (Wounded in nose at Griswoldville)
Private R. M. Whitten
Private P. M. B. Williams (Wounded at Griswoldville)
Private William C. Wisdom

Company K—Randolph County
Captain Talbert Wimberly (Wounded in arm at Griswoldville)
1st Lieutenant James T. Philllips (Wounded in hand at Griswoldville)
Sergeant J. P. Leonard (Missing at Griswoldville)
Private S. Beckey (Wounded in thigh at Griswoldville)
Private D. C. Bellingein (Missing at Griswoldville)
Private J. J. Branford
Private T. Castleberry (Wounded in leg at Griswoldville)

Private T. W. Duggan

Private E. G. Freeman

Private Thomas N. Gibson

Private James Gilmore

Private John B. Griffin

Private Samuel Mills

Private Henry T. Murphy

Private W. L. Owen

Private W. N. Payne

Private James T. Phillips

Private John M. Proctor (Wounded knees
and arms at Griswoldville)

Private John B. Riley

Private L. J. Storey

Private Charles Togity (Missing at
Griswoldville)

Private John C. Wade

Private J. H. Willis (Wounded shoulder and
arms at Griswoldville)

Private Abner Wimberly

4th Brigade

Brigadier General Henry Kent McCay

10th Regiment

Colonel Charles M. Davis

Major Thomas Ransom (Captured at
Griswoldville)

Company A—Spalding County

Captain R. F. Mann

Sergeant D. A. Cochran (Wounded in neck
and thigh at Griswoldville)

Sergeant George T. Marshall (Wounded in
shoulder at Griswoldville)

Corporal F. M. Green (Wounded at
Griswoldville)

Corporal C. F. Kaigler (Wounded in knee at
Griswoldville)

Private Eli Aycock

Private H. B. Brown

Private S. J. Buchanan

Private Henry Craft

Private B. W. Ellis

Private E. S. Harris

Private G. O. Hill

Private J. E. Hunter (Wounded arm and hip
at Griswoldville)

Private Jesse D. Jarnigan (Wounded in head
at Griswoldville)

Private J. C. T. Jordan (Wounded in leg at
Griswoldville)

Private C. C. Kercy (Wounded in hand at
Griswoldville)

Private C. P. Kitchen (Wounded in ankle at
Griswoldville)

Private A. A. Paul

Private J. M. Powell

**Company B—Lee, Whitfield, &
Randolph Counties**

Captain C. C. Yarbrough (Wounded and
lost leg at Griswoldville)

1st Lieutenant George Davis (Wounded in
neck at Griswoldville)

2d Lieutenant E. G. Cox (Wounded in
finger at Griswoldville)

3rd Lieutenant J. T. Jenkins (Wounded in
arm at Griswoldville)

Private Milton J. Bellflower

Private Thomas R. Brown

Private J. J. Buckholt

Private James W. Bynum

Private Clem Coates

Private W. H. Coleman

Private Martin Cooper (Died 14 September
1864 of unknown causes)

Private Richard J. Cosby

Private Nathan T. Crozier

Private Riley Fillingame

Private Walter A. Hobbs

Private A. M. Laukin

Private J. W. Lee

Private Abe McKinney

Private David Merritt (Wounded in arm at
Griswoldville)

Private Andrew J. Moye

Private Henry Pittman (Wounded in side at
Griswoldville)

Private William Henry Rigell

Private Lucius W. Stewart
Private C. C. Yarbrough
Private George H. Yarbrough

Company C—Harris County
Lieutenant H. Perry (Killed at Griswoldville)
Sergeant John Chancey (Killed at
  Griswoldville)
Private James W. Alexander
Private John Bird (Wounded in head and
  neck at Griswoldville)
Private G. B. Cross
Private Thomas Lanier (Motally wounded at
  Griswoldville)

Company D—Spalding County
Captain John Stewart
Lieutenant William Crawford (Wounded at
  Griswoldville)
Corporal Walter Watts (Wounded right
  shoulder at Griswoldville)
Private J. E. Albriton (Killed at
  Griswoldville)
Private W. D. R. Crawford
Private Clark A. Dickinson
Private E. C. Grant
Private A. Peterson (Wounded right shoulder
  at Griswoldville)
Private John F. Rish (Missing at
  Griswoldville)
Private O. C. Shivers

Company E—Murray County
Captain J. Oates
Private S. Butler (Wounded in arm at
  Griswoldville)
Private J. H. Freeman
Private John J. Johnson (Died 10 September
  1864 of unknown causes)
Private Neil McCorquodale
Private Benjamin F. Powell
Private O. B. Stevens

Company F—Butts, Henry, Worth, &
Whitfield Counties

Captain Hal H. Kendall (Resigned August
  1864)
1st Lieutenant D. McClelland
2d Lieutenant Thomas Young
1st Sergeant William J. Ford (Wounded in
  breast and arm at Griswoldville)
1st Corporal J. H. T. Calhoun
2d Corporal Barney Barrs
3rd Corporal Gordon Sumner
4th Corporal Jackson Williams
Private William Ammond
Private Moses A. Bick (Killed at
  Griswoldville)
Private William Black
Private Andrew Martin Brett
Private Wesley Brooks
Private William Bunch
Private S. B. Castleberry
Private C. K. Chestnut
Private William H. Eady
Private Thomas W. Fillyaw (or Philyaw)
Private Adam J. Fowler
Private John H. Goodman
Private John M. Hall
Private Jordan Hancock
Private W. H. Harden
Private Thomas J. Harris
Private John Henderson
Private William Henderson (Wounded in leg
  at Griswoldville)
Private Augustus Hill
Private Jesup R. Hill
Private Josiah Hill
Private R. A. Hill
Private M. C. Horn
Private William J. Johnson
Private William W. Johnson
Private E. J. Jones
Private Henry Kirkendall (Deserted 20
  November 1864)
Private S. G. Lang
Private Charles Lidden
Private Charles Long
Private G. S. Long
Private Washington Moree

Private G. E. Powers
Private Horace Powers
Private Thomas J. Ragland
Private Edward Reynolds (Disability discharge, October 1864)
Private James Rouse
Private Stephen W. Rouse
Private John Shiver
Private John Spring
Private George S. Sumner
Private James J. Taylor
Private Columbus C. Turnbull
Private Moses F. Tyson
Private Grit Tyson
Private Theophilus W. Tyson (Detached as physician, 1864)
Private Andrew J. Walker
Private Z. W. Watson
Private Benjamin Willis
Private Daniel Willis
Private Joseph Willis

Company G—Marion County
Captain William C. Gill
1st Lieutenant A. A. Paul (Wounded in arm at Griswoldville)
2d Lieutenant George C. Edwards
1st Sergeant George Garrett
Sergeant W. Martin (Killed at Griswoldville)
Corporal B. F. Lanier (Mortally wounded at Griswoldville)
Private James W. Alexander, Sr.
Private James W. Alexander, Jr.
Private W. H. Baldy
Private Wilk Brooks
Private Samuel Scrutchin
Private John W. Bryan
Private G. W. Dawson (Wounded in hip at Griswoldville)
Private James Ellison
Private Robert G. Freeman
Private J. M. Griffin (Wounded in hand at Griswoldville)
Private William A. Green
Private T. B. High

James B. Hooks
Private J. H. Bunk Hudnell (Mortally wounded at Griswoldville)
Private Thomas Kendrick
Private John Langford
Private (Dr.) H. B. Lipsey
Private J. M. Martin
Private Asa McBee (Died 10 September 1864 of unknown causes)
Private Almorine V. McLeod (Wounded at Griswoldville)
Private J. W. McLeod
Private J. G. Miller (Killed at Griswoldville)
Private Noel J. Pace
Private Dupree Peacock
Private D. A. Pettis (Wounded at Griswoldville)
Private Samuel Scrutchins
Private J. W. Sessions
Private Cicero Speight
Private John L. Thomas (Wounded in neck at Griswoldville)
Private W. J. Tillman
Private A. J. Tison
Private William Ward (Wounded in breast and hip at Griswoldville)
Private John Wells
Private Frank Williams
Private Given Williams
Private Jonathan Williams
Private S. M. Wilson (Wounded in knee at Griswoldville)

Company H—Gwinnett & Schley Counties
Captain Reuben F. Simmons
Lieutenant N. Corquodale (Wounded in shoulder at Griswoldville)
Sergeant J. B. Boynton (Lost arm at Griswoldville)
Corporal T. W. Todd (Killed at Griswoldville)
Private Demetrius A. Cochran
Private Richard R. Davis

Private William Isler (Died 29 August 1864 of unknown causes)

Private D. Merrit (Wounded in hand at Griswoldville)

Private Marcus A. Perry

Private R. F. Simmons

Private E. J. Thigpen (Wounded in jaw and wrist at Griswoldville)

Company I—Sumter County (Commander not recorded)

Sergeant George W. Kendrick (Wounded in head at Griswoldville)

Private John K. Hall (Wounded in hip at Griswoldville)

Private Thomas J. Kitchens

Private J. W. McClellan (Detailed sixty days from 7 October 1864 with Captain R. K. Harris)

Private James E. Philips (Wounded both legs at Griswoldville)

Private Charles L. Shaw (Wounded in shoulder at Griswoldville)

Company K—Dade, Newton , Pickens, Randolph, & Pike Counties

Captain John B. Pollock

Private Charles F. Barry

Private Henderson Bass

Private A. J. Boon (Missing at Griswoldville)

Private W. Bridges (Missing at Griswoldville)

Private Nathan T. Crozier

Private George D. Ferguson

Private J. R. Ferguson (Wounded in forehead at Griswoldville)

Private John T. George

Private Alex B. Hendry

Private Daniel McFather

Private Angus McLeod (Missing at Griswoldville)

11th Regiment

Colonel William T. Toole

Lieutenant Colonel James B. Pickett (Wounded left side at Griswoldville)

Lieutenant Colonel Timothy M. Furlow

Major David L. Wicker (Wounded left leg at Griswoldville)

Regimental Staff

Captain L. E. M. Williams

Captain Jacob Ellis

1st Lieutenant G. R. Hagin

2d Lieutenant A. E. Miller

3rd Lieutenant Solamon Hagin

4th Lieutenant William Greiner

Sergeant Major J. W. Wells (Wounded right side at Griswoldville)

Private Robert Collins

Private James Dixon

Private Jasper Dixon

Private Abner Donaldson

Private John Ellis

Private James Green

Private William Green

Private Timothy Hollaway

Private Ben Holloway

Private Morgan Holloway

Private Ben Mercer

Private Basil Oliff

Private Ben Parrish

Private Jackson Ruie

Private Frank C. Thompson

Private James Tillman

Private Terrell Trapnell

Private Ben Turner

Company A—Macon County

Captain William A. Wilson (Wounded and captured at Griswoldville)

Lieutenant J. A. Turner244

Sergeant William F. Flowers (Killed at Griswoldville)

Private J. H. Cantrell

Private Henry L. Dyer

Private W. J. Farmer

Private William F. Foster
Private John Godwin
Private Thomas A. Granberry (Killed at
  Griswoldville)
Private Joel Horne
Private Helton Ingram
Private James E. Little
Private Merritt R. Lyon
Private Jesse C. McClendon (Killed at
  Griswoldville)
Private A. F. McDonald
Private John W. McNeil (Wounded at
  Griswoldville)
Private John R. Owen
Private William L. Parham
Private Daniel K. Ryder
Private Joshua Smith (Killed at
  Griswoldville)
Private W. J. Thomas
Private John Tomlinson (Killed at
  Griswoldville)
Private James P. Walker
Private James E. Wimpee

**Company B—Sumter & Webster
  Counties**
Captain A. J. Smith
Captain E. P. West
Captain Robert White (Commanded from
  July 1864)
1st Lieutenant W. F. Lowry245
2d Lieutenant J. J. Oliver (Wounded in
  hand at Griswoldville)
Sergeant J. H. Riddick (Killed at
  Griswoldville)
Corporal W. E. H. Holloman (Wounded
  hand and abdomen at Griswoldville)
Private Arthur D. Applewhite (Wounded in
  buttocks at Griswoldville)
Private Francis Marion Bozeman
Private J. H. Campbell
Private J. H. Cantrell
Private Thomas S. Chappell
Private Francis E. Christian
Private Thomas S. Chappell

Private James R. Coker
Private S. G. Cox
Private A. A. Dantzler
Private N. W. Dozier (Wounded in breast at
  Griswoldville)
Private Joseph L. Free
Private G. W. Glover
Private C. E. Grubbs
Private B. F. Holcombe
Private Allison Jordan
Private Andrew Lowery
Private J. W. F. Lowery
Private L. B. Monroe
Private W. J. Morris
Private J. T. Nicholson (Wounded in face at
  Griswoldville)
Private J. S. Nix
Private Jacob H. Reddick
Private O. J. Reynolds
Private John H. Rumph
Private John Sellers
Private R. T. Sharman
Private Andrew J. Smith
Private James R. Stapleton
Private F. G. Thompson
Private Thomas F. Turner
Private Thomas J. Williams

Company C—Webster & Macon Counties
Captain L. Harp (Wounded right arm and
  neck at Griswoldville)
Private S. B. Addis
Private William I. Ammons
Private A. M. Avery
Private Jonathan Bridges
Private E. L. Duckett
Private R. E. Eubanks
Private R. C. Flanigan (Wounded in groin at
  Griswoldville)
Private W. F. Foster
Private J. I. Gilder
Private T. A. Golden (Wounded left thigh at
  Griswoldville)
Private Levi Hangabook (Wounded left
  hand at Griswoldville)

Private Peter Hester
Private John Hollomon (Wounded left knee
    at Griswoldville)
Private John W. Jones
Private W. F. McClelland
Private W. J. McClelland
Private D. W. Nations
Private T. L. Nations
Private Barton H. Overby
Private T. W. Roberson
Private R. C. Shackelford (Wounded in hip
    at Griswoldville)
Private O. B. Stevens
Private T. D. Taylor
Private M. L. Woods
Private L. C. Woodward
Private M. Young (Died 18 September 1864
    of unknown causes)

Company D—Sumter County
Captain George A. Brown
1st Lieutenant David A. Mayo (Wounded
    left leg at Griswoldville)
Sergeant W. H. D. Cook (Wounded in
    mouth at Griswoldville)
Sergeant Charles W. Morgan (Killed at
    Griswoldville)
Private W. W. Ash
Private C. B. Burruss
Private A. P. Davis
Private Arch Gaddis
Private William Gooch
Private W. H. W. Gurley
Private W. W. Hammond
Private J. H. Hill
Private Jewell Houston
Private W. P. Ingram
Private John A. McDonald (Wounded left
    thigh at Griswoldville)
Private Milledge McLeod (Lost hand at
    Griswoldville)
Private William H. Morgan
Private Thomas R. Murphy
Private Harvey Pitner
Private James R. Robertson

Private John Robinson
Private George D. Rogers
Private Joshua Smith (Killed at
    Griswoldville)
Private L. J. Snellgrove
Private Young Snipes
Private J. H. Westmorland
Private Alexander Wheeler
Private James A. Yeoman
Private M. W. Yeoman
Private M. W. Youmans

Company E—Stewart County
Captain Charles Christian Humber
    (Wounded at Battle of Atlanta, 22 July
    1864 and again at Griswoldville) 246
Captain C. A. Farwell (Killed at
    Griswoldville)
Sergeant S. S. Johnson (Wounded in head at
    Griswoldville)
Ordnance Sergeant Neal Johnson
Sergeant R. E. Shipp (Wounded left foot at
    Griswoldville)
Private John B. Armor
Private J. R. Armstrong
Private Nathaniel Bowers
Private P.S. Bryan(Killed at Griswoldville)
Private W. C. Bryan
Private J. N. Colley (Wounded left thigh at
    Griswoldville)
Private J. F. Copper
Private Robert L. Dent
Private C. A. Dunaway (Wounded left side
    at Griswoldville)
Private George B. Gaddis
Private Young Grindle
Private Lucius F. Humber
Private M. H. Johnson
Private James Jones (Wounded left arm at
    Griswoldville)
Privtae Ed Joiner
Private Allison Jordan
Private George W. Kenyon
Private Alfred Lee (Wounded leg and hand
    at Griswoldville)

Private B. L. McElroy
Private Alladin Thomas Newsom247
(Wounded in hands and thighs at
Griswoldville)
Private B. H. Overby
Private John R. Parramore (Wounded in
thigh at Griswoldville)
Private Wiley Pope (Wounded left thigh at
Griswoldville)
Private B. F. Porter (Wounded left knee at
Griswoldville)
Private Silas Smith
Private James P. Snow
Private Daniel Terry
Private Samuel Lee Terrell

Company F—Brooks County
Captain William Cook (Wounded in face at
Griswoldville)
1st Sergeant A. D. Jackson
Private C. H. Allen
Private W. W. Ash
Private John Beck
Private Joe Chambers
Private G. W. Christy
Private William Couch
Private J. R. Glaze
Private J. K. P. Heard
Private W. P. Ingram
Private F. Jackson (Wounded face and shoulders at Griswoldville)
Private E. B. Magness
Private Alex Miller
Private James M. Mitchell
Private William Perkins (Killed at
Griswoldville)
Private R. Philips (Wounded right hip at
Griswoldville)
Private William Ramey
Private B. T. Ray
Private J. F. Saine
Private M. W. Saine
Private Elisha Seabolt
Private Sam Shoemaker

Private A. J. Smith (Wounded and missing
at Griswoldville)
Private J. M. Taylor
Private F. M. Williams

Company G—Laurens & Macon Counties
Captain Hiram Toliver Gaines
Private A. Baker
Private Thomas Coagle (Wounded in thigh
at Griswoldville)
Private Samuel H. English
Private A. W. Fleming
Private J. B. Hill
Private Isaac Jessup
Private E. Killebrew (Wounded in foot at
Griswoldville)
Private Thomas J. Peterson
Private William A. Underwood (Wounded
left hand at Griswoldville)
Private J. J. Worsham (Wounded left side at
Griswoldville)

Company H—Schley County
Captain William G. Womack
Sergeant Lucius W. Stewart (Wounded right
forearm and hip at Griswoldville)
Private Arthur A. Adams
Private B. F. Blasingame
Private J. H. Bridges
Private W. T. Eason (Wounded in leg at
Griswoldville)
Private Joseph M. Kendrick
Private G. M. Milner (Wounded right
forearm at Griswoldville)
Private Henry Stewart

Company I—Lowndes & Ware Counties
Captain James L. Wilson (Killed at
Griswoldville)
Lieutenant O. A. Crittenden (Wounded
right shoulder at Griswoldville)
Lieutenant W. R. Stewart (Captured and lost
leg at Griswoldville)
Lieutenant J. T. Lockhart (Killed at
Griswoldville)

Sergeant P. W. McLane (Wounded left side at Griswoldville)

Private James Stacy Bailey (Captured at Griswoldville)

Private David M. Bennett

Private R. McD. Bennett

Private J. B. Carr

Private James Carr (Wounded right knee at Griswoldville)

Private G. W. Crawford

Private O. A. Crittenden

Private J. H. Daniel

Private L. B. Formby

Private Private G. W. Glover (Missing at Griswoldville)

Private Arnold Goodwin (Wounded right wrist at Griswoldville)

Private B. B. Hammond

Private E. T. Iseral

Private Jackson Kenney

Private David Miller

Private J. B. Rigdon

Private James Stephens (Missing at Griswoldville)

Private Jacob Stroman (Died 10 September 1864 of unknown causes)

Private Eli Taylor

Private F. G. Thompson

Private W. C. Thompson

Private W. C. Turner

Private Isaac L. Wilson

Company K—McIntosh County

Captain William A. Wilson (Wounded in hand at Griswoldville)

Lieutenant John W. Lowrey

Private P. J. Allen

Private A. M. Bolton

Private E. J. Brooks

Private Robert Burton

Private William L. Blackshear

Private Alfred Dorman

Private J. H. Dupree

Private William P. Finch

Private T. A. Granberry (Killed at Griswoldville)

Private William B. Hays

Private Jesse McClendon (Killed at Griswoldville)

Private J. W. McNeil (Wounded at Griswoldville)

Private John J. Murphy

Private John W. Murphy

Private Miles L. Patrick

Private A. J. Pennington

Private Amos K. Schumpert

Private Joshua Smith (Killed at Griswoldville)

Private H. H. Story

Private W. C. Thompson

Private John Tomlinson (Killed at Griswoldville)

Private Joseph J. Turner

Private B. T. Weaver (Finger shot off at Griswoldville)

Private J. L. Wilson

Private William A. Wilson

Private William G. Womack

Captain A. T. Bennett's Company— Clarke County

Captain A. T. Bennett

Private Augustus D. Eberhart

Private W. R. H. Statham

Captain William Cook's Company— Dougherty & Quitman Counties

Captain William Cook .

Private Alex Miller

Private R. T. Ray

Captain Robert Patton's Company— Worth County

Captain Robert Patton

Private G. W. Bowen

Private Ira Cox

Private James Glen

Private Thomas Griffin

Private J. P. Kimsey

Private Richard Kimsey
Private J. M. Meaders
Private J. L. Nix
Private John Robinson
Private J. P. Thurmond
Private George Turner
Private E. P. West

12th Regiment
Colonel Richard Sims
Lieutenant Colonel Henry Mitchell
Major Patrick H. McGriff
Sergeant John Mitchell, Adjutant

Company A—Brooks County
Captain S. L. Moore (Wounded in side at
Griswoldville)
Lieutenant J. R. Edminston (Wounded in
chin at Griswoldville)
Lieutenant W. W. Grover (Wounded at
Griswoldville)
Private G. J. Bennett
Private D. W. Brooks
Private Joel Burgess
Private Reuben Culp
Private Thomas Drew
Private J. W. Haddock
Private Lewis Hemphill
Private William R. Holloway
Private J. T. S. Humphries
Private William E. Hunter
Private Asa Kemp
Private J. A. McCormac
Private Robert McCoy (Wounded in arm at
Griswoldville)
Private George McMullen
Private Colin C. McRae (Wounded in side
at Griswoldville)
Private S. B. Miller
Private Henry O'Neal
Private Wiley T. Patterson
Private Owen Ramsey
Private Richard Ramsey
Private W. A. Reddick
Private J. G. Scruggs

Private James Simmons
Private Richard J. Stansel
Private William Strickland
Private Thomas G. Wade
Private J. H. White
Private Kinch Williams
Private James Wood (Wounded in leg at
Griswoldville)
Private J. B. Wooten (Wounded at
Griswoldville)
Private C. Yates (Wounded in jaw at
Griswoldville)

Company B—Berrien & Echols Counties
Captain T. M. Ray
Private Felix Banks
Private Benjamin S. Boatwright
Private James A. Bulloch
Private B. E. Chastain
Private Hugh Connell
Private James M. Gramling
Private Joe McCormick
Private E. Murphy
Private Killey Murphy
Private John W. Robinson
Private Joseph Rogers (Wounded in arm at
Griswoldville)
Private J. N. Strickland (Wounded in arm at
Griswoldville)
Private John Tomlinson (Wounded in thigh
at Griswoldville)
Private James Madison Turner
Private Isom Walker
Private J. H. White

**Company C—Mitchell & Thomas
Counties**
Captain J. J. Ivey
1st Lieutenant Patrick Dickey
2d Lieutenant Henry McClendon
3rd Lieutenant William J. Dickey (Wounded
in hip at Griswoldville)
Lieutenant William Hubert
1st Sergeant Fairfax Everett
2d Sergeant Thomas Harwick

3rd Sergeant Robert Madre
4th Sergeant John Mitchell
Sergeant William W. Heir (Wounded at
  Griswoldville)
Corporal John Cochran
Private William Akins
Private John Arnold
Private D. R. Atkinson
Private William Ayers (Wounded in arm at
  Griswoldville)
Private W. Barwick
Private E. S. Birel
Private James M. Blackshear
Private Thomas Blackshear
Private Caswell Braswell (Wounded at
  Griswoldville)
Private Sam Braswell
Private Alva Brown
Private Burwell Brown
Private Robert Brown
Private William Burney
Private Shade Carter
Private E. K. Cochran
Private William Cochran
Private Mike Conan
Private Dudley Cox
Private Isaiah Dekle
Private Henry Dickey
Private John Dickey
Private Robert Donaldson
Private Henry Dunbar
Private James Eberhart
Private William Flanigan
Private Eli Futch
Private Moses Futch
Private William Garnto
Private L. Griffith
Private Bartow Hambleton
Private W. B. Hamilton (Wounded in elbow
  at Griswoldville)
Private John Hancock (Discharged for
  underage at fourteen years)
Private Isaac Thomas Henderson
Private Juniper Hill

Private Henry Hopkins (Drummer boy dis-
  charged at Lovejoy's Station)
Private Hillary Humphries
Private William James
Private A. J. Kleckley
Private William Mathews
Private M. McIntosh
Private Mark McKinnon (Mortally wounded
  at Griswoldville)
Private Kenneth A. McLean
Private Fletcher McQueen
Private William Miles
Private James Miller
Private Henry Mitchell
Private Nelson Mitchell
Private Richard Mitchell
Private Thomas Mitchell
Private John L. Montgomery (Wounded at
  Griswoldville)
Private John Parker
Private James Perry
Private John Pittman
Private J. J. Ragan
Private John Ragans
Private Robert Rainer
Private David Singletary
Private Lewis Singletary
Private Travis Singletary
Private John Slater
Private William Smallwood248
Private William Smith
Private J. N. Strickland
Private Pleasant Vickers
Private Thomas Vickers
Private Alex Wattles
Private Thomas Williams
Private Thomas Young

Company D—Berrien County
Captain Henry A. Knight
Private Eli Brogdon
Private J. D. Dupree
Private J. L. Gufford
Private David Hudson
Private Riley Mathews

Private H. M. McNabb
Private James Parrish
Private Thomas Prescott
Private Isaac Weathers

Company E—Thomasville & Thomas County
Captain Thomas N. Gandy
1st Lieutenant John Stack
3rd Lieutenant A. J. Bulloch
2d Lieutenant Thomas B. Whitfield
(Wounded in forehead at Griswoldville)
Private Jasper Barwick
Private W. Bass
Private T. W. Braswell
Private M. W. Broadway
Private W. P. Burney
Private Jasper Cannon
Private Ben Chastain
Private Mark Collins
Private Hugh Connell
Private William Cox
Private Charles Dekle
Private John Dugger
Private A. G. W. Edwards (Wounded in hip at Griswoldville)
Private Newton Franklin
Private Art Gandy
Private D. Goff
Private L. Griffith (Died 27 August 1864 of unknown causes)
Private Frank Hagan
Private R. Haven
Private G. B. Havers (Wounded in arm at Griswoldville)
Private Daniel Horn
Private William Hubert
Private I. G. Humphries
Private Pleasant Hutchinson
Private A. A. J. Johnson
Private Sam Johnson
Private L. O. Jones
Private W. L. Lance
Private J. G. Mallette
Private Joe McCormick

Private H. D. McCullers
Private Dan McDonald
Private John McDougall
Private Thomas McIntosh
Private Kenneth McKinnon
Privtate M. D. McKinnon (Wounded in thigh at Griswoldville)
Private Robert McMurray
Private Joe McRae
Private Jasper Miles
Private Nathaniel Miller
Private W. B. Mise
Private Thomas Mundy
Private E. R. NeSmith
Private W. Page
Private D. Patterson
Private Delmar Peacock
Private Malcolm Peacock (Wounded in head at Griswoldville)
Private Wiley Pierce
Private C. M. Pilcher
Private J. F. Pilcher
Private Alfred Pollard
Private D. S. Ragan
Private E. Ramsey
Private Tom Ramsey
Private I. I. Reagan
Private Buck Roberts
Private John Rushin
Private Haines Singletary
Private Harrison Singletary
Private Travis Singletary
Private William Singletary
Private Willis Singletary
Private Nathaniel Spangler
Private John Stendard
Private P. Suber
Private Madison Turner
Private Addison Way
Private J. H. Whaley
Privtate I. H. White
Private Moses Williams

Company F—Miller County
Captain L. Q. Sanders

Lieutenant T. J. Cross

Private A. N. Ard

Private Isaac A. Bush

Private P. H. Carter (Wounded in shoulder at Griswoldville)

Private John Duce (Wounded at Savannah, 12 December 1864)

Private William B. Everett

Private Thomas Gordon

Private J. J. Henry (Captured [IN?] Savannah, December 1864)

Private Henry Ivey (Wounded in head at Griswoldville)

Private E. Kerr (Died 11 September 1864 of unknown causes)

Private Thomas Lane (Killed in trenches of Atlanta, 17 August 1864)

Private John T. Norman

Private Emanuel Phillips

Private Silas M. Phillips

Private Albert Pierce

Private John M. Pilcher

Private James E. Roberts

Private L. Q. Saunders

Private J. H. Sheffield (Wounded in leg at Griswoldville)

Private Andrew P. Smith

Private John Stegall

Private Albert Williams

Private Albert J. Williams

Private B. B. Wilson (Wounded in thigh at Griswoldville)

Company G—Colquitt County

Captain Hiram Gay (Wounded at Griswoldville)

Private Isiah Barton

Private John Gay

Private M. L. Gay (Wounded in hand at Griswoldville)

Private S. C. Gregory

Private John D. Hancock

Private Solomon Hiers

Private D. Highsmith (Wounded in shoulder at Griswoldville)

Private Thomas P. Hulsey

Private John Johnson

Private Julius M. King

Private William Mathis

Private James I. Oliver

Private William Owens

Private R. F. Pope

Private Ransom C. Smith

Private Mathew Tucker

Private J. A. Whitley

Private George Wilkes (Wounded in thigh at Griswoldville)

Company H—Decatur County

Captain J. B. Coochman

Lieutenant J. A. O'Neal

Corporal M. O'Neill (Wounded in arm at Griswoldville)

Private J. H. Bailey

Private J. S. M. Donaldson

Private N. J. Edwards

Private Jessey Everitt (Wounded right leg at Griswoldville)

Private R. Galaway (Killed at Griswoldville)

Private Sam Gardner

Private James Giddens

Private John Gilbert

Private Elbert Griffin

Private Joseph Jones

Private W. M. Linson (Contusion of arm at Griswoldville)

Private D. W. Long (Wounded in leg at Griswoldville)

Private John R. McCranie

Private James Park

Private T. A. Parramore (Wounded in foot at Griswoldville)

Private Jethro Patten

Private H. M. Philips (Wounded left arm and face at Griswoldville)

Private H. N. Philips (Killed at Griswoldville)

Private John Ragan

Private Jorden Ragin (Wounded both arms at Griswoldville)

Private Thomas Ray
Private L. R. Rehberg
Private T. J. Rick (Wounded in hip at
   Griswoldville)
Private Sam Smith
Private John T. Wilkerson
Private Jesse Wilkinson
Private Malcom Wilkes (Wounded in arm at
   Griswoldville)
Private John Williams
Private T. J. Worsham

**Company I—Lowndes, Mitchell, &
Talbot Counties**
Captain J. D. Keaton
Captain Jason Maxwell
Lieutenant Mark Griffin
Private J. P. Anderson
Private Henry Connell
Private M. H. Culpepper
Private William H. Culpepper
Private J. W. Glenn
Private Samuel Hudson
Private Joseph C. Jones
Private Mathew Pope
Private Green Spence
Private C. G. Whittel

ANDERSON'S LIGHT ARTILLERY
BATTERY 249

4 12-pounder Napoleons
Captain Ruel W. Anderson
Assistant Surgeon James Leffers
1st Lieutenant Henry Shorter Greaves250
   (Absent without leave from 21 November
   1864, but present at surrender)
2d Lieutenant Robert H. Brown
2d Lieutenant Willis G. Allen
1st Sergeant D. Homer Brown
2d Sergeant John L. Brown
3rd Sergeant Marshall Hill
3rd Sergeant H. F. Manning
4th Sergeant David F. Mathews
5th Sergeant James M. Willis

Corporal Jesse D. Horne
Corporal James Malloy
Corporal Paul Meadows
Corporal E. L. Moran
Corporal William R. Sanders
Corporal David Willis
Private Stephen Akins (Deserted 22
   November 1864 on march from Macon
   to Griswoldville)
Private William Akins (Deserted 22
   November 1864 on march from Macon
   to Griswoldville)
Private William R. Akins
Private W. C. Allen (Killed at Griswoldville)
Private William J. Allen
Private J. J. Anderson
Private James W. Ansley
Private Lemuel Henry Ansley (Returnedned
   to duty from Ocmulgee Hospital 14
   November 1864)
Private Berry Armstrong
Private Dock Arnold
Private Senate Arnold (Wounded at
   Griswoldville)
Private Marcellus E. Barkwell
Private Elisha Barlow
Private Harrison H. Barlow
Private Joseph Barlow
Private H. L. Barron (Deserted 22
   November 1864, before Battle of
   Griswoldville)
Private James P. Barrs
Private C. A. Bell
Private Joseph Bell
Private John Blount
Private Spire M. Blount
Private Stephen Blount
Private T. M. Brady
Private James Branham
Private J. W. Britton
Private C. P. Brown
Private Calvin R. Brown
Private George W. Brown
Private John W. Brown
Private Samuel Brown

Private Burrell Bryant
Private W. W. Clemens
Private Andrew Coleman
Private John A. Coleman
Private James Coody (Deserted 22
  November 1864)
Private Lewis Coody
Private Richard Coone
Private Benjamin Coudy
Private Stiron B. Coudy
Private John A. Crow
Private Burrell Crumley
Private John M. Crump
Private J. E. Crumpton
Private F. S. Daniel
Private Bryant Davis
Bugler W. F. Dorris
Private Thomas H. Dunn
Private J. M. Dupree
Private Thomas R. Dupree
Private M. E. English
Private G. W. Evans
Private Wade Evans
Private John T. Evers
Private James H. Fenn
Private Archibald Floyd
Private Frederick Floyd
Private Shade Floyd
Private James Forehand
Private Samuel Forehand
Private Perry Gentry
Private Benjamin Giddens (Mortally
  wounded at Griswoldville)
Private James Giddens
Private John N. Giddens
Private V. B. Gosden (Wounded at
  Griswoldville)
Private Joshua Grantham (Deserted 28
  October 1864 from Macon)
Private Louis W. Gregory
Private G. J. R. Grimsley
Private J. Crawford Grimsley (Sent to hos-
  pital in Macon 23 November 1864 by
  Captain Anderson)
Private William Grimsley

Private Cornelius Grissum
Private Frederick Grist
Private John J. Hanley
Private L. Hartman
Private Henry J. Harvey
Private John P. Harvey
Private Augustus Haskins
Private William B. Haskins
Private Joseph Hayes
Private J. J. Henley
Private James Holland
Private William Holland
Private James F. Horne
Private Thomas J. Horne (Deserted 22
  November 1864, before Battle of
  Griswoldville)
Private Robert Jones
Private Hiram J. Jump
Private E. M. King
Private S. B. Lawson
Private Jordan Lee
Private John Lucas
Private Benjamin Maddox
Private William Maloy
Private Thomas McCullough
Private Andrew H. Metts
Private T. A. Mullis
Private David Nichols
Farrier Henry P. Palmer (Deserted 28
  October 1864 from camp at Macon)
Private H. L. T. Parkerson
Private Union Pickern
Private Amos Pipkin
Private Edward Pipkin
Private John Pipkin
Private John Porter
Private Uriah Porter
Private G. F. Powell (Deserted 25 November
  1864 from Macon)
Private J. M. Pritchett
Private James Rodgers (Deserted 22
  November 1864 before Battle of
  Griswoldville)
Private Robert Rodgers (Severely wounded
  at Griswoldville)

Private James W. Rosier

Private Meady Rozier (Deserted 25 November 1864 at Macon)

Private Malta Scarborough (Wounded by accident at Doctortown GA, 3 December 1864)

Private Beverly A. J. Simmons

Private Murdock J. Simmons

Private William Simmons

Private Eli D. Smith

Private J. G. Smith

Private D. Washington Southerland

Private D. L. Stewart

Private J. D. Stewart

Private L. W. Stewart

Private McDonald Stewart

Private Thomas Stewart (Absent without leave from 25 November 1864 since reported to be sick)

Private J. S. Thomas

Private Elihu Thompson

Private J. E. Trippe

Private Jesse Wade

Private William Wade

Private Willis Wade

Private A. J. Walker

Private George W. Walker

Private Gus M. Walker

Private W. B. West

Private Robert White

Private Vincent White

Private M. M. Willis

Private John G. Woods

Private Joseph F. Wynne

ATHENS LOCAL DEFENSE BATTALION [251]

Major Ferdinand W. C. Cook (Shot in head and killed near Daley's Farm 11 December 1864, during the Siege of Savannah)

Chief Surgeon E. J. Eldridge

Acting Surgeon R. M. Smith

Acting Surgeon George M. Duggan

Captain Francis L. Cook

Captain William N. Pendergrass252 (Wounded at Griswoldville)

Captain W. H. Sims

Captain _____ Elliott (Commanded Company D at Griswoldville)

1stLieutenant Wiley F. Hood

1st Lieutenant James Griffith

1st Lieutenant A. M. Wyng (Wounded left arm at Griswoldville)

Lieutenant _____ Mainus253 (Wounded at Griswoldville)

1st Lieutenant J. H. Hunter (Killed at Griswoldville)

1st Lieutenant Thomas E. Middlebrooks (Wounded in knee at Griswoldville)

2d Lieutenant T. J. Fitzpatrick

2d Lieutenant Thomas Cooper

3rd Lieutenant H. S. Snow

2d Lieutenant J. Salisbury

2d Lieutenant A. P. Hand (Wounded in head at Griswoldville)

Sergeant _____ Framer (Wounded at Griswoldville)

1st Sergeant L. M. Hand (Captured 21 December 1864, at Savannah)

1st Sergeant J. C. Jackson

1st Sergeant Charles Stevens

2d Sergeant Samuel Bailey

2d Sergeant F. J. Snow

3rd Sergeant J. A. Cooper

4th Sergeant W. H. Freeman

4th Sergeant W. W. Smith

5th Sergeant John Harper

Corporal J. W. Bagnon

Corporal _____ Booth (Wounded at Griswoldville)

1st Corporal Joseph Bull

1st Corporal John Dormer

1st Corporal John Zedaker

2d Corporal Allen Brena

2d Corporal H. H. Goodwyn

3rd Corporal W. J. Conley

3rd Corporal W. P. Wayne

4th Corporal R. M. Breedlove

4th Corporal George Collins
4th Corporal T. M. Lampkin
Private S. H. Adams
Private J. W. Anthony
Private W. Atkinson
Private W. T. Aughtry
Private J. A. Baker
Private C. Bandeloff
Private Samuel Bassett
Private J. R. Bates
Private J. H. Beall (Missing at Griswoldville)
Private R. Beall (Mssing at Griswoldville)
Private W. A. Beall
Private James Bearden (Wounded at
    Griswoldville)
Private Joseph Bearden
Private J. C. Bell
Private R. W. Bell (Wounded in hand at
    Griswoldville)
Private W. T. Bell
Private Thomas Bible (Wounded at
    Griswoldville)
Private Charles Bier
Private M. R. Boggs (Wounded in arm at
    Griswoldville)
Private J. C. Bone
Private J. A. Booth
Private S. W. Booth
Private M. T. Boyce
Private W. M. Boyce
Private James Brack (Wounded at
    Griswoldville)
Private Z. Brake
Private James Brane (Wounded in mouth at
    Griswoldville)
Private C. Braselman
Private J. F. Breedlove
Private J. W. Breedlove
Private James Brewer
Private Raleigh Brimm
Private D. A. Brown
Private G. C. Brown
Private G. W. Bryan
Private W. J. Brymer
Private James Burpee

Private William Burrows
Private J. R. Cawthres (Missing at
    Griswoldville)
Private John Chancy (Killed at
    Griswoldville)
Private W. Childers
Private C. Clearland (Killed at
    Griswoldville)
Private A. J. Cleveland
Private D. M. Clower
Private T. L. Clower
Private A. Cochran
Private Fulcher Comer
Private J. R. Comer
Private R. Comer
Private Harry Cook
Private Jesse Cook
Private C. B. Cooper
Private John Cosley
Private W. C. Craft
Private W. Creighton
Private C. C. Curry
Private E. Damron
Private J. F. Darby
Private Frank Davenport
Private S. L. Davenport
Private W. Davenport
Private M. L. Davis
Private George DeBue
Private J. Dorand
Private William Dorand (age fourteen)
Private Green Dottery
Private T. Douglass
Private J. H. Dudson (Wounded in hand at
    Griswoldville)
Private J. W. Dunn
Private H. W. Durham (Wounded in
    stomach at Griswoldville)
Private M. G. Durham (Missing at
    Griswoldville)
Private Joseph Emerick
Private M. Eppes
Private William Estes
Private P. D. Farrerr
Private Jacob Fesler

Private James Few (Wounded in foot at
Griswoldville)

Private L. C. Franks

Private Jack Freeman (Missing at
Griswoldville)

Private David Gann

Private J. C. Gant

Private J. R. Gardner (Wounded in foot ast
Griswoldville)

Private Thomas Gean

Private _____ Gellart (Wounded at
Griswoldville)

Private A. Gillen

Private John Gilliland

Private A. Gilmore

Private J. M. Ginn (Wounded in hand at
Griswoldville)

Private G. W. Gordon

Private J. C. Grant

Private J. A. Grebold

Private G. W. Green

Private Robert Gribbs

Private S. B. Griffin

Private J. F. Hails

Private J. H. Hale

Private J. M. Hale

Private W. T. Hale

Private J. T. Hall

Private Thomas Hall

Private W. C. Hall (Wounded in breast at
Griswoldville)

Private Alexander Hamilton (Wounded at
Griswoldville)

Private H. L. Harper

Private William Hartly

Private Joseph Heffley

Private John Hembree

Private F. M. Hernden

Private R. W. Herod

Private J. W. Herrod

Private Charles Hester

Private T. L. Hewson

Private William A. Hinton

Private David Hodges (Wounded at
Griswoldville)

Private Joseph Hodges

Private Thomas Hodges

Private R. H. Howard (Mortally wounded at
Griswoldville)

Private W. J. Howington

Private R. J. Hughes

Private Job Hunter

Private W. James

Private Jabers Johnes

Private T. G. Jordan (Wounded in arm at
Griswoldville)

Private David Knott

Private James Leary

Private James Linsey

Private G. W. Long

Private Robert Loony

Private B. S. Mahaffey

Private D. S. Marett

Private S. A. Marett

Private S. H. Marett

Private T. C. Marett

Private W. G. Marett

Private J. F. Marsten

Private A. Mass (Wounded at Griswoldville)

Private J. L. Mathews

Private J. P. McAlister

Private T. McCardle (Wounded in hand at
Griswoldville, age sixteen)

Private W. B. McCay

Private M. Melton

Private E. W. Merrett

Private J. R. Michaell

Private J. Middlebrooks (Wounded at
Griswoldville)

Private W. L. Milholan

Private B. H. Milican

Private J. L. Miller (Wounded at
Griswoldville)

Private J. P. Mills

Private M. A. Millsas (Wounded both thighs
at Griswoldville)

Private J. A. Moody (Wounded in hand at
Griswoldville)

Private John Moody

Private Robert Moore

Private John Morris

Private Frank Narbon

Private J. R. Nichols

Private A. Norris

Private Jack O'Farral

Private Ira D. Oglesby (age fourteen)

Private J. G. Oglesby

Private S. H. Oglesby

Private E. O'Neil

Private W. O'Neil

Private W. B. Owen

Private C. D. Parker

Private S. T. Parker

Private J. Parks

Private N. M. Parks (age fourteen)

Private William Parks (Missing at
   Griswoldville)

Private James Patat (age fourteen)

Private W. M. Payne

Private W. T. Pitman

Private H. C. Pollard

Private Henry Pruit

Private John Rawson

Private W. A. P. Reed

Private J. W. Rhodes

Private N. E. Rhodes (Wounded at
   Griswoldville)

Private D. Richardson (Wounded in hand at
   Griswoldville)

Private H. P. Richter

Private E. W. Riley

Private F. Robinson (age fourteen)

Private Jesse Robinson

Private W. M. Rudolph

Private W. A. Sanders

Private Frank Sannoner

Private S. S. Saunders

Private John Saylers

Private W. Simpson

Private J. F. Sims

Private W. J. W. Skelton

Private E. A. Smith

Private A. D. Snow (Missing at
   Griswoldville)

Private J. W. Starr

Private W. B. Stockdale

Private William Stone (Wounded at
   Griswoldville)

Private B. Stonecypher

Private W. W. Stribbling

Private C. C. Swan

Private W. A. Talmadge

Private W. R. Tanney (Missing at
   Griswoldville)

Private R. O. Thurman

Private Thomas Trainer

Private W. M. Treadway

Private Eli Treadwell

Private E. F. Tribble

Private J. B. Turner

Private B. F. Venable

Private J. C. Vickers

Private Isaac Vincent

Private W. S. Walker

Private William Walker (Wounded at
   Griswoldville)

Private W. M. Walkins

Private W. J. Wallace (Wounded in foot at
   Griswoldville)

Private T. C. Warner (Wounded at
   Griswoldville)

Private W. H. Watkins

Private B. W. Watters (Wounded at
   Griswoldville)

Private J. S. Wayne

Private J. W. White (Wounded at
   Griswoldville)

Private L. M. White (Wounded in thigh 21
   November 1864 at Macon and deserted
   19 December 1864)

Private Samuel M. White (Wounded both
   thighs at Griswoldville)

Private J. C. Wilkins

Private W. W. Wilson

Private J. J. Wood

Private James Wright

Private John M. Wright (Wounded at
   Griswoldville)

Private S. M. Wright

Private D. P. Young

THE AUGUSTA BATTALION [254]

Major George T. Jackson
Surgeon W. B. Cheesborough
Private William C. Cartright

Company A

Captain T. H. Holleyman
Lieutenant T. A. H. Meyer (Wounded in hand at Griswoldville)
Private Simeon Buford (Wounded in arm at Griswoldville)
Private William Churchill (Wounded in shoulder at Griswoldville)
Private John Copeland (Wounded in foot at Griswoldville)
Private W. O. Dunbar (Wounded in arm at Griswoldville)
Private R. J. Morrison (Wounded in leg at Griswoldville)

Company B

Captain Jacob Adams (Wounded at Griswoldville)
Lieutenant G. P. Weigle (Wounded in shoulder at Griswoldville)
Corporal _____ Job (Missing at Griswoldville)
Private _____ Goodyear (Wounded in shoulder at Griswoldville)
Private J. Witherington (Wounded at Honey Hill)

Company C

Captain A. T. Smith
Lieutenant S. Poole (Wounded in head at Griswoldville)
Sergeant W. H. Murden (Wounded in thigh at Griswoldville)
Private J. D. Andrews (Wounded in shoulder at Griswoldville)
Private W. C. Cartwright (Wounded in leg at Griswoldville)

Private D. Gaunt (Wounded in shoulder at Griswoldville)
Private Jerry Gleason (Wounded in leg at Griswoldville)
Private E. Lublin (Wounded in head and thigh at Griswoldville)
Private John Scales (Missing at Griswoldville)
Private M. P. Scales (Missing at Griswoldville)
Private George Shiver (Missing at Griswoldville)
Private James Walker (Missing at Griswoldville)
Private W. H. Woods (Wounded in head at Griswoldville)

Company D

Captain James C. Sentell
Sergeant J. H. Tice (Wounded in shoulder and neck at Honey Hill)
Corporal _____ Welch (Wounded in leg at Griswoldville)
Private A. Belcher (Killed at Griswoldville)
Private H. Frydell (Wounded in leg and arm at Griswoldville)
Private D. Halslop (Wounded in neck at Griswoldville)
Private James Herring (Wounded in hip at Griswoldville)
Private Joseph Hudson (Wounded in arm at Griswoldville)
Private J. Lemore (Wounded in hand at Griswoldville)

Company E

Lieutenant _____ Shackleford (Missing at Griswoldville)
Private George Tomens (Wounded at Griswoldville)
Private Henry Reeves (Wounded at Griswoldville)

CASUALTIES AT THE BATTLE OF GRISWOLDVILLE 22 NOVEMBER 1864 [255]

Total casualties more than 500; c. 2,300 present

1st Division Georgia Militia
Brigadier General Pleasant J. Philips, Commanding 1st Brigade—Detached

2d Brigade
Colonel James N. Mann

4th Regiment
Colonel James N. Mann

Company A
Captain Samuel Harben (no casualties found)

Company B
Captain Wilson Davis (no casualties found)

Company C
(Commander not recorded)
Private William Whatley–wounded

Company D
Captain R. F. Pitman
(no casualties found)

Company E
(Commander not recorded and no casualties found)

Company F
Captain J. W. Payne
Private William F. Burroughs–wounded in head
Private James Credille–wounded

Private Porer Fears–wounded
Private Joseph Few–wounded
Private George Stovall–wounded in neck
Private Seaborn Walker–wounded in thigh
Private Walter L. Zachry–wounded in leg

Company G
Captain J. M. Lane (no casualties found)

Company H
Captain Dock Owens
Captain Joseph J. Prather–wounded
Lieutenant William Mitchell–Mortally wounded
Private James Long–wounded
Private Joseph Long–wounded
Private George Malcom–captured
Private John Nunnally–wounded
Private Junius Williams–wounded

Company I
(Commander not recorded and no casualties found)

5th Regiment
Colonel Henry H. Floyd
Lieutenant Colonel John Thomas Bowdoin–wounded in foot
Lieutenant J. M. Bonner–killed
Sergeant Major William A. Gatewood–wounded in leg
Private William Hawkins–wounded in hip
Private H. Raldin–wounded in neck

Company A
Captain J. P. A. DuPont
Sergeant W. C. Caldwell–Mortally wounded

Company B
Captain H. S. Parks (no casualties found)

Company C
Captain D. G. Johnson (no casualties found)

Company E

Captain Arch Pittman–killed
Captain George Walker–wounded

Company F
Captain William A. Harris (no casualties found)

Company G
Captain C. E. Clark (no casualties found)

Company H
Captain Benjamin F. Adams
1st Sergeant J. A. Davis–killed
Private J. M. Adams–wounded in arm
Private Howell Baldwin–wounded
Private Carroll Caswell–killed
Private William Hawkins–killed
Private Ralph Jones–wounded in foot
Private Asa Martin–wounded in side
Private James Middleton–wounded in shoulder
Private A. S. Mosley–missing
Private D. A. Savis–killed
Private William Seals–killed
Private Elijah Wheeler–killed
Private Paul Wheeler–killed
Private John Wilson–killed

Company I
Captain Fleming Jordan
Private John W. Grubbs–wounded
Private Thomas Piper–wounded

Company K
Captain James Bostwick (no casualties found)

6th Regiment
Colonel J. W. Burney
Lieutenant Colonel Frank George–Mortally wounded

Company A
Captain T. C. Reedy (no casualties sustained)

Company B
Captain Washington Mann
Private Samuel Barron–Mortally wounded
Private Jack Clark–wounded
Private William Willis–wounded

Company C
Captain John Phillips
Private E. J. Dooling–wounded and lost leg

Company D
Captain James Wiggins
Private J. Smith–wounded

Company E
Captain T.M. Peeples
Private S.H. Cannon–wounded

Company G
Captain W. H. Bryam (no casualties)

Company H
Captain Fleming Ward (no casualties found)

Company I
1st Lieutenant R. B. Johnson (no casualties found)

Company K
(Commander not recorded and no casualties found)

Company L
Captain M. B.Holland (no casualties found)

3rd Brigade
Brigadier General Charles D. Anderson–wounded in hand and had two horses shot from under him

7th Regiment
Colonel Abner F. Redding–killed
Captain _____ Adams–wounded
Lieutenant _____ Hamilton–wounded

Company A
Lieutenant Wiley Sikes–wounded in leg
Sergeant Thomas Dumas–wounded in arm
Private William Evans–wounded in foot

Company B
Captain J. T. Collier
Corporal A. C. Colvard–wounded in foot
Corporal J. A. G. Phinizy–wounded in breast
Private J. T. Childs–wounded in foot
Private R. Whatley–wounded in thigh
Private John Winn–missing

Company C
Lieutenant Lewis "Gipp" Willcox
Lieutenant Walter T. McArthur–wounded
Lieutenant W. Wilcox–wounded in thigh
Sergeant John W. McArthur–wounded in side
Sergeant William R. Ryals–wounded in knee
Private Thomas B. Adams–wounded head
Private Groves Connor–killed
Private Addison C. McArthur–killed
Private John J. McArthur–wounded and missing
Private W. D. Penick–wounded in foot
Private William Ryals–killed
Private M. K. Wilcox–wounded

Company D
Captain J. G. Green
Corporal T. G. King–killed
Private Obadiah Edge–wounded in ankle
Private T. L. Turk–wounded in arm
Private James White–wounded in foot

Company E
Captain John Power
(no casualties found)

Company F
Captain R. G. Fulgam–wounded in leg
Lieutenant A. C. McPhail–wounded and missing

Sergeant D. H. Henley–wounded in thigh
Private John King–wounded in arm

Company G
Captain S. D. Fuller
Private J. A. Gibbs–wounded and missing
Private R. A. Gibbs–wounded in shoulder
Private Darling Grain–wounded and missing
Private Allen Marshall–wounded in thigh
Private W. D. Swain–wounded and captured
Private George W. Young–wounded and missing

Company H
Captain Charnel C. Hightower–wounded in foot
Private Jack Bussey–wounded in shoulder
Private James E. Coppedge–wounded in thigh
Private George Gardner–killed

Company I
Captain Daniel Fraser McRae–wounded in arm
1st Lieutenant John A. Powell–Mortally wounded
2d Lieutenant Thomas McDuffie–Mortally wounded
Sergeant William F. Williams–wounded in breast
Corporal Thomas J. McRae–wounded in hand
Private James H. Lindsey–wounded in right shoulder
Private John C. McLean–killed

Company K
Captain W. T. Morgan–wounded
Captain S. H. Singleton–wounded in head
Sergeant Blanton Nance–wounded, shoulder and neck
Private E. Erwin–missing
Private Peyton Horton–wounded in leg
Private H. Johnson–missing
Private Arthur Newton–wounded in head

Private William Warren–missing
Private D. Wartz–missing

8th Regiment
Colonel William B. Scott
Captain M. E. Boatwright, Adjunt[???]

Company A
1st Lieutenant B. F. White–wounded both
  knees
Private W. T. Braswell–wounded both lungs
Private James Bryant–wounded
Private James Fry–wounded
Private O. T. Myoch–wounded in shoulder
  and missing
Private C. F. White–Mortally wounded

Company B
(On detached service)
Captain D. A. Green

Company C
1st Lieutenant M. Jones
Sergeant B. F. Fenney–wounded in jaw
Private C. Catton–wounded in leg

Company D
Captain Eli Cummings
Sergeant William R. Ryals–wounded in knee
Private Urias E. Adkins–Mortally wounded
Private Andrew Chambers–wounded in
  thigh
Private James M. Manson–killed
Private W. H. Ogburn–wounded
Private O. H. P. Rawls–wounded in thigh
Private J. J. L. Smith–wounded left side
Private W. L. Smith–wounded in hand

Company E
Sergeant_____ Beckom
Private Elias Champion–killed
Private J.D. Tharp–wounded in arm
Company F
1st Lieutenant G.W. Thames
2d Lieutenant Henry Edmondson

Private S.F. Bryant–wounded
Company G
1st Lieutenant _____ Hollaman
Corporal W. R. Gilbert–wounded in both
  thighs
Private M. Dominac–wounded in both arms
Private Joel Harris–wounded in leg
Private A. Vinson–wounded in leg
Private Ben Vinson–wounded in side

Company H
Captain R. H. Barron
Lieutenant Jonathon Baker–wounded in
  wrist
Lieutenant Jonathon Humphrie–wounded
  in left hand
Private William H. Jolly–killed
Private N. Morris–wounded in right arm
Private Wiley Vinson–wounded in side

Company I
Captain John T. Lingo
Private Henry A. Wood–captured

Company K
Captain T. M. Hunt
2d Lieutenant John Baker–wounded in left
  arm
Private W. Cairy–wounded in hand
Private W. D. Darm–wounded in side and
  arm
Private J. Hawkins–wounded in hip
Private J. Van Zant–wounded both knees

9th Regiment
Colonel John M. Hill
Lieutenant Colonel T. S. Sherman–wounded
  in shoulder
Major W. A. Turner–wounded in leg
Surgeon J. S. Henry–wounded

Company A
Captain James L. Turner
Private Z. T. Crawford–wounded in thigh
Private J. C. Forbes–killed

Private John Leaker–missing
Private S. L. Lorger–wounded left arm
Private A. W. Phillips–killed
Private L. Shell–wounded in thigh
Private R. D. Smith–wounded in elbow

Company B
Captain W. H. Hinton
Corporal W. T. Bussey–wounded in both
feet and arms
Private James Callaway–killed
Private L. M. Chunn–wounded in shoulder
Private T. J. Hardaway–wounded right knee
Private Thomas Hattaway–Mortally
wounded
Private John R. O'Cain–wounded in
shoulder
Private John B. Pope–wounded in shoulder
Private P. Strozier–wounded in hip and
shoulder

Company C
Captain W. H. Chambliss
Lieutenant J. B. Chamblis–wounded in both
feet
Sergeant R. M. Canton–wounded in arm
Private J. W. Hammock–wounded head and
hand
Private W. Rothermel–Mortally wounded
Private H. M. Smith–Mortally wounded
Private H. M. Snead–missing
Private A. Teal–missing

Company D
Captain Clark Mattox
Lieutenant L. Farmer–killed
Lieutenant _____ Semms–Mortally
wounded
Lieutenant Thomas Swint–wounded
1st Sergeant _____ Lee–wounded in hip
Private John Anderson–wounded
Private _____ Dykes–wounded
Private J. R. Getton–wounded in leg
Private Ira Scoggins–wounded
Private John I. Scoggins–wounded right foot

Company E
Captain E. F. Strozier–killed
Sergeant Thomas Michain–wounded in arm
Private John W. Matthews–wounded in
thigh
Private Wade Stewart–wounded

Company F
Lieutenant William C. Bray
Sergeant R. B. Lyle–missing
Sergeant R. F. Patillo–wounded
Corporal H. M. Jackson–missing
Private H. T. Butts–killed
Private G. W. Childs–wounded in thigh
Private W. I. Cole–Mortally wounded
Private T. A. Dallas–missing
Private C. H. Green–wounded
Private B. G. McKenney–wounded

Company G
Captain John Kennon
Private James Blow–missing
Private Benjamin Boddi–wounded
Private Bennett Boddie–Mortally wounded
Private Abe Coates–wounded
Private John Copeland–wounded
Private David Evans–wounded
Private James H. Freeman–missing
Private Thomas H. Freeman–wounded
Private C. M. Grant–wounded
Private Wilkerson Grant–wounded
Private William A. Harris–killed
Private James Hubbard–wounded hip and
arm
Private Jonathon H. Hubbard–wounded
Private Hartwell Passmore–wounded in knee
Private Joe Pollard–missing
Private W. S. Saxon–wounded in leg
Private C. Williams–missing

Company H
Captain B. Gray–wounded
Lieutenant J. D. Thurman–wounded
Sergeant J. B. L. Watson–wounded
Sergeant A. N. Camp–wounded

Corporal G. Hall–wounded
Private J. R. Cotton–wounded
Private J. W. Moore–wounded
Private J.W. Odom–wounded

Company I
Captain H. E. Moss–wounded
2d Lieutenant E. G. Tucker–wounded
1st Corporal A. F. Truett–wounded
Private Andrew Clines–killed
Private J. W. Davidson–killed
Private Thomas Dillamer–killed
Private Thomas DeLoach–killed
Private John S. Goodman–wounded
Private Wilson Hargett–Mortally wounded
Private Joel A. Hulling–wounded in leg
Private J. R. McDaniel–wounded in hand
Private A. C. Tuett–wounded in nose
Private P. M. B Williams–wounded

Company K
Captain Talbert Wimberly–wounded in arm
1st Lieutenant James T. Phillips–wounded in
    hand
Sergeant J. P. Leonard–missing
Private S. Beckey–wounded in thigh
Private D. C. Bellingein–missing
Private T. Castleberry–wounded in leg
Private John M. Proctor–wounded knees
    and arms
Private Charles Togity–missing
Private J. H. Willis–wounded shoulder and
    arms

4th Brigade
Brigadier General Henry Kent McCay

10th Regiment
Colonel Charles M. Davis
Major Thomas Ransom–captured

Company A
Captain R. F. Man
Sergeant D. A. Cochran–wounded in neck

Sergeant George T. Marshall–wounded in
    shoulder
Corporal F. M. Green–wounded
Corporal C. F. Kaigler–wounded in knee
Private J. E. Hunter–wounded in arm & hip
Private Jesse D. Jarnigan–wounded in head
Private J. C. T. Jordan–wounded in leg
Private C. C. Kercy–wounded in hand
Private C. P. Kitchen–wounded in ankle

Company B
Captain C. C Yarbrough–wounded and lost
    leg
1st Lieutenant George Davis–wounded in
    neck
2d Lieutenant E. G. Cox–wounded in finger
3rd Lieutenant J. T. Jenkins–wounded in
    arm
Private David Merritt–wounded in arm
Private Henry Pittman–wounded in side

Company C
Lieutenant H. Perry–killed
Sergeant John Chancey–killed
Private John Bird–wounded in head and
    neck
Private John Lanier–mortally wounded

Company D
Captain John Stewart
Lieutenant William Crawford–wounded
Corporal Walter Watts–wounded right
    shoulder
Private J. E. Albriton–killed
Private A. Peterson– wounded right shoulder
Private John F. Rish–missing

Company E
Captain J. Oates
Private S. Butler– wounded in arm

Company F
1st Lieutenant D. McClelland
1st Sergeant William J. Ford–wounded in
    breast

Private Moses A. Blick–killed
Private William Henderson–wounded in leg
Private Andrew J. Walker

Company G
Captain William C. Gill
1st Lieutenant A. A. Paul–wounded in arm
2d Lieutenant George C. Edwards
Sergeant W. Martin–killed
Corporal B. F. Lanier–Mortally wounded
Private G. W. Dawson–wounded in hip
Private J. M. Griffin–wounded in hand
Private J. H. Bunk Hudnell–mortally
  wounded
Private Almorine V. McLeod–wounded
Private J. G. Miller–killed
Private D. A. Pettis–wounded
Private John L. Thomas–wounded in neck
Private William Ward–wounded in breast
  and hip
Private S. M. Wilson–wounded in knee

Company H
Captain Reuben F. Simmons
Lieutenant N. Corquodale–wounded in
  shoulder
Sergeant J. B. Boynton–lost arm
Corporal T. W. Todd–killed
Private D. Merrit–wounded in hand
Private E. J. Thigpen–wounded in jaw and
  wrist

Company I
(Commander not recorded)
Sergeant George W. Kendrick–wounded in
  head
Private John K. Hall–wounded in hip
Private James E. Philips–wounded both legs
Private Charles L. Shaw–wounded in
  shoulder

Company K
Captain John B. Pollock
Private A. J. Boon–missing
Private W. Bridges–missing

Private J. R. Ferguson–wounded in forehead
Private Angus McLeod–missing

11th Regiment
Colonel William T. Toole
Lieutenant Colonel James B.
  Pickett–wounded left side
Major David L. Wicker–wounded left leg
Sergeant Major J. W. Wells–wounded right
  side

Company A
Captain William A. Wilson–wounded and
  captured
Lieutenant J. A. Turner
Sergeant William F. Flowers–killed
Private Thomas A. Granberry–killed
Private Jesse C. McClendon–killed
Private John W. McNeil–wounded
Private Joshua Smith–killed
Private John Tomlinson–killed

Company B
1st Lieutenant W. F. Lowry
2d Lieutenant J. J. Oliver–wounded in hand
Sergeant J. H. Riddick–killed
Corporal W. E. H. Holloman–wounded in
  hand
Private Arthur D. Applewhite–wounded in
  buttocks
Private N. W. Dozier–wounded in breast
Private J. T. Nicholson–wounded in face

Company C
Captain L. Harp–wounded right arm and
  neck
Private R. C. Flanigan–wounded in groin
Private T. A. Golden–wounded left thigh
Private Levi Hangabook–wounded left hand
Private John Holloman–wounded left knee
Private R. C. Shackelford–wounded hip

Company D
Captain George A. Brown

1st Lieutenant David A. Mayo–wounded left leg

Sergeant W. H. D. Cook–wounded in mouth

Sergeant Charles W. Morgan–killed

Private John A. McDonald–wounded left thigh

Private Milledge McLeod–wounded and lost hand

Private Joshua Smith–killed

Company E

Captain Charles Christain Humber–wounded

Captain C. A. Farwell–killed

Sergeant S. S. Johnson–wounded in head

Sergeant R. E. Shipp–wounded left foot

Private J. N. Colley–wounded left thigh

Private C. A. Dunaway–wounded left side

Private James Jones–wounded left arm

Private Alfred Lee–wounded leg and hand

Private Alladin T. Newsom–wounded

Private John R. Parramore–wounded in thigh

Private Wiley Pope–wounded left thigh

Private B. F. Porter–wounded left knee

Company F

Captain William Cook–wounded face and shoulders

Private F. Jackson–wounded face & shoulder

Private William Perkins–killed

Private R. Philips–wounded right hip

Private A. J. Smith–wounded and missing

Company G

Captain Hiram Toliver Gaines

Private Thomas Coagle–wounded in thigh

Private E. Killebrew–wounded in foot

Private William A. Underwood–wounded left hand

Private J. J. Worsham–wounded left side

Company H

Captain William G. Womack

Sergeant Lucius W. Stewart–wounded forearm & hip

Private W. T. Eason–wounded in leg

Private G. M. Milner–wounded right forearm

Company I

Captain James L. Wilson–killed

Lieutenant O. A. Crittenden–wounded right shoulder

Lieutenant W. R. Stewart–captured and lost leg

Lieutenant J. T. Lockheart–killed

Sergeant P. W. McLane–wounded left side

Private James Stacy Bailey–captured

Private James Carr–wounded right wrist

Private G. W. Glover–missing

Private Arnold Goodwin–wounded right wrist

Private James Stephens–missing

Company K

Captain William A. Wilson–wounded in head

Private T. A. Granberry–killed

Private Jesse McClendon–killed

Private J.W. McNeil–wounded

Private Joshua Smith–killed

Private John Tomlinson–killed

Private B. T. Weaver–finger shot off

Private P. W. H. Weaver–missing

Captain A. T. Bennett's Company

Captain A. T. Bennett (no casualties found)

Captain William Cook's Company

Captain William Cook (no casualties found)

Captain Robert Patton's Company

Captain Robert Patton (no casualties found)

12th Regiment

Colonel Richard Sims

Company A

Captain S. L. Moore–wounded in side
Lieutenant J. R. Edminston–wounded in
  chin
Lieutenant W. L. Grover–wounded in hip
Private Robert McCoy–wounded in arm
Private Colin C. McRae–wounded in side
Private James Wood–wounded in leg
Private J. B. Wooten–wounded in neck
Private C. Yates–wounded in jaw

Company B
Captain T. M. Ray
Private Joseph Rogers–wounded in arm
Private J. N. Strickland–wounded in arm
Private John Tomlinson–wounded in thigh

Company C
Captain J. J. Ivey
3rd Lieutenant William Dickey–wounded in
  hip
Sergeant William W. Heir–wounded
Private William Ayers–wounded in arm
Private Caswell Braswell–wounded
Private W. B. Hamilton–wounded in elbow
Private Mark McKinnon–mortally wounded
Private John L. Montgomery–killed

Company D
Captain Henry A. Knight (no casualties
  found)

Company E
Captain Thomas N. Gandy
2d Lieutenant Thomas B.
  Whitfield–wounded
Private A. G. W. Edwards–wounded in hip
Private G. B. Havers–wounded in arm
Private M. D. McKinnon–wounded in thigh
Private Malcolm Peacock–wounded in head

Company F
Captain L. Q. Sanders
Private P. H. Carter–wounded in shoulder
Private Henry Ivey–wounded in head
Private J. H. Sheffield–wounded in leg

Private B. B. Wilson–wounded in thigh

Company G
Captain Hiram Gay–wounded
Private M. L. Gay–wounded in hand
Private D. Highsmith–wounded in shoulder
Private George Wilkes–wounded in thigh

Company H
Captain J. B. Coochman
Corporal M. O'neill–wounded in arm
Private Jessey Everitt–wounded right leg
Private R. Galaway–killed
Private D. W. Long–wounded in leg
Private W. M. Linson–contusion of arm
Private T. A. Parramore–wounded in foot
Private H. M. Philips–killed
Private Jorden Ragin–wounded both arms
Private T. J. Rick–wounded in hip
Private Malcolm Wilkes–wounded in arm

Company I
Captain J. D. Keaton
(no casualties found; company apparently
  consolidated with Company H before
  battle)

ANDERSON'S BATTERY
Captain Ruel W. Anderson
Private W. C. Allen–killed
Private Senate Arnold–wounded
Private Benjamin Giddons–killed
Private V. B. Gosden–wounded
Private Robert Rogers–mortally wounded

ATHENS BATTALION
Major Ferdinand W.C. Cook

Company A
Captain Sims
Lieutenant A. P. Hans–wounded in head
Lieutenant A. M. Wyng–wounded left arm
Private R. W. Bell–wounded in head

Private J. M. Ginn–wounded in hand
Private J. A. Moody–wounded in hand
Private William Parks–missing

Company B
Lieutenant Mainus–wounded
Lieutenant J. H. Hunter–killed
Private M. R. Baggs–wounded in arm
Private James Bearden–wounded
Private Thomas Bible–wounded
Private James Brack–wounded
Private James Brane–wounded in mouth
Private C. Clearland–killed
Private J. H. Dudson–wounded in hand
Private H. U. Durham–wounded in stomach
Private James Few–wounded in foot
Private J. B. Gardner–wounded in thigh
Private _____ Gellart–wounded
Private R. H. Howard–Mortally wounded
Private T. McCardle–wounded in head
Private J. Middlebrooks–wounded
Private J. L. Miller–wounded
Private M. A. Millsass–wounded both thighs
Private W. J. Wallace–wounded in foot
Private T. C. Warner–wounded
Private B. W. Waters–wounded
Private J. W. White–wounded
Private Samuel M. White–wounded both
  thighs

Company C
Captain _____ Pewdergrass–wounded
Sergeant _____ Framer–wounded
Corporal _____ Booth–wounded
Private S. M. Bassett–missing
Private J. H. Beall–missing
Private R. Beall–missing
Private J. B. R. Cawrhres–missing
Private Alex Hamilton–wounded
Private David Hodges–wounded
Private A. Mass–wounded
Private N. E. Rhodes–wounded
Private A. D. Snow–missing
Private O. Stone–missing
Private William Stone–wounded

Private W. R. Tanney–missing
Private William Walker–wounded
Private John M. Wright–wounded

Company D
Captain _____ Elliott
Lieutenant _____ Middlebrooks–wounded
  in knee
Private John Chancy–killed
Private M. G. Durham–missing
Private Jack Freeman–missing
Private W. C. Hall–wounded in breast
Private T. G. Jordan–wounded in arm
Private D. Richardson–wounded in hand

AUGUSTA BATTALION
Major George T. Jackson

Company A
Captain T. H. Holleyman
Lieutenant T. A .H. Meyer–wounded in
  hand
Private Simeon Buford–wounded in arm .
Private William Churchill–wounded in
  shoulder
Private John Copeland–wounded in foot
Private W. O. Dunbar–wounded in arm
Private R. J. Morrison–wounded in leg

Company B
Captain Jacob Adams–wounded
Lieutenant G. P. Weigle–wounded in
  shoulder
Corporal _____ Job–missing
Private _____ Goodyear–wounded in
  shoulder

Company C
Captain A. T. Smith
Lieutenant S. Poole–wounded in hand
Sergeant W. H. Murden–wounded in thigh
Private J. D. Andrews–wounded in shoulder
Private W. C. Cartwright–wounded in leg
Private D. Gaunt–wounded in shoulder

Private Jerry Gleason–wounded in leg
Private E. Lublin–wounded in thigh and head
Private John Scales–missing
Private M. P. Scales–missing
Private George Shiver–missing
Private James Walker–missing
Private W. H. Woods–wounded in head

Company D
Captain James C. Sentell
Corporal _____ Welch–wounded in leg
Private A. Belcher–killed
Private H. Frydell–wounded in leg and arm
Private D. Halslop–wounded in neck
Private Joseph Hudson–wounded in arm
Private J. Lemore–wounded in hand

Company E
Lieutenant _____ Shackleford–missing
Private Henry Reeves–wounded
Private George Tomens–wounded

GEORGIA STATE LINE

Lieutenant Colonel Beverly D. Evans–wounded

1st Regiment
Private W. H. Roberts, Company B–killed
Private Leonidas W. McKinney, Company D–wounded in wrists & bowels

2d Regiment
Lieutenant Stanton D. Porter, Company E–captured & released from Fort Delaware in 1865.
Corporal S. A. Thompson, Company G–wounded
Private L. H. Borders, company E–wounded
Private A. N. Grant, company E–wounded
Private Alphonza J. Jackson, company G–wounded
Private J. W. Wright–wounded left arm

CASUALTIES AT BATTLE OF HONEY HILL, 30 NOVEMBER 1864

8 killed, 42 wounded; 1,400 present; below lists incomplete[256]

1ST BRIGADE GEORGIA MILITIA

Colonel James N. Willis

1st Regiment
Lieutenant Colonel T. A. Walton
Lieutenant E. A. Burgess, Company G–wounded in leg
2d Lieutenant John Coswell, Compnany F–wounded
Corporal Robert Davy, Company K–wounded shoulder
Private T. O. O'Keef, Company A–wounded in back
Private H. J. Wolfe, Company A–wounded
Private J. W. Smith, Company B–wounded in shoulder
Private Peter Wright, Company B–wounded left thigh
Private G. W. Martin, Company B–wounded in breast
Private Richard Foster, Company B–wounded in back
Private Elijah Norman, Company C–wounded right thigh
Private Joseph D. Byrd, Company K–wounded both feet

2d Regiment
Colonel James Stapleton
Lieutenant James L. Fulcher, Company B–wounded in head
Corporal John Barrow, Company G–wounded in face
Private Lovett McGuire–wounded

Private Moses E. Mead–wounded in face
Private Allen Roundtree, Company
   H–wounded in shoulder
Private Patrick Thomas, wounded & cap-
   tured
Private Joe Tompkins, Company
   G–wounded in face
Private J. Vining, Company G–wounded
   right arm

3rd Regiment

Colonel L. G. Johnston
1st Lieutenant A. S. Butts, Company
   C–wounded left leg
Lieutenant T. J. Fortson, Company H–flesh
   wound in head
Sergeant W. H. Armstrong, Company
   D–wounded left breast
Corporal Thomas A. Orr, Company
   D–unspecified wound
Corporal Oliver Griffith, Company B–killed
Private R. Walter Davis, Company
   C–wounded in groin
Private E. F. Orr, Company D–wounded left
   knee
Private J. Brown, Company E–wounded arm
   and shoulder
Private W. C. Faulkner, Company
   G–wounded left wrist
Private C. R. Hitchcock, Company
   K–wounded
Private W. J. Bell, Company K–wounded in
   back

ATHENS BATTALION

Major Ferdinand W. C. Cook
(no casualties found)

AUGUSTA BATTALION

Major George T. Jackson
Sergeant J. H. Tice, Company D–wounded
   shoulder & back

Private J. Withington, Company
   B–wounded

47th Georgia Confederate Regiment

Major J. S. Cone–wrist broken
Captain J. C. Dodge–wounded right elbow
Private J. Bruer–wounded arm and leg
Private William Busser–wounded neck, wrist
   & head
Private B. R. Gnann–wounded left hand
Private Thomas Harrison–wounded left leg
Private A. Litebridge–wounded in hip
Private E. Norman–wounded right thigh
   and hand
Private E. E. Orr–wounded left knee
Private W. P. Owens–wounded in scalp
Private L. M. Prine–wounded left hand
Private Arthur Ray–wounded left side
Private D. F. Robbins–wounded right
   shoulder
Private Clinton Sapp–wounded right thigh
Private A. Setching–wounded left hip
Private Z. P. Thompson–wounded in leg
Private John Totankins–wounded in face
Private William H. Wise–wounded left arm
Private Thomas Wylly–mortally wounded in
   chest

32d Georgia Confederate Regiment

Lieutenant Colonel Edwin H. Bacon
(no casualties found)

3rd South Carolina Cavalry Regiment

Major John Jenkins
(no casualties found)

Artillery

Captain Hal M. Stuart
(no casualties found)

PRIMARY SOURCES

1. GOVERNMENT DOCUMENTS

A. Confederate States and US Government Documents, Printed and Manuscript

Compiled Service Records of Confederate Soldiers Who Served in Organizations from the State of Georgia. National Archives Microfilm Publication. Microcopy 266.

Kennedy, Joseph C. G., editor. *Population of the United States in 1860.* Washington DC, 1864.

Record of Appointment of Postmasters, 1832–1971. National Archives Microfilm Publication. M841. National Archives. Washington, DC.

"Telegrams Sent, Arsenal, 1862–1865," Records of Ordnance Establishments at Macon Georgia. Chapter 4, volume 101. Record Group 109, War Department Collection of Confederate Records. National Archives. Washington, DC.

US War Department, compiler. *The War of the Rebellion: A Compilation of the Official Records of the Union and Confederate Armies.* 128 volumes. Washington, DC: Government Printing Office, 1880–1901.

B. State of Georgia Documents, Printed and Manuscript

Candler, Allen D., editor. *The Confederate Records of the State of Georgia.* 5 volumes. Atlanta: C. P. Byrd, State Printer, 1909–1911.

Capers, Francis W. *Official Report on Services [of the Battalion of Cadets, Gerogia Military Institute].* Milledgeville GA: n.p., 1864.

Civil War Army Orders, MF 195, GAr 00-282. Georgia Department of Archives and History. Atlanta.

Cornell, Nancy J., compiler. *1864 Census for Re-organizing the Georgia Militia.* Baltimore: Genealogical Publishing Company, 2000.

Georgia Adjutant General's Office. *Annual Report of the Adjutant and Inspector General of the State of Georgia.* Milledgeville GA: Boughton, Nisbet, Barnes, and Moore, 1864.

———. Book of Commissions. Volume B-49. 1861–1865. Georgia Department of Archives and History. Atlanta.

———. Letter Book B-44. 2 volumes. Georgia Department of Archives and History. Atlanta.

———. Statistical Analysis of Militia Enrollment under 1864 Reorganization. Georgia Department of Archives and History. Atlanta.

Georgia General Assembly. *Acts of the General Assembly of the State of Georgia in 1864.* Milledgeville GA: Boughton, Nisbet, Barnes, and Moore, 1864.

———. *Acts of the General Assembly of the State of Georgia in 1864–1865.* Milledgeville GA: Boughton, Nisbet, Barnes, and Moore, 1865.

Georgia Militia/Georgia State Line Miscellaneous File. Box 3337-10. Georgia Department of Archives and History. Atlanta.

Governor Brown's Proclamations and Orders Calling into Active Military Service and Sending to the Front the Civil and Military Officers, and the Reserved Militia of the State of Georgia, to the Army of Tennessee. Milledgeville: Boughton, Nisbet, Barnes, and Moore, 1864.

Governor Joseph E. Brown's Incoming Correspondence. Georgia Department of Archives and History. Atlanta.

Governor's Letter Book, 1861-1865, Georgia Department of Archives and History. Atlanta.

Henderson, Lillian, compiler. *Roster of the Confederate Soldiers of Georgia.* 6 volumes. Hapeville GA: Longino and Porter, 1959–1964.

Reports of the Operations of the Militia, from October 13, 1864, to February 11, 1865, by Maj.-Generals G. W. Smith and Wayne, together with Memoranda by Gen. Smith, for the Improvement of the State Military Organization. Macon GA: Boughton, Nisbet, Barnes, and Moore, 1865.

Statistical Reports of the First Division, Georgia Militia, 31 October and 10 November 1864. Georgia Department of Archives and History. Atlanta.

2. CORRESPONDENCE, MEMOIRS, AND UNIT HISTORIES

Abercrombie, John J. "Battle of Honey Hill, S.C." *Confederate Veteran* 22 (October 1914): 452–54.

Anderson, Charles D., to Charles C. Jones, Jr. 15 August 1889. In Jones's personal copy of *The Siege and Evacuation of Savannah* (1890). Hargrett Rare Book and Manuscript Library. University of Georgia Libraries. Athens.

Andrews, Eliza Frances. *The War-Time Journal of a Georgia Girl.* 1908; reprint, Atlanta: Cherokee Publishing Company, 1976.

Arndt, A. F. R. *Reminiscences of an Artillery Officer.* Detroit: Winn & Hammond, 1890.

Avery, I. W. *The History of the State of Georgia from 1850 to 1881.* New York: Brown & Derby, 1881.

Beauregard, P. G. T., Papers. Special Collections. Duke University Library. Durham NC.

Brown, Joseph E. Parole, 8 May 1865, Joseph E. Brown Papers [Felix Hargrett Typescript]. Hargrett Rare Book and Manuscript Library. University of Georgia Libraries. Athens.

Carr, John M., Collection. Southern Historical Collection. University of North Carolina. Chapel Hill.

Cate, Wirt Armistead, editor. *Two Soldiers: The Campaign Diaries of Thomas J. Key, C.S.A., December 7, 1863–May 17, 1865, and Robert J. Campbell, U.S.A., January 1, 1864–July 21, 1864.* Chapel Hill: University of North Carolina Press, 1938.

Colcock, Charles J., to Charles C. Jones, Jr. 5 November 1867. Special Collections. Duke University Library. Durham NC.

Dahlgren, Madeleine V. *Memoir of John A. Dahlgren, Rear Admiral, United States Navy.* New York: Charles L. Webster & Company, 1891.

Emilio, Luis F. *A Brave Black Regiment: The History of the Fifty-Fourth Regiment of Massachusetts Volunteer Infantry, 1863–1865.* Boston: Boston Book Company, 1894.

Fielder, Herbert. *A Sketch of the Life and Times and Speeches of Joseph E. Brown.* Springfield MA: Press of the Springfield Printing Company, 1883.

Frobel, B. W. Journal of the Siege of Savannah [copy]. 24 November–20 December 1864. Charles C. Jones, Jr., Collection. Special Collections. Duke University Library. Durham NC.

———. Letter to General Martin L. Smith. 25 February 1865. Charles C. Jones, Jr., Collection. Special Collections. Duke University Library. Durham NC.

Gresham, E. B. and J. J., Folder. Georgia Miscellany 1. Special Collections. Robert W. Woodruff Library. Emory University. Atlanta.

Griswold, S. H. "Stoneman's Raid." *Jones County News.* 4 March 1909.

———. "Unwritten History. A Battle Fought in Jones County but Never Recorded." *Jones County News.* 3 July 1908.

Hall, Henry, and James Hall. *Cayuga in the Field. A Record of the 19th New York Volunteers, All the Batteries of the 3d New York Artillery, and 75th New York Volunteers.* Auburn NY: Truair, Smith, & Company, 1873.

Hardee, William J. Letter to Charles C. Jones, Jr. 14 May 1866. Georgia Portfolio. Charles C. Jones, Jr., Collection. Special Collections. Duke University Library. Durham NC.

Hardeman, Ellen Griswold. Manuscript Memoir of Samuel Griswold. In private possession.

Hardy, C. M.. Letter. 18 September 1864. Civil War Miscellany. Georgia Department of Archives and History. Atlanta.

Holliday, A. T., Letters. Mss 116. Atlanta History Center Archives. Atlanta.

Jackson, A. J. "Diary of the War Between the States kept by A. J. Jackson, Company G, Georgia State Line Troops, from February, 1863, to April, 1865 [Manuscript]." Microfilm Box 76-7. Georgia Department of Archives and History. Atlanta.

Johnson, Robert Underwood, and Clarence Clough Buel, editors. *Battles and Leaders of the Civil War.* 4 volumes. New York: The Century Publishing Company, 1887–1888.

Johnston, Joseph E. *Narrative of Military Operations.* New York: D. Appleton Co., 1874.

Jones, Charles C., Jr., papers. Special collections, Duke University Library. Durham NC.

Lee, G. W. "Official Report of the Battle of East Macon, July 30, 1864." 4 August 1864. Cobb Papers. Hargrett Library. University of Georgia Libraries. Athens.

McGriff, Patrick, Letter, 6 June 1864. Private Collection of Chuck Winchester and Steven Brown.

McKee, James Harvey. *Back "In War Times." History of the 144th Regiment, New York Volunteer Infantry.* New York: H. E. Bailey, 1903.

Nichols, George Ward. *The Story of the Great March.* New York: Harper & Brothers, 1865.

Ray, Ruby Felder, editor. *Letters and Diary of Lieut. Lavender R. Ray, 1861–1865.* N.p., 1949.

Reminiscences of the Civil War from Diaries of Members of the 103d Illinois Volunteer Infantry. Chicago: Press of J. F. Leaming & Company, 1904.

Robertson, John, compiler. *Michigan in the War.* Lansing: W. S. George & Company, State Printers, 1882.

Rowland, Dunbar editor. *Jefferson Davis, Constitutionalist: His Letters, Papers and Speeches.* 10 volumes. Jackson: Mississippi Department of Archives and History, 1923.

Sanford, Washington L. *History of the Fourteenth Illinois Cavalry.* Chicago: R. R. Donnelley & Sons, 1898.

Sherlock, Eli J. *Memorabilia of the Marches and Battles in Which the One Hundredth Regiment of Indiana Volunteers Took an Active Part.* Kansas City MO: Press of Gerard-Woody Printing Company, 1896.

Sherman, William T. *Memoirs of Gen. W. T. Sherman.* 2 volumes. New York: Charles L. Webster & Company, 1891.

Stephens, Robert Grier, Jr., compiler and editor. *Intrepid Warrior: Clement Anselm Evans, Confederate General from Georgia; Life, Letters, and Diaries of the War Years.* Dayton OH: Morningside Publishing Company, 1992.

Tarrant, Eastham. *Wild Riders of the First Kentucky Cavalry.* Louisville: Press of R. H. Carothers, 1894.

Taylor, Richard. *Destruction and Reconstruction.* New York: D. Appleton & Company, 1879.

Toombs, Robert, Papers. Hargrett Rare Book and Manuscript Library. University of Georgia Libraries. Athens.

Watkins, Sam R. *"Co. Aytch," Maury Grays, First Tennessee Regiment; or, A Side Show of the Big Show.* 1900; reprint, with introduction by Bell Irvin Wiley, Jackson TN: McCowart-Mercer Press, 1952.

Wills, Charles W. *Army Life of an Illinois Soldier.* Washington, DC: Globe Printing Company, 1906.

Wilson, James Harrison. Civil War Diary. Wilson Manuscripts. Historical Society of Delaware. Wilmington.

———. *Under the Old Flag.* 2 volumes. New York: D. Appleton & Company, 1912.

Wright, Henry H. *A History of the Sixth Iowa Infantry.* Iowa City: Iowa State Historical Society, 1923.

3. GEORGIA NEWSPAPERS & PERIODICALS

Athens Southern Watchman

Atlanta Daily Intelligencer

Augusta Chronicle & Sentinel

Christian Index

Columbus Daily Enquirer-Sun

Columbus Daily Sun

Columbus Times

The Countryman

Macon Telegraph

4. MISCELLANY

Lloyd's Southern Railway Guide. Atlanta, n.p., 1864.

Harwell, Richard Barksdale, editor. *Songs of the Confederacy.* New York, 1951.

Silber, Irwin, editor and compiler. *Songs of the Civil War.* New York: Dover Publishing Company, 1995.

SECONDARY SOURCES

Albaugh, William A., et al. *Confederate Handguns.* Philadelphia: Bonanza Books, 1967.

Allardice, Bruce S. *More Generals in Gray.* Baton Rouge: Louisiana State University Press, 1995.

Bailey, Anne J. *The Chessboard of War: Sherman and Hood in the Autumn Campaigns of 1864.* Lincoln: University of Nebraska Press, 2000.

Bass, James Horace. "Georgia in the Confederacy, 1861–1865." Ph.D. dissertation, University of Texas, 1932.

Bohannon, Keith Shaw. "Cadets, Drillmasters, Draft Dodgers, and Soldiers: The Georgia Military Institute during the Civil War." *Georgia Historical Quarterly* 79 (Spring 1995): 5–29.

———. "'Not Alone Trained to Arms But to the Science and Literature of Our Day': The Georgia Military Institute, 1851–1865." Master's thesis, University of Georgia, 1993.

Boney, F. N. *Rebel Georgia.* Macon GA: Mercer University Press, 1997.

Bonner, James C. *Milledgeville: Georgia's Antebellum Capital.* Athens: University of Georgia Press, 1978.

Boyd, James P. *The Life of General William T. Sherman.* N.p.: Publisher's Union, 1891.

Bragg, William Harris. *Griswoldville.* Macon GA: Mercer University Press, 2000.

———. "The Fight at Honey Hill." *Civil War Times Illustrated* 22 (January 1984): 12–19.

———. "Joe Brown vs. the Confederacy." *Civil War Times Illustrated* 26 (November 1987): 40–43.

———. "The Union General Lost in Georgia." *Civil War Times Illustrated* 24 (June 1985): 16–23.

Brockman, Charles J., Jr. "The Confederate Armory of Cook and Brother." *Papers of the Athens Historical Society* 2 (1979): 76–87.

Brooks, U. R., editor. *Stories of the Confederacy.* Columbia SC: The State Company, 1912.

Carse, Robert. *Department of the South: Hilton Head Island in the Civil War.* Columbia SC, 1976.

Castel, Albert. *Decision in the West: The Atlanta Campaign of 1864.* Lawrence: University Press of Kansas, 1992.

Cawthon, William Lamar, Jr. "Clinton: County Seat on the Georgia Frontier, 1808–1821." M.A. thesis, University of Georgia, 1984.

Colcock, Charles J., Jr. "The Battle of Honey Hill." *Charleston [SC] Sunday News,* 1 December 1899: 10, 16.

Coleman, Kenneth, and Charles Stephen Gurr, editors. *Dictionary of Georgia Biography,* 2 volumes. Athens: University of Georgia Press, 1983.

Coulter, E. Merton. *The Confederate States of America, 1861–1865.* Baton Rouge: Louisiana State University Press, 1950.

Courtenay, William A. "Fragments of War History Relating to the Coast Defence of South Carolina, 1861-'65, and the Hasty Preparations for the Battle of Honey Hill, November 30, 1864." *Southern Historical Society Papers* 26 (1898): 62–87.

———. "Heroes of Honey Hill." *Southern Historical Society Papers* 26 (1898): 232–41.

Cullum, George W. *Biographical Register of the Officers and Graduates of the U. S. Military Academy.* 2 volumes. Boston: Houghton, Mifflin Company, 1891.

Davis, Stephen. *Atlanta Will Fall: Sherman, Joe Johnston, and the Yankee Heavy Battalions.* Wilmington DE: Scholarly Resources, Inc., 2001.

Davis, William C. *The Cause Lost: Myths and Realities of the Confederacy.* Lawrence: University Press of Kansas, 1996.

Derry, Joseph T. *Georgia.* Volume 6 of *Confederate Military History.* Clement A. Evans, editor. 12 volumes. Atlanta: Confederate Publishing Company, 1899.

Dodge, Theodore Ayrault. *A Bird's-Eye View of Our Civil War.* Boston: Houghton, Mifflin Company, 1883.

Dodson, W. C., editor. *Campaigns of Wheeler and His Cavalry.* Atlanta: Hudgins Publishing Company, 1899.

Durham, Roger S. "Savannah: Mr. Lincoln's Christmas Present." *Blue & Gray Magazine* 7 (February 1991): 8–18, 42–53.

Evans, David. *Sherman's Horsemen: Union Cavalry Operations in the Atlanta Campaign.* Bloomington: Indiana University Press, 1996.

Encyclopedia of Contemporary Biography of New York. 2 volumes. New York: Atlantic Publishing and Engraving Company, 1882.

Freeman, Douglas Southall. *Lee's Lieutenants: A Study in Command.* 3 volumes. New York: Charles Scribner's Sons, 1942–1944.

Garrett, Franklin M. *Atlanta and Environs: A Chronicle of Its People and Events.* 3 volumes. New York: Lewis Historical Publishing Company, 1954.

Gary, William A. *Confederate Revolvers.* Dallas: K8 Communications, 1987.

Governor Treutlen Chapter, D.A.R., Fort Valley GA. *History of Peach County, Georgia.* Atlanta: Cherokee Publishing Company, 1972.

Gunnison, George W. *A Genealogy of the Descendants of Hugh Gunnison.* Boston: G. A. Foxcroft, 1880.

Hess, Earl J. "Civilians at War: The Georgia Militia in the Atlanta Campaign." *Georgia Historical Quarterly* 66 (Fall 1982): 332–45.

Hill, Louise Biles. *Joseph E. Brown and the Confederacy.* Chapel Hill: University of North Carolina Press, 1939.

Hitz, Alex M. "Georgia Militia Districts." *Georgia Bar Journal* 18 (February 1956): 1–7.

Holland, Lynwood M. "Georgia Military Institute, The West Point of Georgia: 1851–1864." *Georgia Historical Quarterly* 43 (September 1959): 225–47.

Holmgren, Virginia C. *Hilton Head: A Sea Island Chronicle.* Hilton Head SC: Hilton Head Island Publishing Company, 1959.

Hudson, Leonne M. *The Odyssey of a Southerner: The Life and Times of Gustavus Woodson Smith.* Macon GA: Mercer University Press, 1998.

Hull, A. L. *The Campaigns of the Confederate Army.* Atlanta: Foote & Davies, 1901.

Johnson, Michael P. *Toward a Patriarchal Republic: The Secession of Georgia.* Baton Rouge: Louisiana State University Press, 1977.

Jones, Charles C. Jr. *The Siege of Savannah in December, 1864, and the Confederate Operations in Georgia and the Third Military District of South Carolina during General Sherman's March from Atlanta to the Sea.* Albany NY: Joel Munsell, 1874.

Jones, James Pickett. *Yankee Blitzkrieg: Wilson's Raid through Alabama and Georgia.* Athens: University of Georgia Press, 1976.

Jones, Mary G., and Lily Reynolds, editors. *Coweta County Chronicles for One Hundred Years.* Atlanta: The Stein Publishing Company, 1928.

Kurtz, Wilbur G. "Whitehall Tavern." *The Atlanta Historical Bulletin* (April 1931): 42–49.

Lawrence, Alexander A. "Henry Kent McCay—Forgotten Jurist." *Georgia Bar Journal* 9 (August 1946): 5–29.

———. *A President for Mr. Lincoln: The Story of Savannah from Secession to Sherman.* Macon GA: Ardivan Press, 1961.

McMurry, Richard M. *John Bell Hood and the War for Southern Independence.* Lexington: University Press of Kentucky, 1982.

Northen, W. J., editor. *Men of Mark in Georgia.* 6 volumes. Atlanta: A. B. Caldwell, Publisher, 1907–1912.

Parks, Joseph H. *Joseph E. Brown of Georgia.* Baton Rouge: Louisiana State University Press, 1977.

Patrick, Rembert W. *Jefferson Davis and His Cabinet.* Baton Rouge: Louisiana State University Press, 1944.

Saye, Albert Berry. *A Constitutional History of Georgia, 1732–1968.* Athens: University of Georgia Press, 1970.

Scaife, William R. *The Campaign for Atlanta.* Atlanta: Civil War Publications, 1985.

Sifakis, Stewart. *Compendium of the Confederate Armies: South Carolina and Georgia.* New York: Facts on File, Inc., 1995.

Smedlund, William S. *Camp Fires of Georgia's Troops, 1861–1865.* Lithonia GA: Kennesaw Mountain Press, 1995.

Smith, Gordon Burns. *History of the Georgia Militia, 1783–1861.* 4 volumes. Milledgeville GA: Boyd Publishing Company, 2000–2001.

Stovall, Pleasant A. *Robert Toombs: Statesman, Speaker, Soldier, Sage.* New York: Cassell Publishing Company, 1892.

Sword, Wiley. *Firepower from Abroad: The Confederate Enfield and The Le Mat Revolver, 1861–1863 with New Data on a Variety of Confederate Small Arms.* Lincoln RI: A. Mowbray, Inc., 1986.

Terrill, Helen Eliza et al. *History of Stewart County, Georgia.* 2 volumes. Volume 1; Columbus GA: Columbus Office Supply Company, 1958; volume 2, Waycross GA: A. H. Clark, 1975.

Warner, Ezra J. *Generals in Gray.* Baton Rouge: Louisiana State University Press, 1959.

Welsh, Jack D., M.D. *Medical Histories of Confederate Generals.* Kent OH: Kent State Press, 1995.

———. *Medical Histories of Union Generals.* Kent OH: Kent State Press, 1996.

Whittle, Lewis N. Biographical File. Middle Georgia Archives. Washington Memorial Library. Macon, GA.

Yates, Bowling C. *History of the Georgia Military Institute.* Marietta GA: n.p., 1968.

NOTES

[1] Louise Biles Hill, *Joseph E. Brown and the Confederacy* (Chapel Hill: University of North Carolina Press, 1939) 11-12; Joseph H. Parks, *Joseph E. Brown of Georgia* (Baton Rouge: Louisiana State University Press, 1977) 30.

[2] Parks, *Brown of Georgia*, 39; Hill, *Brown and the Confederacy*, 32, 72; W. J. Northen, "Joseph Emerson Brown" in William J. Northen, ed., *Men of Mark in Georgia*, 6 vols. (Atlanta GA: A. B. Caldwell, 1907-1912) 3:79-80.

[3] Herbert Fielder, *A Sketch of the Life and Times and Speeches of Joseph E. Brown* (Springfield MA: Press of Springfield Printing Co., 1883) 169.

[4] I. W. Avery, *The History of the State of Georgia from 1850 to 1851* (New York: Brown & Derby, 1881) 145–46; Hill, *Brown and the Confederacy*, 41–43.

[5] Michael P. Johnson, *Toward a Patriarchal Republic: The Secession of Georgia* (Baton Rouge: Louisiana State University Press, 1977) 117; Joseph T. Derry, *Georgia*, vol. 6 of Clement A. Evans, ed., *Confederate Military History*, 12 vols. (Atlanta GA: Confederate Publishing Company, 1899) 8, 14; Parks, *Brown of Georgia*, 129-30, 135.

[6] Kenneth Coleman and Charles Stephen Gurr, eds., *Dictionary of Georgia Biography*, 2 vols. (Athens: University of Georgia Press, 1983) 2:1043-44 (Hereafter cited as *DGB*.); Gordon Burns Smith, *History of the Georgia Militia, 1783-1861*, 4 vols. (Milledgeville GA: Boyd Publishing Company, 2000) 1:28; Alex M. Hitz, "Georgia Militia Districts," *Georgia Bar Journal* 18 (February 1956): 1-2; Lyle D. Brundage, "The Organization, Administration, and Training of the United States Ordinary and Volunteer Militia, 1792-1861" (Ed.D. diss., University of Michigan, 1958) 69-70.

[7] William Harris Bragg, *Joe Brown's Army: The Georgia State Line, 1862-1865* (Macon GA: Mercer University Press, 1987) ix-xi.

[8] Allen D. Candler, ed., *The Confederate Records of the State of Georgia*, 6 vols. (Atlanta GA: C. P. Byrd, 1909-1911) 3:193 (Hereafter cited as *CRG*.); Parks, *Brown of Georgia*, 198-99.

[9] F. N. Boney, *Rebel Georgia* (Macon GA: Mercer University Press, 1997) 29-30; Avery, *History of Georgia*, 256-57, 286.

[10] *Report of the Adjutant and Inspector General…for the Year 1862-63* (Milledgeville GA: Boughton, Nisbet, Barnes, & Moore, 1863) 7-8 (Hereafter cited as *AGAR*, with pertinent year.); *AGAR* (1864), 4-5; *CRG*, 2:523-26; James Horace Bass, "Georgia in the Confederacy, 1861-1865" (Ph.D. diss., University of Texas, 1932) 239-40.

[11] *Acts of the General Assembly of Georgia* (Milledgeville GA: Boughton, Nisbet, Barnes, & Moore, 1864) 51-58.

[12] Ibid., 56; http://www.rootsweb.com/~gapicken/census.htm.

[13] *Acts of the General Assembly* (1864), 51-53.

[14] Ibid., 53-55. The manuscript statistical analysis of the enrollment—giving the "census" data by counties and militia districts, with numbers rather than names—Is in the Georgia Department of Archives and History (Hereafter cited as GDAH.), bound as "Georgia Adjutant General, Statistical Analysis of Militia Enrollment under 1864 Reorganization." Lacking from this record are dates from the following counties: Bibb, Campbell, Catoosa, Chattooga, Dade, Franklin, Glascock, Glynn, Habersham, Hart, Henry, Jefferson, Monroe, and Pike. (This statistical analysis—lacking only Catoosa, Chattooga, and Dade counties—was published in *AGAR* [1864] as a large folding chart: "Table No. 1—Enrollment of the Militia under the Act to Reorganize the Militia of the State of Georgia and for Other Purposes, Assented to December 14, 1863"—hereafter cited as Table.) The named records that yielded the statistical

analysis are also at the GDAH, microfilmed as "State of Georgia[,] Office Adjutant and Inspector General[,] List of Men Enrolled in the Georgia Militia by Militia Districts as Required by the Act of 14th December 1863, for Re-organizing the Militia of the State." These have been abstracted, compiled, and indexed by Nancy J. Cornell and published as *1864 Census for Re-organizing the Georgia Militia* (Baltimore MD: Genealogical Publishing Company, Inc., 2000). Some of the counties missing from the statistical analysis are found in the list—and vice versa. Those missing from the lists (and thus from the Cornell book) are the counties of Burke, Catoosa, Chattooga, Dade, Dooly, Emanuel, Irwin, Johnson, Laurens, Montgomery, Pulaski, Telfair, and Wilcox. Unaccountably, Adjutant General Wayne stated (*AGAR* [1864], 4) that no enrollment was made in the counties of White, Lumpkin, Dawson, Union, Towns, Rabun, Walker, Dade, Chattooga, and Catoosa, though all but the last three may be found in the analysis or the lists.

[15] *AGAR* (1864), 4 and Table.

[16] Ibid., 5; US War Department, comp., *The War of the Rebellion: A Compilation of the Official Records of the Union and Confederate Armies,* 128 vols. (Washington, DC: 1880-1902) [hereafter cited as *OR*; all citations are to series 1 unless otherwise indicated] ser. 4, vol. 3, pp. 178-81. Constructive enrollment removed the need for actual enrollment, stating as it did that "from and after the passage of this act, all white men, residents of the Confederate States, between the ages of seventeen and fifty [the age range of the Militia Proper], shall be in the military service of the Confederate States for the war" (*OR*, ser. 4, vol. 3, p. 178).

[17] *AGAR* (1864), 5.

[18] *CRG*, 2:774, 703.

[19] *Governor Brown's Proclamations and Orders Calling into Active Military Service and Sending to the Front the Civil and Military Officers, and the Reserved Militia of the State of Georgia, to the Army of Tennessee* (Milledgeville GA: Boughton, Nisbet, Barnes, & Moore, 1864) 3. This source is hereafter cited as *Governor Brown's Proclamations.*

[20] *AGAR* (1864), 5; *Columbus Times,* 26 May 1864 (quoting the *Atlanta Intelligencer*); *OR*, vol. 38, pt. 3, p. 970.

[21] Private collection of Chuck Winchester and Steven Brown. The governor asserted that men such as McGriff "rendered effective service," observing also that they "constitute[d], in a great degree, the remaining active militia force left to the State by the different acts of conscription." In the view of the manpower-hungry Confederate authorities in Richmond, the state force was certainly not negligible. By late 1864 they estimated that Georgia had exempted from conscription 5,478 civil officers and 2,751 militia officers (*Governor Brown's Proclamations,* 4; *OR*, ser. 4, vol. 3, pp. 869-70).

[22] George W. Cullum, *Biographical Register of the Officers and Graduates of the U. S. Military Academy,* 2 vols. (Boston: Houghton, Mifflin Company, 1891) 2:121-22; *Encyclopedia of Contemporary Biography of New York,* 2 vols. (New York: Atlantic Publishing and Engraving Company, 1882) 2:58-64; Ezra Warner, *Generals in Gray* (Baton Rouge: Louisiana State University Press, 1959) 280-81 [The image that illustrates Smith's entry in Warner's book is of Lawrence O'Bryan Branch, not Smith—a fact that would surely displease someone of Smith's high self-regard.]; Douglas Southall Freeman, *Lee's Lieutenants: A Study in Command,* 3 vols. (New York: Charles Scribner's Sons, 1942-1944) 1:xl, 262; Rembert W. Patrick, *Jefferson Davis and His Cabinet* (Baton Rouge: Louisiana State University Press, 1944) 131-32. The only book-length biography of Smith is Leonne M. Hudson's *The Odyssey of a Southerner: The Life and Times of Gustavus Woodson Smith* (Macon GA: Mercer University Press, 1998).

Smith's health problems apparently contributed to his lackluster career as commander of the militia. William C. Davis argues that Jefferson Davis passed over Smith for Lee because of "disillusionment with G. W. Smith and Smith's…psychosomatic ailments when under pressure" (*The Cause Lost: Myths and Realities of the Confederacy* [Lawrence: University Press of Kansas, 1996] 48). Douglas Southall Freeman's diagnosis was similar: "In action, [Smith] was one of the most unconcerned of soldiers and while under fire he did not even change the pitch of his voice. Consequently, no question of his personal courage could be raised by any one who had seen him in battle. Responsibility it was that shattered his nerves..., and, perhaps the fear that if he failed his reputation was gone" (*Lee's Lieutenants*, 1:262-63, 262 n. 99, 263 n. 100). Though Smith is described as never fully recovering from his wartime illness, myocarditis would kill him in 1896, in his seventy-fifth year (Jack D. Welsh, M.D., *Medical Histories of Confederate Generals* [Kent OH: Kent State University Press, 1995] 199-200).

[23] Gustavus W. Smith, "The Georgia Militia about Atlanta," in Robert Underwood Johnson and Clarence Clough Buel, eds., *Battles and Leaders of the Civil War*, 4 vols.(New York: The Century Company, 1887-1888) 4:332 (Hereafter cited as Smith, "Atlanta," *Battles and Leaders*.).

[24] *OR*, vol. 38, pt. 3, p. 969; *Atlanta Daily Intelligencer*, 4 June 1864.

[25] *Atlanta Register*, 3 June 1864, quoted in *The Countryman*, 21 June 1864, p. 347.

[26] *Atlanta Daily Intelligencer*, 15 June 1864. Stephens, then forty-one, had been lieutenant colonel of the 15th Georgia until ill health forced his return to Georgia. Once recovered, he became an officer in the Georgia State Guard. Sickness would ultimately lead to his resignation as aide-de-camp of General Smith, and Stephens would die prematurely eight years later. In a letter to a friend soon after his appointment to Smith's staff, Stephens gave an interesting description of the general: "A closer acquaintance with the General has elevated his ability in my estimation very much. Mr. Toombs always said that Smith was one of our ablest generals, but it is only lately that I have come to the same conclusion. He is certainly a very agreeable associate. His patience and good temper are a model. He is always polite to everybody without the slightest *affectation* of politeness. He is very warm-hearted and sociable, and is great fellow for standing up to his friends. He has very high *business* capacities, having, unlike most of the West Point people, quit the army...and mingled actively in the business of the world." Stewart Sifakis, *Compendium of the Confederate Armies: South Carolina and Georgia* (New York: Facts on File, Inc., 1995) 214; *OR*, vol. 35, pt. 1, p. 560; I. W. Avery, *The History of the State of Georgia from 1850 to 1851* (New York: Brown & Derby, 1881), 285; Linton Stephens to Thomas Hardeman, 18 August 1864, Adjutant General's Incoming Correspondence, GDAH (hereafter cited as AGIC); Linton Stephens to James Thomas, 19 June 1864, James Thomas Papers, Special Collections, Robert W. Woodruff Library, Emory University, Atlanta GA.

[27] *DGB* 2:988-91; Freeman, *Lee's Lieutenants*, 1:623.

[28] Robert Toombs to Julia Toombs, 15 August 1864, Robert Toombs Papers, Hargrett Library, University of Georgia Libraries, Athens GA (Location hereafter cited as Hargrett Library.). Just over a week earlier, Confederate artillery officer Thomas J. Key had recorded his impression of Toombs and the militia: "Yesterday I saw an aged man of corpulent dimensions riding behind the lines and telling the Georgia troops to 'stand by the artillerists and you will whip the Yankees like the devil.' His remarks 'took' so promptly that an involuntary cheer was raised, and I walked near the individual to get a close view of him. It proved to be Hon. Robert Toombs, of Georgia, who in better times had figured largely on the political stage in the capital at Washington, and who had a wide reputation as a debater and statesman. He is no longer known as a Senator but now goes by the title of General of Militia. It was to the Georgia militia that he was addressing himself" (Wirt Armistead Cate, ed., *Two Soldiers: The Campaign Diaries of Thomas J. Key, C.S.A., December 7, 1863-May 17, 1865, and Robert J. Campbell, U.S.A., January 1, 1864-July 21, 1864* [Chapel Hill: University of North Carolina Press, 1938] 108).

[29] *Atlanta Daily Intelligencer*, 5 June 1864.

[30] *OR*, vol. 38, pt. 4, p. 797.

[31] Smith, "Atlanta," *Battles and Leaders*, 4:332.

[32] Ibid.; Earl J. Hess, "Civilians at War: The Georgia Militia in the Atlanta Campaign," *Georgia Historical Quarterly* 66 (Fall 1982): 343.

[33] *OR,* vol. 38, pt. 5, pp. 867-68.

Johnston's letter appeared to give the militia and Smith himself all the credit even the most delicate of egos might demand. But something not apparent from a careful study of the official records seemed to offend Smith's sensibilities—causing him to devote much of his report on the campaign to lengthy praise of Johnston's successor, John Bell Hood, along with a rather amazing defense of Hood's leadership during the final tragic days of the campaign. Neither were appropriate in the after-action report of an officer who had been subordinate to both Johnston and Hood. Years later, Smith took issue with Johnston's *Narrative of Military Operations* (1874), particularly his description of the withdrawal from the Smyrna to Chattahoochee River Line. Therein, Smith noted, Johnston failed to mention Smith's offer to sacrifice his entire militia force, if necessary, to hold Nickajack Ridge, just north of the River Line. The official records also failed to record Smith's offer, if indeed it was ever made. But this seeming slight apparently prompted Smith to write a scathing indictment of Johnston, which later appeared in his account of the Atlanta Campaign in *Battles and Leaders of the Civil War.*

These discourses by Smith ("Atlanta," *Battles and Leaders,* 4:333-34) are the only significant defenses of Hood's performance around Atlanta, other than those found in *Advance and Retreat* (1880), Hood's own memoirs. But as Richard McMurry repeatedly points out in his biography of Hood, Smith and Hood were kinsmen, and there is a suggestion that, in a related instance, Smith may have taken this protective stance because Hood was related to him (Richard M. McMurry, *John Bell Hood and the War for Southern Independence* [Lexington: University Press of Kentucky, 1982] 185). Whatever Smith's motives for defending Hood, his indictment of Johnston revealed a remarkable lack of understanding of the military situation during the final days before the fall of Atlanta—and was surpassed in contradictions, distortions, and inaccuracies only by John B. Hood's postwar account.

[34] *CRG,* 2:710-12; A. T. Holliday to Elizabeth Holliday, 2 September 1864, A. T. Holliday Letters, mss. 116, Atlanta History Center Archives, Atlanta GA (Hereafter cited as Holliday Letters.).

[35] *OR,* vol. 38, pt. 3, p. 970.

[36] Pleasant A. Stovall, *Robert Toombs: Statesman, Speaker, Soldier, Sage* (New York: Cassell Publishing Company, 1892) 276-77.

[37] A. T. Holliday to Elizabeth Holliday, 12 July 1864, Holliday Letters; William S. Smedlund, *Camp Fires of Georgia's Troops, 1861-1865* (Lithonia GA: Kennesaw Mountain Press, 1995) 140.

[38] A. T. Holliday to Elizabeth Holliday, 16-17 July 1864, Holliday Letters.

[39] Theodore Ayrault Dodge, *A Bird's-Eye View of Our Civil War* (Boston: Houghton, Mifflin, & Co., 1883) 256-59; William R. Scaife, *The Campaign for Atlanta* (Atlanta GA: Civil War Publications, 1985) 59-69.

[40] *OR,* vol. 38, pt. 3, pp. 970-71.

[41] Stovall, *Robert Toombs,* 278.

[42] *OR,* vol. 38, pt. 5, p. 903.

[43] *Augusta* [GA] *Chronicle & Sentinel,* 31 July 1864.

[44] *CRG,* 2:711-12.

[45] J. J. Gresham to "Dear Brother," 21 July 1864, E. B. and J. J. Gresham folder, Georgia Miscellany 1, special collections, Robert W. Woodruff Library, Emory University, Atlanta GA; *CRG,* 2:716.

[46] *OR,* vol. 38, pt. 5, p. 264; *OR,* ser. 2, vol. 7, pp. 418-19; Washington L. Sanford, *History of the Fourteenth Illinois Cavalry* (Chicago: R. R. Donnelley & Sons, 1898) 185-86; *OR,* vol. 38, pt. 1, p. 76, pt. 2, pp. 763, 915, 919, pt. 5, p. 409; *Atlanta Daily Intelligencer,* 4 August 1864; Eastham Tarrant, *Wild Riders of the First Kentucky Cavalry* (Louisville: Press of R. H. Carothers, 1894), 368-69.

For more detailed accounts of Stoneman's Raid, see William Harris Bragg, "The Union General Lost in Georgia, *Civil War Times Illustrated* 24 (June 1985): 16-23; David Evans, *Sherman's Horsemen: Union Cavalry Operations in the Atlanta Campaign* (Bloomington: Indiana University Press, 1996) 291-376; and William R. Scaife, *The Campaign for Atlanta* (Atlanta GA: Civil War Publications, 1985) 77-100.

[47] Evans, *Sherman's Horsemen*, 299-300, 311, 313.

[48] *OR*, vol. 38, pt. 2. p. 916; G. W. Lee, "Official Report of the Battle of East Macon, July 30, 1864," 4 August 1864, Cobb Papers, Hargrett Library; *Christian Index*, 12 August 1864; Evans, *Sherman's Horsemen*, 314, 317.

[49] "Map of the City of Macon, Ga.," RG 77:N 76-3, National Archives; Evans, *Sherman's Horsemen*, 311, 316-17; Albert Castel, *Decision in the West: The Atlanta Campaign of 1864* (Lawrence: University Press of Kansas, 1992) 439.

[50] Evans, *Sherman's Horsemen*, 313-16.

[51] S. H. Griswold, "Stoneman's Raid," *Jones County News*, 4 March 1909.

[52] *OR*, vol. 38, pt. 2, p. 916; *Macon Telegraph*, 2 & 3 August 1864.

[53] Joseph E. Johnston, *Narrative of Military Operations* (New York: D. Appleton & Co., 1874) 370.

[54] *OR*, vol. 38, pt. 3, p. 971.

[55] C. M. Hardy to his sister, 18 September 1864, Civil War Miscellany, GDAH.

[56] Sam R. Watkins, *"Co. Aytch," Maury Grays, First Tennessee Regiment; or, A Side Show of the Big Show* (1900; reprint with intro. by Bell Irvin Wiley, Jackson TN: McCowart-Mercer Press, 1952) 189-90. Not as widely quoted, but probably more objective, is Confederate artillerist Thomas J. Key's impression of 6 August 1864: "Heavy rain fell this evening while the raw militia were in the street preparing to go into the trenches on picket for the first time. They appear ready to do their duty as well as the best fighting they know how. It is laughable, however, to see their awkward motions and blunders at the simple military evolutions. But in two months they will prove good soldiers" (Cate, ed., *Two Soldiers*, 110).

[57] *CRG*, 3:607.

[58] *CRG*, 3:608-609, 612-22.

[59] *OR*, vol. 39, pt. 2, p. 381.

[60] Joseph H. Parks, *Joseph E. Brown of Georgia* (Baton Rouge: Louisiana State University Press, 1977) 296-97.

[61] E. Merton Coulter, *The Confederate States of America, 1861-1865* (Baton Rouge, Louisiana State University Press, 1950) 332, 361, 557-58.

[62] Scaife, *Campaign for Atlanta*, 50, 52; Castel, *Decision in the West*, 551-52.

[63] McMurry, *John Bell Hood*, 162-67, 182.

[64] Anne J. Bailey, *The Chessboard of War: Sherman and Hood in the Autumn Campaigns of 1864* (Lincoln: University of Nebraska Press, 2000) 24-27; Parks, *Brown of Georgia*, 301-304; Governor's Letter Book, 1861-1865, p. 706, GDAH.

[65] Governor's Letter Book, 1861-1865, p. 706, GDAH.

[66] Ibid., 707. Whittle would become first president of the Georgia Bar Association in 1883 (Lewis N. Whittle biographical file, Middle Georgia Archives, Washington Memorial Library, Macon GA).

[67] Governor's Letter Book, 1861-1865, 706, GDAH.

[68] Ibid., 708; "Telegrams Sent, Arsenal, 1862-1865," Records of Ordnance Establishments at Macon Georgia, ch. 4, vol. 101, RG 109, War Department Collection of Confederate Records, National Archives, Washington, DC; Gustavus W. Smith, "The Georgia Militia during Sherman's March to the

Sea," in Robert Underwood Johnson and Clarence Clough Buel, eds., *Battles and Leaders of the Civil War*, 4 vols.(New York: The Century Company, 1887-1888) 4:667 (Hereafter cited as Smith, "March to the Sea," *Battles and Leaders*.). For additional details on this incident, see William Harris Bragg, "Joe Brown vs. the Confederacy," *Civil War Times Illustrated* 26 (November 1987): 40-43.

[69] General Orders, 15 July 1864, 1st Division, Georgia Militia, in Gustavus W. Smith, *Civil War Army Orders*, MF 195, Gar 00-282, GDAH; Smith, "Atlanta," *Battles and Leaders*, 4:333; Avery, *History of Georgia*, 281; *Macon Daily Telegraph*, 24 & 25 November & 7 December 1864; *Augusta Chronicle & Sentinel*, 7 December 1864; *Reports of the Operations of the Militia, from October 13, 1864, to February 11, 1865, by Maj-Generals G. W. Smith and Wayne, together with Memoranda by Gen. Smith, for the Improvement of the State Military Organization* [Hereafter cited as *Reports of Militia Operations*.] (Macon GA: Boughton, Nisbet, Barnes, & Moore, 1865) 14. Unsurprisingly, all four of the militia brigadiers had previously served as the governor's aides-de-camp for the enrollment for the militia reorganization (Cornell, *1864 Census*, 841-42).

[70] "Tri-Monthly Report of the First Division, Georgia Militia, of the Army of Tennessee," 31 October 1864, Georgia Militia/Georgia State Line Miscellaneous File, box 3337-10, GDAH.

[71] Ibid., 10 November 1864.

[72] *AGAR* (1864), 5; *OR*, vol. 38, pt. 3, p. 971. Wayne's precise accounting of the militia's numbers was as follows: "From the Report of General G. W. Smith, his Division proper embraced 9,170 men aggregate, exclusive of the Fulton County Militia, ordered to report to the Military Commander of Atlanta, and the Heard and Troup Counties Militia, assigned to the defence of West Point, and the Militia held for the defence of the State Capitol. It is known that between ten thousand and eleven thousand men were armed, and put into the field" (*AGAR* [1864], 5). G. W. Smith, whose statements must always be used with caution, obviously sought to minimize the estimates of his available force during the Atlanta Campaign. As suggested elsewhere, his ploy may have been—as a partisan of his kinsman Hood—to cast doubt on Johnston's conduct of the Atlanta Campaign, specifically Johnston's stated desire to "move freer and wider" against Sherman with the Army of Tennessee while the Georgia Militia held the Atlanta fortifications (earthworks that Smith argued were insufficient). Stephen Davis notes that President Davis probably interpreted the "freer and wider" as "intimating" Johnston's abandonment of Atlanta. In any case, Johnston telegraphed Davis with his plan on 16 July and was relieved of command the following day. Consequently, the Georgia Militia proved a factor in the elevation of John Bell Hood to command of the Army of Tennessee, and he sought to increase the militia's numbers (and defensive capability) dramatically, to give his own army more freedom of movement (Smith, "Atlanta," *Battles and Leaders*, 4:334; Stephen Davis, *Atlanta Will Fall: Sherman, Joe Johnston, and the Yankee Heavy Battalions* [Wilmington DE: Scholarly Resources, Inc., 2001] 115-16, 166-67).

[73] *AGAR* (1864), 5-6.

[74] Ibid., 6.

[75] Ibid. As early as September 1864, Wayne had been warned by one of the militia brigadiers that care should be taken to find a convenient rendezvous point for the militia once their agricultural leave ended—the rank and file were "reluctant to return to duty" (P. J. Philips to Henry C. Wayne, 27 September 1864, Adjutant General's Incoming Correspondence (Hereafter cited as AGIC.), GDAH.

[76] *AGAR* (1864), 5; *OR*, vol. 38, pt. 3, p. 971.

[77] *Reports of Militia Operations*, 3.

[78] W. C. Dodson, ed., *Campaigns of Wheeler and His Cavalry* (Atlanta GA: Hudgins Publishing Co., 1899) 284-87.

[79] William T. Sherman, *Memoirs of Gen. W. T. Sherman*, 2 vols. (New York: Charles L. Webster & Company, 1891) 2:152.

[80] James P. Boyd, *The Life of General William T. Sherman* (n.p.: Publisher's Union, 1891) 336.

⁸¹ Ibid., 347.

⁸² William T. Sherman, *Memoirs of Gen. W. T. Sherman*, 2 vols. (New York: Charles L. Webster & Company, 1891) 2:166.

⁸³ Franklin M. Garrett, *Atlanta and Environs: A Chronicle of Its People and Events*, 3 vols. (New York: Lewis Historical Publishing Company, 1954) 1:375.

⁸⁴ Sherman, *Memoirs*, 2:171-76; Anne J. Bailey, *The Chessboard of War: Sherman and Hood in the autumn Campaigns of 1864* (Lincoln: University of Nebraska Press, 2000) 48-50.

⁸⁵ Charles C. Jones, Jr., *The Siege of Savannah in December, 1864, and the Confederate Operations in Georgia and the Third Military District of South Carolina during General Sherman's March from Atlanta to the Sea* (Albany NY: Joel Munsell, 1874) 3.

⁸⁶ Sherman, *Memoirs*, 2:178-79.

⁸⁷ *CRG*, 2:799-800.

⁸⁸ Smith, "March to the Sea," *Battles and Leaders*, 4:667; *OR*, vol. 44, p. 859.

⁸⁹ *OR*, vol. 44, p. 866; *Reports of Militia Operations*, 3-4.

⁹⁰ *OR*, vol. 44, p. 870; Ruby Felder Ray, ed., *Letters and Diary of Lieut. Lavender R. Ray, 1861-1865* (n.p., 1949) 13-14; *Columbus Daily Sun*, 29 November 1864.

⁹¹ Jones, *Siege of Savannah*, 11.

⁹² Ibid., 12.

⁹³ *OR*, vol. 44, p. 414, 886; *Macon Telegraph*, 30 November 1864; Hardee to Beauregard, 21 November 1864 (two telegrams), Beauregard Papers, Special Collections, Duke University Library, Durham NC [Hereafter cited as SC-DUL.].

⁹⁴ *OR*, vol. 44, pp. 414–15, 877, 886; mileage tables for the Central of Georgia, Southwestern & Ocmulgee, and Atlantic & Gulf railways, *Lloyd's Southern Railway Guide* (Atlanta GA: n.p., 1864).

⁹⁵ *DGB*, 1:370; William Lamar Cawthon, Jr., "Clinton: County Seat on the Georgia Frontier, 1808-1821" (M.A. thesis, University of Georgia, 1984) 17; Record of Appointment of Postmasters, 1832-September 30, 1971, roll 24, Georgia: Irwin-Putnam Counties, National Archives Microfilm Publication M841, National Archives, Washington, DC [Samuel Griswold's date of appointment as first postmaster of newly founded Griswoldville is dated 18 December 1849]; Hardeman, Ellen Griswold, manuscript memoir of Samuel Griswold, in private possession; *Macon Daily Telegraph*, 2 August 1864.

⁹⁶ *Macon Daily Telegraph*, 5 August 1862; George W. Gunnison, *A Genealogy of the Descendants of Hugh Gunnison* (Boston: G. A. Foxcroft, 1880) 117; William A. Albaugh et al., *Confederate Handguns* (Philadelphia: Bonanza Books, 1967) 33-34; A. N. Gunnison to G. W. Randolph, 14 May 1862, in Wiley Sword, *Firepower from Abroad: The Confederate Enfield and The Le Mat Revolver, 1861-1863 with New Data on a Variety of Confederate Small Arms* (Lincoln RI: A. Mowbray, Inc., 1986) 110; William A. Gary, *Confederate Revolvers* (Dallas: K8 Communications, 1987) 8.

⁹⁷ *OR*, vol. 44, pp. 390, 396, 369, 97-98.

⁹⁸ Ibid., 82-83, 382, 386-87; Henry H. Wright, *A History of the Sixth Iowa Infantry* (Iowa City: State Historical Society of Iowa, 1923) 365.

⁹⁹ *Reports of Militia Operations*, 4-5; Jones, *Siege of Savannah*, 24-25.

¹⁰⁰ Smith, "March to the Sea," *Battles and Leaders*, 4:667.

¹⁰¹ *OR*, vol. 44, pp. 414, 877.

¹⁰² *OR*, vol. 44 pp. 888-89; *OR*, vol. 53, p. 39; *OR*, vol. 44, p. 382.

¹⁰³ *OR*, 53:41; *Athens Southern Watchman*, 12 November 1862; Charles J. Brockman, Jr., "The Confederate Armory of Cook and Brother," *Papers of the Athens Historical Society* 2 (1979), 76-79; George T. Jackson to Charles C. Jones, Jr., undated, Charles C. Jones, Jr., Papers, Duke; *Columbus Daily Sun*, 26

November 1864; *Reports of Militia Operations*, 12-13; A. J. Jackson, "Diary of the War Between the States kept by A. J. Jackson, Company G, Georgia State Line Troops, from February, 1863, to April, 1865 [manuscript]," microfilm box 76-7, pp. 6-7, GDAH.

[104] *OR*, vol. 53, p. 41; Smith, "March to the Sea," *Battles and Leaders*, 4:667.

[105] *OR*, vol. 44, pp. 83, 97-98, 512; *OR*, vol. 53, p. 44; S. H. Griswold, "Unwritten History. A Battle Fought in Jones County but Never Recorded," *Jones County News*, 3 July 1908; *Reminiscences of the Civil War from Diaries of Members of the 103d Illinois Volunteer Infantry* (Chicago: Press of J. F. Leaming and Company, 1904) 154; Henry H. Wright, *A History of the Sixth Iowa Infantry* (Iowa City: State Historical Society of Iowa, 1923) 366.

[106] Richard Taylor, *Destruction and Reconstruction* (New York: D. Appleton & Company, 1879) 210-11.

[107] *Reports of Militia Operations*, 12.

[108] Ibid.

[109] Ibid., 14.

[110] Ibid., 13.

[111] Ibid., 14.

[112] Wright, *Sixth Iowa*, 365-66; *103d Illinois*, 154; *OR*, vol. 44, pp. 83, 98, 407; *Macon Telegraph*, 24 November 1864; A. F. R. Arndt, *Reminiscences of an Artillery Officer* (Detroit: Winn & Hammond, Printers, 1890) 8; A. F. R. Arndt, After-Action Report, 27 November 1864 [Missing from the *Official Records*], in John Robertson, comp., *Michigan in the War* (Lansing MI: W. S. George & Company, 1882) 523; *OR*, vol. 46, p. 42.

[113] Arndt, *Reminiscences*, 8; Arndt, *After-Action Report*, 523; *OR*, vol. 46, p. 42.

[114] Wright, *Sixth Iowa*, 366-67; *103d Illinois*, 155.

[115] *OR*, vol. 44, pp. 105-106; *OR*, vol. 53, pp. 42-43; Wright, *Sixth Iowa*, 367; *103d Illinois*, 155.

[116] *OR*, vol. 53, pp. 43-44.

[117] Ibid.; S. H. Griswold, "Unwritten History. A Battle Fought in Jones County but Never Recorded," *Jones County News*, 3 July 1908; Charles W. Wills, *Army Life of an Illinois Soldier* (Washington, DC: Globe Printing Company, 1906) 324; *OR*, vol. 53, p. 29; Wright, *Sixth Iowa*, 367; *103d Illinois*, 155.

[118] *OR*, vol. 53, pp. 43-44; *OR*, vol. 44, p. 108.

[119] Wright, *Sixth Iowa*, 368; *OR*, vol. 44, p. 105; *OR*, vol. 53, p. 42; Jack D. Welsh, *Medical Histories of Union Generals* (Kent OH: Kent State University Press, 1996) 356-57; Diary of Captain John M. Carr, Co. G, 100th Indiana Infantry, entry of 23 November 1864, John M. Carr Collection, Southern Historical Collection, University of North Carolina, Chapel Hill NC.

[120] *OR*, vol. 44, p. 105; Eli J. Sherlock, *Memorabilia of the Marches and Battles in Which the One Hundredth Regiment of Indiana Volunteers Took an Active Part* (Kansas City: Press of Gerard-Woody Printing Company, 1896) 157; *OR*, vol. 53, p. 43. Colonel Catterson was recommended for a promotion to brigadier general for his conduct at Griswoldville (*OR*, vol. 47, pt. 1, p. 250).

[121] George Ward Nichols, *The Story of the Great March* (New York: Harper & Brothers, 1865) 64; Sherlock, *Memorabilia*, 163; *OR*, vol. 53, pp. 42, 44.

[122] Wright, *Sixth Iowa*, 363.

[123] Wills, *Army Life*, 324.

[124] Helen Eliza Terrill et al., *History of Stewart County, Georgia*, 2 vols. (vol. 1, Columbus GA: Columbus Office Supply Company, 1958; vol. 2, Waycross GA: A. H. Clark, 1975) 1:551-52; Wills, *Army Life*, 323.

[125] *OR*, vol. 44, p. 106.

[126] Ibid.,105.

[127] *Reports of Militia Operations*, 15; *OR*, vol. 44, pp. 97-98, 414; *OR*, vol. 44, p. 368; *OR*, vol. 53, pp. 40-43.

[128] *OR*, vol. 53, pp. 41-42.

[129] *OR*, vol. 44, p. 414.

[130] *OR*, vol. 53, p. 39.

[131] Ibid., 40.

[132] "Philips, Pleasant J., File," roll 405, *Compiled Service Records of Confederate Soldiers Who Served in Organizations from the State of Georgia* (Hereafter cited as *CSR*.), National Archives Microfilm Publication Microcopy 266, National Archives, Washington, DC (Hereafter cited as NA.); Stewart Sifakis, *Compendium of the Confederate Armies: South Carolina and Georgia* (New York: Facts on File, Inc., 1995) 241; Robert Grier Stephens, Jr., comp. and ed., *Intrepid Warrior: Clement Anselm Evans, Confederate General from Georgia; Life, Letters, and Diaries of the War Years* (Dayton OH: Morningside Publishing Company, 1992) 104; Bruce S. Allardice, *More Generals in Gray* (Baton Rouge: Louisiana State University Press, 1995) 182-83; P. J. Philips to Henry C. Wayne, 28 June 1863, AGIC, GDAH; *Columbus Daily Enquirer-Sun*, 13 October 1876; *Columbus Daily Sun*, 20 June, 8 July 1862; P. J. Philips to Henry C. Wayne, 26 December 1863, AGIC, GDAH; *Atlanta Daily Intelligencer*, 5 June 1864.

[133] *Columbus Daily Enquirer-Sun*, 13 October 1876; *Columbus Daily Sun*, 20 June, 8 July 1862; P. J. Philips to Henry C. Wayne, 26 December 1863, AGIC, GDAH; *Atlanta Daily Intelligencer*, 5 June 1864.

[134] "McCay, Henry K., File," roll 272, *CSR*, NA; "Henry Kent McCay," in *Men of Mark in Georgia*, 3:432; Alexander A. Lawrence, "Henry Kent McCay—Forgotten Jurist," *Georgia Bar Journal* 9 (August 1946) 8-9; *OR*, vol. 5, pp. 462-63; "Anderson, C. D., File," roll 272, *CSR*, NA; "Charles David Anderson," in *Men of Mark in Georgia*, 3:108-10; Joseph T. Derry, *Georgia*, vol. 6 of Clement A. Evans, ed., *Confederate Military History*, 12 vols. (Atlanta GA: Confederate Publishing Company, 1899) 469-70; Governor Treutlen Chapter, D.A.R., Fort Valley, Georgia, *History of Peach County, Georgia* (Atlanta GA: Cherokee Publishing Company, 1972) 76-78; Charles D. Anderson to Charles C. Jones, Jr., 15 August 1889, bound after p. 18 in Jones's personal copy of *The Siege and Evacuation of Savannah* (1890), Hargrett Library; "Carswell, R. W., File," roll 490, *CSR*, NA; "Reuben W. Carswell," in *Men of Mark in Georgia*, 3:108-10. The ages of the Philips, McCay, Anderson, and Carswell at the time of the Battle of Griswoldville were forty-five, forty-four, thirty-seven, and thirty-six, respectively.

    A note on spellings: The surnames of both Philips and McCay are almost always misspelled as Phillips and McCoy in secondary sources. The spellings used herein (Philips and McCay) are those that appear on the generals' tombstones and on letters signed by them. The misspelling of McCay's name is partially explained by the fact that it was pronounced "McCoy" (Lawrence, "Henry Kent McCay," 5).

[135] A. L. Hull, *The Campaigns of the Confederate Army* (Atlanta GA: Foote & Davies, 1901) 80 [The battle "saved Macon from the fate of Atlanta."]; *CRG*, 3:698–69 [Joseph E. Brown to James A. Seddon: "Thus 'abandoned to her fate' by the President, Georgia's best reliance was her reserve militia and State Line…. Without them much more property must have been destroyed and the city of Macon…must have shared the fate of Atlanta and Savannah, while Augusta…must also have fallen."]; Mary G. Jones and Lily Reynolds, eds., *Coweta County Chronicles for One Hundred Years* (Atlanta GA: the Stein Printing Company, 1928) 154 ["…he was killed at the Battle of Griswoldville, November 22, 1864, where it is said drunken officers pitted these reserves …against the whole of Sherman's army."]; S. H. Griswold, "Unwritten History. A Battle Fought in Jones County but Never Recorded," *Jones County News*, 3 July 1908 ["It was said at the time that the brigade commander was drunk."]; Jones, *Siege of Savannah*, 27.

¹³⁶ On the other hand, Sherman's clever strategy also obviously contributed to the fiasco, and the failure of Wheeler's cavalry to carry out adequate reconnaissance to the east of Macon helped make Sherman's strategy work.

¹³⁷ Wilbur G. Kurtz, "Whitehall Tavern," *Atlanta Historical Bulletin* (April 1931): 46; James Horace Bass, "Georgia in the Confederacy, 1861–1865" (Ph.D. diss., University of Texas, 1932) 254–55.

¹³⁸ Irwin Silber, comp. and ed., *Songs of the Civil War* (New York: Dover Publishing Company, 1960) 186.

¹³⁹ *OR*, vol. 4, pt. 3, p. 48; *Macon Telegraph*, 24 November 1864.

¹⁴⁰ "Tri-Monthly Report of the First Division, Georgia Militia, of the Army of Tennessee," 10 November 1864, Georgia Militia/Georgia State Line Miscellaneous File, Box 3337-10, GDAH; Jones, *Siege of Savannah*, 90; George T. Jackson to Charles C. Jones, Jr., [undated], Charles C. Jones, Jr., papers, special collections, Duke University Library, Durham NC. The order of battle is drawn from various places in the pertinent volumes of the *Official Records*, as well as from newspaper accounts and memoirs.

¹⁴¹ *OR*, vol. 44, p. 97.

¹⁴² Smith, "March to the Sea," *Battles and Leaders*, 4:667; William Harris Bragg, *Griswoldville* (Macon GA: Mercer University Press, 2000) 139, 172 n. 155.

¹⁴³ Robert Carse, *Department of the South: Hilton Head Island in the Civil War* (Columbia SC: The State Printing Company, 1961) 22, 71–72; Virginia C. Holmgren, *Hilton Head: A Sea Island Chronicle* (Hilton Head SC: Hilton Head Island Publishing Company, 1959) 92–98.

¹⁴⁴ *OR*, vol. 39, pt. 3, p. 740; *OR*, vol. 35, pt. 2, p. 328; *OR*, vol. 44, p. 547.

¹⁴⁵ *OR*, vol. 44, p. 586; Charles C. Jones, Jr., *The Siege of Savannah in December, 1864, and the Confederate Operations in Georgia and the Third Military District of South Carolina during Germinal Sherman's March from Atlanta to the Sea* (Albany NY: Joel Munsell, 1874) 34–35.

¹⁴⁶ *OR*, vol. 44, pp. 421–22.

¹⁴⁷ Ibid., 420.

¹⁴⁸ Jones, *Siege of Savannah*, 35–36; Smith, "March to the Sea," *Battles and Leaders*, 4:667; *OR*, vol. 44, pp. 414–15.

¹⁴⁹ Richard Taylor, *Destruction and Reconstruction* (New York: D. Appleton & Company, 1879) 213.

¹⁵⁰ Ibid., 213–14.

¹⁵¹ Smith, "March to the Sea," *Battles and Leaders*, 4:667.

¹⁵² *OR*, vol. 44, p. 906.

¹⁵³ Ibid., 415.

¹⁵⁴ Ibid. General Richard Taylor gives a different and more humorous (though quite dubious) account of what happened in Savannah, starring himself and Robert Toombs: "The railway from Savannah to Charleston passes near the coast. The officer commanding at Pocataligo, midway of the two places, reported an advance of the enemy from Port Royal, and that he must abandon his post the following morning unless reinforced. To lose the Charleston line would seriously interfere with the concentration [of Hardee's, Bragg's, and other forces] just recommended. Hardee said that he could ill spare men [to protect the rail line], and had no means of moving them promptly. I bethought me of Toombs, Smith, and Governor Brown's 'army.' The energetic Toombs had frightened the railway people into moving him, and, from his telegrams, might be expected before dawn. Hardee thought but little of the suggestion, because the ground of quarrel between Governor Brown and President Davis was the refusal of the former to allow his [Georgia troops] to serve beyond their state. However, I had faith in Toombs and Smith. A short distance to the south of Savannah, on the Gulf road, was a switch by which

carriages could be shunted on to a connection with the Charleston line. I wrote Toombs of the emergency, and sent one of Hardee's staff to meet him at the switch. The governor's army was quietly shunted off and woke up at Pocataligo in South Carolina.... Toombs enjoyed the joke of making them unconscious patriots" (Taylor, *Destruction and Reconstruction*, 215).

[155] Smith, "March to the Sea," *Battles and Leaders*, 4:668; Jones, *Siege of Savannah*, 36. For Col. Colcock's regiment, see Charles J. Colcock, Jr., "The Third South Carolina Cavalry," in U. R. Brooks, ed., *Stories of the Confederacy* (Columbia SC: The State Company, 1912) 219–33.

[156] William A. Courtenay, "Fragments of War History Relating to the Coast Defence of South Carolina, 1861-'65, and the Hasty Preparations for the Battle of Honey Hill, November 30, 1864," *Southern Historical Society Papers* 26 (1898): 76; Charles J. Colcock, Jr., "The Battle of Honey Hill, *Charleston* [SC] *Sunday News*, 1 December 1899, 10; Charles J. Colcock to Charles C. Jones, Jr., 5 November 1867, Charles C. Jones, Jr., Collection, SC-DUL (Hereafter cited as Colonel Colcock's Letter.). The excellent account by Charles J. Colcock, Jr.—son of Colonel Colcock—cited above, was exhaustively researched and tells the story of the battle in satisfying detail. Colcock, who mined most of the published accounts and corresponded with both Confederate and Union veterans of the battle, also includes a map of the battlefield.

[157] *OR*, vol. 44, pp. 422–23.

[158] James Harvey McKee, *Back "In War Times." History of the 144th Regiment, New York Volunteer Infantry* (New York: H. E. Bailey, 1903) 185–86; John J. Abercrombie, "Battle of Honey Hill, S.C.," *Confederate Veteran* 22 (1914): 452.

[159] Ibid.; *OR*, vol. 44, p. 422.

[160] *OR*, vol. 44, pp. 422, 425; Abercrombie, "Honey Hill," 452.

[161] Colonel Colcock's Letter, SC-DUL; Courtenay, "Fragments of War History," 84.

[162] Madeleine V. Dahlgren, *Memoir of John A. Dahlgren, Rear Admiral, United States Navy* (New York: Charles L. Webster & Company, 1891) 480; McKee, *Back "In War Times,"* 186; Henry Hall and James Hall, *Cayuga in the Field. A Record of the 19th New York Volunteers, All the Batteries of the 3d New York Artillery, and 75th New York Volunteers* (Auburn NY: Trueair, Smith, & Company, Printers, 1873) 211; *OR*, vol. 44, p. 435.

[163] *OR*, vol. 44, p. 422; Charles Barnard Fox, *Record of the 55th Regiment of Massachusetts Volunteer Infantry* (Cambridge MA: Press of J. Wilson & Son, 1868) 42; Colonel Colcock's Letter, SC-DUL; Abercrombie, "Honey Hill," 452; McKee, *Back "In War Times,"* 197; Hall and Hall, *Cayuga in the Field*, 211.

[164] Colcock, "Honey Hill," 10, 16. Colcock further described the militia's part of the line: "This organization defended the left extremity of the main breastwork...and like all the Georgia militia, went into position like their native gophers, using canteens, knives and bayonets to throw up [dirt] for repairing the broken-down embankment, on whose top, in common with all the militia, they quickly placed short cross-pieces, supporting large logs, forming excellent protection against small arms, while their fire could be delivered through the space made between log and parapet" (Colcock, "Honey Hill," 16). Colcock's allusion to gophers refers to the gopher tortoise, an inveterate digger of deep burrows.

[165] Colonel Colcock's Letter, SC-DUL; Colcock, "Honey Hill," 10. Interestingly, on the day of the Honey Hill battle, Smith is reported to have referred to that time in Virginia in 1862 when, having taken over the Confederate army because of the wounding of General Johnston, he was "prostrated by a long and serious illness and was paralyzed." The subject came up "when mounting a horse at Grahamville depot, which proved too spirited for him." Major John Jenkins, to whom the comment was directed, "exchanged with him, loaning his own horse, which was easy-going and safe-footed. This gave the General great satisfaction on their ride together to the battlefield" (Courtenay, "Fragments of War History," 79–80).

[166] *OR*, vol. 44, p. 423; Luis F. Emilio, *A Brave Black Regiment: The History of the Fifty-Fourth Regiment of Massachusetts Volunteer Infantry, 1863–1865* (Boston: Boston Book Company, 1894) 242–44.

[167] Colonel Colcock's Letter, SC-DUL.

[168] *OR*, vol. 44, p. 435; Colcock, "Honey Hill," 16.

[169] *OR*, vol. 44, p. 421.

[170] Emilio, *A Brave Black Regiment*, 243.

[171] *OR*, vol. 44, p. 426.

[172] Ibid., 431–32.

[173] Ibid., 433–35.

[174] Ibid., 423.

[175] Ibid., 416, 425; William Harris Bragg, "The Fight at Honey Hill," *Civil War Times Illustrated* 22 (January 1984): 19.

[176] George T. Jackson to Charles C. Jones, Jr., undated, SC-DUL.

[177] *OR*, vol. 44, p. 416; Smith, "March to the Sea," *Battles and Leaders*, 4:668–69.

[178] Ibid., 417.

[179] Colonel Colcock's Letter, SC-DUL; William A. Courtenay, "Heroes of Honey Hill," *Southern Historical Society Papers* 26 (1898): 232.

[180] Emilio, *A Brave Black Regiment*, 248.

[181] Colonel Colcock's Letter, SC-DUL.

[182] *OR*, vol. 44, p. 417.

[183] *Acts of the General Assembly of Georgia* (Milledgeville GA: Boughton, Nisbet, Barnes, & Moore, 1865) 86. The order of battle is drawn from various places in the pertinent volumes of the *Official Records*, as well as from newspaper accounts and memoirs.

[184] Charles C. Jones, Jr., *The Siege of Savannah in December, 1864, and the Confederate Operations in Georgia and the Third Military District of South Carolina during Germinal Sherman's March from Atlanta to the Sea* (Albany NY: Joel Munsell, 1874) 101–103.

[185] Ibid., 111–12.

[186] Ibid., 74.

[187] *OR*, vol. 44, p. 921.

[188] Wayne County Historical Society, *History of the Battle for Doctortown Railroad Trestle* (n.p., n.d.) 4–5; *OR*, vol. 44, pp. 150, 388, 921; Bobby M. Martin, ed., *Wayne County, Georgia: Its History and Its People* (Dallas GA: n.p., 1990) 92; Buddy Sullivan, *Early Days on the Georgia Tidewater: The Story of McIntosh County & Sapelo* (Darien GA: McIntosh County Board of Commissioners, 1990) 322.

[189] Joseph LeConte, *'Ware Sherman: A Journal of Three Months' Personal Experience in the Last Days of the Confederacy* (Berkeley: University of California Press, 1937) 17.

[190] Ibid., 18–19.

[191] Ibid., 21; Wayne County Historical Society, *History*, 22; Discharges, nos. 3337-01 & 3337-02, Boxes 1-3, passim, Adjutant General's Records, GDAH; Martin, ed., *Wayne County, Georgia*, 92; Frederick H. Dyer, *A Compendium of the War of the Rebellion*, 3 vols. (1908; reprint, New York: T. Yoseloff, 1959) 3:1738.

[192] *OR*, vol. 53, pp. 32–36; Smith, "March to the Sea," *Battles and Leaders*, 4:669; Jones, *Siege of Savannah*, 90.

[193] Lt. Col. B. W. Frobel to Maj. Gen. M. L. Smith, 25 February 1865, Jones Collection, SC-DUL.

[194] Smith, "March to the Sea," *Battles and Leaders*, 4:669; Jones, *Siege of Savannah*, 75; *Reports of Militia Operations*, 27–28.

[195] Jones, *Siege of Savannah*, 90.

[196] *OR*, vol. 44, p. 208.

[197] Jones, *Siege of Savannah*, 109.

[198] Alexander A. Lawrence, *A Present for Mr. Lincoln: The Story of Savannah from Secession to Sherman* (Macon GA: Ardivan Press, 1961) 193; Jones, *Siege of Savannah*, 131–32.

[199] Roger S. Durham, "Savannah: Mr. Lincoln's Christmas Present," *Blue & Gray Magazine* 7 (February 1991): 44.

[200] Ibid.; *OR*, vol. 44, pp. 236–37, 800, 962–63; Jones, *Siege of Savannah*, 133.

[201] Jones, *Siege of Savannah*, 133–35; Frobel to Smith, 25 February 1865, Jones Collection, SC-DUL.

[202] Lt. Col. B. W. Frobel's Journal of the Siege of Savannah [copy], 24 November–20 December 1864, Jones Collection, SC-DUL.

[203] Ibid.

[204] *Report of Militia Operations*, 29; Jones, *Siege of Savannah*, 149, 175; Durham, "Savannah," 48; William J. Hardee to Charles C. Jones, Jr., 14 May 1866, Georgia Portfolio, Jones Collection, SC-DUL.

[205] *OR*, vol. 47, pt. 2, pp. 999–1000.

[206] *Report of Militia Operations*, title page.

[207] Ibid., 23–24.

[208] *OR*, vol. 47, pt. 2, p. 1071.

[209] *OR*, vol. 47, pt. 2, pp. 1093, 1122; *CRG*, 3:707.

[210] *CRG*, 3:707–709.

[211] Ibid., 709–10.

[212] James C. Bonner, *Milledgeville: Georgia's Antebellum Capital* (Athens: University of Georgia, 1978) 187–88, 196; Louise Biles Hill, *Joseph E. Brown and the Confederacy* (Chapel Hill: University of North Carolina, 1939) 243; Horace Montgomery, *Howell Cobb's Confederate Career* (Tuscaloosa AL: Confederate Publishing Co., 1959) 128–31; *Macon Telegraph*, 2 December 1864; *Historic Macon Building Survey*, 12:2787, History and Genealogy Room, Washington Memorial Library, Macon GA.

[213] *CRG*, 2:800–801; *CRG*, 805–809. Brown's precedent—the French Revolution's *levée en masse* of 1793—was, like Brown's version, "more than conscription," but the French levy was also actually much less broad, since it embraced only unmarried men, ages eighteen to twenty-five (Richard Holmes, ed., *The Oxford Companion to Military History* [New York: Oxford University Press, 2001] 504).

[214] *CRG*, 3:676–77. Wright's proclamation, noted as "Not Found" in both the *CRG* and the *OR*, is printed in Jones, *Siege of Savannah*, 19–20; Wright there signs himself as "President of the Senate, and *ex officio* Governor during the disability of Governor Brown" (20). The provision for the president of the Senate taking over for the governor dated back to the Georgia Constitution of 1798. The constitutional office of lieutenant governor was created by the Georgia Constitution of 1945 (Albert Berry Saye, *A Constitutional History of Georgia, 1732–1968* [Athens: University of Georgia Press, 1970] 175, 399).

[215] *CRG*, 3:677–79.

[216] Bernard Suttler, "Ambrose Ransom Wright" in William J. Northen, ed., *Men of Mark in Georgia*, 6 vols. (Atlanta: A. B. Caldwell, 1907–1912) 3:319; *CRG*, 2:814–16.

[217] *CRG*, 2:818–19, 825–26, 841–42.

[218] Ibid., 851.

[219] *Macon Telegraph*, 13 March 1865.

[220] James Pickett Jones, *Yankee Blitzkrieg: Wilson's Raid through Alabama and Georgia* (Athens: University of Georgia Press, 1976) 28–34, 84–89, 110–12.

[221] *CRG*, 3:712.

[222] Ibid., 713–14; *OR*, vol. 49, pt. 1, p. 391; Montgomery, *Howell Cobb's Confederate Career*, 221; Jones, *Yankee Blitzkrieg*, 132–33, 141–43.

[223] Jones, *Yankee Blitzkrieg*, 160–63.

[224] Eliza Frances Andrews, *The War-Time Journal of a Georgia Girl* (Atlanta: Cherokee Publishing Company, 1976) 158; Montgomery, *Howell Cobb's Confederate Career*, 131–32; Jones, *Yankee Blitzkrieg*, 166–68; James Harrison Wilson, *Under the Old Flag*, 2 vols. (New York: D. Appleton & Company, 1912) 2:278.

[225] Jones, *Yankee Blitzkrieg*, 175; Joseph H. Parks, *Joseph E. Brown of Georgia* (Baton Rouge: Louisiana State University Press, 1977) 324–25.

[226] Dunbar Rowland, ed., *Jefferson Davis, Constitutionalist: His Letters, Papers and Speeches*, 10 vols. (Jackson: Mississippi Department of Archives and History, 1923) 6:567.

[227] Hill, *Brown and the Confederacy*, 250–51.

[228] Parks, *Brown of Georgia*, 324–25; *CRG*, 3:715; *CRG*, 2:878–79.

[229] James Harrison Wilson, entry for 7 May 1865, diary, Wilson Manuscripts, Historical Society of Delaware, Wilmington DL; *CRG*, 3:716. For public consumption, General Wayne provided the Milledgeville *Confederate Union* with a summary of two "interviews" he had conducted with General Wilson in Macon on 2 May on various topics relating to the end of the war. He prefaced his summary with a reminder to readers that he and General Wilson "as *West Pointers*…conversed with the frankness that our Military Education and professional candor had taught us to deal with each other" (Henry C. Wayne to J. H. Nisbet, 4 May 1865, in the Milledgeville *Confederate Union*, 9 May 1865).

[230] Wilson, *Under the Old Flag*, 2:350–53.

[231] Ibid., 354–56.

[232] Parole, Joseph E. Brown, 8 May 1865, Joseph E. Brown Papers [Felix Hargrett Typescript], Hargrett Library.

[233] This roster is a composite based on a variety of sources. Many of the records of the Georgia Militia were destroyed in an 1865 fire, and the roster is at best an incomplete reconstruction based on available sources. The major manuscript sources are located in the Georgia Archives, Morrow, Georgia, in documents of the Adjutant and Inspector General's Office in Record Group 22. Particularly important were records in Unit 97-2583A, Location Numbers 3337-06 (Box 1), 3337-08 (Box 1), 3337-11 through 3337-15, 3341-07, and 3342-04 through 3342-05 (Boxes 20-24). Supplemental information came from contemporary newspapers and the *Official Records*, as well as the following sources: *Compiled Service Records of Confederate Soldiers Who Served in Organizations From the State of Georgia* (National Archives Microfilm Publication Microcopy No. 266); I. W. Avery, *The History of the State of Georgia from 18500 to 1881* (New York: Brown & Derby, Publishers, 1881) [in particular, Appendix A, "Georgia Officers Who Served in the Civil War of 1861-5 in the Confederate Service, Including General and Regimental; Field Officers and Captains," pp. 657–94]; Juanita S. Brightwell, comp., *Index to the Roster of the Confederate Soldiers of Georgia, 1861–1865* (Spartanburg SC: The Reprint Company, 1982); Nancy J. Cornell, comp., *1864 Census for Re-Organizing the Georgia Militia* (Baltimore MD, Genealogical Publishing Company, 2000); Lillian Henderson, comp., *Roster of the Confederate Soldiers of Georgia, 1861–1865*, 6 vols. (Hapeville GA: Longino and Porter, 1944–1964); Janet B. Hewett, ed., *Georgia Confederate Soldiers, 1861–1865*, 4 vols. (Wilmington NC: Broadfoot Publishing Company, 1998); Charles Edgeworth Jones, *Georgia in the War, 1861–1865* (Atlanta GA: Foote & Davies, 1909); Stewart Sifakis, *Compendium of the*

Confederate Armies: South Carolina and Georgia (New York: Facts on File, 1991); and Virgil D. White, *Index to Georgia Civil War Confederate Pension Files* (Waynesboro TN: National Historical Publishing Company, 1996).

[234] Name also appears on roster of Company K, 5th Regiment.

[235] Commanded at Griswoldville.

[236] Commanded at Griswoldville.

[237] Commanded at Griswoldville.

[238] Commanded at Griswoldville.

[239] Commanded at Griswoldville.

[240] Commanded at Griswoldville.

[241] Commanded at Griswoldville.

[242] Commanded at Griswoldville.

[243] Original casualty report read, "wounded in side [of head?], but family records indicated "in ear."

[244] Commanded at Griswoldville.

[245] Commanded at Griswoldville.

[246] Charles Christian Humber was appointed captain of Company E in July 1864 and was furloughed home following his wound at the Battle of Atlanta, 22 July 1864, then returned to duty in time to resume command of the company at Griswoldville, following the death of Captain C. A. Farwell. At the Battle of Griswoldville, he was again wounded while carrying Alladin Newsom from the battlefield.

[247] Alladin T. Newsom was Stewart County purchasing agent for the Confederate States Army, and, though overage for military service, he joined the militia as a private prior to the Battle of Griswoldville.

[248] Record states he was a physician.

[249] This roster comprises artillerists serving with the 1st Division, Georgia Militia, during the campaigns of 1864–1865. It is drawn from Compiled Service Records of Confederate Soldiers Who Served in Organizations From the State of Georgia (hereafter CSR-GA), National Archives Microcopy No. 266, Roll 98, "Captain Anderson's Battery, Light Artillery." Excluded from the roster as printed herein are men whom the records indicate left the battery before the beginning of the Atlanta Campaign, or whose records do not extend to or include the period from mid-1864 until war's end. The names of many of Anderson's men appear on the muster role of the surrendered Confederates paroled at Greensboro, North Carolina.

[250] Greaves, a native of nearby Clinton, no doubt absented himself to see how his family was faring during the invasion. S. H. Griswold, however, gives him credit (apparently erroneously) for being with his battery during the battle.

[251] Although not a part of the 1st Division Georgia Militia, this battalion was assigned to Gustavus W. Smith's command at the Battles of Griswoldville, Honey Hill, and the Siege of Savannah and is included for convenience in this order of battle. Most members of the battalion were employees of Cook and Brother Armory in Athens or were mechanics, blacksmiths, and leather workers detailed from the Confederate army. The names are drawn principally from rosters of the battalion found in the *CSR-GA*, National Archives Microcopy 266, Roll 354. These rolls date from September–October 1863, when the Athens Battalion temporarily became part of the Georgia State Guard. At that time, the men were divided among three companies, each named for their captains: Francis L. Cook, William N. Pendergrass, and W. H. Sims. By the time of the Savannah Campaign, however, the battalions comprised four companies, lettered A through D. Additional names have been added from newspaper casualty lists. Although most of the men listed were identified as employees of Cook and Brother Armory, Athens, Georgia, other names belong to detailed mechanics and leather workers attached to the battalion during fall 1863, some of whom appear to have stayed with the battalion. Some other names represent blacksmiths and machinists

detailed from the army and a few others are of Athens residents, not employed at the armory, who also joined the battalion. A few names, dating from the Savannah Campaign, have been added from another, very abbreviated listing in the *CSR-GA*, National Archives Microcopy No. 266, Roll 577, "Cook's Battalion, Georgia Infantry, Reserves."

[252] Commanded Company A at Griswoldville.

[253] Commanded Company B at Griswoldville.

[254] Although not a part of the 1st Division Georgia Militia, this battalion was assigned to Gustavus W. Smith's command at Griswoldville, Honey Hill, and the Siege of Savannah and is included for convenience in this roster. Drawn from Col. George W. Rains's 1st Regiment, Local Defense Troops, most of its members were employees of the Augusta Arsenal and Powder Works and were frequently mobilized and disbanded with changes in personnel and unit designations that make impossible a meaningful reconstruction of the battalion in 1864–1865. Records of the 1st Regiment, Local Defense Troops are found in *CSR-GA* (Microcopy 266, Rolls 125–28). The listing for "Augusta Battalion, Georgia Infantry" that appears in *CSR-GA* (Microcopy 266, Roll 577) includes only two individuals, both of whom appear in this roster.

[255] This casualty list is drawn principally from lists in the following newspapers:

Macon Daily Telegraph and Confederate, 24, 25, 29 November 1864; *Augusta Daily Constitutionalist*, 30 November 1864; *Augusta Chronicle and Sentinel*, 7 December 1864; *Columbus Daily Sun*, 25 November 1864; *Athens Southern Banner*, 30 November 1864.

Although G. W. Smith variously reported the casualties at Griswoldville as being "a little over 600" (6 December 1864) and "51 killed and 472 wounded" (26 January 1865), the data herein, though incomplete, suggest that the killed may actually have numbered around 80 (*Reports of the Operations of the Militia* [Macon GA: Boughton Nisbet, Barnes, and Moore, 1865] 5, 15).

[256] This casualty list is drawn principally from lists in the following newspapers: *Macon Daily Telegraph and Confederate*, 7 December 1864; *Augusta Chronicle and Sentinel*, 7 December 1864.

GENERAL INDEX

INDEX TO ROSTERS AND CASUALTY LISTS

Landrum, William 262
Lane, J. M. 273, 317
Lane, Thomas 308
Lane, W. S. 257
Lane, William 280
Laney, John 297
Lang, S. G. 299
Langford, A. A. 262
Langford, Carter 263
Langford, John 300
Langford, W. B. 267, 271
Langford, William 280
Langford, William A. 274
Langston, S. S. 292
Langston, William G. 258
Lanier, B. F. 299, 322
Lanier, John 322
Lanier, Thomas 298
Lankford, Joe Henry 261
Lankford, Joseph 261
Lansdell, William 257
Larkin, George E. 258
Lasetor, O. R. 260
Lashley, J. W. 281
Lassiter, Orin D. 264
Laukin, A. M. 298
Lauson, Jesse 280
Lawrence, Jerry 278
Lawreull, H. T. 278
Lawson, John 295
Lawson, S. B. 311
Lay, John W. 262
Layton, James W. 295
Leaker, John 293, 320
Leary , James 314
Ledbetter, Abner 297
Ledbetter, John W. 268
Ledbetter, S. 261
Ledlaw, Baldwin 267
Lee, ___ 294, 320
Lee, Alfred, 303, 323
Lee, Benjamin 264
Lee, J. H. 280
Lee, J. W. 298
Lee, Jordan 311
Lee, Larkin 282
Lee, Moore 286
Lee, Thomas J. 280
Lee, Walter 289
Lee, William B. 272
Lee, Zachariah 289
Leffers, James 309
Leggett, Abraham 283

Lemons, A. 276
Lemore, J. 316, 326
Leonard, Charles E. 278
Leonard, J. P. 297, 321
Lesley, David 264
Leslie, T. C. 287
Lester, Edward A. 282
LeSueur, David 276
Leverette, Reid, 278
Lewis, I. C. 269
Lewis, Joseph 272
Lewis, Obediah 288
Lewis, Thomas 282
Lewis, William 281
Lewis, William G. 289
Lidden, Charles 299
Lilse, James 280
Linceford, Strozier 269
Lindsey, James H. 287, 319
Lindsey, John T. 259
Lingo, John T. 292, 320
Linsey, James 314
Linson, W.M. 309, 325
Lipsey, H. B. 300
Litebridge, A. 328
Little, Davis 278
Little, Frank L. 268
Little, J. M. 261
Little, James E. 301
Little, T. A. 276
Little, Thomas 261
Little, W. F. 278
Littlejohn, Samuel Floyd, 271
Litty, Frank 291
Livingston, Henry 295
Lockhart, J. T. 304, 324
Lockhart, William 266
Lockhart, William H. 266
Lockheart , J.T.
Logan, W. H. 271
Long, Charles 299
Long , D.W. 309, 325
Long, G. S. 299
Long , G. W. 314
Long, J. F. 273
Long, James 274, 317
Long, Joseph 274, 317
Looney, J. P. 275
Loony, Robert 314
Lord, J. H. 289
Lord, T. 269
Lorger, S. L. 293, 320
Lott, Mation 276

Lott, Robert 259
Lott, Thomas W. 264
Lovejoy, John D. 279, 281
Lovette, Moses 286
Lovett, William L. 286
Low, Nile 264
Lowe, Thomas J. 287
Lowery, Andrew 302
Lowery, George V. 263
Lowery, J. W. F. 302
Lowrey, John W. 304
Lowry, W. F. 301, 323
Loyd, Thomas P. 268
Lozier, William 269
Lublin , E. 316, 326
Lucas, James T. 288
Lucas, John 311
Lumsden, Richard P. 271
Lumsford, C. G. 281
Lunceford, Bolen F. 261
Lunceford, David H. 261
Lunsford, Si 280
Lunsford, William 274
Lyle, Byrd, 276
Lyle, David 276
Lyle, R. B. 294, 321
Lyle, William 276
Lynch, Calvin 286
Lynch, E. S. 261
Lynch, Grief 279
Lynch, James W. 272
Lynch, John 265
Lynn, John 283
Lyon, Merritt R. 301
Lyon, T. E. 283
Lyons, George 277

M

Mabry, W. H. 272
Mack, Thomas 267
Mackey, Fernando 282
Madden, R. A. 276
Maddox, Benjamin 311
Maddox, Emory 282
Maddox, James G. 265
Maddox, Notley 265
Maddox, Robert G. 260
Madre, Robert 306
Magness, E. B. 303
Mahaffey, B. S. 314
Mainus, ___ 312, 325
Major, Daniel P. 263
Malcom, George 274, 317